NORTON

NORTON

Mick Woollett

Published in 1992 by Osprey, a division of Reed International Books, Michelin House, 81 Fulham Road, London SW3 6RB and Auckland, Melbourne, Singapore and Toronto

Reprinted 1997

© Mick Woollett

All rights reserved. Apart from any fair dealing for the purpose of private research, criticism or review, as permitted under the Copyright Designs and Patents Act, 1988, no part of this publication may be reproduced, stored in a retrieval systemn, or transmitted in any form or by any means, electronic, electrical, chemical, mechanical, optical, photocoping, recording or otherwise, without prior written permission. All enquiries should be addressed to the Publisher.

Cataloguing in Publication Data is available from the British Library.

ISBN 185532 700 7

Editor Shaun Barrington
Page Design Gwyn Lewis
Phototypset by BAS Printers Limited, Over Wallop, Hampshire
Printed and bound in Great Britain by The Bath Press, Bath

DEDICATION
This book is dedicated to Cyril Smith and Edgar Strub and to all who raced Nortons.

FRONT COVER Mike Hailwood in action on a Manx Norton at Aberdare Park in 1939.

BACK COVER 1948 Model 18, 490cc, and below, Trevor Nation on the JPS Norton rotary, 1991.

HALF TITLE Ralph Cawthorne in the paddock at the 1922 Senior TT astride the first overhead valve Norton to compete in the Isle of Man.

TITLE PAGE A picture that epitomizes an era – John Hartle at speed on a Manx Norton during the 1956 Senior TT.

ABOUT THE AUTHOR

Mick Woollett's interest in Nortons began when his elder brother Ian acquired a 1931 Model 18 in 1944. He bought his own Norton as soon as he could afford it, a 1938 350cc Model 50. It was followed by two 350cc Internationals and a 1948 350cc Manx. In 1956 he became a full-time professional sidecar passenger – first with 1952 World Champion Cyril Smith, and then with Belgian Jack Wijns and later with Swiss Edgar Strub. Successes included wins at Mettet and Chimay in Belgium, second at Hockenheim, Germany, and Hedemora, Sweden. While passengering, Mick drifted into journalism – first with Cyril Quantrill's *Motor Cycle News*, then with *Motor Cycling* and finally, when the magazines merged, with *Motor Cycle*. He is the only man ever to have been sports editor of all three main British weeklies and was editor-in-chief of *Motor Cycle Weekly* (successor to *Motor Cycle*) and *The Classic Motor Cycle*. He has written a number of books including *The Grand Prix Riders*, and, for the Japanese, *Honda Racers in the Golden Age*.

Contents

Foreword by Murray Walker

I was a bit put out at the British Motor Cycle Grand Prix this year when someone came up to me in the pit lane and aggressively said 'what are you doing here? You're a car man.' So maybe I ought to establish my credentials for having been done the honour, by my friend Mick Woollett, to write the foreword for his superb definitive story of Norton.

My father, Graham Walker, later to ride for Sunbeam and Rudge-Whitworth and become the Editor of *Motor Cycling*, was the post World War One Competitions Manager for the great Bracebridge Street concern. He starred on Nortons in innumerable trials, sprints and hillclimbs and rode Nortons in the TT from 1920 to 1923 (second to the great Freddie Dixon in the Sidecar race). It was through him and my many visits to the Isle of Man, where I saw so many epic Norton victories, that I became a motor cycle sport aficionado. In a pathetic attempt to emulate him I rode a 500T trials Norton and was lucky enough to win a Gold Medal in the 1949 International Six Days Trial. Together we were the BBC's motor cycle commentary team from 1949 to 1962 and I carried on after my much-loved father's death.

When I was a little boy staying at the Castle Mona Hotel in Douglas with the Norton TT team Jimmy Guthrie was my 'Uncle' and so were Stanley Woods, Tim Hunt, Jimmie Simpson and Wal Handley. Artie Bell was my personal friend, as were Mike Hailwood and Bob McIntyre. Geoff Duke and John Surtees still are.

So Norton has been an important part of my life, is very dear to me, and I like to think that I know a fair amount about it, its history and its many great personalities. I well remember by Dad telling me, for instance, how, when Gilbert Smith had been a lowly storeman at Norton, he had said 'One day Graham I'm going to be Managing Director here.' How right he was: and a jolly good one too!

Norton is one of the truly great motor cycle manufacturers of all time with charisma like no other, before or since. As such its story was crying out to be told in the thoroughgoing but truly entertaining way that Mick Woollett has done. I can think of no one better qualified than him to have recorded its history. His personal background in motor-cycling journalism, his dedicated probing into how what happened and when and his putting the events in the context of their time

has made a rivetting story that anyone with an interest in motor cycling will find hard to put down. It has certainly brought back a flood of happy memories for me. Well done indeed Mick!

I can only hope that you enjoy reading it and learn as much from it as I have.

Author Mick Woollett passengering with Swiss Edgar Strub on a Norton outfit at the Dutch TT in 1957. They finished 4th.

Acknowledgements

The first step for me in the production of this book was to slog through the bound volumes of *The Motor Cycle* and *Motor Cycling* at the British Library Newspaper Library in Colindale – and I would like to thank the Museum for the facility and the staff who were unfailingly helpful on the 71 days that I spent researching there.

I must also thank Dave Fenner of the Norton Owners Club who provided a vital link in the chain of research by letting me have the address of Mrs Grace Stocks, Pa Norton's surviving daughter. Despite the recent death of her husband, Mrs Stocks provided a fascinating insight into the character of her father and kindly allowed several family photographs, the majority taken by her father, to be reproduced here.

My plan was to interview as many top Norton people as I could and the next was that great Irishman Stanley Woods who rode for Nortons from 1926 to the end of 1933. He told his story with humour and clarity. Thanks to Dennis Howard I next tracked down John 'Crasher' White who was in the team from 1935 to 1939. Charlie Edwards, who started work at Bracebridge Street as a boy in 1933 and later worked as a race team mechanic under Joe Craig, gave fascinating insights into what went on both before and after the war.

Ken Bills took up the story of the early post-war scene and the incomparable Geoff Duke was kind enough to expand on points raised in his book 'In pursuit of Perfection'. John Hudson, the father-figure of the Norton Owners Club, assisted with recollections of the final years in Birmingham and the switch to Woolwich and Doug Hele spoke about his three spells at Nortons – starting under Joe Craig soon after the war and only ending in 1991 when he retired.

TT winner Peter Williams told of how he helped develop the Commando for racing in the early 1970s and of the days of the first John Player Norton team; while Mike Jackson, a key member of Dennis Poore's management group, patiently explained the rise and fall of the complex Manganese Bronze Holdings Norton-Villiers-Triumph conglomerate.

Moving to modern times I went to the new Norton works at Shenstone where David Garside talked about his 22 years work on the Norton rotary while Brian Crighton, who had recently left the factory, spoke about how the rotary racing project got under way. Frank Westworth, editor of *The Classic Bike Guide* and a Norton rotary owner, detailed how the latest machines to bear the famous name perform on the road.

Others I must thank include Bob Holliday, author of 'The Norton Story', Peter Roydhouse for supplying production figures, Tiny Ayres of the Sunbeam Club for letting me look at Norton catalogues dating back to 1914, Titch Allen for allowing me to quote passages from the excellent Norton series he wrote for *Motorcycle Sport*, Dennis Howard, author of Ballantine's Norton, Elwyn Roberts, Don Morley and Helmut Krackowizer of Austria, the National Motor Museum Beaulieu and EMAP for the loan of historic photographs and of course Murray Walker for writing the foreword.

Finally I must thank my agent Chris Forster for suggesting the original approach to the subject; Nick Collins of Osprey for taking over when the original publisher faltered; editor Shaun Barrington for seeing the job through – and keeping calm in times of crisis – and my wife Peta for putting up with my moods when things were going wrong and for helping with the time-consuming job of indexing.

I won't pretend this is the complete story. To tell that would take many more books of this size. What I do claim is that this volume, illustrated by over 350 photographs and drawings, is the most comprehensive Norton history written so far. I'm also certain that it is the most thoroughly researched. So I do hope that you'll enjoy it and I again thank all who helped me with it.

Mick Woollett

CHAPTER 1

A remarkable man: James Lansdowne Norton

Geoff Duke was not the first Norton rider to contest the Isle of man TT in a skintight racing suit. An eye-witness at the 1909 race reported: 'Mr J.L. Norton appeared at the start clad from neck to ankle in a close fitting garment of black woollen material. The costume appeared more suitable for an acrobat than a motor-cyclist but Mr Norton's explanation, that it minimised wind-resistance, indicates how thoroughly he had thought out everything.'

The Mr Norton concerned was James Lansdowne Norton, founder of the company that was to become the most famous name in motor-cycling; his younger daughter Grace, speaking to me in 1990, clearly remembered the get-up: 'We used to call it his teddy-bear suit. It was a tight-knit woollen outfit.'

Unfortunately the Norton he rode, powered by his first design of single-cylinder side-valve engine, let him down and he retired near the end of the race when, in the words of a reporter from *The Motor Cycle*, 'the lubrication failed'.

Norton was a remarkable man. His life, achievements, adventures and agonising death would make a superb film. Born in Birmingham in 1869, he was brought up in a strictly religious middle-class family. His father was a skilled cabinet-maker and wood carver whose work included pulpits and other furnishings for the churches and chapels that were built in such numbers during the second half of the nineteenth century.

But James Lansdowne Norton's talents lay in a different direction. He was intrigued by all things mechanical, and when he was 12 he built a model steam-engine with upright boiler of the stationary type. The story has it that young Norton used to run the engine in the front window of the family home, where it attracted such large crowds that the police came and asked him to move it because the people were causing an obstruction. Grace confirms that she heard this tale as a girl, and she also throws some light on the family background.

I believe that my father was the eighth in line to be christened James Lansdowne. We were told that his grandfather was the son of a Lord Norton but he had been a bit of a ne'er-do-well who had been thrown out of the family when he married a maid or housekeeper. She was a very fine woman apparently, but the family would never speak to us children about it.

Young James was apprenticed to a toolmaker when he left school and was soon involved in making bicycle chains. Work was interrupted when he went down with a severe bout of rheumatic fever when he was 19. The attack was so bad that the family doctor advised that a sea trip would be the best form of convalescence, and in 1888 he went to New York and back on one of the new transatlantic liners. It helped, but he suffered ill health all his life which prematurely aged him and led to him being nicknamed 'Pa' while still a TT competitor.

The next milestone came in 1898 when, aged 29, he set up his own business, the Norton Manufacturing Company in Bromsgrove Street, Birmingham. It was an eventful year, for in October he married Sarah at the Salvation Army Citadel in Birmingham and took her back to the family home which they shared with his widowed father until JLN died in 1925.

The Norton Manufacturing Company, a small concern, initially made chains; but Norton was a great talker and visionary and he and an expanding group of friends were soon meeting to talk about all things mechanical and particularly about a new form of transport, the motor-bicycle, that was taking over from cycling as the sport of the middle and upper classes.

One of his circle was Charles Riley Garrard, a wealthy entrepreneur who decided that the new craze was a potential money-spinner. At that time the French were the pioneers, and early in 1902 Garrard concluded a deal to import Clement engines which he would build into bicycles and market as the Clement-Garrard. In those days the bulk of powered two-wheelers were simply heavy-duty bicycles with an engine bolted on wherever the designer thought was the best place.

The Clement was the best 'clip-on' of its day. It was a four-stroke of 160 cc with an overhead exhaust valve and what was known as an 'automatic' inlet valve – which meant it was sucked open and the fresh fuel mixture vacuumed into the cylinder as the piston fell. It developed just over one horsepower at 1100 rpm yet weighed only 21 lb, and the complete Clement-Garrard tipped the scales at 75 lb ready for the road along which it would cruise at 20 mph – well above the 12 mph legal limit of the day.

The Norton Manufacturing Company was soon building the frames for Garrard, and in November 1902 advertised the first Norton. This was named the Energette and it was claimed to be 'the ideal doctor's bike' and 'suitable for business, touring or racing'. Why the name Energette was chosen is not known – and why it was thought ideal for medical men is not explained. But we do know that it was almost identical to the Clement-Garrard except that it had a longer wheelbase, a design feature much favoured by JLN in his later machines and which gave rise to the nickname 'ferrets'.

It is unlikely that more than a handful were built. At that time Garrard was running an aggressive advertising campaign in the motorcycle press, whereas the very few Norton advertisements that appeared were small. If you did want an Energette, it could be supplied with belt or chain drive and with either single or two-speed gear. In other words, the Energette was a sideline, a machine built to order and to your specification.

Soon after that first advertisement the works moved from Bromsgrove Street to Bradford Street. There Norton continued to build frames for Garrard and to operate the official repair depot for all Clement-Garrard machines sold in the UK – the customer simply despatching the machine through the very efficient rail system of the day.

Clement were riding high at this time. The factory built a racer powered by a V-4 engine and sent their works rider Maurice Fournier over to compete at the Canning Town track. There, on the concrete cycle track, he beat the local aces and averaged over 50 mph for a three-mile, flying-start event.

That was in 1903, and it is interesting to note that although car and motorcycle auctions were already being held (Friswells Great Motor Auctions at Albany Street, London), it was almost impossible to buy petrol on a Sunday. In answer to a reader's plea, *The Motor Cycle* reported that: 'The premises of Mr J. Draper of 124 Marylebone Lane, London are open on Sunday for the sale of petrol.'

At the same time readers were warned, under the heading 'How not to carry a passenger', that pillion riding would never catch on.

Two London riders carried out a successful Continental tour on a motor-bicycle converted into a tandem by the simple expedient of fitting a makeshift seat on the luggage-carrier over the rear wheel. They are to be commended on their enterprise but at the same time we do not in the least anticipate that this novel method of carrying a passenger is ever likely to seriously rival the trailer or forecar.

This emphasizes just where the development of the motorcycle had got to in 1903. No pillion riding, no sidecars and the majority of machines still powered by bought-in 'motor sets'. The roads were, in the main, rolled stones and the general public, especially horse owners, often hostile. Motorcyclists were seriously encouraged to carry light whips with which to fend off fierce dogs. Pioneering days indeed!

However, progress was rapid and during 1903 Parliament decided new laws were required to control the

ABOVE **James Lansdowne Norton in his Salvation Army uniform in the studio of E. S. Baker and Son, Bristol Street, Birmingham, circa 1889 – nine years before he founded the Norton Manufacturing company.**

ABOVE RIGHT **Believed to have been taken in 1921, this famous picture of Pa Norton hung in the Norton boardroom until the move from Bracebridge Street in 1963. It is now in the Sammy Miller Museum in New Milton, Hants.**

RIGHT **The early Nortons were powered by a French 160 cc Clement engine. This 1902/3 model has chain drive to a two-speed gearbox with belt final drive. Top speed was 20 mph.**

NORTON

fast-expanding market for motor vehicles of all types. After a great deal of debate it was agreed that as from 1 January 1904 all machines would have to be registered and carry numbers both front and rear, the speed limit should be raised to 20 mph and the minimum age for drivers/riders be 14.

Before this, anyone could be out on the road in a powered vehicle. In fact, a Peugeot advertisement of 1903 boasted of a nine-year-old who drove one of the new 'baby' Peugeots, a delightful little two-seater that was setting the trend. But there was no driving test. The licence could be obtained, according to Iliffe's *Motor Cycles and How to Manage Them*, 'by anyone over the age of 14 years without demur upon application to the County Council of the district in which the intending motor cyclist resides, for a fee of five shillings [25p]'.

The main means of transport, apart from the railways and canals, continued to be the horse, and written into the Motor Car Act of 1903 was a proviso that the motorist 'must stop, and remain at a standstill, for as long as may be reasonably necessary if a policeman or any person in charge of a horse requests him to stop or signifies the same by holding up his hand'.

In addition to building frames for Garrard and his own Clement-engined Energette, Norton had been expanding the components side of the business and in a small advertisement in *Motor* in 1903 the company offered 'Motor components, accessories, motor-cycles, variable-speed gears for cycles and motors, trailers and fore-carriages, engine sets', and ended: 'Manager: J.L. Norton AMCEI, The Norton Manufacturing Co, Manufacturers and Factors, Motor-Cycle Engineers'.

ABOVE **Believed to be the only surviving 1902 Clement-engined Norton, this machine has been carefully restored in Holland.**

RIGHT **The first Norton display advertisement appeared in the classified section of *Motor Cycling*, 19 November 1902. It plugs the lightweight Clement-engined Energette as 'the ideal doctor's bike' without explaining why! At that time the company's main business was as a factor to the motor trade.**

Obviously Norton had decided to diversify. The name Energette was dropped and in November 1903 came the first hint of a larger machine. In a very small advertisement in *The Motor Cycle*, tucked away among the classifieds, the following appeared under the Norton banner: 'Belt or chain, single or two-speed, 1⅓ to 4½ single and twin-cylinder machines. The Trade House for all Motor Components'.

It was not clear what the power units were. Clement were by this time offering a small V-twin, virtually a double-up of the little single, but they did not make a big 4½ hp unit. It is probable that Norton was 'flying a kite' to see what response there would be. Certainly, had you contacted him he would have built a machine to your specification – that was the way the smaller manufacturers operated in those days.

It is almost certain that the 4½ hp referred to was the Peugeot twin. The French were still leading the way and in 1904 Lanfranchi covered the flying kilometre at 76.5 mph. His Peugeot was powered by a massive 1490 cc V-twin with steel pistons, forked connecting rod and wooden wheel rims – the whole

NOVEMBER 19TH, 1902. *ADVERTISEMENTS.* **Motor Cycling.**

SIMPLE. **2¼ H.P.** **GRACEFUL.**

SAROLEA

Fast. MOTOR BICYCLE. **Powerful.**

RELIABLE. **2¼ H.P.** **ECONOMICAL.**

96, 97 & 98, Leadenhall Street, London.

HERBEL, two-cylinder voiturette, 5 h.p., carry two, pneumatic tyres, electric ignition, £50, or offer: trial by appointment. 57, Preston Road, Leytonstone. 795a

BENZ, two-speed, 3½ h.p., just overhauled, spare accumulator, lamps, and every requisite, thoroughly perfect and in good condition; exchange good motor-cycle or tricycle and cash, or pony and trap. T., 60, Church Hill Road, Walthamstow. 806a

6 h.p. MOTORCAR, seat four, Dunlop tyres, pump, spare parts, £100; would take good motorcycle as part payment. Farish, 615, Old Kent Road. 825a

MOTORCAR, 4 h.p. Benz engine, seat four, three speeds, extra chains, inner tubes, rugs, etc., £95. Bryant, 18, London Road, Brighton. 856a

10 h.p. TONNEAU car, seat four or five, double cylinder, new pneumatic tyres, 3½ in., £180; or will accept motor-bike, quad, and cash. A. C. C., 2, Addington Road, Bow. 837b

The Following are Trade Advertisements:

STEAM car, Locomobile, centre steering, perfect condition, Clincher pneumatic tyres, practically new, £70. The Motor Mart, Limited, 108, Euston Road, London. 797a

4½ h.p. BENZ, gear driven, three speeds, forward and reverse, hood and apron, in good condition, a bargain, £80. Mathew. 852a

5 h.p., TWO-CYLINDER Petit Duc Mors, three speeds, forward and reverse, seat three, £140. Mathew and Co., 105, High Street, Beckenham. 852a

SIRENE tonneau, 4½ h.p. double-cylinder engine, artillery wheels, licensed tyres, engine at present disconnected, price as it stands, £100, in running order £110. The Motor Mart, Limited, 108, Euston Road, London. 799a

BENZ and Star cars from £40 upwards. See adverts. in "Motor Car Journal" last issue. The Motor Mart, Limited, 108, Euston Road, London. 800a

GENUINE Leon Bollee, £55; racing De Dion, £85; Mayfair voiturette, £75; Benz brougham, £70; 9 h.p. Benz, £120. The Motor Mart, Limited, 108, Euston Road, London. 801a

Motor Tandem.

CENTURY tandem (5 h.p. Aster engine), equal to new, perfect condition, Clincher tyres (uncut, unpunctured), £85. Ernest Quinton, Needham Market, Suffolk. 842a

Mottet.

SALE or exchange privately, Mottet, by British Motor Syndicate, free engine, three speeds, electric ignition, spray carburetter, adjustable governor and Dunlop tyres, new accessories include three gas lamps, spare accumulator, horn, tools, etc.; thoroughly overhauled this month, seats two, very compact and ready for use, inspection invited, and trial given any evening after eight, or morning before nine, reason for sale or exchange given to purchaser, photograph if desired, price £45, or would exchange for either new Singer tricycle, new genuine De Dion tricycle, or small reliable Benz car. Apply by letter for appointment, in first instance, to Mr. Hermann, 64, High Street, Notting Hill Gate, London, W. 789b

Miscellaneous.

ONE pair switch handles, complete, new, 4s 6d; one lever and collar for 1⅛ in tube, 5s 6d, accept, 3s 6d; Bassee and Michel coil, in box, with clips, 1⅛ in tube, new, 17s 6d; set of wires, new, 3s 6d; belt rim, 20 in dia. 3s 6d.; Minerva transparent two way lubricating pump, new, 12s. 6d.; twisted raw hide belt, new, 4s. 6d.; P and R. 6 D accumulator, new, 18s. 6d., take 13s. 6d.; interrupter and plug, 1⅛ tube, 1s. 6d.; Minerva shape tank, 19½ in. by 9 in. by 2½ in., compartments for lubricating oil, P. and R. accumulator, tools. What offers? Green, Stephenson Terrace, Felling-on-Tyne. 853a

MITCHELL 2 horse motor, on English frame, Warwicks, £33; Minerva 1¾ horse, Palmers, £33; both perfect order, ridden 200 miles. Saloon, Whitley. 854a

COMPLETE set motor castings, 2½ by 3 stroke, piston turned cylinder bored, complete inlet and exhaust valves, fly-wheels turned, set crank cases, bargain, 26s. J. Green, 83, Albert Road, Blackpool. 790a

"MOTOR CYCLINGS" for sale, Nos. 4 to 39, best cash offer, post free. Lee, 631, Commercial Road, London, E. 811a

"MOTOR CYCLING," complete, except two numbers, best offer within four days secures lot. A., 50, Gresham Road, London, S.W. 823a

HANDSOME front seat for quad or trailer, beautifully plated and finished, low price. 9, Ringstead Road, Catford. 847a

ROUBEAU spray carburetter, new, £1. 9, New Street, Brightlingsea. 864a

The NORTON

The ENERGETTE **MOTOR BIKE**

Belt or Chain Drive. Single or Two Speeds.

THE IDEAL DOCTOR'S BIKE.

IS OUR SPECIAL WINTER MOTOR.

For BUSINESS, TOURING, or RACING,

Norton, THE GARRARD DEPOT, Bromsgrove St., Birmingham.

Coils, Accumulators, Belts, Chains, Clement-Garrard Motor Sets, etc.

NOW READY!

NOW READY!!

FOR IMMEDIATE DELIVERY,

McCurd's Patent Automatic

MOTOR BICYCLE JACK

(New Pattern)

ORDERED AT SIGHT BY

All the Leading Motor Bicycle Firms.

Attached or detached in five minutes, although intended to be permanently on the machine.

As light as a feather, but as strong as a house. Laterally adjustable to any degree of rigidity. Unnoticeable when out of use, but pretty if noticed. Automatically manipulated with two fingers. Fits any and every Motor Bicycle. Adjustable in all parts. For testing your Motor, making Repairs, and elucidating the occult, it is the only successful device yet invented.

Price 22/6 Carriage Paid.

YOU can fix it if you have a spanner to tighten 3 nuts

W. A. McCURD,

263, STANSTEAD RD., FOREST HILL, LONDON, S.E.

This Jack is made under Patents sealed and pending. BEWARE of useless infringements with which my solicitors are dealing.

NOTE.—Customers owning the old pattern will be liberally treated. Please write. You want this culminating improvement.

YOU CAN SEE

The "***HAMMOND***" Motor Bicycle, Clement-Garrard Engine, at

National Show, Stand 111.

Price complete, **35** gns. or **£10 5**s. down, balance **£2 11**s. **3**d. per month.

T. W. HAMMOND,

9, Lower Addiscombe Road, Croydon.

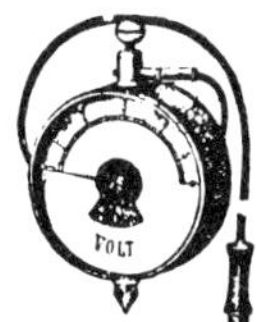

CHAS. PEACOCK & CO.,

35, Clerkenwell Road, London, E.C.

Telephone No. 159 Holborn.

Cheapest reliable pocket voltmeter in the market, also other measuring instruments.

Agents for the well-known Woven Glass Accumulators, and other Motor Car Accessories, High Tension Wires, Coils, Sparking Plugs, Tremblers, etc. Send for List.

EMPIRE MOTOR CYCLE BELT,

3-ply, V Shape, Copper Sewn,

Of Best Material and Workmanship,

13/- each, complete.

"Transmo" Motor Cycle Belt,

Full ½-inch Twist, Tough, High Quality, and Well Stretched,

6/6 each, complete.

F. L. ANDERSON, 1, Furnival St., London, E.C.

The following are Trade Advertisements:

TYRES! Patent motorcycle covers, fitted with 24oz. Para rubbers, price 15s. 6d. Freeman and Co., Tyre Manufacturers, Paddington, Liverpool. 70 b

EXPERT advice free. Valuations, etc. Six years' practical experience, eight club awards. E. J. Coles, 7a, Princes Street, Oxford Circus, London, W. 754zzz

CASTINGS in aluminium phosphor bronze, gunmetal, etc., also finished specialities made to drawings; repairs, petrol, etc. John Bromilow, William Street Brass and Aluminium Works, Heywood. zz

TO CLEAR. Six De Dion surface carburetters, 15s. each; six De Dion battery cases, 5s. each; 2¼ Automoto engine, new, fitted with belt pulley, suitable for bicycle, £6. King, Motors, Cambridge. 788a

FOR SALE, patent rights of friction chain for driving motorcycles, motorcars, and other machinery, light, strong, flexible, and possessing good grip, can be made cheap. Apply, C. Willis, 103, Wolverhampton Street, Bilston. 859a

ENGINES, engines. De Dion pattern, 1½, 2, 5 h.p., also motor-bicycles, with Carlton combined carburetter inlet valve, sets of castings, catalogue free. Carlton Motor Co., 19 Elm Grove, Cricklewood, N.W. 876a

SETS of castings, sets of castings, not the cheapest but the best, 2, 5 h.p., water-cooled cylinders, rough or finished. Stand 3, Minor Hall, Stanley Show. Carlton Motor Co., Elm Grove, Cricklewood, N.W. 876a

GENUINE De Dion tricycle, 1¾ h.p., electric ignition, tyres in good condition, guaranteed perfect working order, £17 10s., spot cash. Iverna, 44, King's Road, Reading. 855a

FREESTONE'S variable gear for motor bicycles and tricycles, free engine, several speeds, comfortable seat and foot rests, tandem seat, three times the power with same engine, started with handle, tricycles converted to carriages. South Road, Saffron Walden. 852b

ALUMINIUM CRANK CASES FOR MOTOR CYCLES.

Castings made from your own patterns in one day . . . .

Best Work at the Lowest Possible Price. Send a Trial Order.

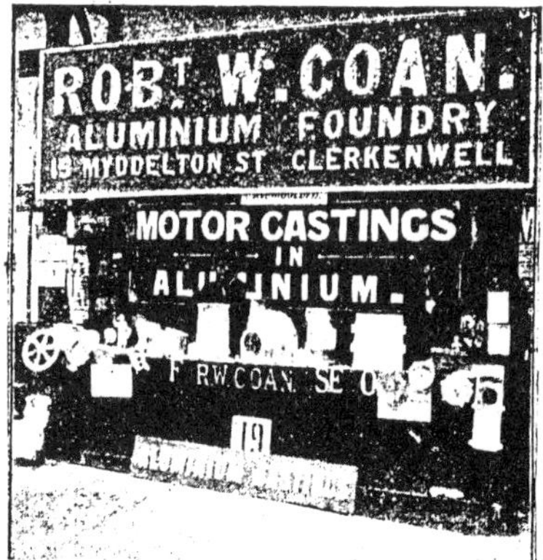

R. W. COAN, 15, Myddelton St., Clerkenwell, E.C.

A31

THE NORTON

Designed and built to combine comfort with reliability, and durability with economy and accessibility of parts

THE NORTON DRUID SPRING FORK steadies the steering, greatly enhances the comfort, durability, reliability, and safety of the motor. We fit them to any machine.

The above illustrates our 3½-4¼ with **NORTON DRUID SPRING FORKS.** We build also 5-6 and 7-8¼ twin, and 2¾-3¼ and 3½-4¼ single cylinder magneto or accumulator ignition.

THE NORTON MANFG. CO.
MOTOR CYCLE ENGINEERS,
BRADFORD ST.
BIRMINGHAM

machine weighing only 110 lb (50 kg).

The French had also invented a pneumatic, pump-up crash helmet, and a continental troupe had devised the first 'Wall of Death' using a motorcycle in a circus act. Discounts are nothing new: The Rex Company of Coventry, then the largest British manufacturer, who regularly took four pages of advertisements in the two motorcycle magazines (compared to Norton's one inch of a single column), offered enormous discounts or part exchanges on new machines. Meanwhile Norton was helping Garrard with a new Clement-powered machine – a true lightweight motorcycle rather than a bicycle with clip-on engine. The sports version was called the Phoenix Park model after early successes at the Dublin venue, and on one of these models Norton achieved a speed of over 40 mph in a contest in Birmingham.

But the new model did not stop the decline of Garrard's business and during 1904 Norton decided to concentrate on building complete machines under his own name rather than making frames and factor components. At first he favoured lightweights, and a slightly larger advertisement that appeared in *The Motor Cycle* in July 1904 stated: 'We build light and heavy motors but prefer THE NORTON light motor bicycle. You don't have to get off and push, you get all the speed you want, its efficiency is in the design and build, not in a big engine.'

However, public demand was for the larger and more powerful bikes. Competition was fierce with over 20 major manufacturers vying for a market that was expanding relatively slowly – registrations rising only from some 29,000 at the end of 1904 to 34,706 by mid 1905 – yet Rex claimed to be making 4500 machines a year. The BAT Company of south London, one of the pioneers of the industry and famous for sporting successes, actually went bankrupt though it was later rescued and the name lived on for a few more years.

Things were not easy. Norton battled on and early in 1906 launched a range of mainly Peugeot-engined machines. Ambitiously JLN listed no less than seven models in the Buyer's Guide that appeared in *The Motor Cycle* in April 1906. These ranged from a 330 cc single-cylinder utility model priced at £32, to a mighty

LEFT **The first real Norton motorcycle, the Peugeot-engined twin that appeared in *The Motor Cycle* in November 1906. It shows the low, racy lines with long wheelbase which was the hallmark of the early Nortons.**

BELOW **The first recorded Norton sporting success, April 1906 at the Birmingham MCC's hill-climb at Rose Hill, Rednal, where Peugeot-engined Nortons finished fourth, fifth and sixth. Black-bearded J. L. Norton and his white-bearded father third and fourth from the right. J. L.'s Wife Sarah is standing behind the rear wheel of the central machine.**

985 cc twin which weighed only 152 lb (69 kg) and cost £51. The only non-Peugeot was a Clement-engined lightweight of 200 cc which cost more than the Peugeot 330 cc. For good measure a chain-drive, two-speed Peugeot-powered three-wheeled forecar was offered for £78. Just how many of these were actually built and, more importantly, sold, we simply do not know. One of the early single-cylinder Peugeot-engined bikes has survived and is currently on show at the Sammy Miller Museum in New Milton, England. This is understood to be JLN's personal machine and was kept at the Bracebridge Street factory until Norton moved to Woolwich in 1963.

Those 1906 models were all, except the forecar, belt-driven machines without clutch or gearbox – the drive went direct from a pulley on the end of the crankshaft to the rear wheel. This meant that to start you had to run alongside and vault aboard once the engine fired. When you stopped, the engine stopped. The brakes were of bicycle type and were virtually useless, and the two controls most used were the throttle lever (twist grip throttles were not fitted to Nortons until the late 1920s) and the valve-lifter. This raised the exhaust valve off its seat so that the engine could continue to fire but not produce any power, the force of the firing stroke escaping down the exhaust pipe. This was used when starting and to control the machine downhill.

That same month Norton machines achieved their first, modest, competition success when no less than five twins competed in the Birmingham MCC's members' hill-climb up Rose Hill, Rednal. The Open class was won by Rem Fowler, then riding for the Rex factory, but Norton twins finished fourth, fifth and sixth. All the events were on handicap and no fastest time of day was given, but it was noted by *The Motor Cycle* reporter that: 'Seymour Smith on a Norton climbed the hill at terrific speed.' Later a photograph appeared showing the five Nortons with JLN and his wife Sarah standing amid the group.

Motor-cycling was by this time booming. After the lull of the previous year, registrations had shot up from the 34,706 of mid 1905 to 45,735 and many of the famous names of the day were extolling the virtues of the powered two-wheeler. Sir Arthur Conan Doyle (of Sherlock Holmes fame) wrote: 'I consider a motor bicycle indispensable and a splendid means of locomotion. In a word I regard the motor-bike much as the owner of a yacht looks upon a steam launch.' His personal machine was a single-cylinder Roc.

The Honourable C.S. Rolls agreed: 'The reason I went in for motor-cycling was because I was not very fond of cycling.' He in fact was a two-wheeled pioneer and rode a German-built Wolfmüller in the 1890s.

In November 1906 Norton took his first big advertisement – a half-page display in *The Motor Cycle* focusing on the Peugeot-powered model with twin-cylinder engines of either 480 cc or 660 cc capacity. The illustration shows a good-looking machine with long wheelbase and Druid sprung front fork. Pedals were retained and could be used to start the machine, especially if you were on a slight downhill gradient.

Peugeot had a good name, and factory rider Henri Cissac used a twin, enlarged to 1760 cc, to clock a world record 85.98 mph in France in 1906. Later that year he came over for a sprint along the promenade at Blackpool where he was credited with a speed of 77.37 mph. No doubt the publicity did Norton good, for the firm prospered in its own small way.

The boom of 1906 was followed by a glut of machines as production again outstripped demand, and towards the end of the year Rex were offering their well-engineered 500 cc single for just £26.50 – cheaper than the little Clement-Garrard of just a few years earlier. Norton did not show at the big London exhibitions at the end of the year but he did have a stand at the Birmingham Show in Bingley Hall in January 1907, and it was there that he offered a bike to Rem Fowler for the Tourist Trophy which was to be run for the first time in the Isle of Man in June.

Fowler accepted and it was agreed that Norton would go over to the island to look after the machine and to act as pit attendant. Before the TT, Norton won the big class at the Birmingham club's hill-climb at Rednal, beating Seymour Smith by five seconds (both rode Peugeot-powered Norton twins). This win was followed by the first Norton success advertisement, which appeared in *The Motor Cycle* dated 15 May 1907. It was the first of many.

From Rem Fowler's own collection this photograph shows him, cap reversed, on the grid at the start of the 1908 TT. Facing him, in cap and coat is J. L. Norton. Fowler, winner the previous year, noted on the back in pencil: 'Retired through stretching valves'.

CHAPTER 2

The unapproachable Norton: TT victory 1907–1909

The Isle of Man TT race of 1907 marks a turning point in motorcycle history. Until then French machines had by and large dominated the racing scene. The international rules of the day led to the development of a strange breed of machine as the makers packed more and more power into bikes which were not allowed to weigh more than 110 lb (50 kg) ready to race! For some reason the governing body refused to change the regulations which had led to dangerous, freak machines. The British decided to go it alone and, with racing banned on their own roads, turned to the Isle of Man. There the authorities had already passed legislation that allowed the roads to be closed to the public.

In fact a motorcycle race had been held on the island in 1905 when the British selection trials for the International Auto-Cycle Cup Races (to be held later in the year in France) were run. The course was a long one, including the Snaefell section but extending right down to Ballasalla in the south of the Island. It was run under the 110 lb formula and the winner, from a field of 19, was J.S. Campbell on an Ariel powered by a JAP (J.A. Prestwich of Tottenham, London) V-twin, the best British engine of the day.

The International Auto-Cycle Cup Races were a shambles that year, with allegations of all manner of cheating – including one which claimed that a manufacturer had strewn nails over the course once his machines had passed! This, together with the weight formula, spurred our own Auto Cycle Club into action. They decided to run their own race. It would be open to fully equipped roadster machines with two classes – single and twins. Virtually the only restriction was that the twins had to cover 75 mpg and the singles 90.

The circuit was a triangular one in the west of the island. The start was in St John's by Tynwald Hill and ran east to Ballacraine where it turned left and followed the present course to Kirkmichael. There riders negotiated a hairpin left-hander and followed the coast road down to Peel before turning left to complete the lap – nearly 16 miles of tough going that had to be covered 10 times.

Neither Fowler nor Norton had ever competed in a road race before. Their only experience of speed events was in the short, sharp hill-climbs of the day. And although entries were slow coming in and totalled only 25 in all, most of the top men of the day started, including the formidable Collier brothers Charlie and Harry on their factory Matchlesses, and the Triumph works riders Frank Hulbert and Jack Marshall.

No one gave Fowler and the untried Norton, the only one in the TT, much of a chance – until the race started. Rem, who had weighed in at 10 st 6 lb (66.2 kg) while the Norton itself tipped the scales at only 182 lb (82.5 kg), shot ahead and led the whole field at the end of the first lap.

Trouble soon struck, however. In the full-page Norton success advertisement that appeared in *The Motor Cycle* the following week, eight stops are catalogued: '. . . came off twice on bad corners; two stops to shorten new belt; punctured, changed front inner tube; broke front mudguard against kerbstone, had to wire and strap it on; changed sparking plug twice.'

However, when reminiscing about the race with motorcycle historian Titch Allen some half century later, Rem recalled no less than 13 stops including six to change plugs. And the puncture was no joke. Reports Allen, writing in *Motor Cycle Sport*: 'The front tyre burst at near 60 mph and fetched him off in a big way. It took him 22 minutes to untangle the old tube from the beaded edge tyre and fit a butt-ended replacement yet he still won the class by half-an-hour.' His time would have placed him third if there had been an overall classification, beaten only by Charlie Collier (Matchless, average 38.22 mph) and Jack Marshall (Triumph).

Rem's speed for the 158-mile race was 36.2 mph and he finished with over two pints of petrol to spare having averaged 87 mpg – an incredible figure for a near 700 cc V-twin being ridden flat out most of the time. Talking to Allen, Rem recalled that the bike went so well that he did not have to use the pedals at all, even up Creg Willey's Hill where many of the competitors were forced to jump off and run alongside to keep their engines going.

Describing the course, Jack Marshall, who finished second on a Triumph in the single-cylinder class, said:

> . . . very dusty in dry weather, mud-covered and slippery in the wet, pretty badly churned up on the stretch from Ballacraine to Kirkmichael . . . plenty of loose stones on the corners. In an attempt to damp down the dust, the officials sprayed the course with an acid solution which was supposed to keep things moist. The acid got on to our clothes and in a couple of days they looked as though the rats had been at them.

LEFT Rem Fowler with his Peugeot-engined Norton after winning the twin-cylinder class of the first Isle of Man TT in 1907. With him is James Lansdowne Norton, designer of the long wheelbase machine which had a top speed of over 60 mph and set a lap record at 42.91 mph.

RIGHT The machines are readied for the 1908 TT – and the bearded figure bottom right is J. L. Norton working on Rem Fowler's bike.

Marshall's factory Triumph had no pedals and he was one of the competitors who had to run up Creg Willey's Hill where a friend would run alongside and tell him his race position! Fowler's Norton was a near standard machine with a 690 cc Peugeot V-twin engine (the French company seems to have offered a wide variety of capacities at this time, ranging from 480 cc to 985 cc, all based on the same crank-case) of 76 × 76 mm bore and stroke.

The only change from standard was the fitting of stronger springs to the automatic inlet valves – up from 4 lb to 8 lb. This reduced bottom-end pull but improved the top speed, which must have been over 60 mph for Rem to set the lap record at 42.91 mph. This was almost a minute better than the best single-cylinder lap, by Harry Collier (Matchless).

Norton enjoyed the TT and, during the race, 'urged Fowler on every time he passed the pits and gesticulated to remind him to use the oil pump'. Very necessary, for in those days the rider had to operate a manual pump every few miles to top up the oil that slopped about in the crank-case – the flywheels dipping in and flinging the lubricant around the engine.

There were the usual advertising claims after the races and Norton reacted angrily to one of them, taking

- INTERNATIONAL -

TOURIST TROPHY RACE.

THE - -

NORTON TWIN WINS.

RELIABILITY

NO MECHANICAL STOP WHATEVER.

ECONOMY

44 ozs. of petrol to spare.

3½ h.p. TWIN.

SPEED,

FASTEST LAP,

42¾ miles per hour.

A private rider, H. Rem Fowler, Esq. (Birmingham Motor C.C.), on a genuine STANDARD NORTON Touring Machine, rode magnificently in this his FIRST RACE, TWICE making FASTEST LAPS, and FINISHING FIRST against the cream of British riders, in spite of following 8 STOPS: Came off twice on bad corners; two stops to shorten new belt; PUNCTURED, CHANGED FRONT INNER TUBE; broke front mudguard against kerbstone, had to wire and strap it on; changed sparking plug twice.

The NORTON MANUFACTURING Co.,

DERITEND BRIDGE,

FLOODGATE STREET, BIRMINGHAM.

This full page success advertisement appeared in *The Motor Cycle* of 5 June 1907 following Rem Fowler's TT win.

an advertisement in *The Motor Cycle* under the heading 'A True Statement' which punched home his message: 'The Fastest machine in the Tourist Trophy was the Norton twin. In spite of misleading statements to the contrary. This is true, a fact and by official figures; we do not perjure ourselves by our statements or advertisements.'

It is difficult to over-emphasize the importance of that TT success. It brought the name Norton to the notice of the motor-cycling public for the first time and gave the company – which had recently moved from Bradford Street to slightly bigger premises at Deritend Bridge in Floodgate Street, Birmingham – a foundation to build on.

Rem Fowler's next outing was on a Norton sidecar outfit in the MMC Team Competition, a 160-mile road trial centred on Daventry. It proved eventful. *The Motor Cycle* reported:

> . . . plagued by a misfire his passenger tried to change a plug on the move. With the aid of a spanner he proceeded, despite numerous shocks from the magneto, to remove one of the fouled sparking plugs from the twin-cylinder engine. His skill however did not prevent a stop, as he could not insert the fresh plug owing to the partially compressed air blowing the plug away every time he brought it in close proximity to the hole in the cylinder . . ..

A story guaranteed to make anyone who has ever received a shock from a plug-lead wince!

Despite the TT success Norton was not completely happy with the Peugeot engine, and as soon as he got back from the TT he completed the designs of the first two Norton engines. The first was a copy of the Peugeot with a number of improvements but the second was an original – the first Norton single cylinder.

Both were ready for the Stanley Show at London's Agricultural Hall in late November 1907 where Norton shared a stand with the Swiss-based Moto Rêve company for whom Norton was by this time sole Midland agent. In a pre-show advertisement, visitors to the exhibition were urged to 'make an appointment to meet our Mr Jas. L. Norton . . . it will probably pay you'.

The Peugeot-inspired Norton twin retained the 76 × 76 mm bore and stroke of the TT winner and the seemingly already outdated automatic inlet valves. However, the plain timing-side bearing was replaced by a ball race so that the crankshaft was supported by ball races on both sides. Other improvements included cleaning up the inlet and exhaust ports, an area where poor design led to a build-up of heat which in turn resulted in broken valve stems – the Achilles heel of early engines. Wrote Allen in *Motor Cycle Sport*:

> Norton tidied up the auto inlet valve pockets, casting them in the heads with inspection caps above, which made for a shorter, less complicated inlet pipe. He redesigned the timing gear to provide separate exhaust cams for each cylinder with hinged lever cam followers which were to be a distinctive feature of Norton side-valve and push-rod engines up to 1948.

The single-cylinder side-valve engine did not have the long stroke that later became a Norton characteristic.

Bore and stroke were 82 × 90 to give a capacity of 475 cc. Both valves were mechanically operated and again Norton paid special attention to the cooling of the exhaust port area.

The press of the day made surprisingly little of the new single. They were far more impressed by a new lightweight Norton powered by a very neat little V-twin 274 cc Moto Rêve engine. Norton reintroduced the name Energette for this machine, which weighed only 76 lb (34.5 kg) complete and had a claimed top speed of 40 mph.

The resurrected Energette was quickly followed, in February 1908, by the Nortonette. This was listed in the Buyer's Guide in *The Motor Cycle* and was powered by a 2 hp single-cylinder engine – almost certainly a 241 cc Swiss-built Motosacoche unit, for Norton was by that time agent for Motosacoche as well as Moto Rêve. Whether any models of either machine were sold or whether they were simply 'show surprises' we do not know. It seems probable that a handful of both were built but nothing more.

On the other hand, the new single was a serious project and was in production in time for a spring sales campaign. The first advertisement appeared in April 1908 warning readers to: 'Look out next week for the announcement of the new Norton $3\frac{1}{2}$ h.p. single-cylinder engine. This engine is entirely our own design and will embody great improvements – the result of our experience in racing and road riding.'

It was quickly followed by a second advertisement with picture and a proud boast to cover both engines: 'The engines are designed on lines of efficiency and durability, eliminating the faults common to the average motor cycle engine.' There was no mention of the lightweight models but there was a testimonial from a satisfied owner of a twin, saying: 'Truly a marvellous jigger'.

And in the very next advertisement appeared the phrase that led to the coining of what became a world-famous slogan. For under a picture of the new Norton was the line: 'My success is due to my unapproachable Norton.' That appeared in the 3 June issue of *The Motor Cycle* in 1908. It does not say who wrote the testimonial, but it was almost certainly Fowler following his TT success of the preceding June.

The Norton Company was growing up. The telephone had been installed (Birmingham 5702) and they had their own telegraphic address of Nortomo for the wire service that was still a very important means of communication. In fact, spares could be ordered from the company by telegram, using a type of shorthand code, right up to the 1950s.

During 1908 the Norton twin was enlarged to 76 × 80 mm, 725.8 cc and a production machine prepared for Fowler to defend his TT title. The races had been switched to September that year but the rules were roughly the same: production singles or twins of

ABOVE LEFT **The 1908 TT judges.**

LEFT **Believed to have been taken in 1908, this picture shows Norton with one of the first 475 cc machines with his own design of side-valve engine.**

ABOVE **The starkly simple lines of the early single cylinder Norton, 1909. Note the steep downward angle of the exhaust pipe, the front mounted magneto with silencer box below and the pedalling gear which was offered as an optional extra.**

ABOVE RIGHT **Norton's Peugeot-inspired twin with automatic inlet valve (sucked open by the descending piston) at the Stanley Show in London in November 1910. It had a bore and stroke of 76 × 80 mm, 725 cc but was never a good seller and was soon phased out of the range.**

any capacity, fully equipped and carrying a minimum of 5 lb of tools. However, pedals were now barred and the fuel consumption rules tightened – singles had to cover 100 mpg while the twins were required to do 80.

Two of the twin-cylinder Nortons were entered, one by Fowler and the other by F.C. Perryman, a Birmingham clubman and friend of Norton. Neither made it to the finish. Perryman ran out of fuel, while Fowler was plagued by stretched valves. In a short autobiography discovered by Allen, Fowler explains what happened: 'The engine was produced in about nine months from drawing board to road. There was not enough time for testing and I failed in this race owing to valves stretching and as our tappets were not adjustable and not having a file with me, it soon overheated, lost its compression and ran to a standstill.' Fowler was not impressed and went back to ride for Rex!

Overheating was a major problem at this time and Norton ran an advertisement: 'Does an air-cooled engine overheat? Not if it's a Norton – the design prohibits it!'

To confuse the lightweight issue, the single was dropped and the Moto Rêve twin, launched as the Energette, was renamed the Nortonette. No wonder Norton historians have sometimes become confused! Additionally a tri-car was listed in 1908 with 725.8 cc twin-cylinder engine and with chain drive to a two-speed gearbox, thence by belt to the rear wheel, price was £75.

At the end of 1908 Norton had his own small stand at the Stanley Show in London on which were displayed just two models – the 76 × 80 mm, 725.8 cc twin and the 82 × 90 mm, 475 cc single. Both retained pedals and both were single-speed direct drive. 'Norton machines look suitable for speed and hard work. The frames are low-built and the wheelbase is long,' noted the reporter for *The Motor Cycle*. The man from *Motor Press* was even more enthusiastic: 'Neatest motor-cycle in the Show' was his comment. But of the lightweight Energette/Nortonette there was no sign.

By this time, helped by the TT and booming British sales, British-built motorcycles were fast gaining a world-wide reputation and in October 1908 Charlie Collier on a V-twin JAP-engined Matchless covered just over 70 miles in 60 minutes to claim the world record for one hour. The machine was the bike ridden in the TT by his brother Harry and the successful attempt was made at the Brooklands track opened the preceding year. His fastest lap was 72.89 mph and he beat the previous record, set by Giuppone on a Peugeot in Paris, by some 6 mph.

Early in 1909 Norton was one of a group of prominent manufacturers who travelled to the RAC in Pall Mall, London, to meet officials of the ACU to discuss the future of the TT races. After a great deal of debate it was decided to abandon the fuel economy restrictions. Instead there would be a single race in which machines with any number of cylinders could compete – the singles limited to 500 cc and the multis to 750 cc. This seems strange by modern-day thinking but in those early years the twins and fours were felt to be less efficient than the simpler and lighter singles. The race was again to be run in September.

Competition was by now taking up a lot of Norton's time. In May he competed in the major hill-climb of the year, the ACU Open at Sutton Bank near Thirsk. In a strong field he took second place in the single-cylinder class, beaten only by Oliver Godfrey, a works rider for Rex who went on to win the 1911 TT for Indian. *The Motor Cycle*'s reporter noted: 'Norton showed great skill in taking the corner . . ..'

At about this time Perryman won a Birmingham club race on the Aston Villa cycle track, beating Rem Fowler on his Rex. Perryman rode his TT twin, and this could well have been Norton's first actual mainland race win as opposed to a hill-climb. Races were gaining in popularity and in May the factory announced that: 'Orders are now being booked for the new special model with shorter wheelbase for track and speed work.'

In the 1909 Buyer's Guide *The Motor Cycle* listed, among a total of over 200 machines, a range of five Norton solos plus a tri-car. The previous lightweights had been replaced by a JAP-powered model of 292 cc (70 × 76 mm) with pedals which tipped the scales at 110 lb (50 kg). Reports suggest that this model was mainly exported to India. The 475 cc single was used in two machines – a basic single-gear and a de luxe version with two-speed hub, selling at £45 and £54.

The 720.8 cc twins were offered in similar specifications at £52 and £62 with the passenger-carrying tri-car, powered by the same engine, at £75. The Norton machines were now being handled by agents and one of the first to advertise them was Maudes Motor Mart of Powell Street, Halifax, whose blurb included the immortal line: 'We can quote you the lowest possible terms.' Little changes.

In July 1909 Norton won his class at the Herts club's hill-climb at Aston Hill near Tring, a still formidable climb off the Halton road. There he beat Zenith Gradua hot-shot Freddy Barnes to win the single-cylinder class in a time that placed him second overall for the day.

The Norton publicity machine was getting into gear. 'We have no use for any "speed thing" which cannot be comfortably used for a holiday tour. As our friends know all our successes are gained on standard machines,' thundered an advertisement of July 1909. This was followed in September by the line: 'There is naught on the market to touch the Norton.'

Working at Floodgate Street at that time was Bob Newey, who later recalled that the 'factory' was a converted three-storey house. The office was on the ground floor, engine building and assembly on the first, while the frames were built on the top floor. The staff consisted of Mrs Williams who did the typing, answered the telephone and generally ran the show, five men and two boys in the engine department, and one brazier and two filers who looked after the frame side of the business. Newey was the tester while 'Pa Norton', as he was by this time known, did the development and design work. Many of the components were, of course, made outside by small engineering works and then brought in to be assembled at the factory, which had no casting facilities or machine shop.

Of Pa himself, Newey wrote:

> He had a flair for cracking jokes, which were interpreted by some people as cutting sarcasm . . . business was a secondary consideration. His thoughts and energies were so often concentrated on the preparation of a machine for some hill-climb or speed trial that output had to take second place. He would sit on his machine and practise getting down to it while I held a straight edge on his back to ensure that his shoulders and rump were parallel to the ground.

Newey, who worked with Norton from 1909 until he joined Levis late in 1910, also said that Norton was 'one of the nicest and most kindly men I have ever been associated with'.

It was in 1909 that Norton decided that a bigger single-cylinder machine, rather than a twin, was the answer for sidecar work. It was easier and cheaper to build, simpler for the owner to maintain and developed the type of slogging power needed to pull heavy loads up hills at, or near, the 20 mph speed limit.

Working under Norton's supervision, it was Bob Newey who actually built the prototype of the machine that was to become famous as the Big Four – the 'Four' indicating the RAC horsepower rating. The 82 mm bore of the 475 cc single was retained but the stroke was lengthened from 90 mm to a mighty 125 mm which gave a swept volume of 660 cc.

THE NORTON

Telephone—5702
Wires—
"Nortomo."

WINNER OF THE INTERNATIONAL TOURIST TROPHY RACE, TWIN CLASS.

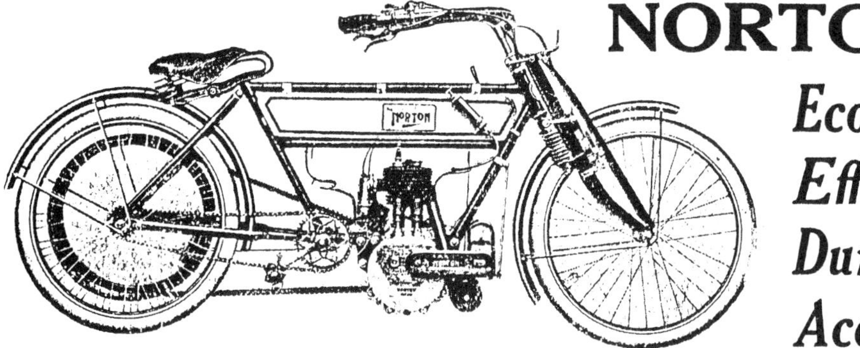

NORTON =

Economy,
Efficiency,
Durability.
Accessibility.

" **My success is due to my un approachable Norton."** **(Testimonial.)**

Engine.—"THE NORTON." Designed on lines of Efficiency and Durability, eliminating the faults common to the average Motor Cycle Engine, **Single-cylinder.**—3½ H.P. Bore 82 m/m x 90 m/m stroke. M.O.I.V. **Twin-cylinder.** 5 H.P. Bore 76 m/m x 80 m/m stroke. A.I.V. **The Bearings** are correctly dimensioned, the main shafts running on balls. **The Frame.**—20in. This has an extremely neat appearance, giving a 58in. wheelbase, a large tank capacity, and very low seat without freakish design. The height from ground to TOP of seat tube is 28½in. **Petrol Capacity** 2 gallons. **Oil Capacity** ½ gallon. **Ignition.**—By High Tension Magneto, unless otherwise ordered. **Control.**—From handle-bar or by tank levers.

SHOWING AT THE SCOTTISH NATIONAL EXHIBITION, EDINBURGH.

THE NORTON MANFG. CO., LIMITED., BIRMINGHAM.

LONDON—Moto-Reve Co., Gray's Inn Rd. EDINBURGH—Alexandra & Co., Lothian Rd, LIVERPOOL—Mersey Light Motor Co., Renshaw St.

Early use of a famous slogan – this advertisement appeared in the 3 June 1908 issue of *The Motor Cycle*. The testimonial is attributed to Rem Fowler after his success in the 1907 TT on a Norton twin – the machine shown is actually a 475 cc single.

While development was going on, Norton went off to the Isle of Man for the TT. Despite the fact that he was by this time aged 40 and in far from robust health (we know from the ACU records that when weighed before the race he tipped the scales at only 9 st 12 lb (62.6 kg)), he had decided to have a crack at the races himself. But while Perryman rode a twin, Norton broke new ground by entering the first single-cylinder Norton in the Isle of Man race. To take advantage of the capacity limit the stroke was lengthened from 90 to 94 mm, to give dimensions of 82 × 94 mm, 496 cc.

This was the year in which Norton, his beard already greying, startled onlookers by appearing on the start line in his 'teddy-bear' suit – and, as reported earlier, retired on the penultimate lap. To take advantage of the 750 cc limit for twins, Perryman's engine had been enlarged to 742 cc (75 × 84 mm) but he ran into all sorts of problems. First the magneto came loose, then the sump plug fell out and finally the exhaust lifter broke. Neither man had been among the front runners.

Interestingly, a six-mile hill-climb up Snaefell was run that year (1909). The start was on the outskirts of Ramsey and the finish near the Bungalow Hotel where the railway track to Snaefell summit crosses today's course. In this Norton did better, finishing seventh in the single-cylinder class. Fastest overall was Charlie Collier who averaged 44.8 mph on his JAP-powered Matchless twin. Brother Harry won the TT on a similar machine and broke Rem Fowler's lap record which had stood for 27 months. He did it in style with a round at 52.27 mph, almost 10 mph faster than Rem – which gives some idea of just how much the machines had improved in such a short time.

By this time the 'unapproachable' slogan was being used prominently in advertising. In the run-up to the Stanley Show, held in London in November 1909, readers were treated to: 'Unapproachable but do not be afraid to approach and inspect the new 1910 models on stand 86'. A second advertisement a week later ran: 'For the steepest hills, the Norton is absolutely unapproachable, either for speed going up or safety in coming down. Unapproachable for the roughest roads.' It ended with news about the new, bigger single: 'We have a specially designed model for sidecar work, a new 4 to 5 h.p. that will give you every satisfaction.'

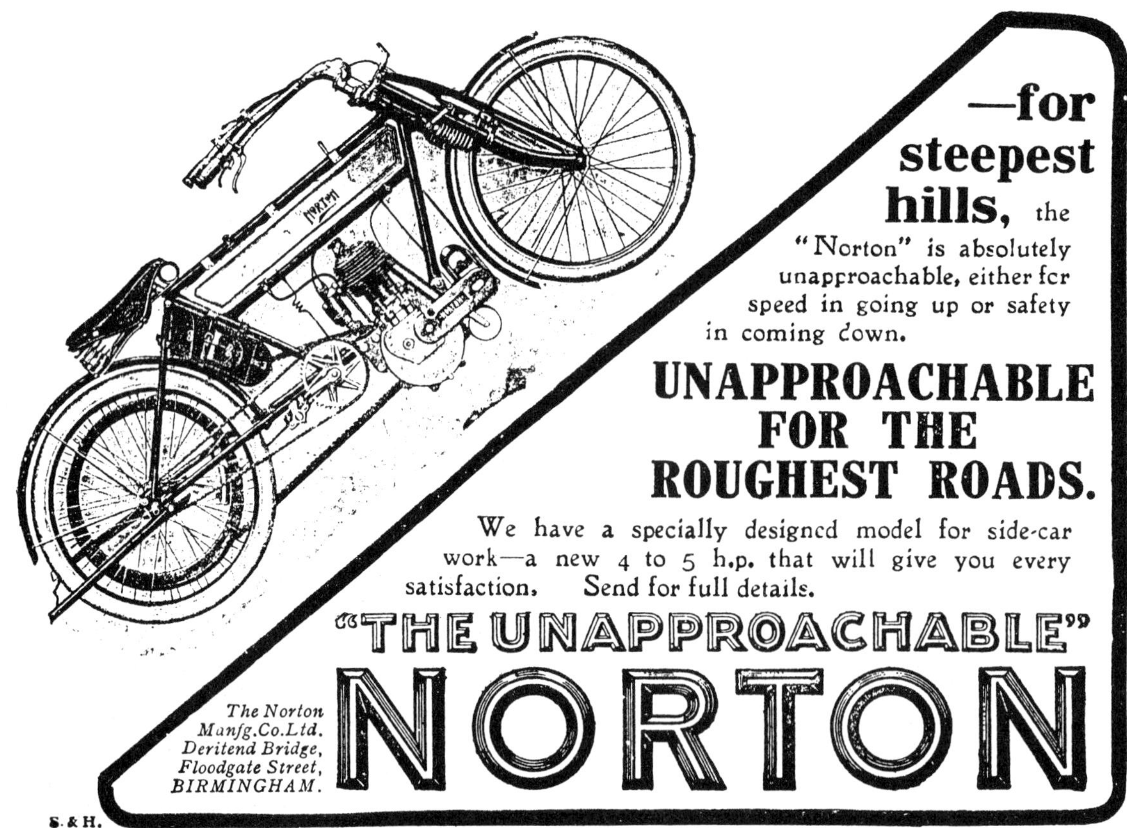

This eye-catching advertisement appeared in *Motor Cycling* in November 1909. The bike shown is the 633 cc Big Four single introduced at the Stanley Show that month – an enlarged version of the original single cylinder Norton.

When the big single appeared, the bore and stroke were 82 × 120 mm. For years Norton gave the capacity as 636 cc but these dimensions do in fact work out to 633.7 cc, and the 1909 Stanley Show marks the birth of the 'Big Four' though that name was not used until the following year.

The capacity of the smaller single had been enlarged from 475 to 496 cc by adopting the 94 mm stroke of the TT machine, and the Peugeot-inspired twins remained in production. As a show surprise Norton had on display a women's model with the little JAP engine and a dropped frame, all finished 'in a delicate shade of green with gold lining'.

These 'ladies' models' were a recurring theme in those Edwardian days. Most of the big manufacturers marketed them and the advertising media were constantly pushing them in an attempt to expand a market that at best was never more than a few machines a week. In general women were, probably very wisely, not interested in the hard-to-start, noisy, smelly and dirty machines of the day.

To ride a motorcycle you had to be prepared to mend a puncture (usually by fitting a butt-ended tube, a straight sausage-like cylinder that could be stuffed into the beaded-edge tyre without removing the wheel from the machine), shorten a stretched belt or replace a broken exhaust valve at any time and with the tools you carried. And with the cart-track roads of the days liberally sprinkled with horseshoe nails discarded by the hundreds of thousands of horses then in use, punctures were the norm rather than the exception. No wonder the cautious steered clear!

CHAPTER 3

Two-strokes and long-strokes 1910–1912

The bearded, prematurely aged figure of Pa Norton was, by 1910, well known to enthusiasts throughout the United Kingdom. Many already looked upon him as the 'father' of the British industry despite the fact that the output of his factory was small compared with the giants of the day. This was largely because he, almost alone among factory bosses, designed, built and raced his own bikes. The Norton Manufacturing Company was not run by some shadowy financier but by a friendly, smiling, intensely practical engineer who was only too ready to down tools and talk about bikes. Far too ready in fact, for money meant little to him, a trait often found in brilliant engineers. Reports of the day speak of 'the ever popular Norton' and note that 'J.L. Norton, the oldest competitor, received an extra-special cheer'. It proved to be an exceptionally busy year.

Variable gears, as they were known, became popular about this time. The Norton singles were, in the main, direct belt drive though the pedalling gear had been phased out (still available as an optional extra). But the twin-cylinder range were fitted with an expanding pulley on the main shaft. This allowed the rider to 'free' the engine by opening the pulley and allowing the belt to slip. The drive was then taken up by closing the faces of the pulley on to the belt. It was in fact a crude but simple clutch, as well as varying the gearing by altering the size of the pulley on the main shaft.

The TT had been moved from September back to June. Again a single race was held, contested on level terms by 500 cc singles but with the capacity for the twins reduced to 670 cc following the JAP–Matchless success of the previous year. Again only two Nortons, to be ridden by Pa Norton and Percy Brewster, were entered in the field of 83 – but only Norton started. Both were on 82 × 94 mm singles but Brewster came off during practice and was too seriously hurt to race. Pa then summoned Bob Newey by telegram, but the top came off his Norton's piston while he was out learning the course and with no spares available he was forced to scratch. That year the start was held up by an unusual incident. *The Motor Cycle* reported:

> A farmer, just to show he had the right to be on the road, drove down the line [of riders and machines] and naturally met with some opposition, which he in turn resented. Shouts of derision arose, and when he tried to use his whip on those objecting to his presence and it was taken away from him, the welkin rang with cheers.

Eventually the crowd took matters into their own hands and, removing the pony from the shafts, pushed the cart on to the green by Tynwald Hill. This left the farmer 'using language which was far more forcible than polite. Yells of derision followed, mixed with reports from a toy pistol, which set the animal plunging and smashed Bentley's front number plate'.

The Bentley mentioned was none other than W.O. who later came to fame as the builder of the Le Mans-winning Bentley cars. He rode an Indian that year but failed to finish. A similar fate awaited Norton. He stopped after just two laps with a broken inlet cam follower.

By this time the Big Four was in production and Norton turned his fertile mind to designing a little single-cylinder two-stroke engine to power a true lightweight motorcycle. This had a bore and stroke of 55 × 65 mm, 154 cc, which, unusually for those days, had a roller bearing big-end. The complete bike, which inherited the Nortonette name from the earlier four-stroke lightweights with bought-in engines, weighed just 65 lb and was offered for sale at £33 – expensive when you could buy a serviceable 500 cc for under £50.

The press followed the development of the two-stroke with interest. It was reported that the prototype had carried two men from Birmingham to Stafford and back and that it had a top speed of 35 mph. A later item stated that it was 'designed for potterers'.

The engine was on display at the Olympia Show in November 1910 while a complete machine was pictured in the 29 November issue of *Motor Cycling*. Said the caption: 'The Norton two-stroke lightweight (in unfinished state) which is going to be marketed next year at a weight not exceeding 60 lb. It may create a new tendency in lightweight design.' The picture showed a lengthened bicycle with tiny engine mounted in front of the pedals with a 'torpedo' fuel tank slung under the top frame tube.

Earlier in the year Norton had written an article for *Motor Cycling* about the characteristics of engines and how to make them develop flexible power. Later he reported a brisk demand for both his single- and twin-cylinder motorcycles, 'although it is late in the season'. It may be that this demand led to a slackening of interest in the two-stroke for it had faded from the Floodgate Street programme by the end of the following year and despite all the publicity it is unlikely that it ever went into production.

Certainly there was a booming market at this time. *Motor Cycling* described Coventry, where the big manufacturers were, as the 'Motoropolis of the Midlands' and reported that Triumph production was up to 100 machines a week. Contests pitting motorcycles against aeroplanes were popular and a report from France claimed that: 'A new role for military motorcyclists has been found. They will be utilized for the purpose of following aeroplanes in time of war and riders are being recruited – crack marksmen preferred.'

In competition, Pa Norton continued to excel. Ranging far afield from his Birmingham base he competed in the Streatham club's hill-climb at Titsey Hill. The actual venue was kept secret and no practising was allowed. Despite this he won his class and made third-fastest climb of the day, competing against the locals who obviously knew the hill. 'The way in which the ever popular Norton made short work of Titsey Hill evoked enthusiastic applause. He told us afterwards he felt rather uncomfortable as not knowing the hill he did not realise the bends were so easy,' reported *The Motor Cycle*.

The Norton advertisements in 1910 had started on a rather vague note. In March a half-page display in *Motor Cycling* claimed 'The Norton Manufacturing Co being probably the oldest commercial motor-cycle builders in the Kingdom', quoting from an item that had appeared in the *Motor and Cycle Trader*. Later came 'Norton Notions No 1' which featured the piston fitted to the single-cylinder machines. Designed by Pa Norton and made of cast iron, it was unusual for the number of grooves it carried. Said the advertisement:

> The piston, a sketch of which we give, is notable for the large number of oil grooves with which it has been provided. There are no less than ten in number, two of which are on the two broad piston rings. The last named have a rebate joint. It is these little notions that help to make the Norton 'unapproachable'.

The idea of the grooves was to trap oil and assist lubrication. The two piston rings ran in a single slot. Unfortunately the 'Norton Notions' series was short lived – perhaps the agency had difficulties finding novelties on what were well-engineered but hardly pioneering designs.

The Motor Cycle had a definite scoop when they reported in their 1 November issue that: 'The new 1911 Norton single and the TT model will be of the long-stroke type, the dimensions being 79 × 100 mm. This is to come within the 500 cc limit.' However, this engine

did not make it to the Olympia Show which opened later that month. There the standard 500 was still 82 × 94 mm and now fitted with an expanding pulley gear to give ratios from $3\frac{1}{2}$ to $6\frac{1}{4}$ to 1. The Big Four was offered with a heavy-duty Roc two-speed hub gear and a similar but lighter Griffin-Simplex two-speeder was an optional extra for the smaller machine. Both gears were similar to the well-known Sturmey-Archer hub fitted to millions of bicycles.

The ladies' model, with JAP engine, was still in the catalogue and there was in *The Motor Cycle* more news about the little Nortonette two-stroke:

> . . . the big-end has a roller bearing. The flywheel is outside, and the crankshaft has a single, long plain-bearing. The combustion chamber is spherical one way and flat the other, that the incoming gases may assist to expel the exhaust without mixing with it. The magneto is chain driven. The lubrication is from an annular groove, into which the piston dips. From here it flows to the main bearing, where a quick-pitch groove prevents it leaking out and returns it to a well in the bottom of the crankcase.

No petroil mix for Pa Norton.

News of the progress of the 79 × 100 mm engine came in February 1911 when *Motor Cycling* reported:

> Although the TT race does not take place until the middle of June Mr J.L. Norton and his colleague, Mr Brewster, are already turning their attention to their racing machines, the dimensions of which will be 79 × 100 mm. This long stroke engine will have several novel features about it, and will probably be the pattern for the 1912 Norton. It will be fitted with a steel piston, only weighing 13 ounces, and a new type of mechanical lubricator, which has at present only reached the experimental stage . . . .

By today's standards the piston looks unusual. It was waisted, with a deep, thick groove at gudgeon pin height, and there were other grooves both above and below the single, deep piston ring. The small oil-retaining grooves of the earlier piston were retained on both the piston ring and the skirt.

The 79 × 100 mm dimensions were to become world famous and were retained, on one model or another, until the ES2 was given a face-lift at the end of 1963. The first competition outing for the 79 × 100 mm was in March 1911 when E.B. Ware rode one, without success, at Brooklands.

Brewster's debut on his TT machine was more impressive. He went to the Bristol club's hill-climb where the road ran from near Bath town centre up a very steep hill to the old racecourse. There he made the fastest single-cylinder climb of the day and finished

Election Result

for Premiership.

The Right Unapproachable

Norton (Motor Cycle)

returned unopposed. No Change.

Deritend Bridge, Floodgate Street, Birmingham. STAND 34, MANCHESTER SHOW.

LONDON AGENTS— Maudes' Motor Mart, 136, Gt. Portland St., W.

S.&H.

"THE UNAPPROACHABLE" NORTON

NORTON NOTIONS, No. 1.

The Piston, a sketch of which we give, is notable for the large number of oil grooves with which it has been provided. There are no less than ten in number, two of which are on the two broad piston rings. The last named have a rebate joint. It is just these little notions that help to make the Norton "unapproachable."

Illustrated List, with full details, sent free. The Norton Manufacturing Co., Ltd., Deritend Bridge, Floodgate St., Birmingham. London—Maudes' Motor Mart, 136, Great Portland Street, W.

S. & H.

NORTON NOTES

A STUDY IN HARMONY OF PARTS.

NOTE—the unique footboards, giving more comfort.

NOTE—the position of toolbag, giving accessibility.

NOTE—the neat and accessible engine.

NOTE—the very low seat—handle-bar control—adjustable pulley.

NOTE—to send for list. NORTON MANFG. CO., Ltd., Deritend Bridge, Floodgate Street, BIRMINGHAM.

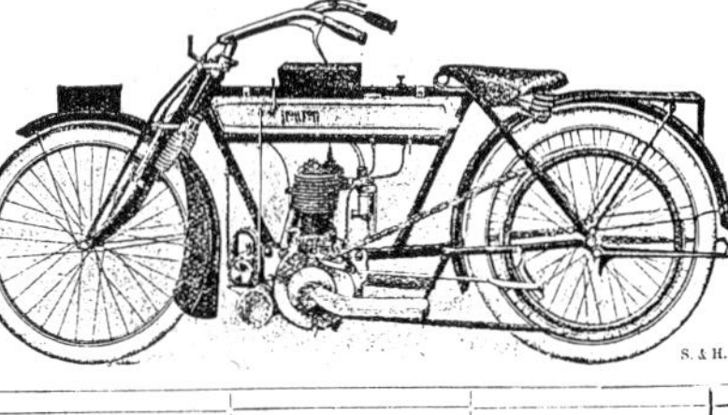

S. & H.

LEFT Pa Norton, hand on chin, chatting to rival Freddy Barnes of Zenith at the Streatham Club's hill climb at Titsey Hill, October 1910. Despite being a newcomer to the hill (no practising was allowed) Norton won the 500 cc racing machine class on his TT machine.

The topical advertisement (top) appeared on 7 February 1910. By September the approach was more technical (middle) but this series was short-lived and in February 1911 it was back to generalities (bottom).

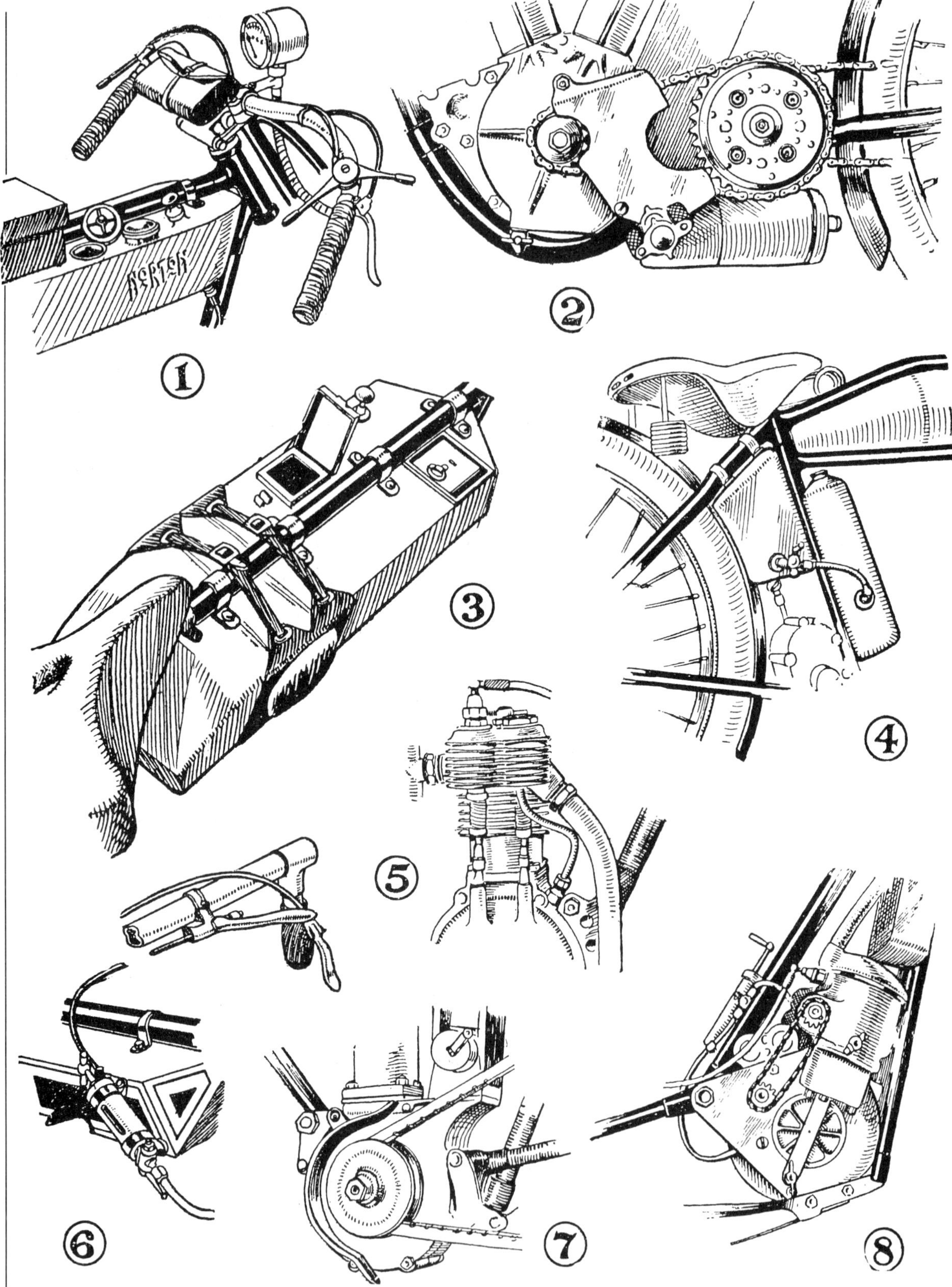

Novel mechanical fittings for the T.T. (1) Norton handlebars and quick-opening filler caps. (2) Chain guard on the two-speed Indians. (3) The Rudge two-gallon tank and special fillers. (4) The extra oil tank on the Indian machines: note the connection to the gearbox. (5) Pipe from the crankcase of a Dot machine to cool the exhaust valve. (6) Handlebar pump control on the Ariel. (7) Pulley shield on a Premier machine. (8) Rotary distributing valve fitted to the Scott machines.

The American Invasion

—of distinctly American motor cycles—of distinctly American design—built for distinctly American conditions, should prove a warning to the wideawake Britisher. Machines manufactured abroad of foreign material, and designed for service under different conditions, never **can** be as reliable and efficient as a British Built

"THE UNAPPROACHABLE"

NORTON

—made in England—of British Material by British workmen —designed for British service. Have a "Norton" with every up-to-date refinement.

Machines on show at Olympia.

THE NORTON MFG. CO., LTD., Deritend Bridge, Floodgate Street, Birmingham.

ABOVE **Knocking copy is nothing new – this example appeared in *The Motor Cycle* in November 1911, soon after American-built Indian twins had taken the first three places in the 1911 TT, the first over the Mountain circuit.**

LEFT **This lovely spread of technical drawings from the TT appeared in *Motor Cycling* in July 1911. Number 1 shows the handlebar and tank layout of the 490 cc.**

second overall. The only man to beat him was Arthur Moorhouse, later to die in a crash at Brooklands, who was riding a 7 hp twin-cylinder racing Indian. Certainly Brewster impressed the *Motor Cycling* reporter:

The spectators, who had been calmly walking up the hill in batches, did not seem to realise the necessity of keeping the course clear, and it was only when the roar of Brewster's Norton was heard in the distance that they thought of moving. However, when they saw the black figure bent low over the Norton tearing up the hill like an express train, the crowds quickly parted and let Brewster through. He was going at a tremendous speed, with his engine, as was afterwards calculated, turning at 3500 rpm. One could see him set his teeth at the corner, which he took magnificently without cutting out, sending a thrill through the crowd of spectators.

Norton himself was unable to compete. In fact, his left shoulder gave him trouble all winter – so much so that there was talk he had retired from competition. He refuted this in a letter in *Motor Cycling* in May 1911.

I should like to correct an impression that, as someone has put it, 'I have decided to let motor-cycling and competitions severely alone – for my health's sake.' This impression has doubtless arisen from the fact that for some six or seven months, since the Streatham hill-climb, in fact, I have been incapacitated from riding by an injury to my shoulder and arm sustained on Snaefell during TT week.

A keen rider who used a motorcycle as his everyday transport until chronic ill health forced him on to four wheels in the early 1920s, Norton continued:

. . . although not in the first bloom of youth, I am never better than when riding. Usually suffering from insomnia and nerves, after a run I almost invariably sleep well, and can certainly recommend motor-cycling as beneficial to one's general health. Contrary to giving up, my efforts are aimed at getting flexibility of the injured member in time to enable me to compete in the TT.

To ride in the 1911 race was not a decision to be made lightly, especially for a 42-year-old who was not in the best of health. For that year the races moved from the St John's circuit to the Mountain course, roughly the same as that used today. The decision was not welcomed by the majority of riders or manufacturers who, after a meeting during the Olympia Show week late in 1910, had urged the ACU not to make the move. They considered the longer circuit too demanding and dangerous.

Tragically, they were proved right even before a race

was held. Vic Surridge, who had recently set a new one-hour 500 cc record of just over 60 mph at Brooklands, crashed with fatal results. The accident occurred at Glen Helen. He skidded, hit the wall and when help arrived it was found, in the words of a contemporary report, 'that his skull was cracked and the poor fellow lifeless'.

That year, for the first time, there were two separate races held on different days – a Junior TT (for singles of 300 cc and twins up to 340 cc) and a Senior TT (500 cc singles/585 cc twins). Despite the moans the entry was up to 104, double that of the preceding year.

The Norton factory prepared two of their standard 79 × 100 mm sports roadsters for Norton and Brewster, the latter's engine having the cylinder lapped out by a half-millimetre to bring it closer to the 500 cc limit; racing was a very serious business even in those days.

To cope with the demands of the Mountain circuit, which included the 1400 ft climb from Ramsey to Brandeywell on the flank of Snaefell, and then the plunge down to Douglas, gears were fitted by Norton to the TT bikes for the first time; both sporting Armstrong Triplex three-speed hubs plus Blumfield quickly adjustable pulleys which were used to take up drive-belt stretch.

The course was little better than a cart-track. In Geoff Davison's *Story of the TT*, Frank Applebee, who later won the 1912 Senior for Scott, said:

> . . . there was no tar on the roads at all, except perhaps in Douglas. Dust was our main trouble, although of course we got plenty of mud, particularly under trees . . . at the end of the race many competitors had to be lifted from their machines . . . a rider was considered amazingly fresh if he could stand at the end of a race.

No wonder then that, according to *The Motor Cycle* report, 'J.L. Norton, the eldest competitor, received an extra-special cheer' as he got away from the start, then situated at the bottom of Bray Hill. But he was out of luck, a seized piston putting him out at Ramsey on the second lap.

Poor Brewster had a tougher time. He crashed at Quarter Bridge on the third lap, remounted and was then flung from his machine when the Armstrong Triplex hub gear seized solid as he was flying down the Mountain at close to 70 mph. American-built Indian machines with chain primary drive to a conventionally placed gearbox with clutch and final chain drive dominated the race to take the first three places.

On the mainland, Dan Bradbury clocked over 70 mph to win the Sheffield and Hallamshire flying kilometre competition – the first time this speed had been achieved by a 500 cc machine and a fine tribute to the Norton because Dan, later to become a leading Norton agent, tipped the scales at over 14 st (89 kg). In a testimonial letter used by Norton in an advertisement, Bradbury said:

HARRODS

HAVE IN **STOCK**

the finest assortment of **MOTOR CYCLES** in London at the **BEST PRICES**, amongst which are the following:

$2\frac{1}{2}$ h.p. "Elswick," F.E.
$3\frac{1}{2}$ h.p. "Matchless"
4 h.p. "Norton" (Big Four) 2 speed F.E.
$3\frac{1}{2}$ h.p. "Norton"
$3\frac{1}{2}$ h.p. "Rudge," F.E.
$3\frac{1}{2}$ h.p. "Rudge," Multi-speed
$3\frac{1}{2}$ h.p. "Singer," F.E.
$2\frac{1}{2}$ h.p. "Singer"
4 h.p. "Singer," 2 Speed F.E.
$3\frac{1}{2}$ h.p. "Zenith Gradua"
8 h.p. "Bat," 2 Speed

THE ABOVE ARE OFFERED SUBJECT TO BEING UNSOLD ON RECEIPT OF ORDER.

50 Machines in Stock to select from.

End of Season Special Bargains
at very favourable rates.

THE HOUSE for CYCLECARS

Any make supplied on Deferred Payments.

WRITE FOR SPECIAL LIST OF SECOND-HAND MACHINES.

HARRODS LTD. RICHARD BURBIDGE, — Managing Director. —
BROMPTON ROAD, LONDON, S.W.

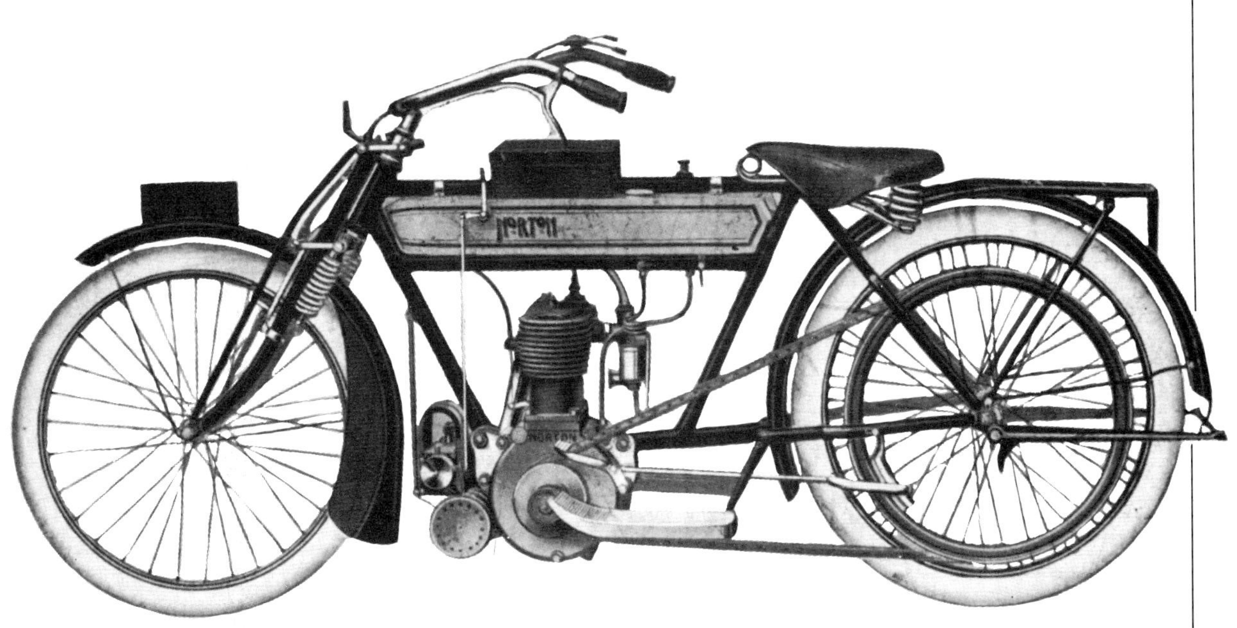

ABOVE **By 1911 the pedals had disappeared but the single cylinder side valve engine, available with capacities of 496 cc, 490 cc and 633 cc, was little changed. Note the aluminium footboards which Pa Norton preferred.**

LEFT **In 1912 Harrods was one of London's biggest motorcycle dealers; this advertisement appeared in *The Motor Cycle* in August that year.**

I should like to draw attention to the fine performance of my 1911 standard 3½ h.p. Norton with 79 mm by 100 mm engine . . . the speed works out at over 70 mph . . . . I should like to express my delight with the all-round excellence of the Norton. The engine is beautifully flexible, and it seems impossible to make it knock.

Recovered from his TT shaking, Brewster won the racing machine class, on handicap, at the famous Shelsley Walsh climb and made the second-fastest climb of the day. Hill-climbs were still popular but there were already signs that the sport was attracting the 'types not cared for'. A writer to *Motor Cycling* complained: 'On our way with our NSU and sidecar to Kop Hill for the Herts AC hill-climb two riders flew past without the slightest intimation that they wished to do so, thereby causing my wife to remark what a set of bounders motorcyclists were in general.' Shrewd woman!

Things then went a little quiet on the Norton front. There was no Norton stand at the show of 1911 but some bikes were on display on the Wall and Wilton stands. Following Indian's superb display in the TT and the sales drive that followed, Norton had a lovely 'knocking' advertisement in *The Motor Cycle* which stated:

The America Invasion – of distinctly American motor cycles – of distinctly American design – built for distinctly American conditions, should prove a warning to the wideawake Britisher. Machines manufactured abroad of foreign material, and designed for service under different conditions, can never be as reliable and efficient as a British built machine – made in England – of British material by British workmen – designed for British service.

The reasoning behind this tirade is not explained. Regrettably, it has proved inaccurate.

Despite not having a stand, Norton followed up with a full-page advertisement in *The Motor Cycle*, the first time the factory had taken such a large space. It was headed 'The sum total of Norton success is efficiency', and listed successes during the year together with the good points of the range, including: 'Note the very low seat, enabling you to plant both feet firmly on the ground' and 'Note the footboards giving perfect comfort and grip. Note the toolbag giving accessibility whilst riding. Note the neat and accessible engine, and the extreme get-at-ableness of all parts.'

The twins, never very good sellers, had been dropped completely as had the two-stroke, the JAP-powered lightweight and the ladies' model. Pa Norton had decided to concentrate on his beloved singles and offered three basic models – the new 79 × 100 mm, 490 cc, the older 82 × 94 mm, 496 cc, and the Big Four of 82 × 120 mm, 633 cc. The cheapest was the direct drive 82 × 94 mm at £48, the most expensive the 633 cc with Roc two-speed gear.

The company had drifted into financial problems. As noted earlier, Pa Norton had no interest in money and this, coupled with his love of constantly building new machines and competing in events, led to the bread-and-butter side of the business being neglected. In his book *Norton Story* Bob Holliday says it was in 1913 that Norton moved from Floodgate Street to Sampson Road North, but the advertisements prove otherwise. They show that it was during the winter of 1911–12 that the company name was changed from the Norton Manufacturing Company to Norton Motors. An advertisement that appeared on 23 November 1911 uses the old name, but one dated 28 March the following year has the simple title Norton Motors in the bottom right-hand corner, no Company and no Limited.

Incidentally the latter advertisement focused on the success of Oxford undergraduate A.C. Hardy who had just won the Oxford University hill-climb. This was run up Horsepath Hill near Wheatley that year and Hardy had a field day, winning the TT class and the Open category and making the second-fastest climb of the day, 'beating high powered twins'. In the bottom left-hand corner of the advertisement, under the heading 'London Agents', are listed Harrod's Stores, Brompton Road, S.W. and Robertson's Motor Agency, 157 Great Portland Street. The connection with Harrod's, which claimed at that time to have 'The finest assortment of motor-cycles in London', was maintained until the First World War.

The actual move from Floodgate Street to Sampson Road North came in August 1912. The company had been saved by R.T. (Bob) Shelley, a well-known Birmingham businessman of the day, who bought the company at auction. Sensibly he realised that Pa Norton was the company's greatest asset and he kept him on as joint managing director and installed Walter

The Norton team at the 1912 TT! At the controls is Pa Norton, on the pillion works rider Jack Emerson while the wicker sidecar is occupied by Pa's father. The machine is Pa's personal Big Four 633 cc single.

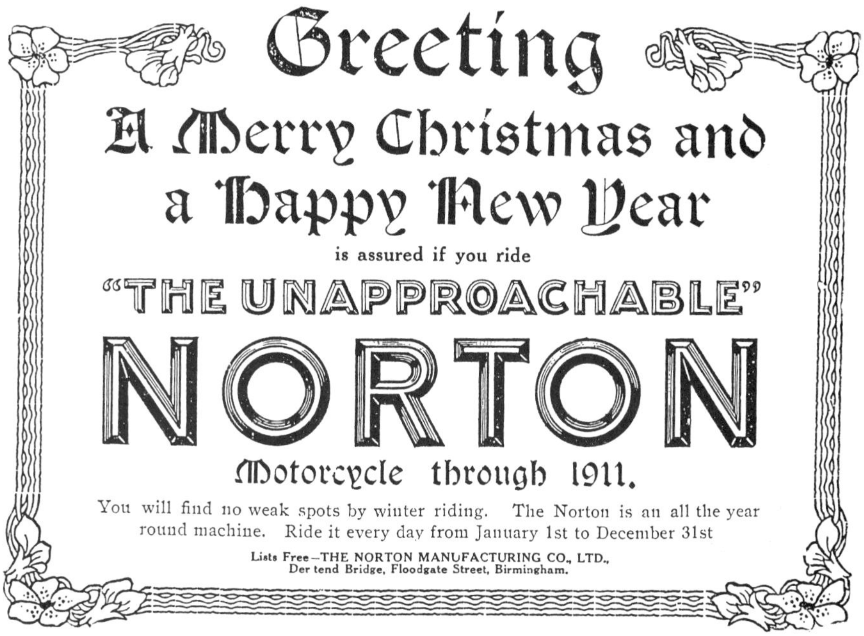

RIGHT This cheery advertisement appeared in *Motor Cycling* in December 1910.

Greeting

A Merry Christmas and
a Happy New Year

is assured if you ride

"THE UNAPPROACHABLE"

NORTON

Motorcycle through 1911.

You will find no weak spots by winter riding. The Norton is an all the year round machine. Ride it every day from January 1st to December 31st

Lists Free—THE NORTON MANUFACTURING CO., LTD.,
Der tend Bridge, Floodgate Street, Birmingham.

BELOW Typical TT going in 1912 as Frank Applebee negotiates the gate at Kate's Cottage. His machine is a two-stroke Scott and he won the Senior TT that year.

Mansell (known to most as Bill), one of his bright young henchmen, to keep an eye on the financial side of things.

As luck would have it, Mansell was already a Norton owner and enthusiast. After discarding two earlier machines he had bought a second-hand Norton for £11 the year before and was well satisfied with it. The Sampson Road North premises were still multi-storey but they were more spacious, and nearby Shelley had a factory where engine parts could be made so that Norton became largely independent from outside suppliers as far as the basic machine went.

Back-tracking a little, Norton had produced the first 350 cc with a Norton engine earlier in the year for Hardy to ride as a member of the ACU's team in the first English–Dutch trial. He did not in fact make the squad himself but rode as a member of the reserve team and finished the course without loss of marks.

Over the years the question of when Norton's first 350 cc was built appears to have puzzled motorcycle historians, but the evidence to be found in the technical press of the day seems conclusive. Some claim that the machine was powered by a JAP unit but Norton, in a success advertisement, talked of: 'Mr F.A. Hardy on the 2½ h.p. Norton Lightweight.' Later in the year, in a Buyer's Guide, there is listed a 2½ hp Norton with Armstrong three-speed hub gear and under the heading 'engine' the make is given as 'Norton' with bore and stroke of 70 × 90 mm, 346 cc. Having said that, the Hardy machine was a one-off produced for the trial and probably exhibited to see what the response would be. It certainly never went into production.

The 1912 TT was yet another Isle of Man disaster as far as Nortons were concerned. Two 490s, now with Sturmey-Archer hub gears, were entered to be ridden by Jack Emerson and P.W. Owen, with both Pa Norton and Brewster giving the race a miss. Emerson had what can be described as an interesting race, changing the plug four times, securing a loose magneto and retiming the ignition. After repairing a puncture he retired. Owen was also in plug trouble. His broke and part fell into the engine where it jammed and bent a valve.

Students of journalism may be interested to learn that the media of the day were already using the now time-honoured phrase: 'Mona's Isle, the motorcyclist's Mecca.' It was coined by a scribe in *Motor Cycling* in July 1912.

Pa Norton's daughter Grace remembers the early days at Sampson Road North and tells a delightful story.

> We children were not encouraged to go to the factory though we lived close to it but I remember that my father had a guard dog there, a fierce terrier. It was named Norton and it soon became known among the workers and visiting tradesmen as the Unapproachable Norton!

Jack Emerson with his 490 cc Norton on which he won the British Motor Cycle Racing Club's 150 mile Senior TT at Brooklands, September 1912, breaking three world records. The next day he rode the bike back to his home in Hull!

CHAPTER 4

Brooklands 1912–1914

Norton's greatest success in 1912 and the years leading up to the First World War were achieved at the Brooklands circuit. This, the first purpose-built motor-racing track, had been built on flat meadowland between Weybridge and Byfleet in Surrey. Today the remains of the vast concrete circuit are still impressive; in June 1907 when the track opened it was one of the wonders of the modern world.

It was wide, very steeply banked at both ends and nearly three miles around. Right up to when it closed for ever at the outbreak of the Second World War in September 1939, motorcycles could, by the very brave, be held flat out all the way round – the two inhibiting factors being the weather and the bumps which worsened over the years as the hastily built track settled.

Even so, John Cobb lapped at 143.44 mph in his 24-litre Napier-Railton while the motorcycle record stands for ever to the credit of Noel Pope. Riding a supercharged 998 cc JAP-powered Brough Superior he clocked 124.51 mph in 1939 in poor conditions, a strong wind slowing him down on one straight and causing the machine to weave and dance on the banking. In the days before the First World War, any machine could be held against the stop all the way for as long as it held together.

Certainly it was a marvellous facility for racing, record breaking and, perhaps even more importantly, for testing. Weather permitting, the track could be used virtually every day of the year. The first motorcycle meeting had been held early in 1908 but it was not until 1912 that a Norton set a world record there.

Early in the year a tragedy had occurred involving the Indian rider Moorhouse who had finished third in the preceding June's Senior TT. Just days after raising the outright one-hour record to over 70 mph, he suffered a fatal crash while out practising on his eight-valve Indian V-twin. Reported *The Motor Cycle*: 'He crashed into a telegraph pole which bears the imprint of his goggles. The cause of the accident was that splendid self-confidence without which daring deeds can never be done.'

This did not deter Norton regular Percy Brewster, and in July 1912 he set a new 500 cc record for the flying mile at 73.57 mph. More success followed in September when Jack Emerson, a Norton dealer from Hull, rode his 490 cc machine from his home to Brooklands to compete in the BMCRC Senior TT – a marathon 150-mile event.

It was a flat-out blind and Emerson set three 500 cc long-distance records – the 100 miles, the two hours and the 150 miles. The Norton ran without trouble, averaging about 64 mph. Emerson decided to keep going at the end of the race, hoping to add the three-hour record, but the rear tyre had had enough and burst just five minutes from the end. Just what he felt like after hammering round the already bumpy concrete track on a rigid frame machine with two-inch tyres pumped rock-hard to keep them on the rims is difficult to imagine, but the next day he rode home to Hull!

In October he was back. *The Motor Cycle* reported: 'Emerson's long-stroke Norton ran like a dream, winning the Senior Hour race by over a lap . . ..' He averaged 64 mph and beat, among others, Matchless star Charlie Collier and Indian expert Oliver Godfrey.

For those interested in technicalities, four valves per cylinder were in vogue at this time, just as they are in the car world today. Godfrey's 500 cc Indian had a four-valve head and George Stanley, riding a factory Singer with four valves, pushed the 500 cc hour record up to 67.4 mph at Brooklands in October 1912.

At the final meeting of the year in November, Godfrey on his Indian beat Brewster in the 500 cc race but Emerson came out on top in the one-lap 500 cc time trial, averaging 67.72 mph – the seemingly technically inferior side-valve proving faster than the sophisticated American rival. Strange to think that some forty years later the boot was to be on the other foot, with overhead camshaft Nortons competing against side-valve Indians!

It was a time of reorganisation and rationalisation at Norton. Only four models were listed for 1913 and one of these was the 70 × 90 mm, 346 cc machine which was never produced, apart from the prototype ridden by Hardy in the trial in Holland. The simple range consisted of two 79 × 100 mm, 490 cc bikes, a tourer and a TT sports model, plus the Big Four 633 cc for sidecar work. Pedals were finally out. They were no longer listed even as an extra, but you still could not buy a Norton with a 'proper' gearbox and clutch. If you wanted gears your only option was the Armstrong three-speed hub.

The Norton recovery was not aided by a glut of machines. Production had again outpaced demand and in March 1913 Harrod's had a clear-out, advertising

EVERYBODY KNOWS that a

specially tuned machine by a good maker, ridden by a picked rider, whose business in life is to do nothing else, can accomplish a good performance in a hill-climb or race, but there is only one make, of motor cycle that, taken from stock exactly as supplied to the public, will equal the performance mentioned in the following extracts from a customer's letters. That machine is, of course,

SCOTTISH BORDER The **UNAPPROACHABLE** **NORTON**

M.C.C. OPEN HILL CLIMB, July 12th (3½ h.p. long stroke, 490 c.c.)

FASTEST SINGLE CYLINDER, beating 6 & 8 h.p. twins easily

Extracts from customer's letters :—

July 10.

I am riding at Hawick on Saturday, but am not going to do any special tuning, as I want to see what a machine as received from the makers can do.

Yours faithfully, ROY G. MACGIBBON.

July 12th.

As I mentioned in my last letter I rode out to Jedburgh on Saturday, and took part in the hill-climb organised by the Scottish Border M.C.C. . . . The results you will see in "The Motor Cycle," but for your information I may say I won class 4 (open) and class 9 (general) making **fastest single-cylinder time of the day.**

Yours faithfully, ROY G. MACGIBBON.

I may say that I adhered to my plan of not touching the engine. . . . . which shows that one firm at least send out their machines properly tuned up and run in.

POWER and plenty of it!

NORTON MOTORS
Sampson Road North,
BIRMINGHAM.
Telegrams—"NORTOMO."
Telephone—481 Victoria.

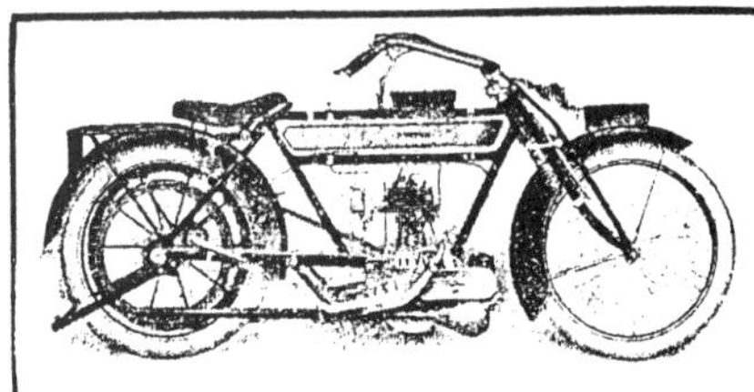

ENGLISH-DUTCH INTERNATIONAL TRIAL.

TWO

NORTON

riders gained

HIGHEST POSSIBLE AWARDS

in the Reserve Section, Private Owners, Mr. F. A. Hardy on the 2½-h.p. NORTON LIGHTWEIGHT, and Mr. Seymour Smith on the 3½-h.p. NORTON STANDARD.

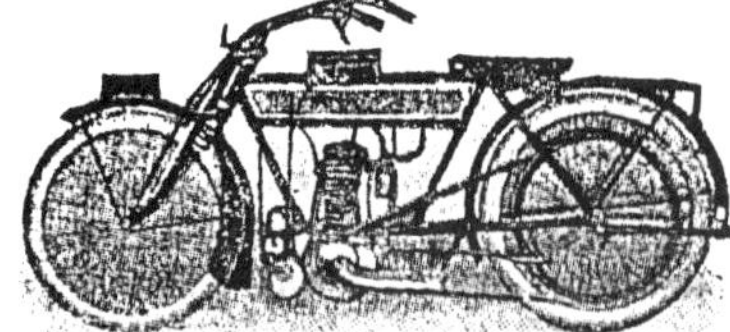

Norton Catalogue free on request.

NORTON MOTORS.
(note new address)
Sampson Road North, BIRMINGHAM.
London Agents—Harrods Stores, Brompton Rd. S.W. and Robertsons, Great Portland St., W.

ABOUT THE "BIG 4."

SHEFFIELD,
Aug. 10th, 1912.

MESSRS. THE NORTON MANUFACTURING CO., LTD.

Dear Sirs,

My wife end I have just completed a tour of 1,133 miles on the Norton "Big Four" and sidecar, and I thought it would be of interest to you to know that the machine ran perfectly.

We went from Sheffield to Edinburgh, Aberdeen, Perth, visiting Loch Tay, Crianlarich, Loch Lomond, Helensburgh, Glasgow, Ayr, Ballanbrae, Shonair, Dumfries, Carlisle, Penrith, Shap, Kendal, Settle, Shipton, Doncaster to Sheffield.

We had not the slightest trouble, and ALL the hills (and as you will know many of them are very stiff ones) were negotiated on the top gear (4¾ to 1) The engine is truly a marvel, and I am very pleased with the combination.

The petrol consumption for the tour was 90½ miles to the gallon.

Yours faithfully,
FRANK W. LAND

A test such as this, in the hands of a private user, emphasises clearly the NORTON'S

RELIABILITY, POWER, ECONOMY.

STRENUOUS WORK—

as opposed to "sprint" records. can only be accomplished by a machine in which every part has been carefully designed and constructed to stand maximum stresses for long periods. The **still unbeaten record** standing to the credit of the

UNAPPROACHABLE NORTON

3½ h.p. long stroke 490 c.c.
(T.T. MODEL £50)

150 MILES IN 140 MINUTES

could only have been made by the Norton. No other engine **even in the 750 c.c. class** has ever done anything like it. Think it over and write for 1913 Catalogue (2nd Edition now in the Press).

NORTON MOTORS,
Sampson Road, North,
BIRMINGHAM.

Telephone—481 Victoria.
Telegrams—"Nortomo, Birmingham."

ABOVE June 1913 – Jack Emerson who had set the records does not get a mention.

ABOVE LEFT This 1912 advertisement emphasises that the Norton successes were achieved on standard machines.

LEFT 22 August 1912. F. A. Hardy rode an experimental 350 cc Norton in the Anglo-Dutch Trial. The factory had moved from Floodgate Street.

a long list of cut-price bikes including the Big Four which was offered for £51 against the list price of £63.

That same March *The Motor Cycle* ran a feature in which prominent personalities were asked to predict what motorcycles would be like ten years hence. It was obvious that Pa Norton was under no illusions, for he wrote: '. . . how very crude and wasteful our usual present methods are, and for this, if for no other reason, they will not and cannot survive'. He forecast that 'forced lubrication' would replace the crude wet-sump systems of the day and that single-gear machines like the basic Norton would be unknown except 'perhaps for track work'. Which, as any speedway follower knows, is true to this day.

Earlier that winter Pa Norton had written an article for *Motor Cycling* under the heading 'Cooling Systems Compared' in which he came out strongly in favour of air cooling. Said he: 'There appears a general tendency, in spite of ideas to the contrary, to make the motor-bicycle too complicated, to require too much of it, and to add too much to it,' and he finished in punchy style: '. . . if as much thought be devoted to perfecting direct cooling as has been employed to bring car radiators up to their present state of efficiency, we shall all look upon water-cooling for motor-bicycles as being as necessary as the proverbial knocker upon a pig-sty door'. And in an advertisement that appeared around this time, Norton claimed: 'The unapproachable Norton, holder of 7 world records, is the most distinctive motor-cycle constructed on accepted lines. No freak designs, no freak fittings – just good substantial British engineering.'

The TT was under fire. After only two years on the Mountain circuit *The Motor Cycle* suggested, in a powerful editorial, that 'a safer course should be found . . . the course is admittedly bad and the arrangements for conveying man and machine to and from the Island are indescribably bad'. Regular visitors to the TT will smile ruefully at this early criticism!

And the supporters were already in deep trouble. Under the heading 'Last Chance for the TT' *The Motor Cycle* ran the following news item: 'In order to avoid desecration of the Sabbath, a strong ground of complaint, no motor vehicles will be allowed to use the roads on the Sunday preceding the races.' In other

THE NORTON 'BIG FOUR.'

The first long stroke big single engine introduced to the motor cycling world has astonished engineers by its remarkable development of SMOOTH POWER.

It has created a new and simple class of passenger vehicle, and the Norton Co. may well feel flattered by the numerous attempts to emulate their sound practice.

The Engine is of 82 × 120 bore and stroke = 636 capacity. Thirteen air ducts pass through those parts of the cylinder most subjected to heat, a uniformity of temperature approximating to water cooling being thereby obtained without additional weight or complication. Note the exceptionally clean design of crankcase and the capacious oil well, the perfectly straight exhaust tube, and the simple external exhaust valve lifter.

Extract from *The Scottish Motor Cyclist*, Dec. 10th, 1913.

"Now that there is a growing tendency to increase the cubic capicity of the "one lunger," special interest is attached to the big Norton single, in view of the fact that the 636 c.c. engine was introduced by the Norton Company as far back as 1908; in fact, points of design introduced by Mr. Norton in 1899 may be found in more than one 1914 engine, and we saw at the Norton works the other day a ten-year-old cylinder which had the air space between cylinder wall and valve pocket, which is such an excellent feature of the present Norton engine. This feature is, of course, largely responsible for cool running, and explains to some extent the way in which the Norton can be run at high speed for long periods without overheating."

NORTON MOTORS, BIRMINGHAM.

London: Robertson's, Great Portland Street.

NORTON

BIG FOUR

FOR SIDECAR WORK

Telephone
4 8 5
Victoria.

NORTON MOTORS,
SAMPSON ROAD NORTH, BIRMINGHAM.

Telegrams—
NORTOMO
Birmingham

words, it was completely taboo to ride your motorcycle on the Isle of Man on that day – which became known to enthusiasts as 'Dead Sunday'. What a contrast to present times when visitors are positively encouraged to ride around the circuit, part of which is made one-way for the day, on what is now called 'Mad Sunday'. Certainly this brings home the hostility against which the early manufacturers and riders had to battle.

Three Nortons were entered in the 1913 TT to be ridden by Brewster, Emerson and Bernard Shaw (not *the* Bernard Shaw, though the famous playwright was a keen motorcyclist and despite his 56 years had ordered a new Lea-Francis at Olympia in November 1912). All three retired. Shaw on the first lap when he crashed at Glen Mona and the others on the second lap – Brewster with a broken piston ring and Emerson with tyre trouble. But the Nortons were noted as fast by *The Motor Cycle* reporter: 'Undoubtedly the fastest ascent of the hill (Creg Willey's) was made by Brewster (Norton) who came up at an extraordinary pace and easily passed Alexander (Indian) on the way, though the latter was going very well.' Alexander in fact finished third in a race won by Tim Wood on a two-stroke Scott. There were 96 starters that year riding 32 different makes.

Norton were represented in the Birmingham–Land's End trial by Rem Fowler, Bill Mansell and Emerson but torrential rain plagued the event and all three ran into trouble. On the speed front, R. Flint won the Scarborough Speed Trials when he covered the flying kilometre at 74.53 mph on his 490 cc Norton.

One of the benefits of the link with Shelley was that a young tuner-rider by the name of Daniel O'Donovan, brother-in-law of R.T. Shelley, switched from NSU to Norton after riding one of the German machines in the TT. He first appeared on a Norton at a Brooklands meeting in August 1913 and on 30 September broke four world records – the 500 cc flying-start five miles at 71.54 mph and the standing start ten miles at 68.08 mph – both fast enough also to beat the 750 cc records.

Reported *Motor Cycling*: 'The Norton machine ridden by D.R. O'Donovan has an interesting history. The machine succeeded in capturing the 2h and 100 mile records last year and was then thrown on the scrapheap. O'Donovan found the parts dismantled and re-

ABOVE LEFT *The Motor Cycle*, 8 January 1914, and Pa Norton's favourite, the lusty 'Big Four'.

LEFT *Motor Cycling* (17 March 1914), the 'Big Four' with the sidecar added to the range in 1913.

RIGHT O'Donovan used a Binks carburettor on his 490 cc Norton when he broke eight world records, including 81.05 mph for the flying kilometre.

81 Miles

per hour on a
3½ h.p. Single
NORTON with

BINKS MOUSETRAP

Carburettor

by Mr. DANIEL O'DONOVAN.

On Monday last, Mr. Daniel O'Donovan, at Brooklands, broke no less than 8 records, accomplishing on his 3½ h.p. "Norton," fitted with Binks Carburettor, the incredible and hitherto impossible speed of over 81 miles per hour. Mr. O'Donovan selected the Binks Carburettor because he proved it to be faster than any other; he was out to break records, and his using this carburettor was not the subject of any money bargain.

The celebrated record breaking "Mousetrap" Carburettor,
Price £5 - 0 - 0

IF YOU WANT TO GO FASTER OR GET BEAUTIFUL SLOW RUNNING AND JUST A TICK OVER WHEN FREE, OR TO WIN HILL-CLIMBS AND RACES, AND DO ENORMOUS MILEAGE PER GALLON, YOU MUST GET A BINKS YOU CANNOT DO IT ANY OTHER WAY. SPECIFY IT ON YOUR NEW MACHINE, OR IMPROVE YOUR OLD ONE.

SEND FOR LIST AND TREATISE ON CARBURATION.

C. BINKS, LTD., ECCLES.

BINKS

MORE WORLD'S RECORDS

British Motor Cycle Racing Club Meeting,
Brooklands Senior T.T. Race, 150 Miles,

Mr. J. L. E. Emerson on a 79 x 100 — 490 c.c.

NORTON

(the smallest engine in the field)

WON, setting up the following

WORLD'S RECORDS:

100 MILES—
1 hour, 33 min., 25·4 sec.

150 MILES—
2 hrs., 20 min., 27 sec.

2 HOURS—
127 miles,
645 yards.

The LONG STROKE

UNAPPROACHABLE

NORTON

The marvellous regularity with which the NORTON ran can be appreciated from the fact that each of these records represent an average speed of about 64 miles per hour.

REMEMBER—
The NORTON holds the
1 MILE WORLD'S RECORD
73·57 MILES PER HOUR
made by Mr. P. Brewster. July 20th, 1912.

NORTON MOTORS,

Sampson Road North,
:: BIRMINGHAM. ::

LONDON AGENTS: Harrod's Stores, Brompton Rd., S.W.; Robertson's Motor Agency, 157, Great Portland Street, W.

assembled them himself, tuned the machine and proceeded to make new records.'

This indicates that it was the same machine used by Emerson, but why it had been discarded is not explained. More likely O'Donovan found it partly dismantled at the Norton works. Capitalising on the records, Norton ran half-page advertisements under the heading 'O'Donovan Did It on the Unapproachable Norton'. He continued to do it in impressive fashion and quickly became established in Norton folk lore.

For the record, his machine was fitted with an AMAC carburettor, Lyso belt and Continental tyres, and it ran on Wakefield oil and Pratt's motor spirit. Nortons were not slow to take advantage of the link with Brooklands and O'Donovan. Less than two months after his record-breaking spree, a Brooklands Special model was on the Norton stand at Olympia.

Said *The Motor Cycle* report: 'A special feature of the Norton exhibit is the Brooklands Special model and each machine leaving the works is guaranteed to have exceeded sixty-five miles per hour for one lap at Brooklands, and a Brooklands certificate to this effect is supplied with each machine.' It could be had either with single-speed direct belt drive or with a Sturmey-Archer hub three-speed gear.

An innovation was that Norton offered their own sidecar for sale, bolted to the Big Four, which by this time had sidecar lugs brazed into the frame, one of the first to have integral rather than clamped-on lugs. Other features included aluminium rubber-covered footboards (Pa Norton much preferred the comfort of these footboards to the more popular footrests), glass-topped filler caps and black celluloid-covered handlebars. Looking to the export market, Norton offered a 'Colonial' model with increased ground clearance.

An item in *Motor Cycling* hinted at a 980 cc big twin: 'It is also intended to market a big V twin composed of two of the 79 × 100 mm cylinders at a not far distant date.' As far as we know this was never built. Speaking of the new sidecar (built for Norton by Freddy Watson who later founded Watsonian Sidecars) the same magazine wrote:

> The body is coach built and upholstered in rich, deep-green pegamoid, with spring back and cushions. Below the seat is a capacious cupboard for tools etc. In order to prevent annoying sideswing when turning the body is pivoted at the front in such a manner that only vertical movement of the leaf spring is permitted.

Asides from that period are that Indian had on show at Olympia a V-twin with electric starter, electric horn and lights, while Sir Arthur Conan Doyle wrote enthusiastically of his exploits on a bicycle fitted with a Wall Auto-Wheel (a device with engine and third wheel which could be bolted to any bicycle): '. . . we are in the presence of a complete revolution in the means of locomotion . . . in a year or so they will be everywhere.

THE UNAPPROACHABLE

MOTORCYCLES
1914

THE ORIGINAL LONG STROKE
AND BIG SINGLE

ABOVE **The familiar Norton trademark first appeared on the 1914 catalogue but was not used on the tanks of the machines until 1915. It was designed by Pa Norton and his elder daughter Ethel who was an art student.**

OPPOSITE **Record breaking at Brooklands was big business pre-1914.**

They are cheap, effective and they meet a popular want.'

Just after the show, Norton ran an advertisement that poses more questions than it answers. It claims: 'Norton introductions of 1899 and later are being advertised by "newcomers and manufacturers" for their 1914 models . . .. No other engine has equal power, such smooth power, or is as simple.' In the corner is a box with a quote attributed to the *Cycle and Motor Cycle Trader* which reads: 'Mr J.L. Norton is one of the pioneer designers of motorcycles, and has probably done more than any one man to improve the design and efficiency of the motorcycle engine.'

The 1899 theme was used again early in 1914 when an advertisement quoted *The Scottish Motor Cyclist* as saying:

> . . . in fact points of design introduced by Mr Norton in 1899 may be found in more than one 1914 engine, and we saw at the Norton works the other day a ten-year-old cylinder which had the air-space between cylinder wall and valve pocket, which is such an excellent feature of the present Norton engine. This feature is of course, largely responsible for cool running, and explains to some extent the way in which the Norton can be run at high speed for long periods without overheating.

Certainly Norton was one of the first to realise that the great enemy of performance and reliability in those early engines was overheating. To minimise this he not only designed his engines with an air space between the cylinder wall and the valve chest but also made sure that the exhaust port design allowed the hot combustion gases to escape as easily as possible. In this he was ahead of his rivals, and the ability of those early Nortons to run flat out without overheating was the cornerstone of Norton success.

Just how much motor-cycling was booming is shown

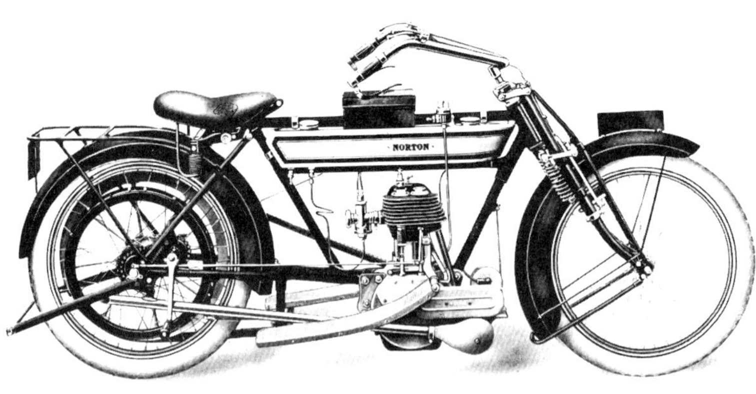

THE NORTON "BIG FOUR"
(Equivalent to the average 6-7 h.p.)

Fitted with Long Stroke Engine of 636 c.c. (82 × 120). Three Speed. Handle-starter. 2½in. Tyres.

Price - £62 0 0

The engine is of the medium compression type and has extraordinary pulling powers on top gear. It DOES NOT knock, and this fact, coupled with the high efficiency, all-round general excellence, and speed of this model, appeals very strongly to all users.

Long, exceedingly comfortable Footboards, Mudguard Valances to front and rear wheels, and Padded Pan Saddle are but a few of the items which give the rider the maximum of comfort under all conditions.

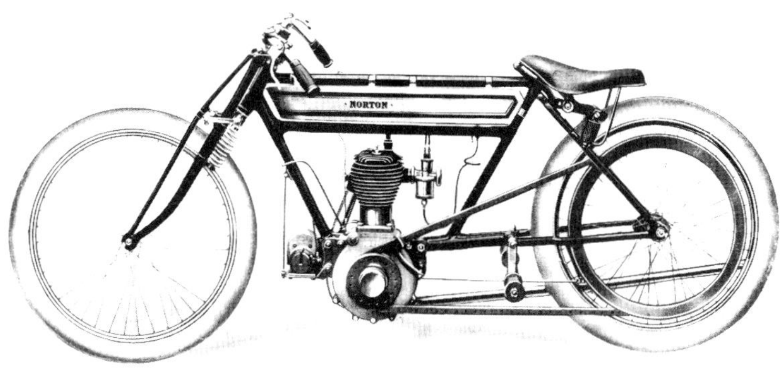

NORTON "BROOKLANDS SPECIAL"

Price - £60 0 0

Each Engine carries a Brooklands certificate, showing that it has officially exceeded a speed of 65 m.p.h. for one lap.

(SEE OPPOSITE PAGE)

ABOVE A page from the 1914 catalogue showing the famous Brooklands Special, sold with a certificate warranting that it had covered a lap of Brooklands at over 65 mph. The road going BRS (Brooklands Road Special) was guaranteed good for 60 mph.

ABOVE LEFT Balloon tyres and a three-speed hub gearbox with hand starter were part of the specification of the 1914 Norton 'Big Four' – together with long footboards and swept-back handlebars.

LEFT This artist's impression of a Norton rider at speed appeared in *The Motor Cycle* of 12 February 1914.

by the fact that the circulation of *The Motor Cycle* touched 90,000 in 1914 – roughly equal to the number of machines on the road. The rival *Motor Cycling* was not far behind so there must have been a massive overlap of readers, but as both titles cost only a penny and were quite lavish productions, with full-colour pictures on the front pages of special issues, this was not surprising.

The motorcycle was still a sporting vehicle for the better-off rather than a means of cheap transport for the masses. An editorial from 1914 poses the question 'Why you should be a motor-cyclist', answering: '. . . it is the best gift of the twentieth century . . . the most enjoyable pastime in the world . . . the beauty spots of Europe within reach'.

In April O'Donovan did it again! This time he really rocked the two-wheeled world when he topped 80 mph for the first time on a 500 cc machine. The record was set at Brooklands on 6 April when the 'Wizard', as he became known, clocked 81.05 mph for the flying kilometre and 78.6 mph for the mile. He had first taken the Norton out with sidecar attached to capture the three-wheeler kilometre record at 64.65 mph and the mile at 62.07 mph. All four beat the existing 750 cc figures so that O'Donovan had bagged eight records in a day.

Even today, 81 mph is fast. When you pause to reflect that it was achieved on a side-valve, single-cylinder machine with cast-iron head and barrel, a cast-iron piston, running on fuel of dubious octane rating on a spindly motorcycle with no rear springing and rock-hard tyres, it is positively startling! And it must have broken the hearts of the designers of the seemingly more advanced four-valve Indian and Singer 500s, not to mention the factory ABC with flat-twin engine on which former Norton star Jack Emerson had recently hoisted the 500 cc record into the high seventies.

O'Donovan's Norton was fitted with a Binks 'rat-trap' carburettor (so called because the curiously shaped air inlet looked like a popular trap of the day), a simple device that the inventor and manufacturer, Mr C. Binks of Eccles, Lancashire, used to advertise extensively, always with a picture of himself pointing menacingly at a drawing of the instrument.

Police persecution was a talking point in those days. Traps to operate the 20 mph speed limit were in force to such an extent that the press carried paragraphs warning readers of their whereabouts. For example: 'A

This is Old Miracle – the long-stroke, side-valve on which Daniel O'Donovan set numerous world records including the flying kilometre at 82.50 mph in 1915.

police trap is being rigorously worked between Acton Vale tram terminus and Ealing with the policemen disguised as fishermen.' *Motor Cycling* even carried a list of towns that were carrying the speed-trap policy to such extremes that readers were urged to boycott them completely. Henley-in-Arden, Kingston, Bromley and

Godalming appeared regularly on this black list and the hope was that traders would notice the loss of custom.

An amusing advertisement offered for sale Dunhill's Bobby Finders, a pair of miniature binoculars that a rider would wear like spectacles and which the blurb claimed 'Will enable you to spot a policeman at half a mile even if disguised as a respectable man'. What they did to the rider's normal vision is not recorded.

By this time the TT was so popular that *Motor Cycling* decided to run a railway excursion to the 1914 races. The train was to leave Euston on the evening of Wednesday 20 May and travel to Liverpool where a steamer would take the enthusiasts over to arrive in good time for Thursday's Senior TT. The return boat would leave Douglas at 4 p.m. and the happy band would get back to London at 2 a.m. on Friday.

The cost was £1 3s (£1.15) and there would be a dining car both ways. As *Motor Cycling* said: 'Every motorcyclist who can absent himself from business on the Thursday will thus be able to witness the Senior race with the least possible inconvenience.' The excursion proved so popular that two trains had to be run, and it was the start of a tradition that was not abandoned until well after the Second World War.

Again Norton's performance on the island was poor. Three bikes were entered, including O'Donovan. He retired, while the Braid brothers finished last and nearly last. Colourful riding gear was creeping in and *The Motor Cycle* reporter commented: 'Some morbid individuals actually had skull and crossbones painted on their helmets. These were very rightly barred.' In fact 1914 was the first year competitors had to wear crash helmets. This ruling followed the death of Rudge rider F.E. Bateman who had died the preceding year after crashing at Keppel Gate.

O'Donovan restored morale when he set four more world records at Brooklands on 17 July. He clocked 75.88 mph for the flying-start five miles and 73.29 mph for the standing-start ten miles. Both were also records in the 750 cc category. The Wizard's best lap was 76.07 mph and nine days later he won a ten-mile 500 cc race at 70.31 mph, beating Stanley on a special Triumph by just a fifth of a second.

War was only days away and while there had been little mention of possible hostilities, once the balloon did go up the press jumped on the bandwagon. *Motor Cycling* was full of warlike articles. 'How to Shoot with Revolver and Rifle', by Walter Winans, champion revolver shot of the world, was accompanied by 'right way' and 'wrong way' photographs. It was followed up by a feature which explained how to use your machine for cover and how to aim from the saddle while travelling at full speed.

Motorcyclists were urged to join the forces and there was a tempting recruitment article which offered £1 15s (£1.75) a week (more than I received as a National Serviceman in 1949), a bounty of £10 on joining (around £500 today) and an assurance that the government would buy the rider's machine at valuation or replace it with a new one. Commenting on the war, an item in *Motor Cycling* claimed: 'The first invasion of Luxembourg by the Germans was carried out by men mounted on motor-cycles.'

CHAPTER 5

Gears, chains and clutches 1914–1918

Initially the First World War made little difference to Nortons. The factory had not been invited to the War Office trials of 1912 held at Brooklands. Obviously the powers that be did not consider the little Birmingham factory, producing very few machines and in serious financial problems, to be worthy of a trial, let alone an actual order.

Among those assessed at Brooklands were bikes from the Triumph, Premier, Zenith, Douglas, Rudge, Royal Enfield, Bradbury and P and M factories. The trials included speed, reliability, cross-country and hill-climbing tests and resulted in massive Army orders for single-cylinder Triumph and flat-twin Douglas solos plus V-twin Royal Enfields for the Machine Gun Corps. The P and M sloper single (later to become famous as the Panther) was favoured by the Royal Flying Corps.

Without the need to concentrate on producing military models, Nortons were left to pursue a normal development programme and in November 1914 announced the 1915 range of machines, which marked a big step forward. For the first time a 'proper' countershaft gearbox and all chain drive were fitted to the two main models – the 633 cc Big Four and the standard 490 cc.

Previously there had been no chain-drive Nortons and the only gears available had been the various makes of hub units (notably Armstrong, Roc and Sturmey-Archer) or the crude expanding-pulley type. An additional benefit of the new set-up was that for the first time the Nortons were fitted with a modern-style clutch. This breakthrough was made possible by the new adoption of a three-speed Sturmey-Archer gearbox with two-plate cork-insert clutch and hand-change which the Nottingham gearbox makers had developed in cooperation with Norton.

Writing in *The Motor Cycle*, Sturmey-Archer designer Jack Cohen enthused about the Big Four Norton and sidecar that he had used to test the prototype gearbox: '. . . over the hilliest roads and tracks it has been possible to find the long-stroke Norton showed to particular advantage in long stretches of low gear work over abominable surfaces, keeping most wonderfully cool under the most trying circumstances.'

In fact he used three Nortons for test purposes between 1913 and 1916 and covered over 50,000 miles on them, ranging from the Peak District near his Nottingham base to Scotland and North Wales. In addition to the all-chain models, Norton offered a chain-cum-belt layout with chain drive to the gearbox then by belt from clutch to rear wheel, preferred by those who claimed the belt gave a smoother, quieter drive.

A basic 490 cc with direct belt drive (rather misleadingly called the TT model) was retained, while the Brooklands model was offered in two guises – the stripped racing Brooklands Special with a 70 mph guarantee and the super-sports Brooklands Road Special, certified to have lapped the famous Surrey oval at 65 mph. Both were direct-belt-drive machines of the type favoured by the 'speed merchants' of the day – no clutch, no gears, although many fitted the Phillipson pulley to the engine shaft, which varied the gear automatically under the influence of speed and torque.

There was already confusion about the two Brooklands models. In January 1915 *The Motor Cycle* tried to clear this up.

> As there appears to be some misapprehension on the point of speed guaranteed by the firm, it may be well to mention the exact figure. The Brooklands Track Special is sold with a guarantee stating that it is capable of 70 mph for one lap of Brooklands and of 75 mph over the flying kilometre. The Brooklands Road Special, which is similar to the Track Special but fitted with mudguards, etc., is guaranteed to do 65 mph for a lap and 70 mph for a flying kilometre. The TT machine, which carries no guarantee, is stated to be capable of 65 mph.

All three machines were powered by basically the same side-valve 79 × 100 mm, 490 cc engine though the two faster machines were fitted with a domed piston to raise the compression ratio.

The first of the 1915 machines had the old-style logo on the tank but this was soon replaced by the 'curly N' trademark still in use today. This first appeared on the front of the 1914 catalogue, a beautifully produced 24-page brochure which spoke of 'an uninterrupted record of production and experience since 1899' and went on to claim that 'The Norton never breaks valves.'

Grace remembered that her father and her elder sister Ethel designed the new logo.

> Both my father and Ethel were very artistic. He wrote poetry and did excellent pencil sketches while my sister went to art school. I remember them sitting at the dining room table sketching various Norton designs until they came up with the one we know today.

Norton

TWO FIRSTS -
TWO SECONDS
ONE THIRD -

AT THE
'All Khaki'
Race Meeting at
Brooklands, Aug. 7th

Again upholding its wonderful reputation for
EFFICIENCY, POWER, AND SPEED.

London: Bartlett & Co., The Parade, Kilburn. **Norton Motors, Birmingham.**

TOP This typical Norton 'Big Four' sidecar outfit was used by the Russian official who came during the First World War to buy motorcycles for the Russian army.

ABOVE Motorcycle sport continued despite the War. August 1915, and a reference to a Brooklands Meeting open only to members of the armed forces.

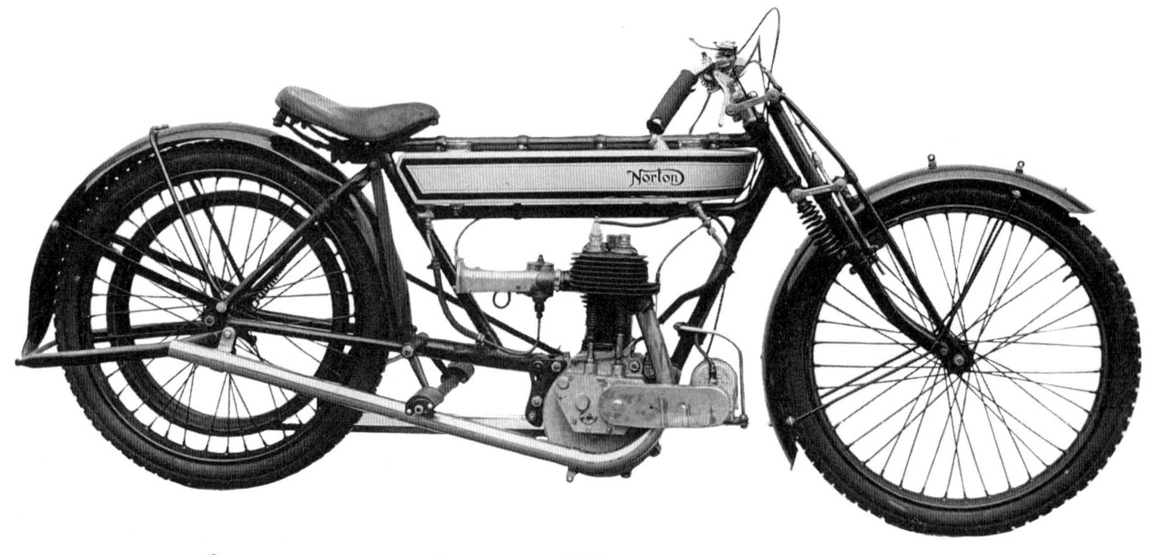

ABOVE Daniel O'Donovan's record breaking 490 cc Norton, 'Old Miracle'. It is said to have set no less than 112 world records during a long Brooklands career that spanned the First World War.

Norton

HIGHEST QUALITY.

SECOND TO NONE.

THE NORTON DOES IT AGAIN

at the **United Services Meeting** at **Brooklands,** and, as at the Khaki Meeting, carried off the PREMIER HONOURS, not only **WINNING** its own class **EASILY,** but also **FIRST PLACE in the UNLIMITED Class,** the little All-British NORTON of 490 c.c. **BEATING SEVERAL FOREIGN MACHINES** of 1,000 c.c., including special racers— ONE WITH PORTED CYLINDERS.

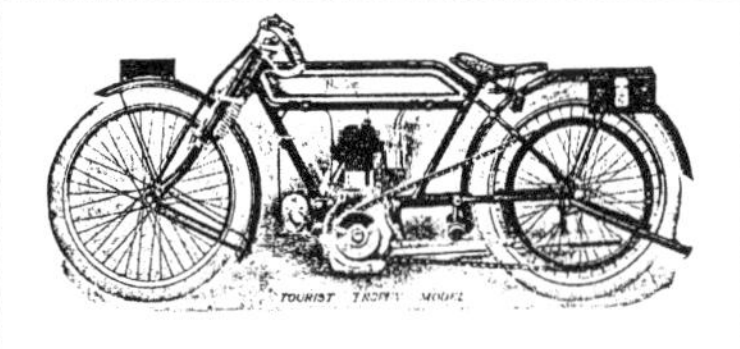

WHY GO ABROAD

for heavy, expensive, and complicated machines when the 490 c.c. SIMPLE SINGLE-CYLINDER NORTON GIVES MORE POWER AND SPEED AND NO TROUBLE.

Keep the Gold in England and buy a NORTON.

Write for Illustrated Catalogue:

NORTON MOTORS, LTD.,
Sampson Road North, Birmingham.
London: Bartlett & Co., The Parade, Kilburn.

LEFT Further Norton successes were gained in a services meeting at Brooklands in September 1915 – and were used by Nortons in this full page advertisement that appeared in *The Motor Cycle*. The 'foreign machines' referred to were American motorcycles which were selling well in England, particularly to munitions workers.

RIGHT Alexander Lindsay, a doctor in the Royal Army Medical Corps, with the Norton he rode in the August 1915 Brooklands meeting. A Norton enthusiast, he extensively modified his machine, fitting special forks and a deeply finned cylinder head. He won the half-mile sprint for machines up to 550 cc.

That was in 1913, in time for the production of the 1914 catalogue, and some 18 months were to elapse before the 'curly N' actually made it on to the tanks and into the advertising. The first advertisement to use it appeared in *Motor Cycling* dated 2 March 1915, and it focused on the new chain drive with fully enclosed chains and cush rear hub – a simple shock absorber with rubber inserts fitted to cushion the snatch of the chain.

By this time Grace was old enough to have retained definite memories of her father and of the home life she enjoyed with her mother Sarah, sister Ethel and three brothers Lansdowne, Spencer and Raymond.

> I adored my father; we all did. He could be very strict. We had to do as we were told but he used to tell us wonderful stories which he made up as he went along. He had a vivid imagination and I remember him starting one tale by saying: 'When I was in the Sahara . . . .' We all knew he had never been there but we enjoyed the story just the same.

Grace remembers occasional outings in the sidecar of the Big Four that her father used: 'I used to feel so proud but unfortunately I didn't get many rides. My mother and the boys came first and then Ethel so I was rather low on the pecking order.' The girls were not encouraged to go to the factory but there was plenty of activity around their home, which was close by the Sampson Road North works: 'Motor-cycles were always coming and going. We used to close our ears to them. They were part of the scenery.'

The technical press was full of war stories. *Motor Cycling* printed a full-page 'artist's impression' showing a despatch rider lying slumped beside his motorcycle, lanced to death by the Hun, while in a later edition the bravery of a French despatch rider, who finished up eating his message rather than let it fall into the hands of the Boche, was detailed.

There were pictures of motorcyclists pursuing Zeppelins (and vice versa, one picture showing a German

airship training a searchlight on a fleeing rider) and of angelic-looking nurses comforting wounded despatch riders as they lay beside their machines on the field of battle. All good recruiting propaganda – and there is no doubt that the motorcycle was doing its bit in France, not only for carrying messages but also for the speedy transport of the Vickers machine guns which were such an important source of fire-power. The Machine Gun Corps used a great many V-twin Royal Enfield and Clyno outfits to transport guns and ammunition from their bases to within a few hundred yards of their firing positions.

All this had passed Nortons by. There was talk of a military model but nothing definite, and there were as yet no orders from the War Office. At home things went on much as before except that the supply of magnetos began to dry up. The Germans had supplied over 90 per cent of the British requirement and there was a period when machines had to be stockpiled in the factories before British production caught up with demand. Even so, in 1915 there was no shortage of bikes for the civilian buyer, and no lack of petrol. The *Motor Cycle* Buyer's Guide lists over 250 machines that year, the great majority British built.

In the spring the Swiss Motosacoche factory had the temerity to beat O'Donovan's Norton record of 81.05 mph for the flying kilometre with a speed of 81.50 mph. Nortons responded and on 14 June O'Donovan regained the record at 82.50 mph and pushed the mile record up to 78.95 mph. The bike he used was the single-geared, belt-driven 490 cc later nicknamed 'Old Miracle' and now owned by the National Motor Museum at Beaulieu. It was an impressive feat, for Brooklands was used by Vickers for testing all types of vehicles and was in poor shape.

There were still sporting events, particularly for riders in the services who, duty permitting, contested two meetings at Brooklands during 1915 – the 'All Khaki' races run in August and the 'United Services' meeting a month later. Norton machines starred at both, with Lt Alexander Lindsay, a doctor serving with the Royal Army Medical Corps, winning the half-mile sprint for machines up to 550 cc and taking second place in the 1000 cc class at the former, while Private Kendall won both classes at the September event, beating a 994 cc Indian V-twin in the big class.

Surprisingly, considering the war situation and the U-boat threat, American machines were flooding in. In addition to Indian and Harley-Davidson, advertisements and editorial appeared for the American Excelsior, Henderson, Yale, Pope, Emblem and Reading Standard machines – mostly V-twins with advanced specifications. There was a good market, for with the majority of British bikes going to the services there was a shortage of machines to meet the demands of a new class of rider – the well-paid munitions worker with money to burn.

Registrations had risen from 123,678 machines at the end of 1914 to 138,496 in 1915, and they climbed to 152,960 the following year, more than the number of cars on the roads. Nortons were selling all they could make. The War Office had done them a favour by ignoring them, for the profits to be made by private sales were certainly in excess of those generated by government contracts. Expanding the market, Nortons launched de luxe and sports sidecars which, after a brief period of being on sale fitted only to new Norton machines, went on general sale.

O'Donovan was still in the news. *The Motor Cycle* pictured him with a chain-driven 490 cc racing machine in September 1915 with the following news item.

> On the occasion of a recent visit to Brooklands we were lucky enough to meet with D.R. O'Donovan, the well known Norton exponent, who showed us his latest chain-driven racing model . . . being designed purely for racing purposes it is provided with a dummy gearbox, serving merely as a support for the bearings of the countershaft.

What the reporter did not point out was that the countershaft allowed a clutch to be fitted in the manner of a modern speedway machine. This would be of benefit for standing-start records and, in emergencies, to free the engine from the rear wheel. It is probable that O'Donovan used this machine, fitted with a sidecar, to beat the five-mile, three-wheeler world record at Brooklands in September 1915 with a speed of 58.78 mph.

This also beat the figures for the 750 cc and 1000 cc classes held by Zenith V-twins, inspiring the Norton advertising copywriter to pen: 'The little engine that beats the big ones. Keep the gold in England and buy a Norton.' This was followed up by: 'Patriotism demands that you should buy a British machine. Economy insists that you should obtain the utmost value for the money you spend. Buy a Norton.'

To stem the tide of American machines an import tax of $33\frac{1}{3}$ per cent was imposed and about the same time the price of petrol went up from 8p to 10p a gallon – which equates to about £5 by 1990 standards.

Amazingly, at this time of increasing strain and tension as the U-boat war created shortages and thousands were slaughtered on the battlefields of France, the chief topic of concern in *Motor Cycling* centred on whether the motorcyclist should wear his cap with the peak at the front or, as favoured by the 'speed merchants', reversed! To be charitable, the original article was written tongue in cheek, but it was followed by weeks of correspondence which was, in the main, deadly serious. The offending article appeared under the heading 'The Wrong Way Round Cap Craze' with the strapline '. . . crusade to abolish the practice of wearing their caps reversed', and it began in fine style: 'The wrong-way-round habit, whatever its attributes, has its serious disadvantages. Thus superior people regard anyone adopt-

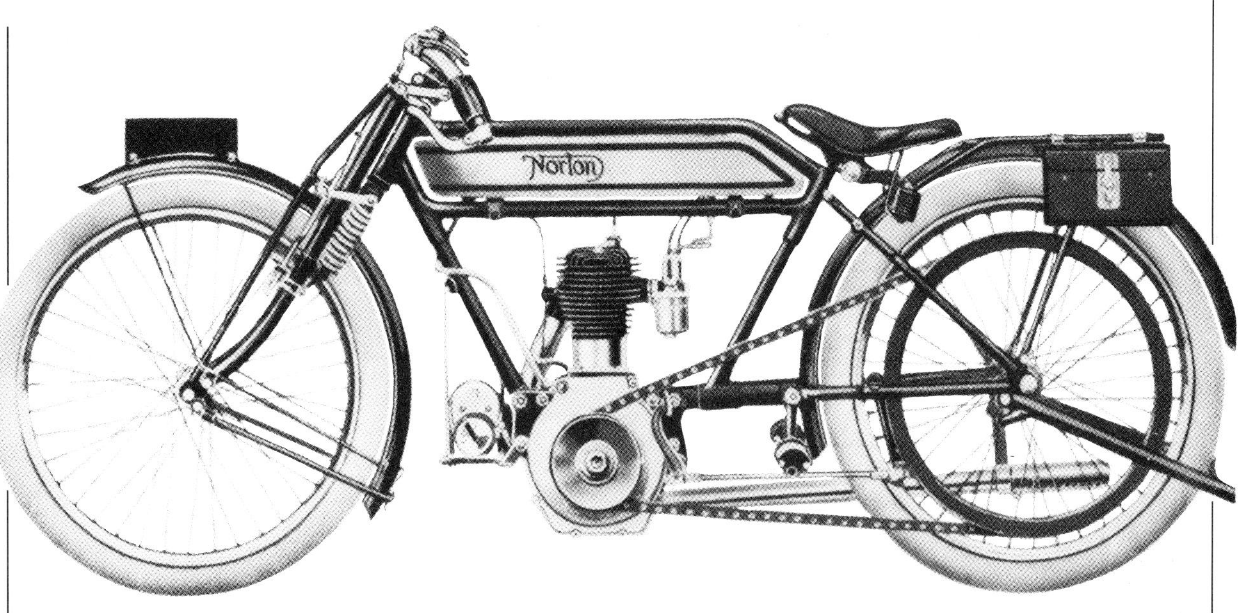

ing this style of headgear as a bounder . . . .'

In December 1915 *The Motor Cycle* printed a letter from Pa Norton in which he commented on a recent article about engine design. His letter ended:

A large diameter piston with short-throw crank must necessarily subject the bearings to greater load or pressure than a long-stroke and small piston with its smaller load, friction (i.e. wear) increasing with the load. This advantage with others of the long-stroke engine must at least be receiving recognition in view of the many models of lengthened stroke now being manufactured.

The year 1916 began with the launch of a model that was to be the backbone of the Norton range until 1954 – the 16H. The first announcement came in *Motor Cycling* on 25 January in a full-page article headed 'A New Norton Model. A countershaft TT machine'. In effect the new bike was the basic 490 cc TT model fitted with the Sturmey-Archer three-speed gearbox and clutch and a fully enclosed chain primary drive thence by belt or chain, as specified, to the rear wheel.

In fact when the machine was launched it did not have a number. Norton started to use these early in 1916 when the range had grown to such an extent that they were needed for quick and easy identification. They first appear in an advertisement in *Motor Cycling* in March of that year when the models are listed as follows:

Model 1	Big Four, 82 × 120, chain-drive	£68	17	6
Model 2	3½ hp, 79 × 100, chain drive	£66	7	6
Model 3	Big Four, chain cum belt	£67	17	6
Model 4	3½hp, chain cum belt	£65	7	6
Model 15	Big Four combination, chain or chain-belt, 3 in tyres	£85	0	0
Model 7	Brooklands Special, certified 75 mph	£68	0	0
Model 8	Brooklands Road Special, certified 70 mph	£63	0	0
Model 9	Tourist Trophy	£52	10	0

Cheapest model for 1915 (first to carry the famous logo on the tank) was the 'TT' model: in fact a basic roadster, with the stock 490 cc engine and direct belt drive to the rear wheel – no clutch and no gears.

The model 16 was added for an advertisement that appeared on 25 April when it was listed along with the brief description 'Countershaft TT £67 0 0'. Writing about the new model, *Motor Cycling* commented: '. . . placed on the market in response to requests from many riders who desire to have a three-speed, countershaft gearbox fitted to a model which, in most other respects, would be similar to the famous TT Norton'. The final paragraph of the article reads:

Probably few men know more about the design of speed engines for motor-cycles than Mr Norton. He has tried every possible design of piston and it is rather remarkable that the one fitted in 1916 is very similar to that of nine years ago, although in the intervening time all types were tried. There have been pistons with one ring, pistons with two, pistons with 'waists', some with webs and some without.

In May 1916 the Norton works moved from Sampson Road North to Phillip Street, Aston, Birmingham which was far bigger than the old premises and close to the main R.T. Shelley works. A photograph that appeared at the time shows workers building bikes on low wooden tables and the caption reads: 'One of the shops in the new Norton Motors works in Phillip

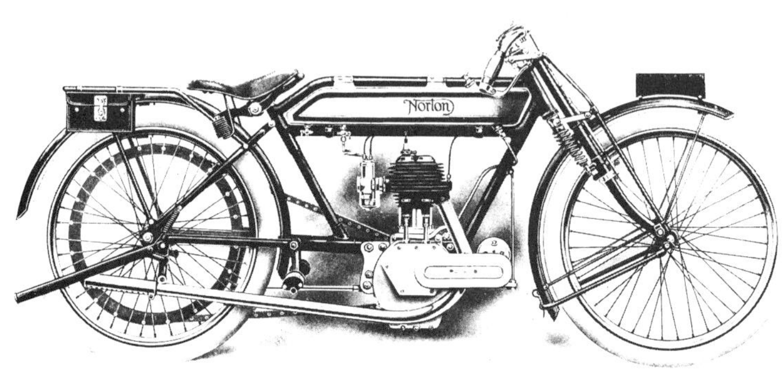

— B. R. S. —

BROOKLANDS ROAD SPECIAL.

2¼ Dunlop Tyres, 79 × 100 = 490 c.c. B. & B. Carburetter.

PRICE - **£60 0 0** With Phillipson Pulley, **£4** extra.

For those who desire exceptional power and speed for competition in a machine suitable for road work. Each engine undergoes a Brooklands test similar to the B.S. (see opposite page) and is CERTIFIED TO HAVE EXCEEDED 65 m.p.h. for a lap. It has grand acceleration, is very flexible and, excepting our B.S., is the fastest machine upon the market. The bearings are in no way "skimped" in order to obtain speed (as so many consider necessary), but are particularly substantial, as in all our models. Durability is in no way interfered with, the engine being designed to withstand the excessive strains due to high speeds. In track parlance, "It will not knock itself to bits."

Model No. 8.—Code Word, "Brookray."

Street, Aston, Birmingham. The new premises are a great improvement upon the old.'

By March the belt was tightening. Imports of motorcycles had been banned and petrol was becoming increasingly expensive. The pages of the technical press were full of articles telling riders how to use various alternative fuels, mainly paraffin, and of advertisements offering various fuels for sale.

Because of air-raids, complicated legislation was introduced to restrict the lights used on vehicles. 'Dimming discs' had to be fitted to the pathetic acetylene headlights in the areas where the Zeppelins and Gothas were most likely to strike. There were in fact three zones – unrestricted, partially restricted and a third where virtually no lights were allowed.

Outings in which clubs took wounded soldiers for runs in sidecars were very popular and much publicised, while *Motor Cycling*, putting a brave face on things, ran a series of articles under the heading 'Motor Cycling for the Maimed'. Nothing squeamish about them! Their rivals on *The Motor Cycle* came up with a more acceptable headline for a similar series: 'Motor Cycling for the Disabled'. Both faced up to the fact that after the war there would be many thousands of limbless ex-soldiers who would want mobility.

Some sporting events were still being held. *Motor Cycling* sponsored the first Public Schools hill-climb in April 1916 at Snowshill near Broadway in Worcestershire. This was won by W.P. Cubitt of Charterhouse on a Norton, who beat his nearest rival on a Rudge by two seconds. There were almost 150 entries. In April

ABOVE Still available – despite the war – the 490 cc Brooklands Road Special as it appeared in the 1915 catalogue. The expanding Phillipson pulley acted both as clutch and gearbox.

RIGHT The first advertisement (2 March 1915) to feature the famouse 'curly N' trademark focusses on the recently introduced chain drive with clutch and three-speed Sturmey-Archer gearbox; both chains fully enclosed.

Captain Scott won the Royal Flying Corps hill-climb at Alms Hill near Henley-on-Thames – his mount was a Big Four.

At the end of May the battle fleets of Britain and Germany clashed at Jutland and Rear Admiral Sir R.K. Arbuthnot, the first private owner in the 1908 TT (finishing third on a Triumph) and later a regular at Brooklands, was killed, one of many famous riders who lost their lives in the war.

Petrol was getting scarcer, and after holding a fuel census the authorities finally introduced a system of rationing in July 1916. At first this limited the majority to half a gallon a week but this was soon increased to a gallon.

Vague mentions of an army machine had appeared from time to time but it was not until late July 1916 that *Motor Cycling* ran a scoop story under the heading 'A Military Model Norton' with the strapline 'Several new and interesting features on projected War Office machine'. The report began: 'Last week we were shown a new machine manufactured by the well known Norton Motors Ltd, Phillip Street, Birmingham, specially designed for military use. In building this machine, Mr Norton has given the greatest care and attention to the requirements of active service motor-cycles.'

The machine was in fact the Model 16 to colonial specification with ground clearance increased to $6\frac{1}{4}$ in, a stronger frame, bigger fuel tank and increased space between tyres and mudguards to allow for the build-up of mud. However, the War Office does not seem to have been impressed for as far as we know no orders were ever placed.

The struggle on the Western Front grew grimmer and grimmer and shortages of just about everything made life at home tough. Eventually in November 1916 the Ministry of Munitions banned the production and sale of new machines for the home market. From then on all the motorcycles produced would go for war service or the factories would be converted to make something the Ministry considered essential to the war effort.

The Russians were by this time good customers for British bikes. The first had been shipped out via the northern route to Archangel and thence by rail to Petrograd (St Petersburg), and a consignment of Humbers had been accompanied by Oscar Brook of that company's testing department. He was one of several factory representatives sent out and *The Motor Cycle* reported:

> The Britishers' task was to teach the Russian soldiers the handling and adjustment of the motor-cycles but they found the Russians slow pupils and, it must be confessed, somewhat unenthusiastic riders . . . the Russian soldiers were depressed with fear by the strict discipline demanded . . . and it is to be hoped that tales of 21 lashes and a diet of bread and water for offenders are not true.

The Russian authorities must have been more impressed than the soldiers, for orders for British machines continued to flow in and, by lucky chance, just at the time they were looking for motorcycles Nortons announced their first military model. Soon the Russian representatives arrived at the Norton works to discuss their specifications, the number of machines Nortons could produce and delivery dates. One of these meetings led to an incident that passed into the Norton family folk lore. Speaking some 74 years after the incident, Grace said:

> As I understand it Dad was court-martialled in his own office. Apparently a Russian officer had picked up a design for a motorcycle and was going to walk off with it. My father

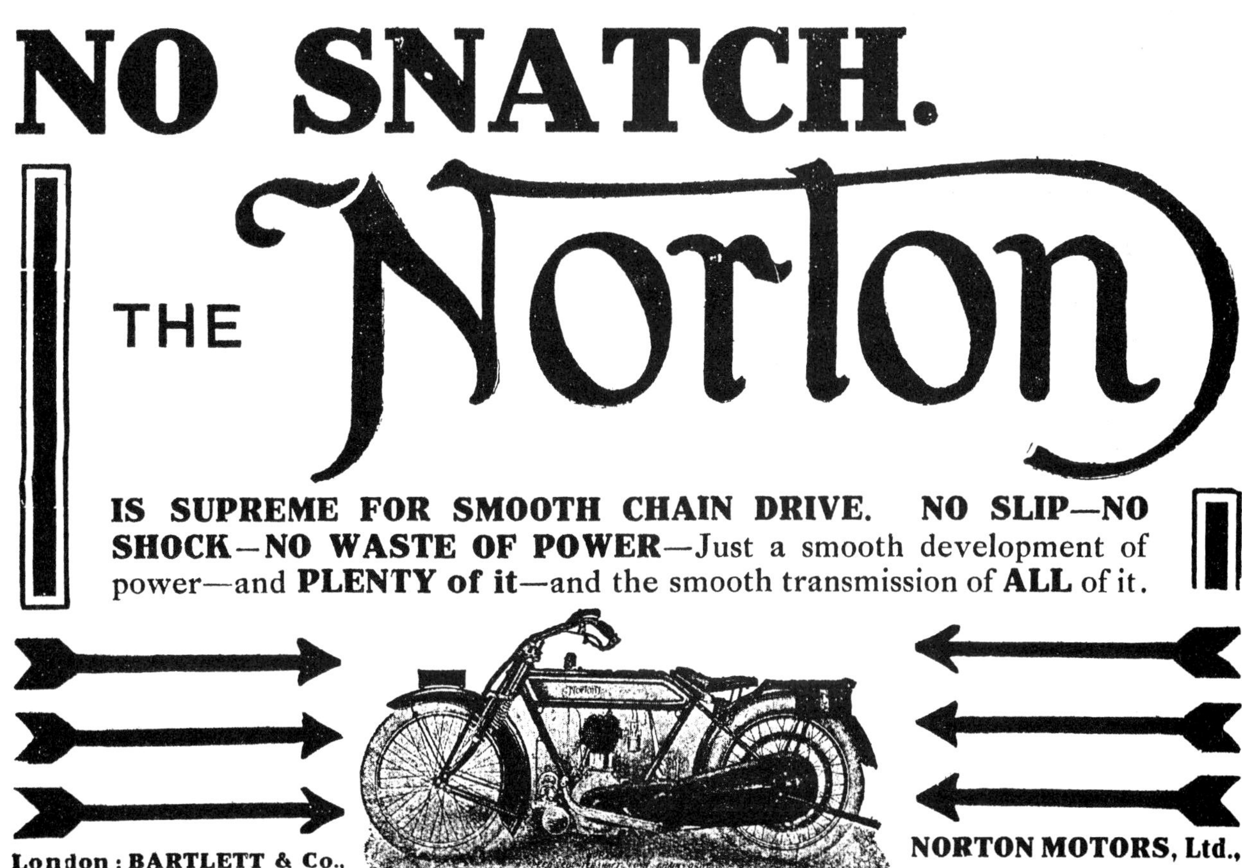

News in Brief (contd.).

A Russian Model.

WE reproduce on this page an illustration of the Norton as supplied to the Russian Government. It will be seen that very complete instructions with regard to the care of this machine are embodied in the lettering on the drawing, a translation of which is the following :—

1. Oil the back hub every 200 miles.
2. Adjust the brake at these points.
3. The change gear lever.
4. Petrol filler orifice.
5. Oil filler orifice.
6. The throttle lever.

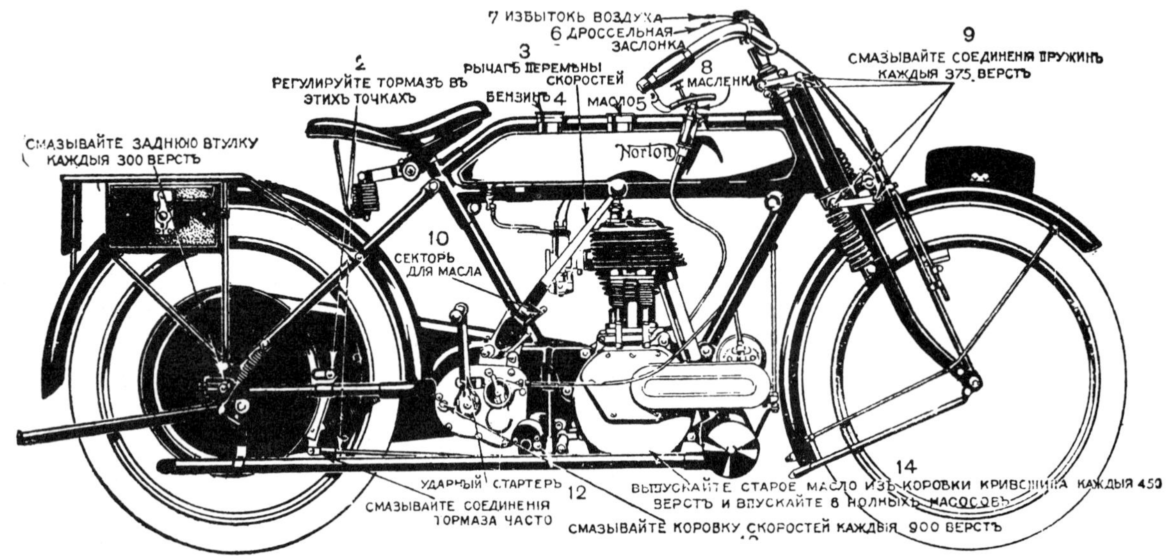

The Russian model of the Norton, and an illustration which will be reproduced in the catalogue in Russian which is being prepared. A translation of the lettering appears above.

7. The extra air lever.
8. The lubricator.
9. Oil the spring fork joints every 250 miles.
10. Oil the quadrant.
11. Brake joints, to be lubricated frequently.
12. The pedal starter.
13. Oil the gearbox every 600 miles.
14. Drain old oil from the crankcase every 300 miles, then put in six pumpfuls of oil.

R.A.C. Prisoners of War Fund.

THE Royal Automobile Club Prisoners of War Fund, started in March, 1916, at the request of the Prisoners of War Help Committee, is in need of further support, owing to many subscribers having gone away. Subscriptions, which should be sent to the R.A.C. at 83, Pall Mall, S.W., will be heartily welcomed, and every penny sent will go directly towards the parcels sent out by the fund to civilian motor drivers interned in Ruhleben, without which parcels, the men write, existence in this camp would be practically impossible.

Enemy Tyre Advertisements.

MOTORISTS coming across the large Continental tyre advertisements which were eyesores in many parts of the country in pre-war days are asked to communicate with the secretary of the Scottish Automobile Club, 163, West George Street, Glasgow, as the club is taking steps to have this pest exterminated.

Procrastinate Saddle Repairs.

MESSRS. J. B. BROOKS and CO. appeal to private customers to withhold, at least for a period, all repairs of motorcycle saddles which are not of vital urgency, thus rendering the utmost assistance to Messrs. Brooks in their effort to carry on under the present adverse conditions.

The Stately Motorcycle.

A WRITER in "Country Life" says:—"If motorists as a whole realized the qualities of the modern motorcycle there would be more people who, when taking to a car, did not hold the mistaken idea that the cycle should be regarded as a somewhat undignified mount."

A New Form of Petrol Theft.

MOTORCYCLISTS carrying extra petrol are warned by a writer in "The Sportsman" against surrendering it to alleged "military representatives" who attempt to commandeer fuel without paying for it or presenting definite authorization. A case in point is described in which a motorist in Hertford, thus accosted, gave up two tins of petrol without payment.

Motor Fuel from Paraffin.

A NEW process of extracting motor spirit from paraffin, by which 60 per cent. is obtained at a cost of 2d. per gallon, was demonstrated recently by Mr. Nat Freeman, at Chesham. The necessary installation cost a large sum, but its inventor is well recompensed by the results. No chemicals are used in the process.

The Motorists' Last Arbiter.

QUERYING whether it were not the duty of the town inspector to prosecute motorists travelling at excessive speed, a member of the Athy Urban Council asked whose duty it was to take up a case of excessive speed. Another member: "It is generally the coroner that takes up such a case." (Laughter.)

The Sincerest Form of Flattery?

WE are much obliged to "The People," "The Field," "The Referee," and "The Globe" for their comments based upon our editorial of the 26th June, relating to the educational value of motoring to the younger generation from a military point of view. Unfortunately, all the publications mentioned omitted to acknowledge the source of their interesting observations.

Motorcycle Saved by a "Kyl-Fyre."

GREAT excitement was caused in Dovercourt recently, when the petrol tank of a motorcycle ridden by a naval officer suddenly burst into flames. Every effort was made to smother the flames, but without success, until a special constable rushed out of his shop with a "Kyl-Fyre" extinguisher and put out the fire. The machine suffered considerable damage.

ABOVE **One of the last sporting events for motorcycles held during the First World War was the Public Schools Hill-Climb at Snowhill. It was won by W. P. Cubitt of Charterhouse, on his 490 cc BRS.**

LEFT **Nortons produced a manual in Russian which was to have accompanied the batch of 633 cc special specification machines ordered by the Russian army. By the time these were built the Russians were in revolt. They were never delivered.**

touched his arm and said: 'I'll trouble you for that,' but because he'd dared to touch an officer he was arrested, though he was later completely exonerated.

There were no hard feelings and a Russian order for machines was placed – not for the 490 cc 'Military Model' but for a similar machine powered by the 82 × 120 mm, 633 cc Big Four engine Nortons were already working on for the colonial market. The Russian model was described in *The Motor Cycle* in March 1917 under the heading 'Norton War Service Machine' with the sub-heading 'The overseas model adopted by an ally'.

The specification included all-chain drive with the Sturmey-Archer three-speed gearbox fitted with a lower than usual first gear, ground clearance increased to 6¼ in, a large 2¼-gallon petrol tank, increased mudguard clearance and roller main bearings in place of the normal ball races.

The Russian Nortons were finished in an attractive light grey-green and, as the picture shows, the end result was a very good-looking mount. Reporting on the order and the progress being made, *The Motor Cycle* said in March 1917: '. . . their manufacture in large numbers is now in progress. This is in response to a special order from the Ministry of Munitions for a regular supply of motor-cycles to a particular specification. Russian Government inspectors are supervising the construction.'

Nortons were only one of a number of British factories working on Russian orders. They included Humber, New Imperial, Royal Enfield, Sunbeam and Royal Ruby. The chief Russian supervisor used a Norton Big Four with sidecar to do his rounds. A picture of this appeared in *The Motor Cycle* in May 1917 together with another showing a batch of around 40 Nortons with the caption '. . . ready for despatch to the Eastern Front, being part of a Russian Government order'.

But the order and the building of the machines had been overtaken by events. Russia was in turmoil. In March 1917 the Czar had abdicated. With Russian resistance to the Germans crumbling and the country split as rival factions fought for power, the export of British motorcycles was put on hold.

Whether an early shipment of Nortons actually got to Russia is not known. It seems unlikely. There were crated machines ready for shipment and an item in *The Motor Cycle* in June 1917 gives more details of the Russian model, with specification uprated to include fully enclosed chain drive, both primary and secondary, and two sets of footrests, 'one normal and one forward so that the rider on a long journey can stretch his legs'. There was no suggestion that shipments would not be made and no reference to the situation in Russia, which was finally settled in March 1918 when a separate peace with Germany was signed.

Obviously Nortons were left with models on their hands and proof of this appeared in a quarter-page advertisement in *The Motor Cycle* dated 28 February 1918. Apparently defying a government order that new machines must not be sold to the public, the advertisement stated: 'Immediate delivery of military models'. A little later the Norton dealer in Hampstead, Rider Troward, listed under new machines a Norton Military Model, 4 hp, 3-speed, £82. So some obviously did get through to the dealers and the high price reflects that new bikes were in short supply.

Meanwhile Pa Norton was regularly quoted in the press. In January 1917 under the heading 'New Year Messages from the Makers of your Machines', he avoided the banalities of the majority of his contemporaries with the following hard-hitting piece.

Through the murk and muddle of things I see, arising out of the victorious peace that is coming to us, a glimpse of a cleaner and stronger England. A saner trade unionism, with a lesser strangle-hold upon the industrial output of the country. A greater appreciation of the need and value of uprightness and integrity to the nation as a more universal and enduring peace based upon reason and righteousness than the tortured world has seen for many a day. These are the gleams of hope I see and these the things I pray for – they lead to prosperity and happiness.

He was of course a devout man, teetotaller, non-smoker and leading light in the Salvation Army. At one time he had been treasurer of his local branch and when the bank in which he had deposited funds collapsed, had made good the money from his own pocket.

Two long articles appeared under his name during 1917. First was 'Efficiency versus Power' in *Motor Cycling* and at virtually the same time he argued his case for the long-stroke engine in a learned three-page piece in the rival, *The Motor Cycle*.

Although there was still no sign of peace he outlined the Norton post-war programme in February 1918, the reporter noting: '. . . they have decided to adhere to the single-cylinder policy and to confine their efforts to three models . . . in place of six or more different varieties'. These were listed as the TT Sports with 490 cc engine and belt drive with variable-pulley gear 'for the speed merchant', a utility mount with the same engine but with three-speed, countershaft gearbox and all-chain drive 'for the average rider', plus a similarly equipped 633 cc Big Four for 'very heavy solo or sidecar work'.

The Motor Cycle reporter finished with: 'It is interesting to note that Mr Norton has been carrying out experiments with aluminium alloy pistons for some time past. He has given a fair trial to a number of different alloys, and so far, only one brand has withstood the test . . . .'

By April 1918 petrol rationing, coupled with the ever-increasing price (17½p a gallon by that time, roughly equivalent to £8 by 1990 standards), had cut the number of motorcycles on British roads from the 152,960 of 1916 to around 27,000 – which gives an idea of just how tough things had become. And when Ludendorff's troops broke through Allied lines in northern France and threatened the Channel ports, it seemed that the Allies might yet lose the war.

The German offensive of April 1918 was finally stemmed, the Allies suffering nearly half a million casualties, and in August Nortons jumped the gun by officially announcing a post-war programme, the first British factory to do so. In a half-page advertisement in *Motor Cycling*, the copy read:

Our post-war programme comprises two types of machine – the light 'sports' model, direct drive with variable pulley, and the 'utility' model, countershaft gear and all-chain cush-drive. Both models – 3½ hp and Big Four – fitted with the Norton long-stroke single cylinder engine – a type accepted by engineers as the most thermally and mechanically efficient, made and proved perfect in practice. Get on the waiting list now.

Three months later the guns fell silent and the economic struggle for survival began. The first shots in this silent battle had already been fired. *The Motor Cycle* had carried a box with bold type headed 'Goods Made in Germany' which read:

The proprietors of this journal, being fully in accord with the recommendations agreed at the Paris Economic Conference, give notice that they will not permit the advertisement of new goods manufactured in enemy countries to appear in this publication either during or after the war.

CHAPTER 6

'Let the other chap chew the dust' 1918–1921

That Pa Norton had a sound grasp of the political and economic scene that was to follow the First World War is well illustrated by his contribution to a series of articles written by the 'captains of industry' for *The Motor Cycle* in January 1919. He ended in brusque, no-nonsense style:

> The demand for motor-cycles for two or three seasons will be scarcely more than met, after which competition will undoubtedly become severe. The prosperity of the motor-cycle industry will depend largely upon its workers, as indeed does the welfare of every industry. At no time in our nation's history has the need for commonsense and sane thinking among the workers been greater than today (thank goodness for some sane thinkers among them) when so many appear to be blindly following the criminal butchers who are out to kill the goose that lays the golden egg productiveness, which means prosperity. Ours will be a happier and even wealthier country if Labour's slogan was 'Unlimited Output'.

That same month Norton announced their range for 1919. There were, as expected, just two basic models, the 633 cc Big Four and the 490 cc of which four versions were offered, ranging from the utility Standard TT with direct belt drive at £63 to the sporty Model 16 with three-speed countershaft gearbox at £85. Delivery was promised 'shortly'; first March was mentioned – then May. In fact, anxious enthusiasts had to wait until July and by that time the prices had increased by some 20 per cent. The Norton advertisement of the time is succinct.

> The pre-war price of the Big Four all-chain drive model was £65. Practically every item in the cost of manufacture of a motor cycle having advanced on an average 100 per cent or more, the logical selling price now should be at least £131. The Norton Company, however, purposes, while the present abnormal conditions continue, to share the increase with their customers, and have therefore fixed the present selling price at £105 only.

Just why it took Nortons so long to switch production from the Russian-order Big Four to the almost identical home-market machine and the very similar 490 cc models is not clear. Bill Mansell, who was running the commercial side of the business as joint managing director with Pa Norton, is said to have bought from the government the stockpile of crated models built for the Russians.

In his book *The Norton Story* Bob Holliday, who knew Mansell well, says that the majority of the crates had been broken open and many components stolen. Obviously the red tape involved in locating, negotiating and finally transporting the machines back to the factory for rebuilding took a long time – probably about a year. But the lack of any machines at all for the home market in the first half of 1919 suggests that motorcycle production at Phillip Street had ceased towards the end of 1917 and that the factory had switched from motorcycles to munitions.

Auctions were in the news at this time. The government had been left with thousands of military machines on their hands and enthusiasts looked forward to getting hold of a serviceable Triumph, Douglas, P and M, Royal Enfield or Clyno for a few pounds. They were disappointed. The bikes were, in the main, in poor con-

BELOW **Nortons announced the 1919 range in this full page advertisement in *The Motor Cycle* in July that year – the copy makes interesting reading.**

ADVANCED **PRICES.** *July 1st, 1919.*

The pre-war price of the Big Four All Chain Drive Model was £65 10s. Practically every item in the cost of manufacture of a motor cycle having advanced on an average 100 per cent. or more, the logical selling price now should be ***at least*** £131. The Norton Company, however, purposes, while the present abnormal conditions continue, to share the increase with their customers, and have therefore fixed the present selling price at £105 only.

Complete List of Prices:

Model No		
1.	Big 4, Chain drive	£105.
16.	3½ T.T. " "	£103.
9.	3½ T.T., Belt "	£80.
8.	3½ B.R.S. " "	£90.
7.	3½ B.S. " "	£97.
	"De Luxe" Sidecar	£33.
	"Sporting" "	£28.

Model No. 9.

Norton Motors Ltd
ASTON,
BIRMINGHAM.

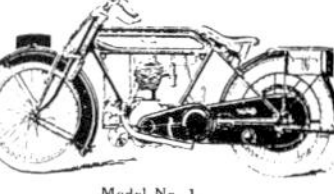

Model No. 1.

dition and the prices fetched surprisingly high. A report of a London auction in *The Motor Cycle* in mid 1919 says:

It had been hoped that the machines offered would be of a better quality than those previously put before a none too enthusiastic public, and also that this sale might mark the decline of the fallacious and exhorbitant prices reached hitherto. Neither of these hopes was gratified.

As far as I could find out, no Nortons were ever offered at any of these auctions, which were held nation wide during 1919. This supports the theory that the British authorities did not buy any, despite the availability of the Big Fours following the collapse of Russia.

It was about this time that Pa Norton, worn out by the long hours he had worked throughout the war, crippled by rheumatism and depressed by the economic situation, suffered a nervous breakdown. Grace said:

He went to the Isle of Man for several months. He had a doctor friend who lived over there and he told father that he had to have tranquil hobbies to take his mind off work. So he took up fly-fishing and when he came home he not only kept this up but also built a wonderful aquarium in a greenhouse in our garden. At one time he had 52 varieties of fish including a tankful of pike. I remember that he had to put a net over them to stop them jumping out. He also had lizards, baby turtles and tree frogs which lived in an area in which water flowed through ferns – we children loved it.

LEFT Crippled by neuritis Pa Norton still managed to ride his beloved Big Four in the Isle of Man in 1920. His wife Sarah is in the sidecar.

ABOVE Pa Norton tops up the oil of Victor Horsman's 490 cc side-valve Norton at Brooklands, September 1920. Horsman broke a number of world records, including the one hour at 71.68 mph.

The Norton advertising changed completely at this time. The first of the 'new look' featured a Red Indian on a horse with the caption: 'The miles fly by joyously, your whole enjoyment is unspoilt by trouble of any sort – for you are on a Norton.' Never mind that it looked at first glance to be a plug for the rival Indian company! Buffaloes, Tigers and Bulldogs featured later, the last with the line: 'Dependability and reliability, very much British qualities, are very much Norton qualities too.'

Later in the year the animals and the virtues they shared with Nortons were dropped and a rather elitist slogan adopted: 'Let the other chap chew the dust, says the powerful sweet-running Norton . . . .'

On the news front the circulation of *The Motor Cycle* exceeded 100,000 for the first time, shooting up from 67,253 in February 1919 to 100,935 at the end of April that year as wartime paper restrictions eased and the

First introduced to the Motor Cycling World *over 10 years ago*. Is still famous as the *Premier* single-cylinder machine for sidecar or solo use.

Delivery can now only be made by our authorised agents. We shall be pleased to forward 1920 catalogue and list of agents on request.

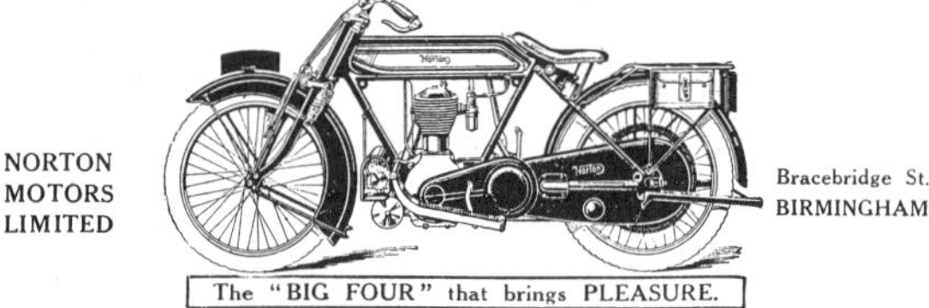

NORTON MOTORS LIMITED

Bracebridge St., BIRMINGHAM.

The "BIG FOUR" that brings PLEASURE.

Messrs. O'Donovan and Beach, at Brooklands, on Wednesday, October 20th, **secured the following Records** on a 3½ h.p. Norton in **Classes C, D, and E:**

	Miles	Yds.	M.P.H.	Miles	Hrs.	Mins.	Secs.	M.P.H
8 Hours	442	716	55·30	450	8	15	23⅕	54·50
9 ,,	494	820	54·93	500	9	5	38⅗	54·98
10 ,,	545	1,286	54·57	550	10	4	20⅕	54·61
11 ,,	598	697	54·40	600	11	1	41⅕	54·40
12 .	651	342	54·27	650	11	58	22⅕	54 27

(Subject to A.C.U. confirmation).

The speeds and times in Class E constitute

10 WORLD'S RECORDS

I.E.—The little 3½ h.p. Norton has travelled over above times and distances faster than any other Motor Cycle in the World, irrespective of size or power.

650 MILES OF PERFECT RELIABILITY ! ! !

NORTON MOTORS, Ltd., Bracebridge St., Birmingham

public's interest in motor-cycling burgeoned.

Sport had been slow to resume. The ACU held a six-day trial based on Llandrindod Wells and it is good to record that Captain Alexander Lindsay, who had done so well in one of the last wartime Brooklands meetings, had survived and rode his Norton in Wales, winning a gold medal. Both he and Vic Horsman, soon to become famous, rode solo Big Fours.

Hopes of running the TT that year had been abandoned but definite plans were laid for 1920 despite strong opposition from many manufacturers. At first the ACU considered it desirable to drop the Senior TT for 500 cc machines because 'of the danger of the course with such fast machines'. It was proposed to run only 350 cc and 250 cc races. However, the interested manufacturers, Norton among them, then persuaded the ACU to keep the programme much as it had been for the 1914 races with a 500 cc Senior TT and a 350 cc Junior.

One major rule change was that factory specials

LEFT This Norton advertisement of 1920 links the 'Big Four' who led the allies to victory in the First World War to the 633 cc Norton 'Big Four'.

BELOW LEFT Yet more World Records for O'Donovan's 490 cc side-valve Norton – including the 12 hour at an average of 54.27 mph. These records were set in October 1920.

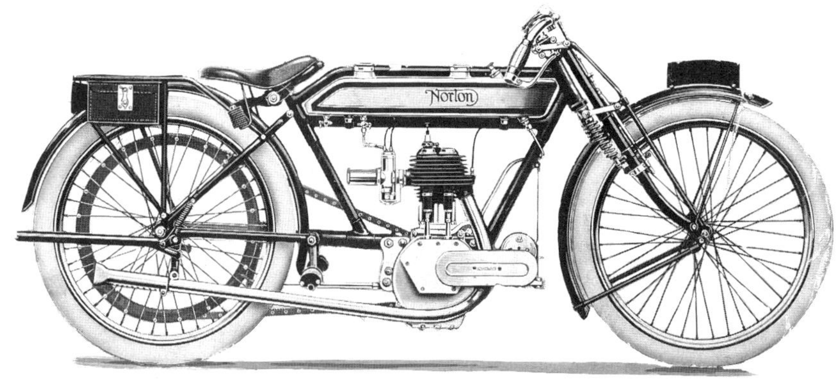

LEFT 1921 Sports $3\frac{1}{2}$ hp.

LEFT Jimmy Shaw at the TT, 1920.

BELOW The Norton workshop at the 1920 TT. Duggie Brown, who finished second in the Senior TT, crouches behind his machine (No 56) while Charlie North (with cigarette) stands behind No 63. The man with the tyre is Norton's works manager Bill Hassall. The machines are the basically standard 16H side-valve models that the team and majority of private entrants used that year.

would be allowed in 1920 – the competing machines no longer had to be catalogue sports models. The basic principle on which the race had been founded had been abandoned and the name Tourist Trophy was already outdated.

By November 1919 Pa Norton was back at work and that month he wrote a letter to *The Motor Cycle* about

ABOVE Record breaker supreme. Daniel 'Wizard' O'Donovan astride a Norton at Brooklands in 1920. Financed by the factory – and by the bonuses received from accessory firms – he ran his own tuning shop at Brooklands from 1913 until he left the company at the end of the twenties to join Raleigh.

RIGHT 1920 Norton 16H with sports/racing sidecar.

sidecar riding technique. After passing on some tips he finished with:

I find, also, that if a high average is required, it is not necessary to 'blind', and I have generally done better in this direction, if I limit my maximum to something like 35 mph, when, provided there are no straggling towns to go through, this will enable an average of something approaching thirty to be made over ordinary roads.

The letter was accompanied by a photograph of Pa astride his Big Four with his father in the sports sidecar alongside.

Interestingly, Pa was inciting readers to break the law, for the speed limit on the open road was still 20 mph, and remained so for several more years. However, it was ignored to such an extent that it had fallen into disuse, though limits in towns, often 10 mph, were still rigidly enforced. One particular policeman gained such a reputation for strictness that his retirement was recorded in *Motor Cycling* under the heading 'Kingston "Terror" Retires', the item reading: 'The menace of the Portsmouth Road – P.C. Beck – is announced to have retired from the force. He was for many years stationed at Molesey, and waged a relentless war against every form of motoring.'

As Norton production had got under way only in mid year, it came as no surprise that there were no new models for 1920. The factory's stand at Olympia in November 1919 focused on the 633 cc Big Four which was said to develop 11 bhp at 2000 rpm. In a report headed 'On the Road with a 1920 TT Norton' a reporter from *The Motor Cycle* wrote of the Model 16: 'It is a mount a sensible rider will very seldom dare to open out to the full on a road.' Then, lapsing into the journalese of the day, he added: 'The machine will burble along like a sucking dove . . . .'

Sadly Sir John Alcock, knighted for his pioneering flight across the Atlantic with Arthur Whitten Brown, lost his life in a flying accident at the end of the year – just six months after his famous crossing. A keen motorcyclist, he had raced a Douglas at Brooklands.

The gloom was carried over into 1920. The men who made the moulds into which the metal was poured to cast motor components were on strike and the industry was grinding to a standstill, fulfilling the fears voiced by Pa Norton in *The Motor Cycle* almost exactly a year earlier. An editorial in that magazine commented: 'Practically every man is now at a standstill . . . there is something wrong with affairs in general when a very small section of the community can jeopardise the foundations of industry.'

It was at this time, early in 1920, that Nortons moved from Phillip Street to bigger premises at an address that became world famous – Bracebridge Street. This was ideally situated for it backed on to the main factory of R.T. Shelley, the parent company who made various components for Nortons.

Bob Holliday records that Bill Mansell used to lunch at the Royal Hotel in Temple Row, Birmingham and that one of his table companions was John Goodman, boss of the Velocette Company which was later developed by his sons Percy and Eugene. One day Goodman said he was going to look at possible new premises and asked Mansell to go with him. The Norton man was amazed when they went to Bracebridge Street for he had no idea the premises there were vacant. When Goodman decided against them, Mansell stepped in.

The brick-built factory was not impressive but it became the centre of the motorcycle racing world in the 1930s and from it came the machines that gained prestige for British engineering around the world. It was to be Nortons' home for 43 years.

The 1920 TT team in Woodbourne Square, Douglas. Seated on the machines (left to right) are Noel Brown, Jimmy Shaw, Duggie Brown, Graham Walker and Charlie North. Behind, team-manager Daniel O'Donovan, Pa Norton and works manager Bill Hassall.

In February Vic Horsman won a gold medal in the tough Paris to Nice road trial, an event in which British riders and machines did well with Kaye Don the victor on a Zenith while Scott two-strokes took the team prize. By March the price of the Big Four had risen from £105 to £120 and the cost of petrol, a bone of public contention to this day, was under scrutiny. Commented *The Motor Cycle* after a report that a Profiteering Act sub-committee was to investigate: '... it is grossly excessive. Control of the world's motor spirit is in the hands of two enormously powerful combines.' The magazine went on to calculate that it should cost 14p a gallon and not the 18p garages were charging.

When 12 leading factories (among them Triumph, BSA, Rudge and New Imperial) made it clear they would not support the TT there was a doubt about whether the 1920 races would take place. Then Norton,

Sunbeam, Douglas, AJS, James and Brough rallied round and the event was saved – no less than 15 of the 31 entries for the Senior being Norton mounted!

The factory riders were Manxman Duggie Brown, Ulsterman Jimmy Shaw, plus Noel Brown and Graham Walker, the future editor of *Motor Cycling* who later achieved fame as the BBC radio commentator at the TT and Ulster – and, incidentally, the father of grand prix commentator Murray Walker. Graham had joined Nortons the preceding year and worked in the competition department when not riding in trials, hill-climbs or road races. Commenting on the Model 16 machines used by the team, *The Motor Cycle* reporter wrote: 'The TT Norton is practically the standard sporting mount. The only changes are a gearbox without a kick-start giving ratios of 4, 5 and 7½ to 1, the substitution of footrests for footboards, a new tool-box and an extra brake.' In fact the stopping power was abysmal, with a block bearing on a dummy belt-rim at the rear and a bicycle stirrup at the front.

While the team were on their way to the Isle of Man, O'Donovan was down at Brooklands and with a Canoelet sidecar attached to a 490 cc Norton with chain-drive, he set no less than 14 world records. These ranged from the 50 miles at 53.05 mph to the three hours at 50.92 mph. Not impressive, but they were the first by Nortons since the war and he did carry a passenger, lying flat, in the streamlined sidecar.

O'Donovan then nipped over to the island, for he was team manager for the factory riders while Graham Walker looked after the private owners. Pa Norton was there too, with his left arm in a sling much of the time due to neuritis (a chronic nerve condition) which caused acute pain. He did not, however, let it stop him riding his beloved Big Four with wife Sarah in the sidecar.

The bikes went well in practice. With full equipment including tools they weighed only 230 lb and down the Mountain O'Donovan calculated that they were revving to 4300 and travelling at some 76 mph. Walker had a nasty moment when he hit a sheep that had strayed on to the course but apart from that, practising was reasonably trouble free.

Things looked good in the race when Brown took the lead on lap three and held it on lap four. Then Tommy de la Hay on a 'built for the race' Sunbeam passed him and pulled away to win. Nortons had the consolation of taking nine of the first 14 places and of fielding only catalogue sports models. This point was rammed home by a two-page Norton advertisement in *The Motor Cycle*: 'All engines were absolutely standard, and the machines have since been sold to private owners through our agents.' In fact all four of the factory-entered bikes finished the race.

The day after the Senior a kilometre speed trial was held on Douglas promenade. The class for TT machines was won by Jimmy Shaw on his Norton at 70.79 mph – a figure which supports O'Donovan's calculated 76 mph down the Mountain.

In July O'Donovan took over the Norton agency for London, operating from premises in Great Portland Street, the prime area for motor traders at that time. His partner was another Brooklands devotee, H.H. Beach, who, on a belt-drive Norton with Middleton sidecar, established a number of long-distance records in September 1920. These included six hours at 49.79 mph, which must have been extremely boring for the poor prone passenger!

By this time Brooklands, neglected during the war and damaged by testing, had been restored to its former

glory. Reported *The Motor Cycle*: 'It has quite regained its old-time condition, and one may see, every day, machines practising or actually attempting to raise the pre-war speed figures . . . .'

Soon after Beach's success, Vic Horsman arrived at the Surrey circuit with Pa Norton to contest the one-hour race for 500 cc machines at a meeting in early September. He went so fast that in addition to winning the race he broke the hour world record (with a speed of 71.68 mph) which had stood to the credit of Jack Emerson on a flat-twin ABC at 67.93 mph.

Fortunately the 500 cc was the last race of the day and as Horsman was going so well Pa Norton organised an extension so that when the other riders were flagged off, Horsman, on the Norton, was left to circulate in an attempt to add further records. He took the 100 miles at 69.07 mph and the two hours at 69.36 mph, but with just three laps to go to complete 150 miles he wobbled in with a flat rear tyre. Rather than lose time changing it he went out again and despite a spill, caused by the tyre, struggled on and crossed the line after 150 miles to beat the record at 65.47 mph. Summing up, *The Motor Cycle* described it as 'the most sensational performance of a 3½ hp solo machine on the track this season'.

It was an autumn of record breaking. In October Horsman returned to Brooklands and raised the hour record to 72.48 mph, using the same Model 16 with

ABOVE **Norton's competitions manager Graham Walker with his 490 cc side-valve 16H at the 1921 TT. While O'Donovan managed the factory team Walker looked after the private entrants. Note the feeble bicycle-type front brake – virtually useless on a machine capable of around 80 mph.**

RIGHT **Victor Horsman on a Norton with wicker sidecar in a sprint event in the Midlands – probably 1921.**

three-speed gearbox he had ridden as a member of the winning Norton team in the Liverpool club's Reliance Trial. O'Donovan joined in and, riding a belt-driven Brooklands Special, he first beat three long-distance records, including the three hours at 63.63 mph, and later, sharing the riding with partner Beach, some even longer-distance records – right up to the twelve hours at 54.27 mph. Nortons were obviously out to prove the endurance of their machines as well as the sheer speed.

The Norton models for 1921 were on display on stand 71 at the Olympia Show late in 1920. There were minor improvements but the range was as before with the price of the Big Four up to £135, just £3 more than the Model 16. The advertising featured the sidecars but the cost of the Big Four with de luxe child–adult sidecar (the offspring accommodated in a 'dickey' seat) had risen to £180 – a year's wages for a working man.

Before the war Nortons had been a small company

selling only a handful of machines a month. Despite the lack of government contracts during the war it had grown by 1920 to be a major force in the industry – not, by any means, one of the biggest but certainly one of the most influential. The sporting successes and the policy of selling machines identical to those raced had created a big following among the sporting riders – and the dealers.

This was proved by an ambitious dealer advertising supplement devoted to Nortons run in *The Motor Cycle* to coincide with the 1920 Show and the launch of the 1921 models. It was the biggest one-make dealer supplement up to that time and ran to eight full pages. The award for the most extravagant praise must go to Laytons of Bicester whose copy ran: 'The Norton is the product of genius . . . the best designed single-cylinder the world has ever seen . . . the memory of happy hours on the Big Four will linger forever, a faithful friend, we know of no equal.' Twenty dealers supported the project, and if you wonder who began the now familiar (in many areas) Dan the Datsun/Nissan man slogan it could just have been Dan Bradbury, the Norton dealer in Sheffield, who in December 1920 used the line 'Dan the Norton man'.

For 1921 the now familiar licence disc was introduced along with the log book which some claimed would wipe out the growing crime of stealing cars and motorcycles. How, they argued, could anyone sell a vehicle without a log book? At about the same time it was made law that the vehicle on the main road had precedence over those coming from a side road. The headline in *The Motor Cycle* read: 'Main Road Riders to have Right of Way' and went on: '. . . thus putting the responsibility on the man entering the main-road and giving the traffic on the main-road the right of way'.

The Norton catalogue for 1921 was detailed and informative. There was a piece about optional extras which included: '. . . aluminium slipper pistons for any model. They increase the silkiness of running, lessen oil consumption and improve acceleration but wear resistance properties are not quite so good as the cast-iron piston.' This was followed by the statement:

> We are frequently asked the difference between the standard TT engine, which may develop record speeds, and the Brooklands Special which does and will attain record speeds. This is our secret; the difference is the reason for the speed, and we must ask our friends to accept the speed as the difference.

By this time the plain big-end bearings of the earlier models had been replaced by a single-row roller big-end but the connecting rods were still drilled for lightness, the 1921 rods having eleven holes. One of the tuning tips of the period was to file these out to an oval to lose yet more weight. The Brooklands Special was still sold with a guarantee that it would exceed 75 mph over the flying kilometre and 70 mph for a lap, with the BRS road version just 5 mph slower. Both retained belt-drive and weighed just over 200 lb (90.7 kg).

O'Donovan had long understood the importance of weight and stature when it came to record breaking. He realised that both he and partner Beach were too big for the serious business that lay ahead and he soon had a tiny jockey of under 9 st (57 kg) on his solo. Rex Judd had joined the firm as a mechanic and his first outing at Brooklands was in the sidecar of a machine ridden by O'Donovan. That was in February 1921 when O'Donovan, using a 490 cc Norton, pushed the flying-kilometre sidecar record up to 69.13 mph and set a new international record, the mean speed of runs over both directions, of 65.81 mph. This was the first year of these two-way runs which the FICM, *Fédération Internationale des Clubs Motocyclistes*, quite rightly, insisted on for true 'world records'. Under the old one-way system the wind and gradient could make a big difference.

Obviously the Wizard had things worked out, for he wrote a short article that appeared in *Motor Cycling*

in early March 1921 in which he said: 'I venture to suggest that, before the end of the year, the following speeds will be recorded at Brooklands – 250 cc 71 mph, 350 cc 81 mph, 500 cc 90 mph, 1000 cc – very little improvement on the 500 cc.'

Judd had in fact already broken his first records on the O'Donovan Norton – now a standard-looking 16H (the H stood for 'home' and had been adopted to differentiate it from the C or Colonial model . . . except that there never was a 16C, the 490 cc overseas bike being catalogued as the Model 17) complete with all chain-drive and three-speed gearbox. On 22 February Judd had raised the flying-kilometre British (one-way) record to 85.35 mph but had failed in an attempt to beat the Indian-held two-way figure of 82.20 mph, the Norton averaging 82.10 mph.

On 29 March the two record breakers were back at Brooklands and this time, despite a wet track and intermittent rain, they slaughtered the records. First Judd clocked 92.44 mph over the flying kilometre to take the British record and then he did the return run to average 86.37 mph, beating the American-held record by over 4 mph. By the next day conditions had improved and with Judd in the sidecar O'Donovan clocked 72.63 mph for the flying kilometre and took the world record at 71.24 mph. So in the space of 24 hours Nortons had

ABOVE Pa Norton (centre) with some of the team at the 1921 TT. Flanking him are Duggie Brown (left) and Dan O'Donovan.

RIGHT A top sports model of its day – the 1921 Model 16H 490 cc side-valve with three-speed Sturmey-Archer gearbox and all chain drive. The catalogue claims it to be the fastest 500 cc machine in production.

FAR RIGHT This picture of the first experimental overhead valve Norton was taken by Pa Norton himself – either late in 1921 or on his return from South Africa early in 1922.

been the first 500 cc solo to beat 90 mph and the first sidecar to top 70 mph.

Betting and bookmakers were part of the Brooklands scene. Imagine, then, the consternation when the judge, sitting by the finish line, gave the wrong result at the first meeting of the year in April 1921! The report in *Motor Cycling* made no bones about it.

In the 500 cc race V. Horsman and P. Kennedy both on $3\frac{1}{2}$ hp Nortons were having matters all their own way, and they flashed over the finishing line almost together, Horsman about one length ahead. For some unaccountable reason the judge, Colonel Lindsay Lloyd, awarded the race to Kennedy and there were stormy scenes between those who had backed Horsman and the bookmakers.

German goods were taboo, and when a German salesman appeared in London he was roundly castigated by *Motor Cycling*.

The Blatant Boche. The story of a German salesman trying to sell a famous German accessory and speaking in broken English shows the cool audacity of our late enemies. It is an insult to the intelligence and patriotism of the motor-trade to endeavour to do business in such a blatant and tactless manner . . . .

It was TT time again and among the many advertising leaflets and brochures was a handy booklet, packed with information, issued by a famous tyre company of the time and entitled 'John Bull's Souvenir'. The issue for 1921 contains this gem: 'While on the promenade at Douglas and Ramsey don't give any rides to young ladies on the carrier. It is bad for the girl, worse for the machine and incidentally is prohibited by the Manx authorities.'

Hopes of a TT success, raised by the second place recorded the preceding year, were dashed when out of 15 Nortons entered only three finished, with the best placed, J. Mitchell on a privately entered Model 16, sixth. Many of the Nortons were eliminated by broken valves – a problem so rare that the company had taunted rival concerns for years with the slogan 'The Norton never breaks valves' in advertising.

Commented *Motor Cycling*: 'Mr Norton could not understand the heads of the valves breaking. When he returns he is going to analyse the metal. For 15 years the 3 per cent nickel steel has never given trouble so that the present complaint is very curious.' It was not the only problem. Of the factory team of three, Horsman retired when his magneto came loose, Jimmy Shaw crashed and it was only Brown who suffered valve failure.

One consolation was that Hubert Hassall (the stepson of works manager Bill Hassall) won the post-TT hill-climb, held that year on a course from Hillberry back up the Mountain to Keppel Gate. And it was Hassall who scored Norton's first major continental success when he won the 1921 Belgian Grand Prix held over the same magnificent Spa-Francorchamps circuit that was used until a few years ago, and part of which is incorporated in today's course.

The continental grands prix were not the short sprints they are today. The Belgian was 20 laps, around 200 miles, and Hassall averaged 56 mph. Officials of the British ACU were at the race and after talks with their Belgian colleagues, hatched a plan to switch the TT races from the Isle of Man to a course near Spa (not the one used for the Belgian GP but a longer circuit using the roads between Spa and Verviers).

The truth of the matter was that the ACU were fed up with the increasing restrictions being placed on motor-cycling visitors to the island, both competitors and spectators, and by the rather offhand manner with which the Manx authorities treated the whole event. A meeting of the ACU's competitions committee voted unanimously in favour of the move and *Motor Cycling*

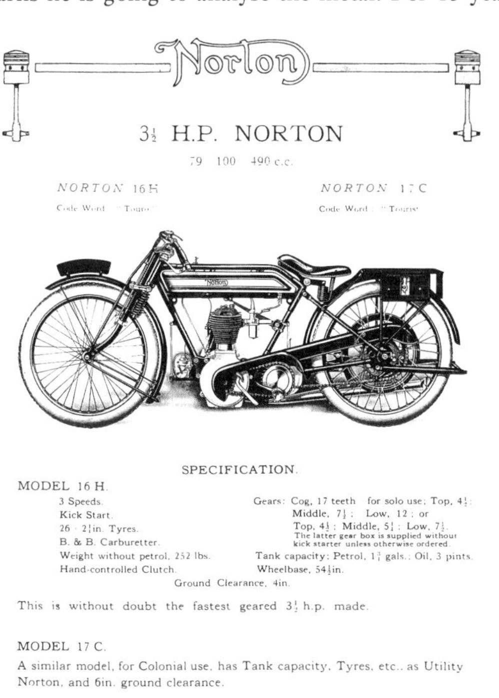
Norton

$3\frac{1}{2}$ H.P. NORTON

79 × 100 490 c.c.

NORTON 16 H — Code Word: "Tour[illegible]"

NORTON 17 C — Code Word: "Tourist"

SPECIFICATION.

MODEL 16 H.

3 Speeds.
Kick Start.
26 × $2\frac{1}{4}$in. Tyres.
B. & B. Carburetter.
Weight without petrol, 252 lbs.
Hand-controlled Clutch.

Gears: Cog, 17 teeth for solo use; Top, $4\frac{1}{2}$; Middle, $7\frac{1}{2}$; Low, 12; or Top, $4\frac{1}{2}$; Middle, $5\frac{1}{4}$; Low, $7\frac{1}{2}$.
The latter gear box is supplied without kick starter unless otherwise ordered.
Tank capacity: Petrol, $1\frac{3}{4}$ gals.; Oil, 3 pints.
Wheelbase, $54\frac{1}{2}$in.

Ground Clearance, 4in.

This is without doubt the fastest geared $3\frac{1}{2}$ h.p. made.

MODEL 17 C.

A similar model, for Colonial use, has Tank capacity, Tyres, etc., as Utility Norton, and 6in. ground clearance.

"The Norton for 1921 differs very little from the machine which last season put up so many brilliant performances. It seems hardly possible that the docile-looking motor cycles, are exact replicas of the hurtling projectiles which have so often lapped the field at Brooklands; yet the fact remains.

Irish Motor Cyclist, December 1st, 1920

ABOVE A happy scene at Brooklands on 17 March 1922 as Rex Judd is carried shoulder high after his first record breaking spree on the new overhead-valve 490 cc Norton. His fastest run over the flying kilometre was an incredible 98.76 mph – a British record – and he averaged 89.92 mph for the two runs, a World Record. Proudly pushing the bike is Pa Norton.

ABOVE RIGHT An early success for the new overhead-valve Norton was the second place scored by Graham Walker in the 1923 Sidecar TT. He used a 588 cc engine and is seen here after the race. Note the braced forks and Hughes racing sidecar.

pointed out that Spa was nearer to London than Douglas.

That put the cat among the Manx pigeons! The final decision was made at a meeting of the ACU in Leicester in October. The Manx authorities sent a strong contingent and after an impassioned appeal, plus no doubt some firm promises as to their future conduct, the meeting voted by a large majority to keep the TT in the Isle of Man. One immediate outcome was that 'Dead Sunday', on which no motor vehicles were allowed out on the roads, was abolished, as was the ruling that no pillion passengers were allowed on the promenades – a fact duly noted in the 1922 John Bull TT Souvenir!

At Brooklands Horsman and his Norton finished the year in a blaze of glory. First, in July, he won the marathon 500-mile race at 62.31 mph and broke five world records in the process – the race lasting some eight hours! Then in October he raised the 500 cc one-hour record to 73.38 mph, and at the end of the year Norton machines held nine out of the 18 500 cc solo records and 16 out of the 17 for 600 cc sidecars.

On the sales front things were tough. Faced by fierce competition, Nortons slashed their prices – the Big Four came down from £135 to £120 and the Model 16 from £132 to £115. The utility TT model with direct belt drive was kept in the range at a bargain £80. Even so, Norton prices remained higher than those of many of their rivals – the Triumph Model H, similar to the 16, selling for £105.

Worse still, Norton were stagnating. The range for 1922 was identical to that offered the preceding year. *Motor Cycling* in October took a kindly view: 'The machines turned out this year have proved so satisfactory that there is practically no alteration.'

Then, late in October 1921, came the first real news that Norton were at last waking up to the challenge. A small news item in *Motor Cycling* read:

> Our readers must not lose sight of the fact that Norton machines, which hold the speed records in the 500 cc class, have all been equipped with side-valve engines. Until he can get no more out of this type of power-unit he intends to stick to it. At the same time there is an overhead valve motor in the background . . . .

The 'he' referred to is O'Donovan and the engine 'in the background' had been built during 1921 by Pa Norton who had been toying with plans for an OHV engine for several years, along with sketches of desmodromic valve gear (in which the valves are closed mechanically as well as opened, a design that eliminates the normal valve spring) and other notions.

That first OHV used a modified SV crank-case and retained the famous long-stroke 79 × 100 mm bore and stroke. The valve gear was supported by pillars which gave ample room for cooling air to flow across the head, and the valves were operated by vertical push-rods. Pa Norton took a picture of this engine in his back garden and thanks to the generosity of his daughter Grace it appears, for the first time, in this book.

CHAPTER

An African odyssey: Pa Norton's epic ride 1921–1923

During the winter of 1921–22 Pa Norton undertook a journey of stunning severity. He decided to visit his brother Harry who was living near Durban in South Africa and then to ride his beloved 633 cc Big Four and sidecar on a 3000-mile trip that would take in all of the Union's major cities – Johannesburg, Pretoria, Bloemfontein, East London, Port Elizabeth and Cape Town.

That he should leave his family and the factory for the best part of six months at a period of intense development seems strange. It may be that his doctor, worried by his continuing health problems, had ordered a complete change and that Pa decided to kill three birds with one stone – convalescing on a two-week cruise, having a holiday with his brother and gaining first-hand knowledge of the 'colonial' market by riding his sidecar on an extensive tour.

It was an ambitious scheme. Even on today's tarred roads such a trip on a 1921 Big Four and sidecar would be an adventure. On the dirt roads of the time and for a man in frail health it bordered on the foolhardy. Certainly his wife Sarah, left at home to look after the five children, was far from happy. 'They were a very devoted couple and she cried for a week after he went,' remembers Grace. 'She never thought that she would see him again.'

As luck would have it, what would have been an epic tour on dry roads turned into a nightmare when South Africa was hit by a series of rainstorms that turned the country into a quagmire – sweeping away bridges, flooding the tracks that passed for main roads and generally causing mayhem.

When he returned to the UK early in 1922 Norton was interviewed by *Motor Cycling* who printed his story under the heading 'A Modern Odyssey – Mr J.L. Norton's extraordinary adventures in South Africa'. The introduction ran:

> Five months ago Mr J.L. Norton, a man of 54, practically crippled with rheumatism, left England in order to explore the possibility of developing the motor-cycle trade and to study the conditions in South Africa. He returned last week, hale and hearty, with a story of adventure, hardship and excitement that few riders would care to experience.

He had sailed out to Durban via the Suez Canal and once in South Africa set out on some excursions around Natal with his brother Harry. On one of these, with Harry on the pillion and a friend, Aubrey Morcom, in the sidecar of the Big Four, they went to Pietermaritzburg. There the local club had organised a climb up a particularly difficult road to a local beauty spot, Howick Falls, where a lunch was held. After they had impressed bystanders by climbing the hill better than the American V-twins in the field, rain began to fall and the party packed up, anxious to get home before the dirt roads became impassable. Pa Norton was one of the last to leave and found the going tough.

> It was absolutely impossible to proceed without assistance, as the wheels clogged solid with mud and had to be freed constantly with tyre levers and screwdrivers. For one mile he rode with the front wheel absolutely locked, and after that had to be frequently dug out by his passengers, who, divesting themselves of boots and stockings, worked . . . to assist him. This mark you, on a main trunk road. To cut a long story short, Mr Norton reached home first, having taken over three hours to do the 14 miles.

Leaving his brother in Pietermaritzburg, Pa set out on the main part of his tour taking with him a native boy, Jim, to assist. It was the rainy season and a particularly severe one – on one occasion over five inches of rain fell in a single night. On the trip to Johannesburg they had to cross 35 rivers, all in flood. Once they made a 60-mile detour only to find the bridge there impassable too, the road having been swept away as the river changed course.

Many of the rivers had to be forded and several times they were almost swept away. Often a bicycle chain had to be wrapped around the rear tyre to give them sufficient grip to continue. At one time Norton could see nothing but water all around and rode for 50 miles in bottom gear, soaked to the skin and praying that the Big Four would keep going. His interviewer recorded:

> The extremely severe conditions encountered may be judged by the fact that Mr Norton was wet through for ten days on end, his luggage, spare shirts and clothes also being soaked. There was no chance of changing but he never suffered any ill-effects. On some days he had nothing to eat, as water was unobtainable, and his tongue was too dry to enjoy food. Another time, with clothes torn by the passage of the machine through the bush and in a semi-conscious condition, Mr Norton, after riding three hours in the dark without a lamp even, found a hut where an Englishman made him comfortable; that cup of tea late at night will be remembered all his life.

LEFT **Pa Norton attempts to ford a flooded stream during his epic 3,000 mile South African tour late in 1921.**

BELOW **While the local Norton agent Aubrey Morcom attempts to pull the 'Big Four' out of the mire, Pa Norton took this picture with his Kodak.**

Despite the conditions, he refused to give in and take the easy option of the train down to Cape Town. The weather had played havoc with his timetable and when it did begin to improve there was no time to have a day off to recuperate. In fact, more miles had to be packed into each day in an effort to recover lost time. When he reached the port of East London on a Saturday in December he apologised to the local motorcycle club, saying that he would not be able to give a talk that evening as he had to leave immediately for Port Elizabeth.

The reporter from *Motor Cycling* then paints a delightful picture of a memorable moment.

> One of the finest performances of the tour was the climbing of the Katsberg Mountains without stopping the engine. The Mountains are 6000 feet high, and had it not been necessary . . . to dig the back wheel out of the mud, the journey would have been made without stopping the road wheels. At the summit Mr Norton astonished his dusky passenger, who was attired in his Sunday best, by cheering merrily and throwing his cap in the air, for he was prouder of his performance than of anything else he had so far attempted.

There were more adventures to come. The rear sidecar connection was shattered by hitting a rock; Jim talked their way out of trouble when they were held up by two belligerent natives and a troublesome cobra was despatched by a rock. Yet the Big Four soldiered on

ABOVE **A troop of monkeys inspect Pa Norton's 'Big Four' 633 cc sidecar combination with the Indian Ocean as a backdrop, just before he set out from Durban in late 1921.**

BELOW **Five local youngsters pose for Pa Norton's camera during his 1921 South African trip.**

and Pa arrived in Cape Town in time to catch his Union Castle steamer home – where, on his arrival, Bob Shelley, chairman of Norton Motors, held a reception at the Midland Hotel in Birmingham where he presented Pa Norton with a 'handsome gold watch as a token of esteem'.

Certainly it was the first, and probably only time that the founding father of a major motorcycle manufacturer had undertaken such a testing marathon. Nortons rammed this home in a full-page advertisement in the two weeklies. Headed 'Across South Africa by Motor-cycle' the copy began: 'The greatest reliability trial ever undertaken was undoubtedly that carried out by Mr Jas. L. Norton when the brought an absolutely standard Big Four and De Luxe sidecar through over 3000 miles of super-colonial conditions.' Few will argue with that summing up, and despite the hardships Pa was soon talking in terms of future fact-finding trips to Australia, New Zealand and Canada.

Just weeks after his return a milestone in Norton history was reached when an overhead-valve Norton appeared in public for the first time. It was wheeled out at Brooklands on 17 March 1922 by O'Donovan for his jockey Rex Judd to have a crack at the British and international flying-start kilometre and mile records. It proved a stunning debut, for Judd upped the one-way British kilometre record to 98.50 mph and the mile to 97.35 mph. He then did the return runs, against a strong wind, to set international figures of 89.92 mph and 88.38 mph.

Pa Norton was at Brooklands to see the fun and both weeklies commented on the first appearance of the OHV. Said *Motor Cycling*:

> At last the long-rumoured overhead valve Norton has made a public appearance and has announced its arrival by putting up some new records for the kilometre and mile over both ways of the course. We must point out the OHV Norton is very far from being a production model at the present time.

The Motor Cycle headlined their similar story 'OHV Norton at last!'.

The Norton joy at their records was short-lived, for the very same day Cyril Pullin on an OHV Douglas flat-twin regained the British records with runs at 98.76 mph and 99.98 mph – unusually his speed over the longer distance being faster. And next day Pullin went one better when he became the first man on a 500 cc machine to beat 100 mph – clocking 100.06 mph over a measured half-mile. This distance was not recognised for official records but it was the first 500 cc 'ton'.

Next mention of the OHV came in April when *Motor Cycling* in their TT News column asked: 'Shall we see the overhead valve Nortons in this year's race? During a recent try-out in the Island it is said that their speed and acceleration [were] much superior to the side-valve engine.' In fact only one was raced in the TT. This was ridden by Ralph Cawthorne who was regarded as

ABOVE **Pa Norton at the controls while sailing at Durban before he set out on his South African tour. Smoking the pipe is the Natal Norton agent Aubrey Morcom.**

BELOW **This full page advertisement detailing Pa Norton's achievements appeared in *Motor Cycling* dated 22 February 1922.**

Across South Africa by Motorcycle

The Greatest Reliability Trial ever undertaken was undoubtedly that carried out by Mr. JAS. L. NORTON, when he successfully brought an absolutely

STANDARD 

& De Luxe Sidecar

through over 3,000 miles of SUPER-COLONIAL CONDITIONS, traversing South Africa during the RAINY SEASON, and performing a feat pronounced IMPOSSIBLE by experienced travellers in that Colony. During the whole of his stay in South Africa Mr. Norton never entered a railway train, yet he arrived with clock-like regularity at his various destinations, after surmounting apparently insuperable difficulties. The only BREAKAGE was that of a sidecar connection bolt, snapped by hitting a boulder at speed. The only REPLACEMENT — a new valve fitted TEMPORARILY after travelling over 50 MILES IN BOTTOM GEAR, because Mr. Norton had no paste with which to grind in the existing valve. The machine finished the journey with its original chains, tyres, etc., intact, and the only attention received by the engine was occasional decarbonizing. The photo gives but a slight idea of the severity of the conditions encountered, but bears ocular proof of the wonderful

Norton Reliability

YOU can purchase from any ***NORTON AGENT*** a machine identical in every detail with that used by Mr. Norton.

Send P.C. for Catalogue and Competition Successes Booklet—Post free.

NORTON MOTORS, Ltd., Bracebridge Street, Birmingham.

Norton's 'most promising novice'. The hastily put together machine did not handle and poor Cawthorne had a real struggle on his hands, eventually falling off, some claimed from sheer exhaustion, at Hillberry on the last lap.

The other four factory entries (Duggie Brown, Hubert Hassall, Norman Black and Jimmy Shaw) stuck to the well-tried Model 16H side-valve. These had been improved by replacing the useless stirrup (bicycle) front brake with a tiny internal expanding drum, though the already outdated dummy belt-rim set-up was retained at the rear. Fuel capacity had been increased by fitting a separate oil tank on the frame below the saddle instead of using part of the main tank. But while others were switching to an oil pump and dry sump, Norton stuck to drip and hand-pump feed with a total loss system.

Judd had used a Ricardo aluminium piston for his successful Brooklands record attempts and these were fitted to the majority of side-valve 16H machines entered for the Senior. However, they gave trouble and *The Motor Cycle* reporter at the TT noted: 'During the week it became necessary to substitute cast-iron for aluminium pistons in the Norton engines, and the camp was busy with the re-balancing.'

Graham Walker was again in charge of the private owners and had been forbidden by Pa Norton actually to race himself. He kept his hand in by trying out a spare OHV model during practice, and when Horsman crashed and put himself out of the race Graham took over his entry and rode a side-valve. In fact in a year when the Nortons were outclassed he finished fifth, first Norton home, and promptly received a telegram from Bracebridge Street congratulating him on his 'splendid finish' despite disobeying orders!

ABOVE After entering only one of the new OHV Nortons in the 1922 TT the factory sent a team to the French Grand Prix at Strasbourg in July. Young Billy Hollowell with one of the new bikes in France.

ABOVE RIGHT The Norton private owners workshop at the 1922 TT. Man on the machine is Ado Carton of Ireland; left to right are Norman Black, R. M. Knowles, Graeme Black, Billy Hollowell, competitions manager Graham Walker, George Tucker and mechanic Harry Homer.

The race had been won by a man who was later to figure prominently in Norton's success story – Irish-born Canadian Alec Bennett who rode a Sunbeam for the last TT win by a side-valve machine.

Royalty attended a motorcycle meeting at Brooklands for the first time that year when the Duke of York, the future King George VI, who had recently been appointed Patron of the ACU, went to the Surrey circuit along with his chauffeur S.F. Wood whom he sponsored on a 500 cc Douglas and a 1000 cc Trump-Anzani. Wood was kitted out in the Duke's racing col-

ours of scarlet jersey with blue stripes and sleeves, and although he did not win that day he did score a royal first on the big V-twin later in the year – possibly helped by a generous handicap.

The two weeklies both road-tested the 16H and the difference in riding conditions is underlined by the *Motor Cycling* reporter who almost proudly admits that he never used the front brake: 'The foot brake was smooth and powerful in action and was never supplemented by the front stirrup brake,' he wrote. The roads were slippery and slimy and the stirrup brakes were poor, so riders just used the rear – and of course the vast majority of cars at that time were not even fitted with brakes on the front wheels.

His rival in *The Motor Cycle* was more original in his road-test phraseology: '. . . tractable as a lamb in traffic it can become a roaring lion at the touch of the throttle'. Times change, but 'road-test speak' goes on for ever.

In July Norton sent a team to contest the French Grand Prix held on an eight-mile circuit near Strasbourg. The course was marshalled by troops with fixed bayonets and in wet and muddy conditions Hubert Hassall took an early lead on an OHV Norton, setting a lap record at 68.69 mph. Then, when well ahead, he pulled into the pits with the rear wheel wobbling. The bearings had worn out. Quick as a flash Pa Norton nipped over to his trusty Big Four which was luckily close at hand, took out the rear wheel and fitted it to the OHV model. Hassall re-started to finish second behind Alex Bennett who repeated his TT win on a factory Sunbeam.

The Belgian Grand Prix was plagued by heavy rain that year (1922). Things looked good initially as Hassall led, chased by Graham Walker. Then Hassall was slowed by tyre problems, eventually finishing third, while Walker went out with a broken crankpin. The race was won by another Sunbeam, ridden by Northerner Alec Jackson, later to be team manager at Wembley Speedway. The race lasted over five hours!

The road-racing season ended in mid-October with the first running of the Ulster Grand Prix and it was there that the OHV Norton scored its first major road-racing success, Hassall winning the 600 cc class at 60.57 mph.

In September O'Donovan masterminded yet another record spree. Partnered by Judd and Horsman he first thrashed a side-valve 490 cc Model 16H round Brooklands for 12 hours on 4 September, averaging 61.77 mph. Then the bike was locked away for the night before completing another 12-hour session. The average for the 24 hours worked out at 60.31 mph and the total distance covered was 1447 miles 839 yards. In all, 19 records were broken.

The 'double 12' was done because night testing at Brooklands was prohibited – noise was becoming an

increasing problem and the 500-mile race, which lasted over eight hours, had to be cancelled because of protests from local residents. However, this did not stop a rash of record breaking just before the Olympia Show in November 1922.

First O'Donovan's partner H.H. Beach set a number of long-distance sidecar records (the longest being the 600 miles at 52.65 mph) on a side-valve 490 cc. Then Victor Horsman, after winning three events at the final race meeting of the year in October (including the 500 cc solo championship in which he rode an OHV model to its first major outright track win at a speed of 82 mph, later in the day taking the all-comers solo championship at 86.22 mph), set flying-start 5-mile sidecar and solo records of 73.55 mph and 89.25 mph.

Then Horsman – a dealer from Liverpool who died at a ripe old age in the 1980s leaving somewhere in the region of £7million – returned in late November and after waiting for four days for fog to clear used the same OHV 490 cc to break a number of sidecar and solo records. Most notable among them were the 600 cc sidecar flying-kilometre world record (mean average of two runs) at 80.24 mph (and remember, he had to carry a passenger) and the solo 500 cc flying-kilometre world record at 93.59 mph. Judd was out too and set a new 500 cc 100-mile record on a side-valve at 74 mph. In

Two types of racing Norton pictured at a Scottish sand race late in 1922. On the left Graeme Black is astride the side-valve 490 cc 16H with stirrup front brake – on the right Norton competitions manager Graham Walker with his factory overhead-valve 490 cc model with tiny drum brake.

six days just before the show no less than 49 records were broken, the majority by Nortons.

By this time the OHV 490 cc in full road trim had been officially launched at the Paris Show in October and *The Motor Cycle* carried a write-up about the machine (yet to be christened the Model 18) in issue dated 2 November 1922, under the headline 'Overhead Valve Norton Modifications'. This began: 'Though the overhead valve Norton has now been with us for a considerable time it is not generally realised that this type has already been standardised and is obtainable by the buying public.' Probably the public did not know because they had never been told!

The height of the engine had been reduced by redesigning the rocker gear, with steel forgings replacing the bronze castings of the original. The rockers pivoted on double-row roller bearings. Following the problems at the TT a new aluminium piston was fitted with a thicker, slightly domed crown and two piston rings – but no oil ring. The revised unit was slotted into a new frame with Druid forks, tiny internal expanding front brake and the old dummy rim brake at the back. The gearbox was a three-speed Sturmey-Archer and the exhaust swept out on the left-hand side.

Interestingly, a problem with the cast-iron heads cracking was cured by drilling a second plug hole on the offside. This was fitted with a simple screw-in blanking plug and evened out the expansion which was the cause of the cracking. The OHV was duly wheeled out at Olympia with a price tag of £98 – the most expensive bike in the Norton range, £14 more than the Big Four, the price of which had been reduced from the £135 of 1920 to £84.

But of a reported 250 cc Norton there was no sign. Back in September *The Motor Cycle* had carried a story headline 'OHV Norton Lightweight. Advance details of a new 250 cc model with a possible speed of 70 mph' which read: 'For some time past it has been known to a select few that the famous house of Norton was likely to produce a small engine for next year. We are now permitted to divulge the main features of the new engine.'

The brief specification included a bore and stroke of 63 × 80 mm to give 249 cc, a detachable cylinder head, aluminium piston, ball-bearing mains and proper expanding hub brakes both front and rear – something the bigger models were still waiting for. It is not known why the 250 cc project was abandoned. Probably when the financial people got down to working out the cost it was found that it would be almost as expensive as a bigger machine to produce yet would have to be priced well below the £98 of the OHV if it was to have any chance of selling in any numbers.

Behind the scenes a tragedy had begun to unfold. After experiencing severe stomach pains Pa Norton had visited a doctor friend in the Isle of Man who, after carefully examining him, told him he was suffering from terminal cancer of the bowel and had only a couple of months to live. The family had to be told sooner or later, and Grace still had a vivid memory of that moment when interviewed in 1990.

I remember him telling us. We were all sitting round the tea-table and I was swotting up some Latin from a book I was holding under the table because I wasn't really allowed to do that, when I suddenly realised everyone had gone very quiet and mother was in tears. He told us then that he'd got two months to live.

In fact will-power kept him going for a further two and a half years, though he suffered terribly towards the end. It was typical of the man that he offered himself to the doctors and told them that if there was anything in the form of a cancer cure they wanted to test then they should try it out on him. He went to London at one stage where he underwent appallingly painful radium treatment. That, of course, was during the final stages of his illness. In 1923 he remained at work and was actively involved in the preparations for the TT. It was during practice for the Isle of Man race that the Norton riders switched from the Druid front fork to the Webb.

Pa Norton was a great supporter of the Druid and at first forbade Graham Walker, who led the revolution, to make the switch, threatening him with the sack if he did. Graham, who was Norton's competitions manager at the time, stuck to his guns. He pulled out of the factory team and raced his Norton as a private entrant.

The Webb was a far better fork. With a single long central spring it had more fork travel and better characteristics. By the time the Senior TT started all but one of the Nortons entered were sporting Webbs! It proved to be an appallingly wet race and this gave the beautifully engineered Douglas twins, purpose built for racing, a tremendous advantage, for they were fitted with the very advanced Research Association brakes both front and rear. These were an early form of disc brake. The friction material was carried on both sides of a disc attached to the wheel. The braking effect was created by a V-shaped aluminium shoe bearing on the disc.

In use it was impervious to rain and, with such a large area of friction material which was out in the open and unshrouded, it cooled very quickly and did not fade. At the end of the first lap the Douglas twins held the first four places but the engines were fragile and only Tom Sheard had a trouble-free run, winning a miserable race at 55.55 mph.

Graeme Black kept going to finish second and with Graham Walker fourth, Tommy Simister fifth and Jimmy Shaw in seventh place, Norton machines filled four of the first seven places and won the Manufacturers' team prize (with Walker going 'private' the team was Black, Simister and Shaw).The bikes they used were carefully prepared standard sports overhead valve Model 18s (after calling the machine the OHV in the early days it had been given the number 18 early in 1923). Nortons did then race 'same as you can buy' bikes, unlike the majority of their rivals who built a batch of special racing machines for the TT.

Norton's mistake had been to keep the old dummy belt-rim brake at the back, for this was useless in the rain. Interviewed after the race, Graeme Black, who finished less than two minutes behind Sheard in a race that lasted over four hours, said that at one time things got so bad that he stopped to try to get the rear brake to work.

The tiny front drum brake, although better than the old stirrup, was far too small to be effective and after the race Black said: 'I drove the rest of the race without any brakes worth mentioning.' In their follow-up technical article, *Motor Cycling* commented: 'The old idea that an effective front brake is dangerous is dead.' Certainly lack of good brakes had cost Nortons their chance of a TT win and it is a curious fact that despite the Douglas success, no one took up the idea of the Research Association disc brake, which simply faded from the scene.

Norton's involvement in the TT that year had been broadened by the running of the first ever Sidecar TT, restricted to 600 cc engines. The legendary Freddie Dixon won the race using a Douglas flat-twin with a hinged sidecar. This allowed the passenger to heel the machine, solo style, into the corners by pulling or pushing a long lever with his left hand.

Nortons ridden by Graham Walker and George Tucker took second and third places. Interestingly, they used 588 cc overhead-valve engines, retaining the 79 mm bore but increasing the stroke to 120 mm, the same as the Big Four side-valve. With two second places and a convincing display of speed and reliability, it had been Norton's best TT since Rem Fowler's win back in 1907. It resulted in a full order book for the Model 18 which was regarded as the fastest catalogue sports model on the market – regardless of capacity.

For the 1923 season record breaker Judd had left O'Donovan to join Cyril Pullin and Douglas – and if you think that pit-to-driver radio contact is something new you will be surprised to learn that Pullin, an early radio enthusiast, built his own transmitting station in his workshop at Brooklands so that he could communicate with Judd (who wore headphones under his helmet) during record attempts!

Another pioneering move was made by Triumph who had so many continental orders that they chartered a plane to air-freight machines to Europe. Said *Motor Cycling*: 'Many manufacturers are finding out the advantages of air-transport for small shipments abroad.'

Judd's place on the O'Donovan bikes had been taken by the equally small Bert Denly – in fact he was only 5 ft 3 in and weighed just 8 st 6 lb (53.5 kg). The regulations of the day required a minimum of 9 st 6 lb (60 kg) so the weight was made up by carrying lead which was attached to Denly's boots to keep the centre of gravity low. He had caught the eye of Brooklands' habitués by the dashing way he rode a 350 cc Douglas while delivering meat for the local butcher – a classic example of being in the right place at the right time.

He was soon in action. In June, riding an

The real significance of this picture of Graham Walker at the 1923 TT is that his overhead-valve Norton is fitted with a Webb fork. Graham had found these to be far superior to the Druid type and when Pa Norton refused to allow him to use them he pulled out of the team and rode as a private owner, finishing fourth. By that time all the other Norton riders, bar one, had switched to Webb forks.

O'Donovan-tuned Model 18, he broke the classic one-hour record at a speed of 82.66 mph and also took the 50-mile record at 83.14 mph. A few days later O'Donovan hitched a sidecar to the Norton and broke four records himself, including the one hour at 67.25 mph and the two hours at 63.60 mph.

By this time all the Brooklands' record machines were using alcohol-based fuels, known as 'dope'. This caused controversy at the time and there is no doubt they bestowed great benefits on the users. They could use a higher compression ratio and the engines ran far cooler and, as record breaker Victor Horsman pointed out in a letter to *Motor Cycling*, the alcohol-based fuel he used, marketed under the brand name Discol, was in fact cheaper than petrol. It was also used by some road racers, notably Douglas whose two 1923 TT winners were both on Discol, though the advantages in longer races had to be balanced against far greater fuel consumption.

In July Denly won the 500 cc class of a 200-mile race at Brooklands at a record 77.61 mph, and the following month he pushed the 100-mile record up to 79.65 mph – a burst tyre putting paid to plans to go for longer records. Then, sharing the riding with Nigel Spring, records for the longer distances were set up to six hours at 71.23 mph.

Record breaking at Brooklands was an industry. Manufacturers and accessory makers, ranging from saddles, chains and tyres to oil and fuel, all paid bonuses based on the number of records broken and the prestige value of the record – for example the classic hour and the outright fastest flying kilometre were worth more than the 100-miles, but they all paid something. This led to intense rivalry between the various camps who all had their tuning shops in or around Brooklands.

On the road-racing front Douglas continued their winning way when Jim Whalley was victorious in the French Grand Prix at Tours. But Hassall, Billy Hollowell and a French rider, Francisquet, the only Norton riders in the race, finished second, third and fourth with Hassall less than a minute behind the winner in a race that lasted 4½ hours.

Hassall was out of luck in the Belgian Grand Prix. A petrol pipe broke and the race was won by Freddie Dixon on an Indian; the American company had abandoned their earlier advanced four-valve OHV in favour of a side-valve. The race that year (1923) was on a very fast road course near Dinant, and the same circuit was used in August for a separate sidecar Belgian Grand Prix. This was completely dominated by George Tucker who, on his 588 cc TT Norton, won both the 600 cc and 1000 cc classes, finishing the 176-mile race 14 minutes ahead of his nearest rival.

Riders were venturing further afield by this time. Ralph Cawthorne took his Model 18 out to Italy to compete in the September meeting at Monza but dropped out with valve-spring failure, a problem that plagued Nortons throughout the 1920s. The race was won by Frenchman Gillard on one of the very fast and technically advanced overhead camshaft Peugeot vertical twins, with a Norton ridden by Eduardo Self in second place.

The road-racing year finished on a high note when Joe Craig won the 600 cc class at the Ulster. It was the very first race the famous Ulsterman ever rode in and the Norton Model 18 he used had been lent to him by a friend. To avoid wear and tear Joe, whose name was to be associated with Norton for over 30 years, did most of the practising on his own ABC twin.

The Ulster that year was run in mid September and about the same time Nortons were venturing on a project which they later claimed, with justification, to be 'the most astounding performance in the history of motor cycling'. The basic plan was to attack long-distance world records with a perfectly standard motorcycle.

To make sure that it was 'same as you can buy', an ACU official went to Bracebridge Street and picked out of the various bins the components needed to build an OHV Model 18 engine. He then watched while the bits and pieces were built into an engine, making sure that no special parts were used and that no modifications were made. After the engine had been fitted into a standard frame the machine was sealed by the ACU observer and was taken to Brooklands. There it was run in for 100 miles and after normal adjustments had been made Denly, Spring and O'Donovan set out on a marathon ride that ended after 12 hours with 18 world records in the bag – averaging 64.02 mph over the whole ride.

It was an impressive stunt and it won for Norton the Maudes Trophy, a new award given by Maudes Motor Mart and observed by the ACU, for the most meritorious performance made by any make of motorcycle during the year.

At Brooklands George Duller, a leading race-horse jockey of the time, caused a stir when (having, as *Motor Cycling* put it, 'caught the Brooklands fever') he turned out with his V-twin New Imperial fitted with footrests shaped like stirrups! Meanwhile, Denly was motoring on. He lifted the hour record first to 85.22 mph and then, in late October, to 85.58 mph during the usual mass attack on the records that took place just before the Olympia Show.

Throughout 1923 there had been rumblings about the TT. In July the competitions committee of the ACU decided to drop the 500 cc class. This was confirmed at the general council meeting in October and that seemed to be the end of the matter. The 500s were deemed to be just too fast for the Isle of Man.

Prices were coming down. Petrol cost 1s 8d (8p) a gallon, the same as it had in 1914 before rising to a peak of 4s (20p) during the war. And for 1924 the price of Norton machines was slashed again. The good old Big Four 633 cc was down from a high of £135 in 1920 to £76 and OHV Model 18, launched at £98 in 1922, was cut to £89.

For the first time an electric lighting system with Lucas magdyno was offered, as an optional extra for any model, at £13 for solos and £14 for sidecars. It was a time for economy and no new models were launched. Commented *Motor Cycling*: 'The OHV model, which is one of the fastest machines on the road, has proved very popular . . . and is being retained for 1924 without alteration . . . other than the fitting of a new silencer.'

CHAPTER 8

Racing the standard product 1924–1925

Major changes were made to the Norton racing set-up during the winter of 1923–24 – and they were to have dramatic consequences. They were sparked off by Castrol's Lonnie Limb who, when he met Norton's chairman of the board Bob Shelley to discuss the coming season and the level of support the famous oil company would provide, complained that Norton were 'missing the boat' because the riders were not good enough.

Writing in a book, *The TT Races – Behind the Scenes*, years later, Gilbert Smith, by that time managing director, said: 'Mr Shelley . . . seemed to have the impression that Nortons were so good that they could win anything and I think he entertained some doubts as to the important part the rider played.' Gilbert had joined the company straight from technical college in 1916 and stayed with Nortons until 1958.

Taking the Castrol man's advice, Shelley told Bill Mansell to contact the leading riders of the day and, if possible, sign one for the season. Freddie Dixon and Alec Bennett were both approached, and Bennett, running his own motorcycle business in Southampton, agreed to join the team. That solved the star rider problem – but what of the machines?

Graham Walker, competitions manager since 1919, had left at the end of 1923 to join Sunbeams. At Nortons he had looked after the private riders as well as competing himself while O'Donovan ran the actual works team. When he went, Mansell reassessed the situation. He realised the team needed a technical man

BELOW *The Motor Cycle*, 28 August 1924; Norton's 'year of firsts'.

BELOW *The Motor Cycle*, January 1924; a standard Model 18 was taken to Brooklands and broke 18 world records.

who could solve mechanical problems as they occurred and he contacted Walter Moore, a well-known trouble-shooter of the day.

Speaking to Titch Allen many years later Moore recalled Mansell telling him that Nortons wanted to win the TT. He replied that they did not have anything to win with – the brakes were useless and the oiling system out of date. Mansell countered by saying they had an excellent engine, and the upshot was that Moore joined Nortons in March 1924 as team manager with special responsibilities on the technical side.

His first task was to do something about the rear brake. When he found nothing suitable on the motor-cycle market he turned to friends in the car trade. There a contact suggested that the eight-inch drums fitted to the latest Ford Model T were good and readily available. Moore bought 40 and had them modified so that they could be spoked into the Model 18 rear wheel.

He tackled the lubrication problem by fitting Best

ABOVE Congratulating Phil Pike (centre) and ACU observer Arthur Bourne after their Maudes Trophy run, October 1924. One of the last pictures taken of Norton who knew he was terminally ill and who died in April 1925.

RIGHT Alec Bennett with his 1924 Senior TT winning Norton in Douglas, with Pa Norton (left) and Walter (Bill) Mansell who took over when Norton died.

and Lloyd pumps. It was not the complete answer but it was the best that could be done in the three months available before the 1924 TT. Then, to gain first-hand experience of what the engines did during a race, he took over as sidecar passenger with George Tucker whom he knew well from his days with Douglas when both lived in Bristol.

Their machine was a 588 cc and one important innovation was that it was fitted with a four-speed gearbox of Norton's own design. Tucker had long felt that a four-speeder would be of great advantage around the TT course, allowing him to use third on the slog up the Mountain and top down the other side – but the solos stuck to the Sturmey-Archer three-speeders.

As usual the machines used by the factory riders (Alec Bennett, Hubert Hassall, Tommy Simister, Graeme Black and Jimmy Shaw) were basically standard machines. Commented *The Motor Cycle*: 'The Norton entry will be absolutely standard as regards all vital parts . . . some of the Norton engines in the process of erection were examined by our representative and were found to differ in no visible respect from the standard productions.'

The team practising on the Isle of Man were encouraged by good news from the Continent. Italian Achille Varzi, on the only Norton entered, had won the Spanish Grand Prix in Barcelona while compatriot Tazio Nuvolari led a Norton clean sweep in the important Circuit de Cremona in Italy – Nortons taking the first five places. Both men later became world-famous grand prix car racers.

To George Tucker and Walter Moore fell the honour of winning the first TT for Nortons since Rem Fowler's 1907 success. Dixon on his Douglas set the early pace but when he retired with engine trouble Tucker took over to win at 51.31 mph. In addition to the four-speed gearbox (ratios 4.5, 6.3, 8.5 and 10 to 1) Tucker also used a twist-grip throttle – not by any means a new invention but not, curiously enough, favoured by many for racing. Bennett in particular preferred the normal lever throttle which, he said, used like a trigger, was quicker acting.

Dixon set off at his usual furious pace in the Senior TT, then ran into a series of problems. He changed a plug to cure a misfire, fell twice at Governors' Bridge and eventually finished in third place.

Bennett made no attempt to stay with Dixon. He said after the race that he had ridden the early laps on three-quarters throttle, saving his machine for the final stages. When they came he was in the lead and cruising to victory. He averaged 61.65 mph – the first time the 60 mph race barrier had been broken. The other Norton riders were never in contention, Hassall finishing the best of them in fifth place; the Castrol man had been proved right.

By this time Pa Norton's health was failing fast. He had kept working as best he could during the winter and in April 1924 had patented a chain-driven overhead-camshaft design in which the valves were closed, as well as opened, mechanically. In his design

ABOVE **Sand racing in Ireland; Jimmy Shaw leads the pack at the start of the 100 mile race at Magilligan Strand, autumn 1924. Riding his factory Model 18 he won the race.**

ABOVE RIGHT **Two completely standard 1924 Norton roadsters in Germany: Model 16H (right) 633 cc Big Four with leg-shields and sidecar (left). Note the swastika.**

a peg in the side of the rocker followed a groove cut in a large cam. The idea was to eliminate valve bounce and to get rid of the valve springs that gave Norton such trouble. The design was called 'desmodromique' and was illustrated in *The Motor Cycle*.

He had been forced to give up riding his Big Four and had bought a car – first an overhead-camshaft Birmingham-built Rhode and then a magnificent Lea-Francis sports tourer which he took with him to the Isle of Man early in 1924. The family went with him and they stayed for several months in a house in Port e Vullen, a mile and a half out of Ramsey. Grace remembers that at TT time he would drive out to a corner and they would then position a chair so that he could sit and watch the action.

That he was a famous figure is clear from an item penned by the columnist of the Isle of Man *Weekly Times* in June 1924.

> Pa Norton, as everyone knows, is the designer of the Norton motor-cycle. He is a very sick man, but he is the most cheerful of persons, despite the fact that doctor after doctor has told him that he must die from cancer. A letter from him – full of hope and courage to those suffering from this dreaded disease – appeared in the *Weekly Times* in which he recommends a special diet as a means of effecting a stay, if not a remedy, of this distressing complaint.

Another journalist wrote:

> Ramsey looks upon him as a sort of honoured guest and everything is being done by the Ramsey folk to make his stay among them as happy as possible. If it should be that a Norton wins the Senior Tourist Trophy this year, Pa Norton will have achieved the ambition of his lifetime.

Imagine Pa's delight when he saw his machines win two TT races in the space of a few days. He attended the Senior prize-giving and *The Motor Cycle* records: 'Everyone was pleased to see Mr J.L. Norton at the TT. He was cheered again and again when, supported by Alec Bennett, he spoke a few words at the presentation of the Senior Trophy.'

In July the City of Birmingham held a civic reception to honour their TT winners. Four races had been won by Birmingham-built machines – the Senior and Sidecar by Nortons and the Junior and Lightweight by New

Imperials ridden by the Tremlow brothers. So that the factory workers could attend, it was held in the evening and started with a parade that left New Street Station at 5 p.m. The winning machines were displayed on the backs of lorries while the celebrities rode in open cars with the workers following in charabancs. Grace remembers the day.

> I rushed from school to Corporation Street to see them drive by. There was a great throng of people and I pushed through, arriving just as father went by in an open car. He saw me and raised his hat. I was sky-high with delight. I felt so proud and the people all around looked at me and obviously wondered why he had acknowledged me!

The procession went to the Town Hall, where it was welcomed by the Lord Mayor. Later, at a dinner at the Midland Hotel, Pa Norton, in response to a toast to the men who made the machines, said that he had been waiting and working for 17 years for this particular moment. It was his last public appearance.

The next big race was the Belgian Grand Prix, back at Spa and run over 28 laps – 275 miles. Bennett won easily at 61.3 mph and then went down to Lyon where the French Grand Prix was held late in July. He won again to become the first man ever to win the three major classic races in a year. In each race he had ridden a different Model 18 Norton – they really were so basically standard that he did not stick to one specially tuned works racer.

Bennett's only defeat in a major race came at the Ulster when he ran out of petrol when leading by the proverbial mile on the last lap. This let Joe Craig, on a similar Norton, through to score his second Ulster win in a race enlivened when a grandstand, on which a band was playing, collapsed as the riders lined up for the start.

At Brooklands all was not well. In May there had been a riders' strike when competitors reacted to a threat to ban noisy machines. Despite the problems Denly had recaptured the hour record at 87.07 mph, beating Horsman who had clocked 86.52 mph on a Triumph just a few days earlier. Then Tucker, fresh from his TT success, won the 200-mile sidecar race in which Nortons took the first five places, and in September Naval Lieutenant R.T. Grogan, riding his own two-year-old Norton tuned by O'Donovan, won the 500 cc class of a long-distance race and set a record for 200 miles at 79.81 mph.

On the stunt front Nortons won the Maudes Trophy for a second year. This time Phil Pike with ACU observer Arthur Bourne (later to become editor of *The Motor Cycle*) in the sidecar of the Big Four 633 cc rode

ABOVE In 1924 Alec Bennett became the first man to win the three major classics – the TT, the French GP and the Belgian GP, each on a different Model 18 OHV Norton – no special works models.

RIGHT Alec Bennett attends to his Model 18 during his winning ride in the 1924 Senior TT. Behind him is Walter Moore the new boss of Norton racing.

from Land's End to John O'Groats and back again – and then repeated the dose to make it four end-to-end runs in a row! The plan was then to ride to Porlock Hill and do 20 runs straight up the infamous climb without a stop.

The driver of an open-topped charabanc had other ideas, however. He managed to crash into the Norton. Luckily neither rider nor passenger was injured. The bike was rebuilt overnight with spares supplied by the local Norton agent. Still stamped and sealed, the original engine and gearbox then completed the test, averaging 20 mph for the final Porlock climb. In all the outfit covered 4088 miles, and despite a total weight of 8 cwt 4 lb (408 kg) the fuel consumption worked out at a quite staggering 68.4 mpg.

The Isle of Man success had resulted in a glut of orders for the Model 18 and the road testers continued to rave over it. *The Motor Cycle* reporter said: '. . . the fastest standard 500 cc machine . . . no doubt 75 mph would have been possible . . . . It pleases on every score, and disappoints on none.' At the end of the year when the 1925 models were wheeled out at Olympia, the majority of the range were fitted with the Ford-inspired rear drum brake and Best and Lloyd mechanical oil pumps which took the guessing out of the older-style hand-pump system – though it was still a wet-sump set-up.

Prices had been cut again. The benchmark Big Four was now £70 or £89 complete with sidecar, while the Bennett-style Model 18 cost £80. Cheapest was the 16H which retained the old brake set-up and was offered at £65. To deter anyone who was thinking of hanging on for a future price reduction, the Norton advertisement warned: 'Prices are fixed and no further reduction will take place.'

Hill-climbs on open roads, popular since the dawn

of motorcycle sport, were under threat following a series of injuries to spectators. One of the last to be held before the ACU banned them was at Aston Hill near Tring on 28 February 1925 when Cambridge beat Oxford in the inter-varsity meeting – a Norton ridden by J.A. Temple making the fastest time of the day. A Norton also won the sidecar class and *Motor Cycling* recorded that 'The electric timing worked without a hitch'.

On 21 April James Lansdowne Norton died at his home in Sampson Road, Birmingham. The obituary in *Motor Cycling* summed up the feelings of the motorcycle industry:

Familiarly known as Pa Norton, there is probably no one in motor-cycling circles who in his life has been more loved and respected, and whose death will be more lamented. All who had met him or were in any way connected with him spoke of him only with the highest praise.

The Motor Cycle spoke in similar vein: '. . . his gentle manner and cheerful outlook endeared him to his fellows'. The funeral was held at Lodge Hill Cemetery on Friday 24 April, and it is nice to record that the grave was recently refurbished by members of the Norton Owners' Club.

His widow Sarah and the family were shattered, and matters were made worse by the way in which they were treated by Bob Shelley and the board of Norton Motors. Grace, 18 when her father died, says that the family have agreed never to speak of the matter but she used the word 'abominably'. The eldest son, Lansdowne, who was working in the drawing office after being apprenticed at the company, was sacked soon after his father's death. He went on to become a designer with the Bristol Aircraft Company, working on the famous monster Brabazon aircraft, before retiring to live in Malta. He died in 1990.

The late Mr. J. L. Norton.

It is with deep regret that we have to announce the death of Mr. James L. Norton, who passed away at his home at Sampson Road, Birmingham, on the 21st inst. Mr. Norton, who was 56, had for the past two years suffered from cancer, and it was only his strong will-power which kept him alive latterly.

Familiarly known as "Pa" Norton, there is probably no one in motorcycling circles who in his life has been more loved and respected, and whose death will be more lamented. All who had met him or were in any way connected with him spoke of him only with the highest praise, and his many friends and acquaintances have sympathized deeply during his long and painful illness.

The late Mr. Norton's life was, we understand, very varied. At an early age he was a toolmaker in the jewellery trade. He then started to make bicycle chains, and was later connected with Clement-Garrard motorcycles, the original Norton Manufacturing Company being founded in 1898. In 1901, he began making cycles, and was engaged in repairs to motorcycles.

The first Norton motorcycles were fitted with Peugeot twin-cylinder and single-cylinder engines, and it was on one of these machines that Rem Fowler won the twin-cylinder class of the first Tourist Trophy race. Later Mr. Norton produced a single-cylinder engine of his own design, and it was one of his dearest ambitions that this machine should win a T.T. race. For many years he waited, but it was not until 1924, when he was already in failing health, that his ambition was realized.

Mr. Norton has in the past contributed many interesting articles to *Motor Cycling*, and the advanced design of motorcycles of to-day has been largely due to his skill and knowledge. From the early days he was always in favour of the long-stroke engine.

The Editor and Staff of *Motor Cycling* join in expressing their deepest sympathy to his widow and relatives.

FAR LEFT **This is the obituary that appeared in *Motor Cycling* dated 29 April 1925.**

ABOVE **The Norton 633 cc Big Four for the 1924 Maudes Trophy attempt is built in the Norton factory from standard parts under the watchful eye of ACU observer Arthur Bourne (left).**

LEFT **Pa Norton (bearded) celebrates the 1924 Sidecar TT win of George Tucker and passenger Walter Moore (recently appointed team manager and technical boss) with Bill Mansell (right).**

On the same page that *Motor Cycling* recorded Norton's death was news of yet more Norton records. Denly, partnered by W. Le Grand on a 500 cc Norton, had bettered 14 long-distance solo figures ranging from five hours at 73.63 mph to ten at 66.95 mph. A few days earlier Nigel Spring, who was taking over as Norton's man at Brooklands, had teamed with Chris Staniland and Pat Driscoll on a 490 cc Norton with sidecar and had captured 14 world records, from 300 miles at 58.27 mph to nine hours at 55.95 mph.

For the 1925 TT Nortons relied on improved versions of the Model 18. The total loss lubrication was gone, replaced by a dry-sump set-up with submerged pump driven by worm gears off the main shaft. The three-speed Sturmey-Archer gearbox was retained and six riders received official support: Bennett, Hassall, Simister, Shaw, Black and Craig, invited to join the team following his impressive Ulster displays.

Things went well during practice, with Bennett beating the lap record by 40 seconds when he went out, in his own words, 'to break the motor'. He lapped at nearly 66 mph which meant that the Norton must have been doing around 90 mph down the Mountain. The engine held together, but things went wrong in the race. Bennett took the lead on the first lap and was well ahead when he slid off at Governors' Bridge and badly bent the offside footrest.

He remounted, rode to the pits and straightened it as best he could but for the rest of the race he was unable to heel the machine over to anywhere near the limit on right-handers. He eventually came home third, just over four minutes behind winner Howard Davies on a JAP-powered HRD. When Bennett had slowed, Craig had taken up the chase but retired with engine trouble. Writing in Geoff Davison's book *The TT Races – Behind the Scenes*, Joe explained:

CB

LEFT Alec Bennett with his Model 18 at the French GP, Strasbourg 1924. He won the 500 cc race to make it three classic wins in three starts – TT, Belgian GP and the French.

ABOVE Soon after the double success in the 1924 TT races the factory offered this nickel-plated facsimile of the TT trophy with handlebar mounting. The mascot cost 10s 6d.

> I was lying second in the Senior Race (though I had no idea where I was) when on the third lap on one of the fastest parts of the course – the descent just previous to the 13th milestone – the connecting rod broke and the jagged end came through the crankcase, accompanied by a startlingly loud crunching noise.

Luckily Bill Mansell was not too upset and after the race invited Craig to go 'on tour' with the team for the French and Belgian Grands Prix.

Thus the week ended without a win. For Len Parker (Douglas) had won the Sidecar TT after George Grinton (Norton) had slowed too much on the final lap. He thought he was so far ahead that he could ease up but overdid things and dropped to third with Bert Taylor (Norton) nipping in for second place. Dixon (Douglas) had again led early on only to blow up and Tucker, who had won for Norton the preceding year, suffered a similar fate.

That year the French was held at Montlhéry on a twisty, hilly road circuit that included one steeply banked end of the speed bowl. Bennett was forced out with tyre problems but Craig kept going to finish second to Jimmie Simpson (AJS).

The Belgian Grand Prix at Spa was a shambles. First the Belgian federation banned the top Belgian factory, FN, because they had entered machines in unauthorised events. The powerful FN company won a legal injunction to allow the team to race. Rather than give in, the federation cancelled the race. FN then showed that sportsmanship was not entirely dead by withdrawing their entries.

By this time it was too late to run the race on the original date of Sunday 2 August and it was rescheduled for the following Sunday. British competitors who went home were paid travelling expenses to return. 'And heartily cheered the FMB for treating them so fairly,' according to *The Motor Cycle* man on the spot.

At first it looked like another win for Simpson, who was out on a full-sized 489 cc AJS and not the 350 cc he had used in France, for after pushing him hard in the early stages Bennett was forced to stop and change a plug in full view of the main grandstand. At the 14-lap half-way stage Simpson still led but Bennett was up to fifth, and by lap 20 of the 28-lap, 250-mile race Bennett was in the lead – and he pulled away to win at 66.6 mph.

Bennett looked set to win in Ireland as he went into the last lap ahead, but again his Ulster bad luck struck and as he wobbled round with a rear-wheel puncture he was passed by fellow Norton riders Craig and Shaw. It was Craig's third Ulster win in succession and his speed of 72.04 mph was a record for a road race.

September 1925 was a busy month. First the veteran O'Donovan used a 588 cc Norton with sidecar to set a world record for the standing-start kilometre at 64.52 mph. Then Norton riders led by Naval Sub-lieutenant H.G. Dodds swept the board in the Amateur

1924–25 Gallery

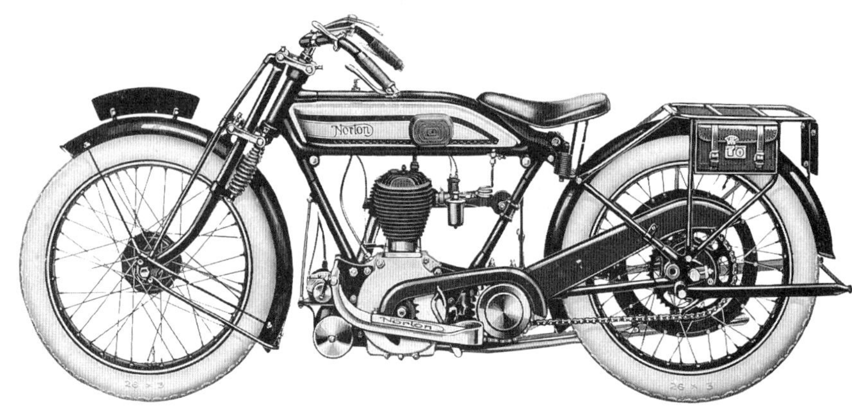

Variations on a theme. This is the 1924 Model 2, a touring version of the 490 cc side-valve 16H with high touring handlebars, footboards and balloon tyres.

For 1924 the Big Four 633 cc side-valve was offered with fully enclosed primary and rear chains and aluminium footboards. The front mudguard was well valanced to keep mud and water off the rider and balloon tyres were fitted.

The top of the range sports Model 18 as offered in 1925 with OHV 490 cc engine, three-speed Sturmey-Archer gearbox and mechanical oil pump. Up front the bone-shaking Druid forks had been replaced by Webbs.

For the family man Norton offered this 633 cc Big Four with de Luxe sidecar in 1924. The luggage compartment of the sidecar extended under the seat and into the nose, room for a set of golf clubs.

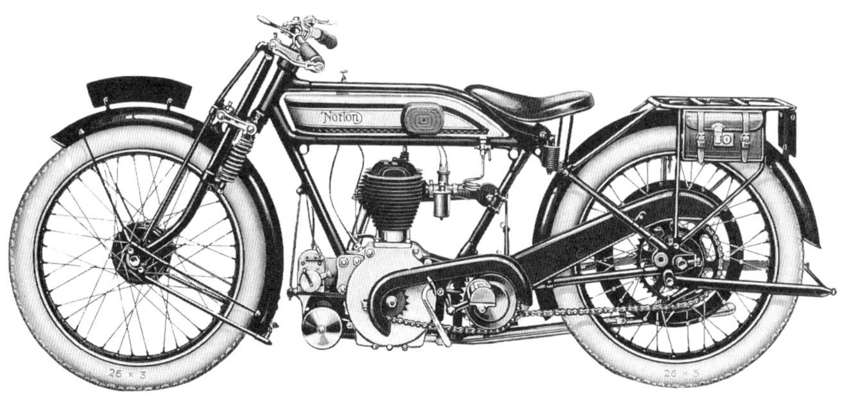

The 1924 490 cc 16H – with drum front brake – which the factory claimed was the fastest side-valve machine on the market. Price £72 – something like 20 weeks wages for a working man.

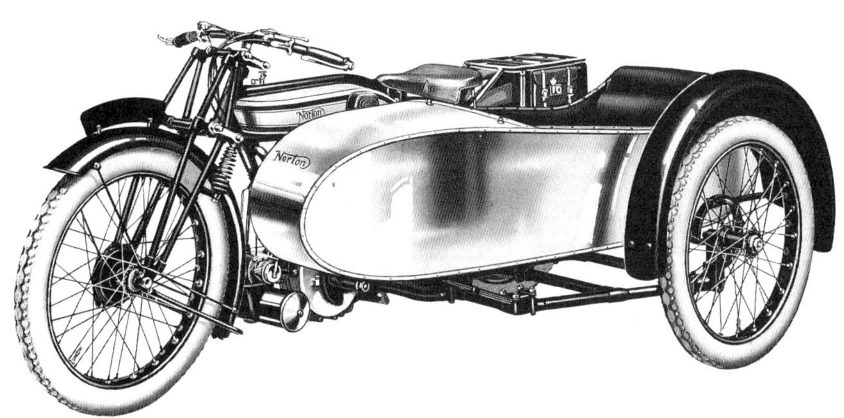

1924 Sidecar with the $3\frac{1}{2}$ hp 16H Sports, for those passengers hardy enough to forego the windscreen (above).

RIGHT Pa Norton at the wheel of his 17/30 Riley tourer, Isle of Man, 1924. Behind him are his wife Sarah and elder daughter Ethel. He only gave up his 633 cc Big Four when he was too ill to handle a sidecar.

BELOW The Norton camp and hangers-on at the 1925 TT. Prominent are designer team manager Walter Moore, standing with hands together behind the broadside bike, Joe Craig (to the right of Moore), 1924 Sidecar TT winner George Tucker (with white handkerchief in coat pocket) and 1924 Senior TT winner Alec Bennett (second from right). The machine (No 11) is Bennett's with braced front fork.

George Tucker and passenger G. Hammond, 1925 TT, 588 cc Norton and Hughes sidecar. They retired on the last lap – a disappointment after Tucker's win the previous year.

TT (forerunner of the Manx GP), and finally the factory launched their Maudes Trophy Challenge.

This time it involved a 490 cc solo ridden by Hubert Hassall and a 588 cc sidecar piloted by marathon specialist Phil Pike. Riding standard bikes built under ACU supervision, they first followed the four classic road-trial routes: London–Exeter, London–Edinburgh, London–Land's End and finally Land's End–John O'Groats. After clocking 3183 miles they made their way to Brooklands and thrashed both machines round the famous speed bowl for one hour – the solo averaging 61.5 mph and the sidecar 53.4 mph. Again the fuel economy was fantastic: the solo recorded 112.1 mpg and the combination 81.1 mpg.

That was not the end of it. The bikes were then locked up under ACU supervision. The following day the engines were stripped and decarbonised, the valves re-ground and new valve springs fitted. The cycle parts were checked over and the chains replaced and then the two machines were wheeled out to attack long-distance world records.

The solo, ridden by Hassall and Denly, broke eight world records including the 12 hours at 67.63 mph, while the sidecar, fitted with a normal road-going chair and not a record 'canoe', took six records, keeping up a steady 54 mph for 12 hours in the hands of Pike and O'Donovan. This epic won Norton the Maudes Trophy for the third successive year.

As if all this activity were not enough, Norton announced new models for 1926. Well actually, one new one, a 588 cc OHV code named Model 19 and fitted with the Norton four-speed gearbox first used by Tucker to win the 1924 Sidecar TT, plus one old favourite updated, the 633 cc Big Four also equipped with the four-speeder. Cheaper versions of both with the three-speed Sturmey-Archer were kept in the range.

One peculiarity of the four-speeder was that the final drive was on the offside. It had been designed that way so that the sidecar rider could get at the chain easily without having to crouch between the bike and chair. The price of the new 588 cc with four speeds (Model 24) was £82 or £77 with three speeds, while the basic Big Four dropped to £65 or £5 more with the new gearbox. By this time most were fitted with the Webb fork though the basic 16H at £59 still had the bone-jarring Druids up front.

CHAPTER 9

Stanley Woods 1926–1927

It was in 1926 that Stanley Woods strode on to the Norton stage, and he was to remain a dominant figure in road racing right up to the declaration of war in September 1939. By great good fortune he has retained vivid memories of those now faraway days and I am indebted to him for a morning-long interview taped in April 1990.

A shrewd, intelligent man, he answered my questions immediately and was able to solve a number of mysteries and to throw a different light on at least one aspect of the evolution of the Norton racing engine. Obviously they are his opinions, but I have always found him to be totally honest and straightforward, and as sole survivor of the men who rode the factory Nortons in those early days, I place great weight on his opinions.

How, then, did this Dubliner, born in 1903 and earning a good living as a commercial traveller (his main 'line' was Mackintosh's toffee and even then he had a company car), come to join Nortons?

Well, Bill Mansell, who was the boss at Nortons, was a real TT enthusiast. Every day he and Walter Moore, team manager at the time, would go out to watch the practice at a different spot and apparently they had spotted me in 1925 when I rode a Royal Enfield in the Junior.

Woods already had a good TT record. He had won the 1923 Junior on a Blackburne-engined Cotton at a faster speed than the rain-sodden Senior and despite his youth had plenty of racing experience on a wide variety of machines. The next step came when Norton's enthusiastic Dublin agent Dene Allen, himself a successful competitor, met Mansell at the Olympia Show in November 1925. There he suggested that Nortons should add yet another Irishman to their squad for 1926 and that young Woods should join Ulstermen Craig and Shaw, not to mention the veteran Bennett who, though raised in Canada, had been born in Ireland.

'When he came back he said that Nortons were sympathetic to the idea and that I must go over and have a chat with Mansell, which I did late in 1925,' Wood recalls. It was agreed that he would join the team for the 1926 TT and as a first step Norton sent him a Model 18, then the basic sports racing machine, for him to ride in Irish events so that he could get the feel of the bike before the TT. Said Woods:

It was a very good machine. I rode it in all types of events including trials. It was lovely to ride in every way. I took it to the island as a hack machine to practise on. It was the first time I'd had a spare bike and I got a lot of laps in at quite high speeds. The roads weren't closed for practice in those days but there was not a lot of traffic about. Later in practising I switched to my race machine and it really went like a bird. The engine seemed to have unlimited revolutions, it just went on and on and never seemed to tire – until the con rod broke!

Walter Moore told Woods not to worry, they would fit a replacement – but this simply would not rev. Woods complained but this time Moore was not sympathetic.

He simply would not listen to me. He said it was exactly the same as the original engine but finally, when practising was over, Moore stripped the engine and found the crankshaft out of line. When I got back from watching the Junior, Moore said that they had found the trouble, and they had although it was never as good as the original engine.

The team had been cut to four for the 1926 TT (Bennett, Shaw, Craig and Woods) and their bikes were virtually standard overhead-valve 490 cc Model 18s with three-speed Sturmey-Archer gearboxes. The compression ratio was up to 6.4 to 1 and an eight-inch brake was fitted at the front as well as the rear.

There had been quite a bit of acrimony over fuel for the TT early in the year. At first the ACU said that there would be no restriction, but the majority of manufacturers were against the use of special 'dope' fuels and in late January the ACU climbed down. For 1926 engines would have to run on 'such fuels as are available to the ordinary rider at wayside garages'.

This did not worry Nortons for they had always used normal petrol in their road-racing machines. At the same time the ACU increased the length of the races from six to seven laps (from 226 to 264 miles) and this focused the designers' minds on fuel-tank size. Norton's answer was to increase the capacity from around $2\frac{1}{2}$ to $3\frac{1}{2}$ gallons by fitting pannier tanks, one on each side of the top frame tube – a first step towards the saddle tanks adopted the following year. A leather tool-box holding spare plugs and other small items was strapped atop the tank.

There was a steering damper, but still no twist-grip. In April *The Motor Cycle* ran a story about throttle control. Under the heading 'The Case for the Twist-grips' the article continued:

LEFT Stanley Woods received a £500 bonus for his 1926 Senior TT win, a victory which made this kind of sales pitch possible.

BELOW When Irish eyes are smiling . . . Stanley Woods in the paddock after winning the 1926 Senior TT on a 490 cc push-rod Norton. Note the larger front brake, small windscreen and the Walter Moore designed oil pump below the timing chest. This bike was capable of around 90 mph.

ABOVE **The 1926 490 cc OHV Model 18 – just about the fastest bike that money could buy. Close ratio gearbox, 2 gallon tank, 3 pint oil tank with mechanical pump (and supplementary hand pump).**

RIGHT **The 1926 Ulster Grand Prix. Alec Bennett left, then Wal Handley and Jimmy Shaw, hand on his Norton. The machine on the left is the Norton on which Joe Craig won the over 500 cc class.**

Merits of a system of control widely used in racing, but against which the riding public exhibits a strange prejudice . . . the twist-grip control has never found favour with British designers and even today the number of machines turned out as standard with twist-grips could be counted on the fingers of one hand.

The Motor Cycle reporter at the TT obviously did not like the look of the new Nortons. The caption under the first picture to appear in TT Notes and News read: 'Beauty has to a certain extent been sacrificed to utility in the case of the TT Norton.' Which is strange, for the 1926 machines look, to modern eyes, far more functional and stylish than the earlier, flat-tank racers.

While Woods was getting in some early TT practice, team leader Bennett and Shaw had taken two of the new Nortons over to Strasbourg for the 249-mile French Grand Prix. There Bennett won at 67.71 mph and Shaw was holding second place when he was forced out near the end with crankshaft problems.

It was Simpson who set the pace early in the 1926 Senior TT – as expected, for he was always a fast starter. On his 498 cc AJS he became the first man to lap the Mountain circuit at over 70 mph (70.43 mph) but it was simply too much for the engine and on the third lap it gave up. Woods took over, with Charlie Hough on another AJS pushing him hard and it was touch and go until Hough crashed near Sulby on the last lap, inspiring *The Motor Cycle* to remark: 'Well, he went down gallantly, risking all for victory.' Fortunately he escaped with cuts and bruises.

Speaking of that TT win (at the record average speed of 67.54 mph) Woods says: 'The handling was excellent. It always was from the time they switched from the Druid forks to the Webb – those Druids were a pig to handle. I'd say that the top speed was about 90 mph – maybe more downhill and with the wind. Probably the output was 30 horsepower or so.' The first prize paid by the ACU was £20 but Norton paid Woods a £500 bonus and offered him a full-time job at £4 a week, racing in the summer and selling bikes to the dealers in the winter.

At first he hesitated. Working for Mackintosh in Ireland he was on £6.50 a week plus expenses plus car, but in September 1926 he agreed to join Nortons full time – not only working for less money but switching from the comfort of a car to an open-air life on the Norton and sidecar with which the company provided him to cover his sales area in northern England.

Meanwhile the team had been to the Continent to contest the Belgian Grand Prix, which was also the Grand Prix of Europe, a title awarded to each major grand prix in succession, supposedly making the event the most important of the year. Things looked good for Nortons when Woods took an early lead, pulling away from Simpson (AJS). After seven laps of the Spa circuit the Irishman was well ahead. Then Simpson gradually caught him and the two of them fought out a great battle until Woods limped into his pit with a front wheel puncture. Said Woods: 'We had spare wheels in the depot but I had trouble re-connecting the front brake cable and lost more time than I should have. I was only able to regain third place – though I did establish a record lap.'

The racing season ended with the Ulster Grand Prix and again things went wrong. Woods had taken an early lead chased by Craig, Walker (Sunbeam) and Bennett. Then the front downtube of Woods' Norton broke. Luckily for him the engine cut out immediately, because the plug lead from the front-mounted magneto ran up and through the integral sidecar lug of the standard roadster frame – and then on to the sparking plug. When the frame parted the lead was snatched from the plug, preventing what could have been a serious accident.

This left Craig ahead and heading for his fourth successive Ulster win, until a rear-tyre puncture dropped him to fifth place and let Walker through for the win, Bennett having stopped with engine trouble. So after a bright start and that record-breaking TT win it was obvious that team manager and technical chief Walter Moore had a busy winter ahead of him.

At Brooklands Bert Denly continued to uphold the Norton name. In April he set 10 world records up to three hours on a 500 cc at 85.70 mph. Then in May he pushed the 500 cc figure for 100 miles over the 90 mph mark for the first time (90.57 mph) while Chris Staniland, on a 588 cc Norton prepared by Nigel Spring, lapped the Surrey circuit at 102.27 mph and set 750 cc records for the flying-start 10 kilometres and 10 miles at 98.96 mph and 99.98 mph respectively – impressive speeds for a single cylinder push-rod engine.

On the trials front Nortons were also prominent, with marathon man Phil Peak riding his 588 cc Norton and sidecar as a member of the three-machine British team which won the major award in the International Six Days Trial that year. After the ISDT had finished with speed tests at Brooklands the Norton was locked away under the supervision of the ACU for Norton's now annual crack at the Maudes Trophy.

This time Pike, again with Arthur Bourne, the ACU observer, as passenger, rode the machine to North Wales and then up and down the steep, poorly surfaced 1½-mile Bwlch-y-Groes (Path of the Cross) 100 times!

ABOVE **Late in 1926 Nortons won the Maudes Trophy for the fourth year in succession – this advert in *Motor Cycling* in March 1927 gets the message across.**

RIGHT **Three truck-loads of machines en route to the Coventry Motor Mart and pictured outside the main offices of R. T. Shelley, Norton's parent company in 1927. The Norton factory was just yards away.**

On the first day 60 climbs were made without stopping the engine. Despite rain and fog and a road that became rutted and, in places, inches deep in slush, another 40 ascents were recorded on the second day. Pike then set out for Edinburgh where he turned round and rode down to Plymouth and on to Land's End before returning to his Plymouth home. In all he clocked 1531 miles without mechanical failure – and won the Maudes Trophy for a fourth time for Nortons.

On the economic front things were grim. It was the year of the General Strike and in an attempt to combat falling sales Nortons launched their own 'Private Hire Purchase System' with a series of whole-page advertisements in the technical press. Previously potential buyers had arranged hire-purchase terms with the dealer of their choice, but now Nortons, a major manufacturer, were offering them a direct deal.

Follow-up advertisements showed a smartly suited potential buyer talking to an equally immaculate Norton representative who answered a series of searching questions before inviting readers to write to Nortons for full details of the scheme. One advertisement was headlined: 'A TT winner for £20 15s (£20.75) balance by monthly payments' and the copy continued: 'The advent of Norton's own private easy payments scheme makes buying an unapproachable Norton the most simple and most convenient affair imaginable. . . . It is entirely financed by ourselves and interest is charged on the balance only.'

Apparently no guarantor was required and no enquiries made as to the financial standing of the customer. It sounds chancy, but those were desperate days and the fact that it continued for several years suggests it was a success. Certainly Nortons survived at a time when the British motorcycle industry was decimated. Part of the strength of the company was that it was one of the group built up by Bob Shelley. Unfortunately he, like Pa Norton, had been stricken by cancer but before he died in 1927 he reorganised his holdings and Nortons emerged as Norton Motors (1926) Ltd.

As part of the sales battle, prices had been further reduced. The basic 16H was marked down to £59.50 in September 1926 while the Big Four was £63.50 and the Model 18 £69. But for the man who was not concerned with price the big news was that Nortons were to build replicas of Stanley Woods' TT-winning 490 cc mount. This was listed at £80 as the Model 25 and,

commented *The Motor Cycle*: 'The TT replicas will be a popular machine with the speedmen. The specification includes a larger tank, a chain lubricator, narrow mudguards and dry-sump lubrication.'

The dry sump set-up was also listed as an optional extra on other OHV models, while the range of machines offered with the Norton four-speed gearbox was expanded to include one with the 490 cc OHV engine – the Model 34. But if you had the 490 cc with dry sump it became the Model 21 . . . what model it was if you had both dry sump and four-speed box is not clear. Certainly the range and the model numbering were getting out of hand – basically the customer could have what he wanted.

That winter of 1926–27 was a tough one for the trade. Stanley Woods, who had taken over his duties as salesman for most of England north of Birmingham after the Olympia Show, remembers that he did not sell a single machine: 'All the agents had put in their orders at the Show. No one bought motorcycles in the winter in those days – they waited until after March 24 when the licensing quarter ended. But I sold a few spares and made contacts – and got fed up with riding a Norton and sidecar!' At that time he reckons Nortons were making about 100 bikes a week.

Early in 1927 Woods escaped from the drudgery of sidecarring and selling when Walter Moore wanted his help in the experimental shop as a mechanic and tester. He got on well with Moore.

He was very easy to work with – no trouble at all. But I don't think that he was a born designer. I know that when he designed the first overhead camshaft Norton in the winter of 1926–27 he had a Velocette and a Chater-Lea in his office – and in my opinion he took the worst features of the two engines. Mind you, I don't think the camshaft engine ever let us down completely but I don't think that we finished a single race with a complete set of bevel gears – there were always a few teeth chipped off. The engine made such a row that it was known as the 'clanker'.

Arthur Carroll, later to design the second camshaft engine, was already at Nortons and worked as Moore's draughtsman. He had in fact joined the company when Pa Norton was still very active and had helped translate many of the founder's ideas into metal.

During that winter Moore had also designed a new cradle frame, and this proved a great success. When the team set out for the island the two prototype camshaft engines were still being built and they took with them 490 cc overhead-valve engines in the new cradle frame – already called the ES2 model though no one can now remember why. One theory is that it was E for extra cost and S for sport and that it was the second version; Moore himself, speaking to Titch Allen in 1970, favoured this explanation.

This full page advertisement that appeared in *The Motor Cycle* in August 1926 outlines the advantages of using the recently introduced Norton private purchase plan. The machine is the 16H.

RIGHT This is the cleaned up production version of Walter Moore's 490 cc camshaft engine that was produced in September 1927 to power the new supersport CS1 roadster.

Moore later claimed that when he finally had the two engines ready he rushed to Liverpool, only to find that he had missed the last boat that day. Anxious to get on with it, he chartered a tug which took him across for £50, enough to buy a motorcycle in those days. When he got there he offered one of the engines to Bennett, who was so impressed with the new frame that at first he turned it down, replying: 'The ES2 will win, the steering is worth 10 mph.'

Stanley Woods has a very different story to tell: 'This tale about a last minute rush and the camshaft engines not being ready until the last minute is rubbish. The first camshaft machine was taken to Germany by myself for the Solitude race outside Stuttgart some weeks before the TT. I led until I had mechanical failure – I think the connecting rod broke. I rushed the machine back to the works so that Moore could see the actual condition of the engine. There was time to modify

Bert Denly at Brooklands on the Nigel Spring prepared 490 cc push-rod Norton in April 1927 after breaking three world records – the 50 km at 97.30 mph, the 50 mile at 96.48 mph and the 100 km at 96.67 mph. Later, with the 588 cc engine, he claimed the 'world's fastest single cylinder record' with speeds of 109.22 mph for the flying km and 107.69 mph for the mile.

With apologies for the poor state of this rare print, this is the camshaft Norton CS1, the replica roadster based on Bennett's 1927 TT-winning machine.

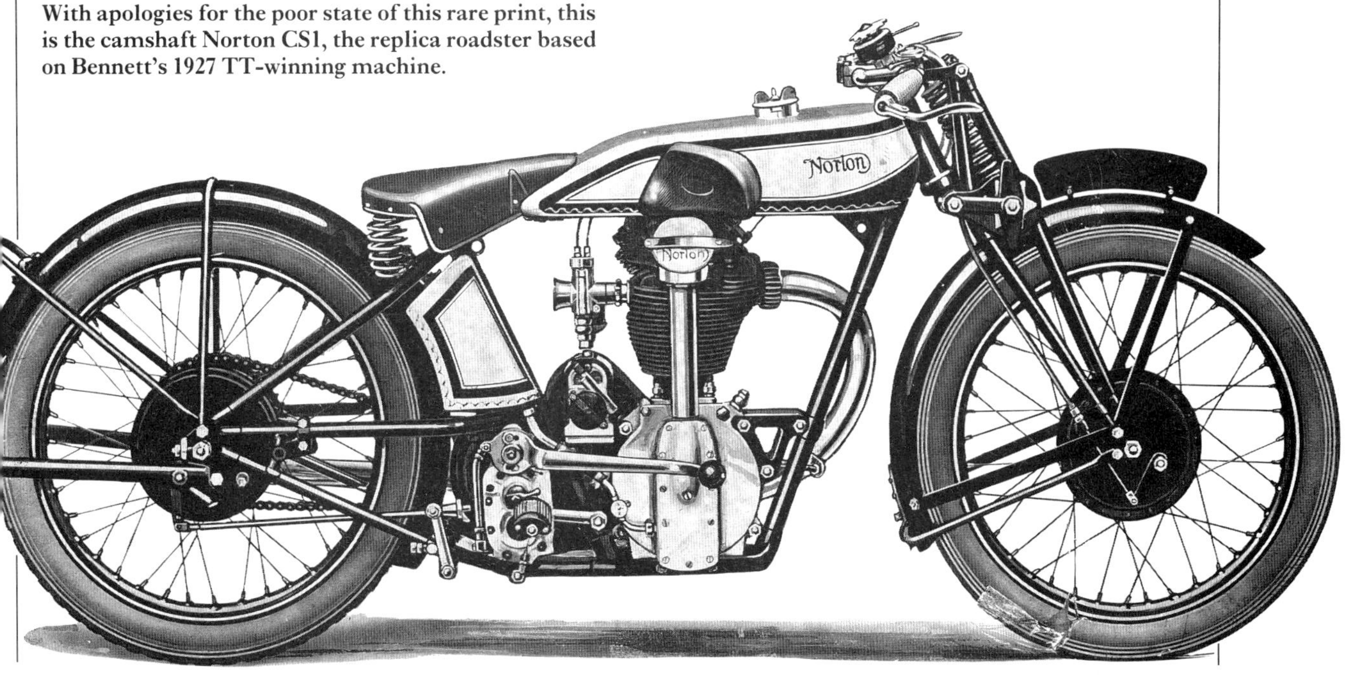

things and the camshaft machines gave no trouble during practising for the TT. As far as I can remember the complete team of racing machines was in the Island for the first or at the very latest the second morning of practising. There were three camshaft machines for Bennett, Craig and myself plus an OHV ES2 for Shaw. Incidentally the ES2 was probably just as fast and it certainly ran more smoothly.'

The Dublin rider's version of events is supported by the journals of the day. The Austrian *Das Motorrad* confirms that Woods competed at Stuttgart on May 22 and led until he retired with a mechanical failure. As was so often the case in those days no mention is made of his machine other than it was a Norton. As far as the TT is concerned the *Motor Cycling* reported on June 15: 'The eagerly awaited Nortons arrived early; there is a selection of camshaft and push-rod jobs but all have the new cradle frame.' Whether Moore was confusing the year or simply spinning a yarn we shall never know but I am certain that Woods' account is the true one. The bottom half of the camshaft engine was virtually the same as the 490 cc OHV unit, and the famous 79 × 100 mm bore and stroke were retained. But the cams and push-rods were replaced by two sets of bevel gears which drove a single overhead camshaft. Moore recalled that he did not have time actually to run the engines on the test bed – he simply built them carefully and set off for the Isle of Man.

ABOVE Joe Craig waits on the grid for the start of the 1927 Senior TT. His push-rod model had the new cradle frame and saddle petrol tank. Note the cast aluminium primary chain case.

RIGHT Dennis Mansell, son of Norton's MD Bill Mansell, competing in the 1927 Victory Cup Trial. He went on to score many trials successes for Norton.

In the prototype engines the Moore-designed oil pump, first used in 1925, was housed in a separate compartment under the lower bevel housing, but in the later, cleaned up, production versions this housing was extended down to take in the oil pump. The magneto was mounted behind the engine – the first time this rather more sensible position had been adopted on actual Norton-engined machines. But the drive was from a sprocket on the main shaft, inboard of the engine sprocket. The new camshaft engine was interchangeable with the push-rod unit in the new ES2 cradle frame and a handsome saddle tank replaced the twin pannier set-up of the preceding year.

There were 45 works entries in the Senior TT that

year, 41 of which were entered by a dozen British factories including, in addition to Norton, Sunbeam, Triumph, AJS, Scott, Calthorpe, New Hudson, Cotton, HRD and OEC. Norton fielded Bennett and Woods on the camshaft models plus Shaw and Craig on ES2s and they also assisted an Australian, Len Stewart.

In TT Topics the *Motor Cycling* reporter on the island noted that the road over the mountain '. . . is now all tar but is covered with loose grit'. He also commented on the new Nortons:

A very interesting TT machine is the Norton model with overhead camshaft . . . the camshaft is driven through a hollow vertical shaft and two pairs of bevels . . . each pair is built up as a unit, which may be removed from the engine without disturbing the meshing of the teeth. The weight of the shaft is carried by the top bevel.

The same magazine had a speed trap on the Sulby Straight and there Woods and Craig were joint fastest at 93.7 mph, which tallied closely with the reading of a speedometer Woods had fitted for one practice session. Whether Craig was out that day on a camshaft model or his OHV race mount I do not know. Probably in sheer top speed there was little in it, the camshaft model scoring on acceleration, despite weighing in at 10 lb heavier – 350 lb as oposed to 340.

From the start of the race Woods went like a rocket. With a record lap at 70.99 mph he drew steadily away and after four laps led Bennett by four minutes – but then the clutch went!

The tongues on the central body of the clutch had sheared. I had no idea that I was leading by so much and was still going as hard as I could. We were still using the Sturmey-Archer three-speeder and I used to change from second to top without de-clutching – just ease the throttle a fraction and knock it through. This put a shock loading on the clutch and it wouldn't stand it.

Later he realised that two avoidable factors had cost him the race – and that Moore should have done something about both of them. Firstly the team should have had a signalling system to let the riders know where they were placed (in which case he would have slowed and in all probability not broken the clutch), and secondly he suspects that Moore knew about the clutch weakness and should have advised him to change the clutch at the end of practice – as he discovered, Bennett, who went on to win, had done so.

When I sat down to think about it I remembered a bantering conversation that I'd had with Alec Bennett as we went up to our hotel rooms the night before the Senior. He had said to me, 'So you think you are going to win tomorrow?' and I'd replied, 'Well, as long as I'm going I'll be ahead of you Alec.' He just smiled and said, 'Time will tell.' Alec knew about the weakness in the clutch. He'd replaced his but he didn't tell me – nobody told me.

Bennett won at the record average of 68.41 mph from Jimmy Guthrie riding an OHV New Hudson prepared by Bert Le Vack, with Tommy Simister, on a Triumph, third. Commented *Motor Cycling*:

Bennett said that he was delighted with the new camshaft Norton and says it steers exceedingly well. The camshaft engine was in perfect condition at the end of the race and was notably free from oil on the outside . . . much of the credit must be given to Mr Moore of Norton's who was responsible for the design of this engine.

No sooner was the TT over than Bert Denly achieved another milestone success for Norton. At the end of June he took a 490 cc OHV to Montlhéry and raised the one-hour record for the half-litre class to 100.57 mph. It was the first time that a 500 had beaten the 'ton' for an hour. Denly also pushed up the figures for the 5-kilometre and 5-mile flying start to 110.56 mph and 110.39 mph, beating his own records. The French track had the advantage that machines did not have to be fitted with the silencers that had become mandatory at Brooklands following noise problems with local residents.

After the TT Woods went to Holland for the Dutch TT. It was the first time the race there was a fully recognised international and he was the lone British factory rider.

It was like taking milk from babies. It was raining for practice so I didn't bother to go out. I had a lap round in a car and when a journalist asked me what I was going to do in the race I told him that I'd follow someone who knew the way.

They were long races in those days – I'd have plenty of time to learn the circuit!

In fact he won the 180-mile event at 67.02 mph and set a lap record at 71.28 mph.

The next race was the German Grand Prix at the brand-new Nürburgring. Woods remembers watching a supporting race at a corner near the pits and thinking that the concrete track looked slippery. He found out just how slippery when a shower wet the concrete and he slid off while leading the 500 cc race. He remounted but despite a record lap could not catch Graham Walker (Sunbeam) who beat him by 57 seconds.

It proved to be a fabulous year. Woods won the Belgian Grand Prix at 71.7 mph with a record lap at over 76 mph, and he won again at the Swiss Grand Prix. Then a tangle with team-mate Craig at the French Grand Prix halted his winning ways. They had roared ahead from the start, went into a left-hander too fast and both slid off, ending up in a ditch. Unhurt, they hauled themselves and their bikes back on to the road but while Craig went on to win Woods was sidelined with a broken throttle lever (still no twist-grips).

There were reckoned to be over 100,000 spectators around the Clady circuit when the Ulster was run in early September. Bennett, who had had a poor season after his TT success, was suffering from a wrist injury and it was Woods and Craig who disputed the lead,

ABOVE **Flanked by Gendarmes Bert Denly (on machine), Nigel Spring and the French Norton importer M Psalty, celebrate breaking the classic one hour World Record for 500 cc machines at Montlhéry near Paris on 28 June 1927.**

RIGHT **Three winners after the 1927 Belgian Grand Prix. Stanley Woods astride the Norton on which he took the 500 cc honours at 71.7 mph, Jimmie Simpson (centre), 350 cc winner on an AJS and Syd Crabtree, 250 cc winner on a Tottenham-built JAP.**

the two Irishmen thrilling the vast crowd as they thundered down the famous seven-mile straight side by side.

The pace was too hot to last. First Craig slowed and then retired with a seized engine, his oil tank empty. Then Woods, who pushed the lap record up to 78.6 mph, lost revs and it was veteran Jimmy Shaw on the third camshaft Norton in the race who won from Frank Longman (Rudge), with Woods third – less than a minute covering the three of them after 205 miles.

That same September young Tim Hunt won the 500 cc class of the Amateur TT on a standard Model 18 that his wealthy father had bought for him. Despite appalling weather he averaged nearly 60 mph.

Moving with remarkable speed, Nortons announced early in September 1927 that a replica of Bennett's TT-winning camshaft model was to be offered for sale at

£95. Said *Motor Cycling*: 'The special cradle frame model which has this year won the Senior TT, Dutch TT, Belgian, Swiss and French Grands Prix . . . has been put into production for delivery shortly.' The overhead-valve 490 cc with cradle frame, which had also appeared for the first time at the TT, the ES2, was also to go on sale priced at £85. Both had saddle tanks – the first time that Nortons had sold a bike with anything but a flat tank.

The rest of the range was little changed. And by the time the 1928 models were wheeled out at Olympia in November the prices of the two TT replica models had been reduced – the camshaft CS1 (for camshaft, model one) down by £6 to £89 and the ES2 by the same amount, to £79. One change to all the machines was that the enamel on the tanks was replaced by cellulose – 'a more durable finish'.

In November *Motor Cycling* started a new series of road tests by riding the CS1. The reporter pointed out that this was available either with a close-ratio three-speed Sturmey-Archer (without kick-start) or with a wide-ratio three-speeder with kick-start. Then he waxed lyrical:

> At low speeds one can liken its performance to that of a steam engine, so sweetly does it gain its revs . . . . It will do 85 to 88 mph without careful tuning and is effortless at 65 to 70 mph . . . candidly the writer has no fault to find with the machine at all. It can be driven like a lamb in traffic or like a lion on the open road . . . .

Nortons had adopted an unusual double-barrelled silencer with fishtail which led to an advertisement focusing on silence. Headed 'Silence is Golden', the Norton copy ran: 'An AA certificate of silence is now supplied with every Norton.'

In what had been a golden year Nortons did suffer one notable setback. Having won the Maudes Trophy four times in succession from the inception of the award

1926–27 Gallery

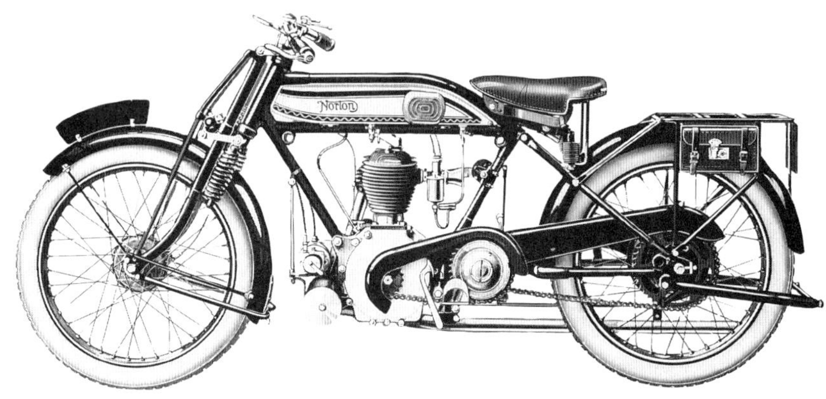

This is the 1926 Model 17C which was designed for 'colonial' use (hence the C) with increased ground clearance and a bigger fuel tank. It weighed 270 lb, cost £63 and was basically a modified 490 cc Model 16H.

In 1926 Nortons offered the Family Sidecar, seen here attached to a 633 cc Big Four, with accommodation for a child on a separate seat ahead of the adult passenger.

The 1926 Model 2 (the touring version of the 16H) does at last have a drum rear brake. It cost £62.

The 1927 Model 19 with 588 cc OHV engine – a functional sporty machine capable of close to 90 mph.

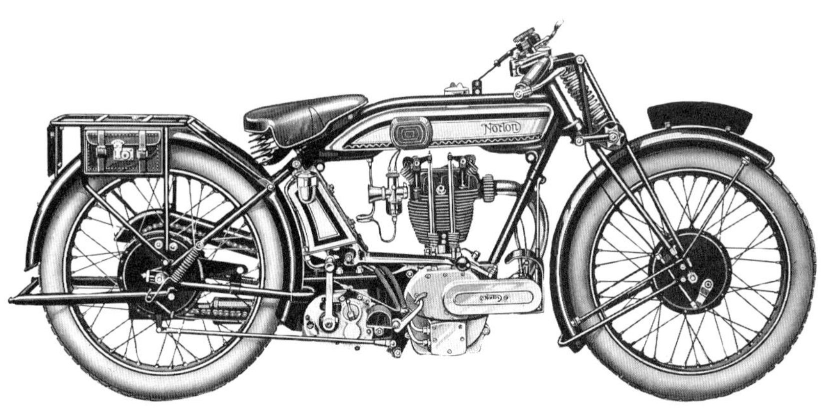

The first Norton to be offered for sale with dry sump lubrication was the 1927 Model 21 – virtually the same as the 490 cc Model 18 but with the Walter Moore designed oil pump (which can be seen under the timing chest) to scavenge the sump.

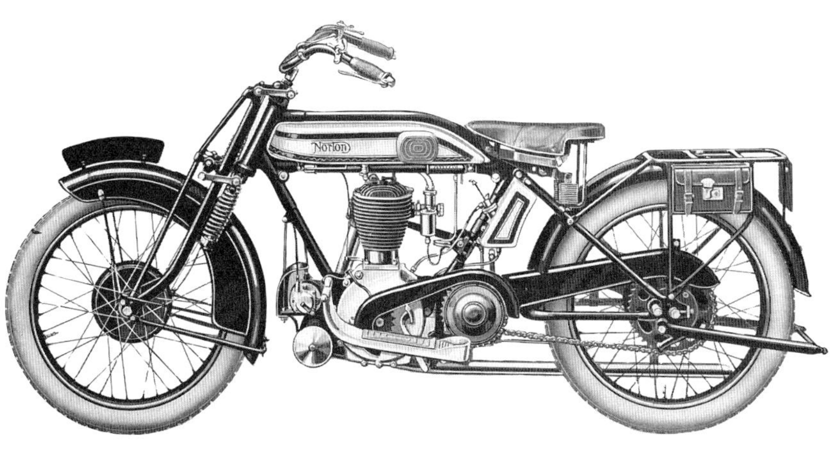

For 1927 the 633 cc Big Four was fitted with a larger front brake but the Druid fork was retained. Lighting of any sort was still an optional extra.

in 1923, they made a fifth attempt in 1927 when an ACU official selected six standard 490 cc OHV engines, sealed them in boxes and sent them down to Brooklands. There each engine was bolted into a slave frame by Nigel Spring's men and Denly then put them through the flying kilometre. All recorded over 80 mph – the slowest clocking 80.47 mph and the fastest 82.85 mph.

After that two engines were selected at random and one was thrashed round Brooklands for two 12-hour stints. Because it was late September the final couple of hours had to be ridden in darkness and the light was provided by a two-litre Lagonda which followed the Norton round the track. The average speed for the double-12 worked out at 62.28 mph.

The second engine had been slotted into Phil Pike's sidecar outfit and he drove it from Land's End to John O'Groats, but he was involved in an accident that smashed the sidecar and crumpled the forks. The machine was repaired and Pike completed 2238 miles but the ACU decided that an Ariel test, in which a machine covered 5000 miles without stopping the engine, was more meritorious.

Nortons went into 1928 full of confidence and with Moore working on plans to expand the Norton range down into the popular 350 cc class with both OHV and camshaft models on the drawing board, sharing the same 71 × 88 mm bore and stroke.

Before news of these appeared, Nortons had cut prices yet again. The cheapest model was the 16H at £56 and the equally old-fashioned-looking Big Four, still with Druid forks and flat tank, was marked down to £60 with the popular sporting Model 18 a seemingly much better buy at £63.50. Electric lighting sets with Lucas dynamo were still an optional extra and a 490 cc camshaft CS1 and sidecar that was used by *The Motor Cycle* reporter to cover the Exeter trial was fitted with this together with a new, massive cast-aluminium primary chain-case. This also covered the chains that drove the magneto (behind the engine) and the separate dynamo, mounted in front. The reporter was delighted: 'Never have I ridden behind a better light on any motor-cycle.' Nortons were still plugging their private hire purchase scheme with the line: 'You can get a Norton for £13 7s 6d [£13.37½p] – think of it. You can have immediate use of a Norton, an unapproachable Norton, for a deposit of only £13 7s 6d!

Dennis Mansell, the 18-year-old son of Norton's boss Bill Mansell, won his first major event in March 1928 when, with CS1 Norton and sidecar, he won the Victory trial outright, and in the same month Graham Goodman scored what was probably Norton's first scrambles/moto cross success when he won the main event at the Camberley Scramble. Wins in trials and scrambles were quickly followed by success in another and even newer sport – dirt-track racing (speedway) – with news of a win by Len Stewart on a Norton at

Geelong in Australia, the same man who had been over to race a Norton in the previous year's TT.

The sport of motor-cycling was attracting enormous crowds to even such boring events as road trials, where

pictures show spectators lining the observed hills 20 deep for long stretches. After the successes of 1927 Nortons looked set to cash in with another great year – but it was not to be.

Alec Bennett after winning the 1927 Senior TT.

CHAPTER 10

Joe Craig 1928–1929

In 1927 Nortons had won six of the seven major international 500 cc races, yet in 1928 they won only one, the poorly supported French Grand Prix. What went wrong? Stanley Woods summed things up.

> During the winter Walter Moore had redesigned the cylinder head and the cams and he'd made a mess of it. Everything went wrong and Moore couldn't sort out the problems. At the time Joe Craig was working in the racing department as well as riding and as I understand it Joe got so fed up that at the end of the season he went to Mansell and told him that he could put things right if Mansell gave him Moore's job. Mansell said, 'Don't be daft', so Joe left Nortons and went back to Ballymena and bought the garage where he had served his time.

The trouble started in the Isle of Man. Nortons entered five riders (Woods, Craig, Shaw, Guthrie and H. Matthews) in the Junior race and this had naturally caused a stir. Commented *The Motor Cycle*: 'Not a little interest has been excited by the decision of Norton Motors Ltd to take part in the Junior TT race this year.' The article, which appeared in May, went on to describe the OHV model Moore was working on. This was a new engine, not a modified 490 cc unit, with the magneto behind the cylinder (the first push-rod Norton to follow the lead of the CS1) and with a Pilgrim-type oil pump mounted on the side of the crank-case, speedway JAP style.

But when the bikes were wheeled out on the island they were all camshaft machines (CJ – camshaft, junior), scaled-down versions of the CS1. They proved so slow in practice that it was not until the eleventh day of training that one appeared among the fastest six. Even then Woods could do no better than fifth, his lap at 65.1 mph comparing badly with the day's best 350 cc lap of 69.2 mph set by Harold Willis on a Velocette which sported a three-speed gearbox with positive stop mechanism.

This system, soon to be adopted by every major manufacturer, was designed so that the foot-change pedal returned to the same position after every gear change. Previously the change lever, usually adapted from a hand change, stayed in a different position after each change which meant that the rider's foot had to travel far further than with the new set-up.

FAR LEFT **In 1928 Nortons contested the Junior (350 cc) TT for the first time with camshaft engined machines. The picture shows Jimmy Guthrie chasing a rival round Governors Bridge. Guthrie was forced to retire when his Norton caught fire during a pit stop.**

LEFT **This push-rod OHV 350 cc was added to the Norton range in February 1929. Known as the Model JE it was initially priced at £68. Bore and stroke were 71 × 88 mm.**

In the Junior TT Guthrie, promoted to the team following his New Hudson ride of 1927, was the best placed Norton in fifth position at the end of the first lap, with Woods seventh. Woods then retired with slipped timing and Guthrie, who had dropped to ninth, was the centre of attention when he came in to refuel.

Recreating the scene, *The Motor Cycle* reported dramatically: 'Suddenly shouts and screams as Guthrie's Norton catches fire when he re-starts from his pit. Firemen dash out with extinguishers and have to play them on the rider too, as he is aflame.' Craig was out with a bent rocker arm, the unknown Matthews was sidelined by a broken valve and finally Shaw, struggling to hold fifth place, crashed at Sulby while peering under the tank to see why his engine had slowed.

Again the problem proved to be a broken valve spring. Describing his departure from the race, *The Motor Cycle* said: 'Another crack out – Shaw retires unhurt at Sulby after writing off the last eminent Norton in a healthy crash.' Summing up, it was noted that: 'The new 350 cc Nortons were fast on downhill slopes though not very quick on the pick-up.' This may be because they were on the heavy side, weighing in at some 340 lb despite an effort to lighten the frames by cutting out the third 'chain stay' which Moore had added to the cradle frame built for the CS1 and ES2.

Bennett won the Junior for Velocette before switching to a factory Norton for the Senior TT – an odd arrangement born in the days before Norton had a 350. But his chances of a double went on the first lap when

a valve dropped in, and Guthrie soon joined him with a broken rocker. The only Norton challenger in the early stages was Craig, who chased Simpson (AJS) hard. Said *The Motor Cycle*: 'Craig plays a lone hand for the proud Norton stable no longer assured of its usual monopoly.'

Simpson stopped on the third lap having blown his motor, but Craig enjoyed the lead for only a few miles before his engine quit near Sulby. Woods, slowed by various problems in the early stages, was by this time gaining ground. 'Stanley Woods, roaring like a lioness deprived of her cubs, is only 3 minutes behind Dodson (Sunbeam) with three laps to go' was how *The Motor Cycle* put it.

The weather was appalling and Woods was in fact in fifth place. He moved up to fourth on the next lap before slowing to finish fifth.

Commenting on gearboxes used in the TT, *The Motor Cycle* technical man said:

Excellent though a four-speed may be for touring purposes, it is not seen at its best in the TT races, where some of its value is discounted by increases in friction and oil-pumping losses, and the fact is even an expert is apt to lose fractions of a second in effecting a change.

Joe Craig used a similar argument when discussing four- and five-speed boxes in the 1950s.

Charlie Dodson on a push-rod Sunbeam won the

ABOVE **Wal Handley (Motosacoche) leads Stanley Woods (Norton) by inches in the 1928 Swiss Grand Prix at Geneva. Woods crashed and Handley went on to win.**

RIGHT **Pat Driscoll was a regular competitor and record breaker with Norton and sidecar at Brooklands in the 'twenties.**

Senior, team-mate Walker retiring on the last lap when well ahead. Walker gained consolation by winning the 500 cc Dutch TT, an event only half-heartedly supported by the British factories. Woods took a pair of Nortons and actually won the 350 cc race at 67.60 mph. Clutch trouble put him out of the bigger class.

After that it was down to Bordeaux for the French Grand Prix and it was there that Woods scored the lone Norton success in the 500 cc class that year, beating TT winner Dodson after a hard-fought 204-mile race. His average speed was 67.62 mph and he clocked a record lap at over 71 mph.

For the German Grand Prix at the Nürburgring Norton fielded a four-man team with Woods and Craig on the big bikes while Guthrie and Italian Pietro Ghersi rode the 350s, the races being run at the same time, as was often the case in the early classics. Both of the 500s went out with problems, Woods engine and Craig chain, but Ghersi won the 350 cc race ahead of Guthrie in a race that lasted over four hours.

Things got worse in Belgium. Early in the race Craig and Woods led but then both slowed and finally retired, Craig with gearbox problems and Woods with an overheating engine which he put down, at the time, to poor fuel. And there was no consolation in the 350 cc division with both Guthrie and Ghersi falling by the wayside.

The Grand Prix of Europe was the Swiss, held at Geneva in late July, and it was, according to *The Motor Cycle*, 'the most truly international motor-cycle event held in the history of the sport'. With the 350 cc race on the Saturday and the 500 cc the next day, Norton entered their star men in both races.

Woods led the 350 cc from the start but was soon passed by Simpson (AJS) who had a good lead when his rear sprocket came adrift. Woods was back in the hunt, battling with Wal Handley on a very fast locally built Motosacoche, a single-cylinder overhead-camshaft machine designed by Dougal Marchant. Then a thunderstorm soaked the circuit and caught out Woods who slid off his Norton as he braked coming

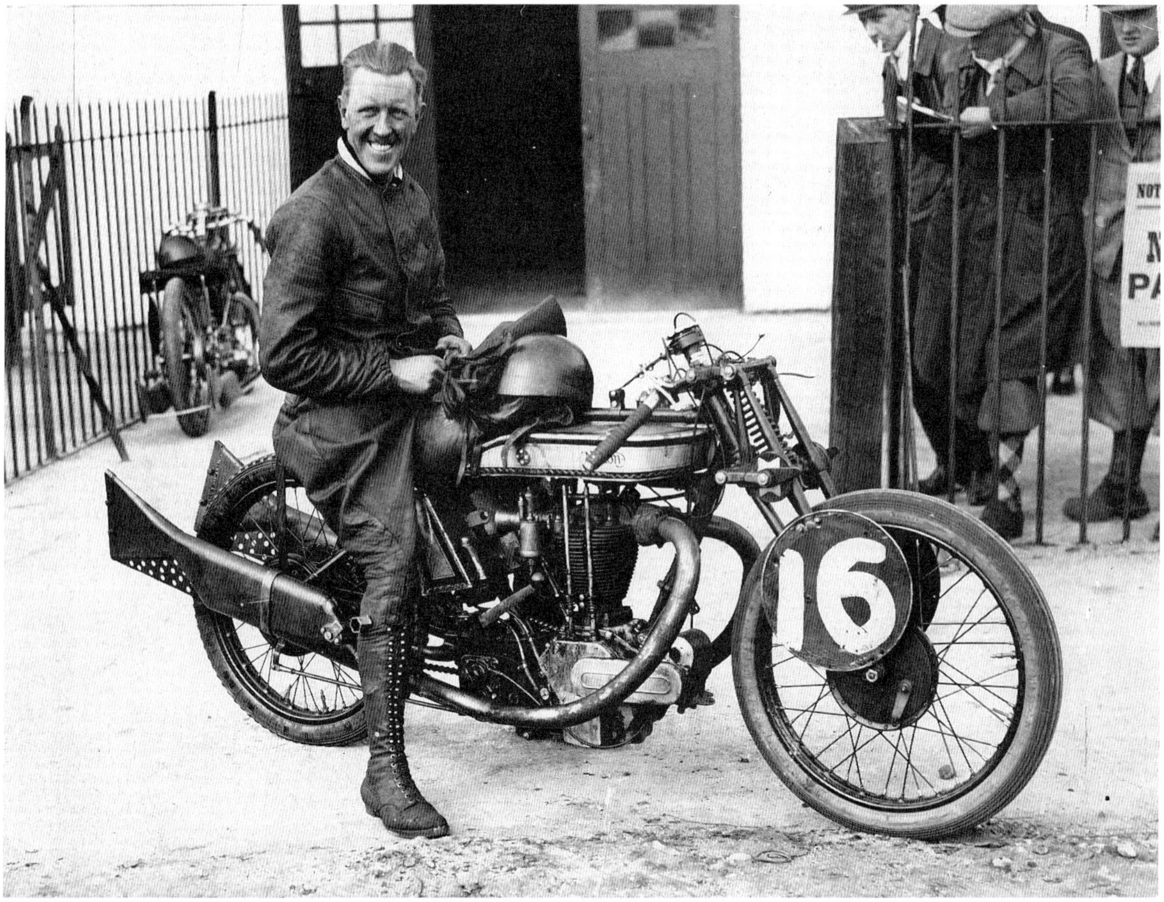
16

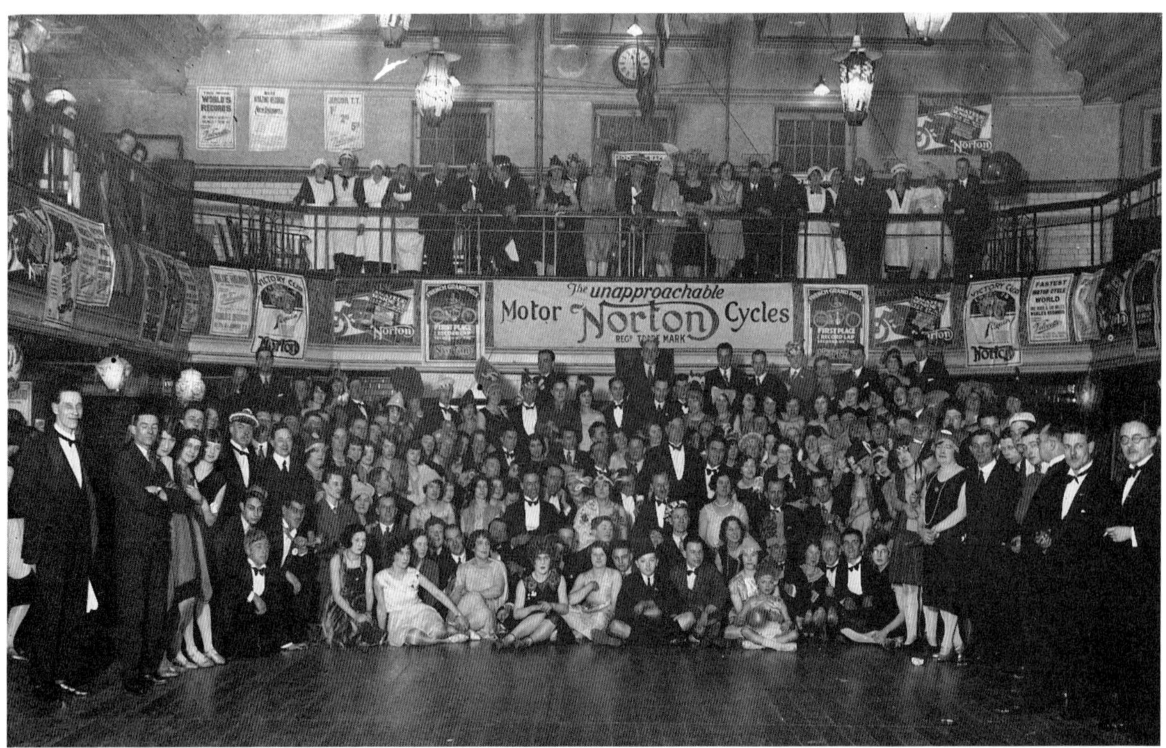

The unapproachable
Motor Norton Cycles
REGD TRADE MARK
Norton

ABOVE LEFT George Tucker ready to do battle at a Brooklands meeting in April 1928. His Norton is fitted with a twin port head with the exhausts leading to two massive silencers – the famous 'Brooklands cans' which had to be used following problems with the local residents.

LEFT In the late twenties Norton's Sheffield dealer Dan Bradbury hosted lavish end-of-season parties – and this is the scene at the 1928 get-together. Prominent in the second row, left of centre in bow-tie is 1928 Amateur TT winner Tim Hunt.

ABOVE Tim Hunt in the paddock after winning the 1928 Amateur TT (forerunner of the Manx Grand Prix) on a camshaft Norton. During the race he lapped at 71.05 mph which beat the outright TT lap record for the Mountain circuit. Earlier he had ridden the same machine in the Scottish Six Days Trial.

RIGHT This advertisement from *The Motor Cycle* of 16 August 1928 punches home the Norton message of speed and reliability. Bike shown is the race-bred camshaft CS1.

When you ride a

you get the thrill of Speed, the economy of Reliability, and the Pride of ownership that only a Norton can inspire

Norton is a *proved* motor cycle in every sense, the supreme achievement of the motor cycle designer. No other motor cycle in the world can boast a record for speed and reliability equal to the Norton's. If you are considering your *first* machine choose a Norton—your safest choice. If you are an experienced motor cyclist you *will* choose a Norton. You can obtain one now for £14 Deposit through our Easy Payment System. May we send you a Catalogue?

NORTON MOTORS (1926) LTD.,
BRACEBRIDGE STREET, ASTON, BIRMINGHAM.

Model C.S.1., O.H.C., 4·90 h.p. - - £89

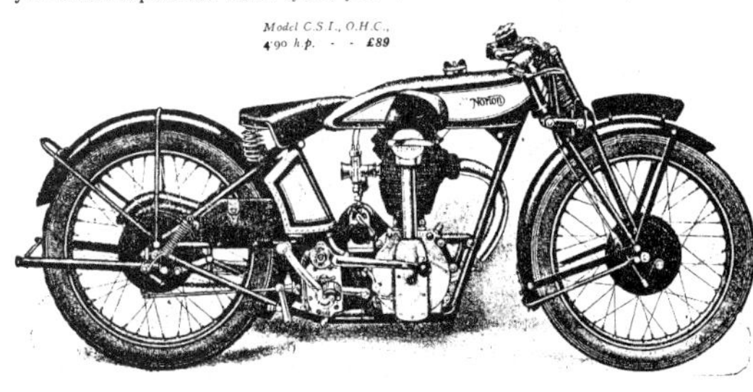

into his pit to refuel. Handley won easily from Guthrie on the surviving Norton.

Handley did the double for Motosacoche in Sunday's 500 cc race in which both Woods and Craig crashed. Despite the relatively short straights Handley's winning average was 74.74 mph and it was claimed that the fastest bikes were achieving speeds of over 100 mph.

The tale of woe continued at the Ulster. There the team was split with Bennett, Woods and Simpson, recruited from AJS, on the 500s and Craig, Shaw and Guthrie on the smaller bikes. Only Shaw finished in the first three – third in the 350 cc.

Young Tim Hunt put a smile back on Norton faces when he not only won the Amateur TT in September but put in a lap at 71.05 mph which broke the out-and-out TT lap record. His mount was a CS1 which he had ridden earlier in the year in the Scottish Six Days Trial. Years later, when I interviewed him shortly before he died, he told me: 'We fitted wide-ratio gears, trials tyres and lowered the compression ratio – that was about it.' He did not enjoy the trial – he much preferred the road – but he did complete the six days and won a silver medal, the highest award for which he was eligible.

His amateur win so impressed Walter Moore that the Norton team manager went straight round to his hotel afterwards and got him out of a steaming hot bath to offer him a works ride for 1929. Moore knew that Tim's father was a wealthy man so he offered him no money, just the bikes and an oil contract with Castrol which Tim finally bargained up from £350 to £700 for the year.

Hunt had no mechanical ability at all. In fact he was later forbidden to lay a spanner on his bikes. He was simply a brilliant, natural rider and Woods acknowledges that when they later rode in the team together Hunt was the man to beat.

Riding for Nigel Spring, described as Norton's racing manager at Brooklands, Bert Denly had been steadily adding to his tally of records during the year. Rather surprisingly they stuck to the well-tried push-rod 490 cc and 588 cc engines and did not experiment with the camshaft engine which, on paper, looked a better bet, especially for the longer distances.

In May 1928 Denly won the 200-mile sidecar race at Brooklands at 78.73 mph, breaking three world records in the process, the fastest of which was the 50 kilometres at 81.47 mph. In June Pat Driscoll, also on a 588 cc push-rod, pushed the 200-mile average up to 87.07 mph and beat all the big twins to win the 1000 cc class as well as the 600 cc.

Denly then took his 588 cc to Montlhéry and not only startled the opposition with a five-mile run at 113.49 mph but also improved on his own one-hour 750 cc record by packing 102.30 miles into the 60 minutes. In August he returned to the French circuit with the 588 cc to break 50-kilometre and 50-mile records and 100 kilometres and 100 miles – all at over 104 mph. Later he fitted a sidecar and pushed the 5-kilometre and 5-mile records over 92 mph.

Teaming with Spring and Driscoll on a 490 cc, he had a hand in upping the 24-hour record to 67.88 mph at Montlhéry – a record which stood for six years. Then, for a grand finale, he took the 588 cc to Arpajon in France where an annual records attempt meeting was held on a long and straight, though narrow and tree-lined, road. There he clocked 111.68 mph for the kilometre and 111.35 mph for the mile – only 13 mph slower than the absolute record for a motorcycle set at the same meeting by Captain O.M. Baldwin on his mighty 996 cc V-twin JAP-powered Zenith.

It was a time of rapid evolution. The 1929 range of Nortons, shown to the public for the first time at Olympia late the preceding year, looked very different from the models they replaced. Gone were the old-style frames with the top tube running over the thin flat tank, replaced on every machine by racing-style saddle tanks as on the CS1 racers at the 1927 TT.

Commented *The Motor Cycle*: 'Saddle tanks with a nicely curved top line are fitted throughout, and a re-designed frame has imposed a distinctly racy appearance.' Sensibly Nortons wanted the success of their sporting machines to rub off on the bread-and-butter mounts, and one way of doing this was for all the bikes to share a common look – what in today's jargon is called a 'corporate image'.

The price of the sports models was reduced – the camshaft CS1 from £89 to £82 and the ES2 from £79 to £73, and as a show surprise Nortons enveiled the Norton Junior, a replica of the 350 cc camshaft machine that had made such a disastrous debut at the 1928 TT. It was the first 350 Norton to go on sale and delivery was promised for February 1929 at £77, with a Lucas lighting set as an extra at £5.25.

By February 1929 Nortons had added a push-rod 350 cc to the range – the JE priced at £68 – and were still pushing the Norton private hire purchase system in their advertisements which included the line: 'Financed entirely by Norton Motors (1926) Ltd . . . there is no interference by a third-party.'

On the sports front Dennis Mansell used a 350 cc camshaft model with sidecar to win the Travers Trial outright, and with Graham Goodman on a Model 18 taking the solo honours it was a good day for Nortons, especially as the two of them teamed with TT favourite Simpson to win the team prize.

The poor racing results achieved in 1928 had led to problems with the team. Following his confrontation

RIGHT The Arthur Carroll/Joe Craig-designed camshaft engine appeared for the first time at the Olympia Show in 1929. The hurried drawing (in *Motor Cycling*, 4 December) distorts the lower bevel housing but the photograph shows the handsome lines.

A LAST-MINUTE SURPRISE—AND OTHER NOTABLE EXHIBITS

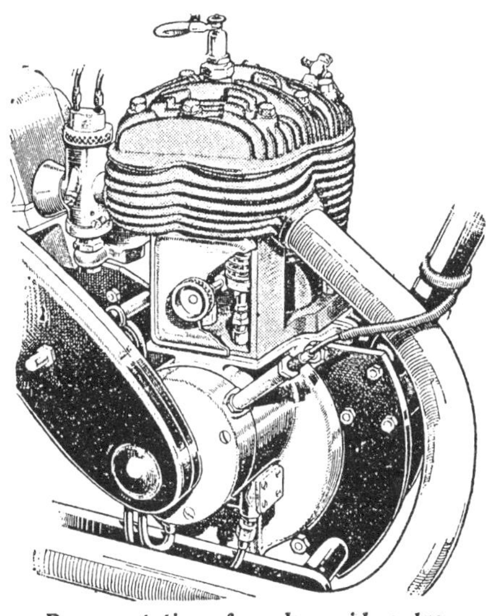

Representative of modern side-valve practice: the 495 c.c. Matchless.

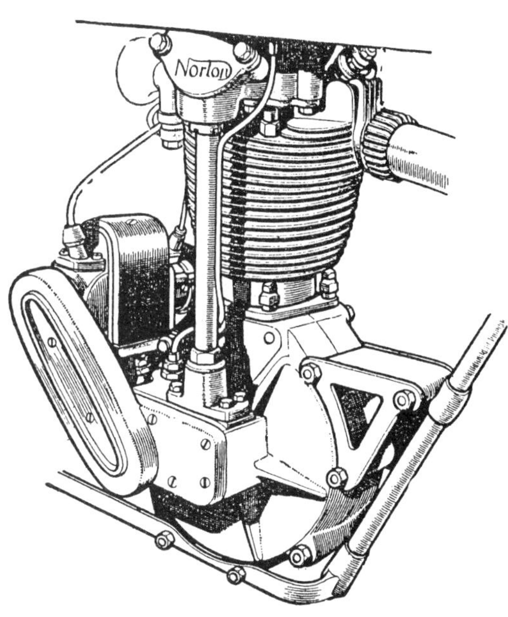

(Above) The new Norton o.h.c. engine, with dry-sump lubrication and off-side magneto drive, and (left) the very clean exterior of the 1930 499 c.c. Rudge-Whitworth four-valve engine.

(Below) A clubman's dream—the latest Camshaft Norton.

with Bill Mansell, Joe Craig, who in addition to riding had been in charge of the test house under the direction of Walter Moore, had decided to pack up. However, despite the lack of success and his views on how the engines could be improved (which were not shared by Moore), Joe remembered his early days with Nortons with affection. In Geoff Davison's *The TT Races – Behind the Scenes*, Joe said: 'I will nevertheless always harbour happy memories of the help and encouragement he [Moore] unstintingly gave me to improve my knowledge of the engineering side, by allowing me to enter into the running of the project in the largest measure possible.'

With Craig gone the team for the 1929 TT was Woods, Hunt, Simpson and Guthrie. The machines were, as *Motor Cycling* put it, '. . . to all intents and purposes, standard productions . . . except for extra large tanks and a modified rear brake anchorage'. However, there was one very major change for when the bikes actually appeared on the Isle of Man they were fitted with a positive-stop foot-change mechanism.

Oddly enough, rumours that Nortons would follow the Velocette lead of the previous year and use such a set-up in 1929 had been denied in *Motor Cycling* early in the TT period. Then, the following week, a picture of the 350 cc machine appeared in TT Topics and though the exposed mechanism atop the gearbox can be seen, together with a shorter gear-change pedal, the caption made no mention of it, referring instead to the bigger tank and the fact that the exhaust pipe now exited from a redesigned cylinder head on the offside of the machine.

However, in the same issue a drawing appeared showing the gear-change mechanism in detail with the caption: 'A pawl and ratchet device is used on some of the Nortons to prevent missing second gear.' At this point it is interesting to note that Hunt was the first of the factory riders to use a twist-grip throttle. The 'baby' of the team, he had always used a twist-grip for racing while his older team-mates stuck to the lever.

The Nortons impressed during training. The *Motor Cycling* reporter went out to watch on the very fast section just before Greeba where 'terrific leaps are made on the bump'. This was at the crest of the hill before The Highlander pub, and he went on to say: 'Generally speaking, of the faster machines – and many were doing about 95 mph – the Nortons seemed to be the steadiest. Stanley Woods and Jimmie Simpson executed prodigious aeriel feats without a flicker of unsteadiness, and were travelling at indecent speeds.'

Guthrie was eliminated by a practice crash, but despite this the Norton camp were optimistic and the week started well when Simpson and Woods led the Junior TT at the end of the first lap. The longer the race went on, however, the slower the Nortons went, and by the sixth lap all three had retired and the race was won by Freddie Hicks (Velocette).

Tim Hunt recalled that competition in the Senior was red hot and that Alec Bennett, who had won for Nortons in 1927 but was on a Sunbeam for the 1929 race, had told Norton boss Bill Mansell that none of his team would finish in the first six. He was nearly right, for Charlie Dodson (Sunbeam) won at a record average of 72.05 mph with Bennett in second place.

The Norton boys had a hectic time. The race started on wet roads and Wal Handley dropped his AJS in a big way at Greeba. A Norton rider, Douglas Lamb, was next along, crashing with fatal results, before Simpson and Jack Amott (Rudge) arrived. Both came off and the first lap ended with Woods the best placed Norton in a lowly fifth place.

On lap two Hunt got cracking and moved up to fourth ahead of Woods. The newcomer to the team was really flying and on his third lap shattered the record by getting round at 73.12 mph – an effort that put him into the lead just 3 seconds ahead of Dodson. So close was the race that Woods, in fifth place, was only 35 seconds behind the leader!

Enthused the *Motor Cycling* reporter: 'Think of it. Over 73 mph round a course which is nowhere better than the road from Edgware to St Albans, Whitby to Scarborough or Edinburgh to Moffat! What a rider! What a machine!' Then, on the fourth lap, Hunt slid off at Quarter Bridge. In the crash he wiped off a footrest but, as the *Motor Cycle* reporter put it: 'Hunt thought more of seconds than bruises, grabbed his prone motor and flung it towards Union Mills with a bark from the exhaust that told of a very wide open throttle.' He crashed again at Waterworks above Ramsey and knocked the other footrest off but at the end of the lap still held sixth place just behind Woods.

Dodson then set the lap record at 73.55 mph, but despite riding without footrests Hunt was up to second place at the end of lap five and was now the lone Norton, for Woods had crashed heavily. Recalling the incident, Woods said: 'Every time I came through the pits they signalled me to go faster. I was driving harder and harder and I finally ran out of road at Kirkmichael. I bloody near killed myself.' The report in *Motor Cycling* agreed: 'Stanley Woods lost some of his youthful charm by leaving a few teeth by the road-side. A little too much daring brought him off after a brilliant ride, and he had to have a number of stitches put in a very badly cut lip.'

Dodson went on to win from Bennett who, in his usual manner, had increased his speed as the race went on, while Hunt was pipped for third place by Tyrell Smith (Rudge) by just 17 seconds. This meant that the Norton tally for the week was a solitary fourth place. Obviously Bill Mansell was far from happy and the pressure was on Moore to produce results – or go.

But, Stanley Woods recalls, things went from bad to worse. In the French Grand Prix, held over the 24-hour car circuit at Le Mans, Dodson won again and

A Norton rider takes a drink during his refuelling stop at a Continental Grand Prix in 1929. The major races in those days were long and arduous – normally over 200 miles.

although Woods finished second he was way behind the push-rod Sunbeam, which actually lapped him. At the Dutch TT he retired in both races and when Hunt joined him for the Belgian Grand Prix they were plagued by the same old trouble – the Nortons were fast in the early stages but got progressively slower.

'There was a gap then before the German Grand Prix and Walter Moore went back to the factory to work on the engines. When he got back he told me that he'd more or less been given an ultimatum by Mansell that if we didn't win the next race he was out,' said Woods. Meanwhile Mansell had spoken to Craig who agreed to rejoin them; in fact he was delighted to do so because his garage venture had proved a fiasco.

At the German Grand Prix over the Nürburgring the Nortons again proved fast early on. After an early dice with Tommy Bullus (Horex) and Tyrell Smith (Rudge), Hunt had pulled away and looked set to win – then he coasted to a standstill with a broken chain. Woods took over for two laps until gearbox trouble slowed him and Tyrell Smith ran out the winner. In the 350 cc race, run concurrently, Pietro Ghersi led on a factory Norton but later slowed and eventually retired.

'That was the end of Walter Moore as far as Nortons were concerned. Mind you, I don't think he was worried. He had already been offered a job by NSU so he walked out of Norton and into the German factory – and took all his bad ideas with him,' said Woods with a smile, adding: 'NSU – we used to say Norton Spares Used or No Sodding Use! The engines he designed for them may have won a few local races but they never did any good in the big events and NSU never achieved anything until they got rid of him.'

Speaking to Titch Allen in 1970 Moore said that NSU had been after him since before Bob Shelley died back in April 1927. He had turned them down then because Shelley had promised him a seat on the board, but later NSU came back and asked him to name his price. By that time his position at Nortons was not as secure so he asked for, and got, £5500 a year – around £100,000 by 1990 standards. What he did not know was that NSU also provided a large house and a team of three gardeners to look after the grounds.

Craig knew what the basic trouble was. He had raced the camshaft models in 1927 and 1928 and so had first-hand experience. Writing in 1949 he said:

. . . one of the main troubles with the engines of 1928 and 1929 emanated from a marked tendency for the cylinder head and piston to attain a temperature out of all proportion to the power output. For example, on the TT course, when one started off down Bray Hill and rounded Quarter Bridge and applied the heat on the short straight towards Braddan Bridge, the device felt quite potent and gave the rider a very favourable impression. By the time one had reached the vicinity of Ballacraine a doubt might be creeping into one's mind that everything in the power-house might not be so 'well harmonised' after all. Towards Sulby Straight, if still in a hurry, the chances were that the favourable impression would be giving place to a doubtful one, and if one arrived at the bottom of the Mountain with everything still working according to 'the book', all doubt would then be quickly dispelled. During the tortuous climb in second gear, a decidedly agitated condition would soon develop upstairs, and if full throttle was still indulged in under these conditions, piston seizure would abruptly assert itself.

At first Moore had accused the riders of over-stressing the engines. Then he had blamed the pistons, and long hours were spent filing off the high spots until the fit was so slack that they rattled in the bore. Craig felt that the real reason for the piston seizures was overheating caused by poor combustion and scavenging. The original Moore engine of 1927 had been successful but the head had been redesigned for 1928 and it was this later head that was at fault.

With the Ulster Grand Prix only weeks away, Craig had to work fast. He went back to the original head design and fitted 'softer' cams. The engines gave the same power on the bench, but in duration tests they did not overheat. Theory was put to the test in Ireland when the Ulster was run in a heatwave on Saturday 6 September. Graham Walker (Rudge) won the 500 cc class at 80.99 mph, the fastest speed at which a road race had ever been won. And this time the Nortons kept going, with Woods taking second place and Hunt third. Craig had come out of retirement to team with Jimmy Shaw in the 350 cc race and he led at the end of the first lap, only to retire on the second, and Shaw dropped out too, with a broken steering column.

The rot had been stopped. The overheating had been cured and the riders had confidence in the machines. But Craig felt that the only long-term answer was a new camshaft engine and, assisted by Arthur Carroll, the chief draughtsman, he got to work on the new unit. Craig had to break off when the team went down to Barcelona for the Spanish Grand Prix, held in October that year (1929) when it carried the prestigious 'Grand Prix of Europe' label.

Stanley Woods remembers that Walter Handley was there and that his Swiss-built Motosacoche was so fast that Craig said, 'Let him go – we'll have to hope that he blows up.' According to Woods:

Tim Hunt replied, 'to hell with that. I'm going to show him the way.' Tim went out in front and he rode like a demon. I tucked in behind Handley but my big-end went. That's how I happen to know that Hunt rode so well. I was able to watch him on a double bend. He never let up and won by a street. He was a fantastic rider and every now and then he'd pull an ace out and no one could hold him.

Hunt also remembered the race:

The Nortons in those days would do about 100 mph and I made a tremendous start. I used the exhaust valve-lifter and not the clutch, took a couple of paces, dropped the lever and the Norton, which had a straight through pipe and not a megaphone, took off. It was a lovely twisty course, tailor-made for me. It was a 225 mile race and I didn't half show them how to go that day!'

The Spanish Grand Prix included a sidecar race and young Dennis Mansell, making a rare road-racing appearance, won the 102-mile event at an average speed of 53.3 mph. These wins, added to Eric Lea's in the Senior Amateur TT, gave Nortons three major successes to advertise, which must have been a relief after a season in which their wins had been confined largely to trials and local events.

Now back to what has become known as the Carroll engine – who actually designed it? Stanley Woods is in no doubt: 'In my opinion Carroll was the draughtsman and Joe Craig was the designer.' Both men played a major part in the design and development of the new unit. In *The TT Races – Behind the Scenes*, Craig himself says:

Arthur Carroll was then in charge of the Design Office and fortunately he and I had formed a very close bond of friendship during my riding career. Now we could get together as a team, each intent on making the maximum contribution possible and neither having any desire to try to steal the kudos – an absolutely essential spirit if the maximum effort is to be made and sustained. Therefore, with Carroll's profound theoretical and practical ability, together with my own reasonably deep store of knowledge regarding the desirable characteristics of a racer, we laid our plans for the construction of machines which we felt could be relied upon to carry the name of the marque and the country successfully to every corner of the world.

While the new racing engine was being designed and built, Norton announced their 1930 range. There were two new models – the 20 and 22. Both followed the sporting trend of the time with twin exhaust port heads and an exhaust system on both sides, but while the cheaper Model 20 had a diamond frame, a steel primary chain-case and the older 490 cc OHV engine with the magneto in front, the Model 22 had the new 490 cc ES2 type engine, the cradle frame and the cast-aluminium chain-case.

The factory had recently installed their own chromium-plating plant and according to *Motor Cycling*, 'all models will be chromium plated except the side-valve machines on which nickel plating will be standard'. At last the valve springs on the 16H and Big Four were concealed (by a neat aluminium casting) and

Prototype of the re-designed 490 cc camshaft engine at Olympia, 1929 – in fact a hybrid with a Walter Moore cambox wedded to the new bevel drive and crankcase.

a gate for the hand-change gearbox was standard on the chromium-plated tanks. A new Norton four-speed box with final drive on the left-hand side was available as an optional alternative on every model, price £5.25.

Gone was the rather curious double-barrelled silencer, replaced by an ungainly one-piece 'squashed diamond' with fishtail. Prices were further reduced, the basic 16H dropping from £56 to just under the £50 mark and the Big Four from £60 to £54. There were similar reductions throughout the range with the top-priced camshaft CS1 ducking under the £80 barrier at £77.50. But electric lighting sets were still an extra.

It was a time of fierce competition and with the depression biting deeper and deeper Nortons sought desperately to instil confidence in potential buyers. Claimed their advertisement at the end of 1929: 'All the resources of a great factory plus unique experience are behind the Norton . . . This explains Norton's supreme reliability.'

The very first Carroll-Craig engine was built into a cradle frame and rushed to the Olympia Show which opened on the last day of November 1929. In fact it was a hybrid unit – a modified Moore top half, complete with circular bevel-housing cover, on the new crankcase. Whether the engine was a 'runner' or simply a mock-up with no internals we do not know, but it was certainly a show surprise. Neither of the weekly journals mentioned it in their previews and little about the new engine appeared in their actual Show reports.

In fact *Motor Cycling* did not mention it in their stand-by-stand write up but carried a rushed and not very accurate drawing of the engine, together with a picture of the complete machine, in the news section, which obviously went to press later. Under the heading 'A Last-minute Surprise' the captions read: 'The new Norton o.h.c. engine with dry-sump lubrication and off-side magneto drive' and 'A Clubman's dream – the latest camshaft Norton'.

The report in *The Motor Cycle* was almost dismissive. Talking about the new camshaft machine it simply said: 'This model has a re-designed crankcase on which the magneto, while still behind the engine, is driven from the timing side.' Little did either magazine realise that this was the engine that would play such a central role in road racing for the next 35 years!

1928–29 Gallery

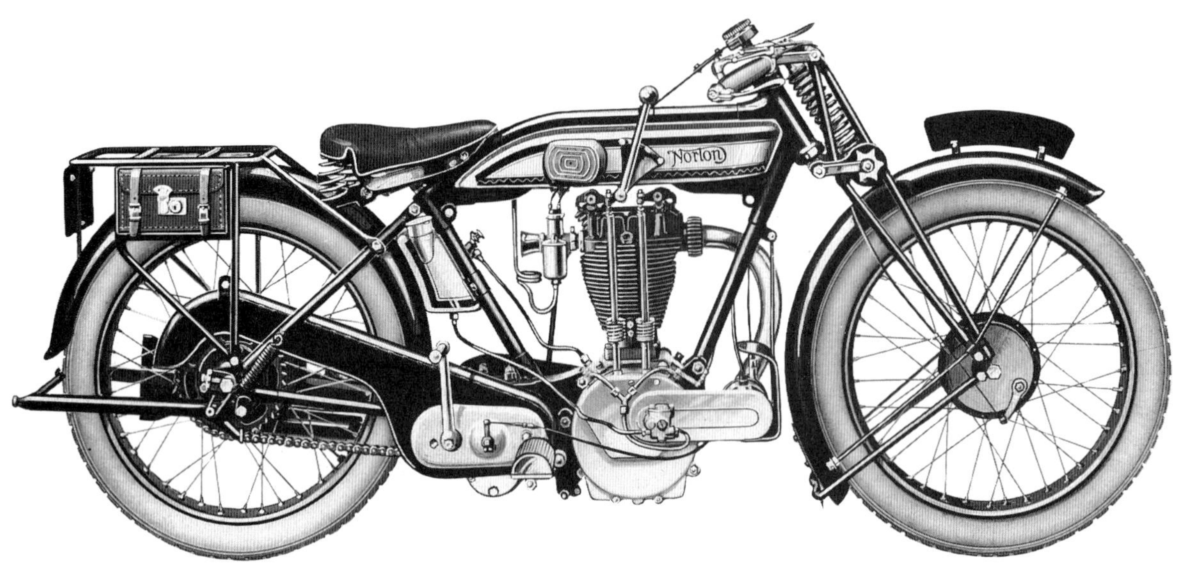

The 588 cc Model 24 of 1928 was fitted with the four-speed gearbox first developed for the Sidecar TT. Final drive is on the righthand side of the machine.

A top sporting mount – the 1928 490 cc camshaft Norton CS1 with a 90 mph top speed. Gearbox was a three-speed Sturmey-Archer.

A catalogue picture of the 1929 490 cc push-rod Model 18 showing the strange double-barrelled silencer adopted by Nortons in the late twenties.

Long and low – the 588 cc OHV Model 19 as shown in the 1929 Norton catalogue.

CHAPTER 11

1930s roadsters 1930–1932

In late April 1930 Tim Hunt and Stanley Woods made their debut with the redesigned camshaft engines at the North West 200 in Northern Ireland – and it was Hunt who scored the first win with the new machine when he romped home in the 350 cc race with a record lap at 72.48 mph. Reported *The Motor Cycle*: 'Hunt's riding, particularly at the bend approaching the start, was spectacular and he was loudly cheered each time he came around.'

The debut of the 500 was not so encouraging. Ernie Nott was out on a new Rudge and he won the race, with Woods back in third place. The Irish race was used by the teams to try out their TT models and as soon as it was over attention shifted to the Isle of Man.

In TT Notes and News in *The Motor Cycle* in May 1930 it was reported that: 'Stanley Woods was to be found batting about Devon and Cornwall on an old camshaft TT Norton. For several weeks prior to the practising in the Isle of Man he gives up making TT Toffee in Ireland and goes into serious training, riding several hundred miles a day.' (The reference to toffee is explained by the fact that Woods had stopped working in the Norton race shop at the end of 1927 and had returned to Ireland where he invested his hard-earned money in a toffee-making venture. This prospered for a while but then, like so many other businesses, fell victim to the depression.)

At the end of May *The Motor Cycle* published a good drawing of the new camshaft engine but the person who wrote the caption did not seem to grasp the significance of the new unit, which was very different from the Walter Moore engine used the preceding year.

The bore and stroke of the original camshaft engines were retained (71 × 88 mm, 348 cc and 79 × 100 mm, 490 cc) but virtually everthing else was changed. While Moore had clearly been influenced by the Chater-Lea layout, Carroll and Craig veered more towards the successful Velocette design though the lower half of their engine was a good deal more robust than that of the Hall Green unit.

Bevel drive to a single overhead camshaft was retained but the plunger oil pump was replaced by a rotary gear unit. The rear-mounted magneto was also retained but was now driven from the timing side, the chain concealed by an aluminium cover. This meant

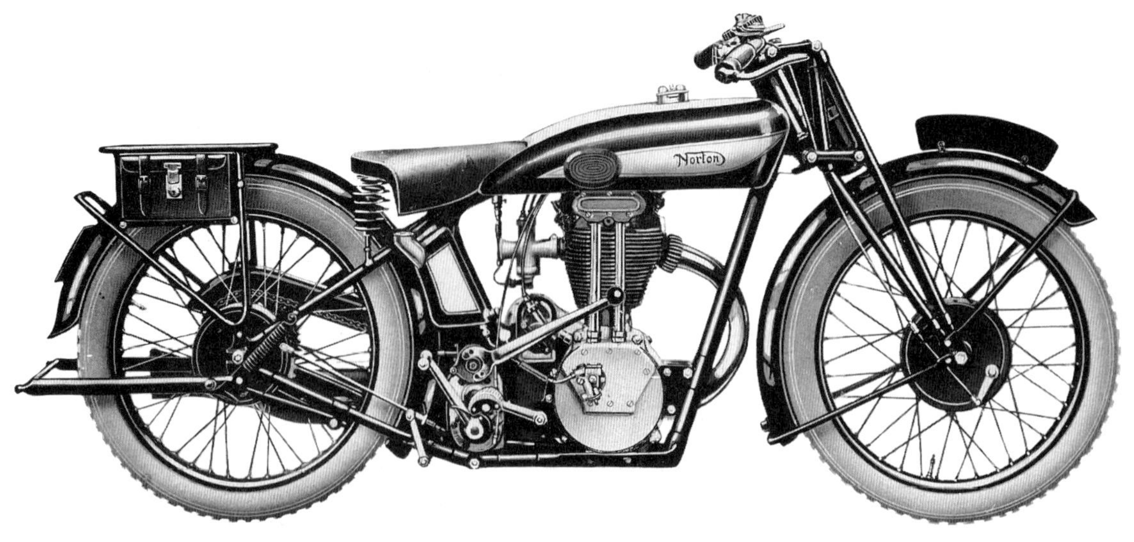

BELOW **The 1930 350 cc Model JE with three-speed Sturmey-Archer gearbox. Basic cost £64, but lights (£5.50) and speedometer (£2) were optional extras.**

RIGHT **The start of the German Grand Prix at the Nürburgring in late June 1930. Just in the foreground is winner Graham Walker (Rudge) with Tim Hunt (Norton, 22) and Stanley Woods (Norton, 23) who finished second.**

that having 'lost' the magneto drive sprocket from the nearside, the mainshaft could be shortened and the engine sprocket positioned close to the crank-case.

Despite the success of Rudge with their four-valve engines, Nortons stuck to two large valves in a hemispherical head (a shape difficult to achieve with four valves). The camshaft was supported by two roller bearings while the rockers rotated on needle roller bearings. The aluminium piston was of the slipper type and using the 50/50 petrol/benzol mixture allowed by the regulations the compression ratio of both units was around 7 to 1.

The three-speed Sturmey-Archer gear boxes were retained and the frames little changed – the 500 still boasting the extra chain stay so that the rear wheel was supported by three tubes converging on the axle on both sides. Things went reasonably well during practice and inspired the *Motor Cycle* tipster to write:

Tim Hunt refuels during the 1930 Senior TT. He retired on the fifth lap – the Rudges were just too fast that year. The small box in front of the cylinder held oil for the primary chain.

Tim Hunt is just about the fastest thing on two wheels and phenomenally consistent. Jimmie Simpson must come home all alone one day when he at last gets an engine stocky enough to stand his furious driving. Woods is the embodiment of grace and elan. . . . The Norton engines are very new but they are built like Mont Blanc, and should produce the reliability for which this factory is famous.

In other words, he did not think they were fast enough to win!

He was right. The new 350 cc Rudge with four valves radially disposed around the hemispherical head, and operated by an ingenious push-rod and rocker layout, proved phenomenally fast straight from the drawing board of George Hack. Aided by a four-speed gearbox they slaughtered the opposition and took the first three places.

The Nortons were never in the hunt. Woods was the best down in sixth place and *The Motor Cycle* summed things up nicely: 'Woods (Norton) is sixth, the same debonair speedster as ever, but yearning for just one more gee-gee.' Hunt trailed in ninth while Simpson ran out of oil and seized at the Gooseneck on the third lap.

In the Senior, run in heavy rain, the Norton trio fared a little better and at least made a race of it. But again the Rudges were supreme. Their bigger engine had a different layout with four valves in a pent-house cylinder head but they also had four-speed boxes, and again they romped away with Wal Handley, who had switched to a Rudge only when his factory FN failed to turn up, the winner from Walker.

Early in the race Hunt led the Nortons in fifth place. Then on lap three Simpson moved up to fourth and he battled on to finish third and to spoil a second clean sweep by Rudge. Hunt dropped out with engine trouble on the fifth lap while holding fifth place, while poor Woods was never in the frame, suffering first from a misfire and then being eliminated when his chain broke as he bump-started after his refuelling stop.

But for Craig and the Norton team there was a glimmer of hope, for not even Simpson, noted for his ability to wreck any racing engine built, had been able to break the Norton. Reported *The Motor Cycle*: 'Simpson can drive most engines to death, but the new Norton stood up to all he could give it, and thrived on it. Jimmy admires its stamina but greedily asks for a few more knots.'

Examined after the race the 490 cc engine proved to be in good shape: 'The internal condition of Simpson's Norton was perfect and no fault of any kind was traceable. Both thrust faces of the slipper piston were beautifully bright; their lubrication had been ensured by a series of fine grooves, designed to retain lubricant.' Pa Norton must have looked down and smiled, for he had advocated grooved pistons since the very early days.

From the TT the team of three (Guthrie had switched to AJS for a season) travelled over to the Nürburgring where the German Grand Prix was held late in June – and there the Nortons proved more competitive. In the 500 cc class Hunt pushed Walker (Rudge) hard for half the race before retiring with engine trouble, while Woods kept going to finish second.

Simpson contested the 350 cc race but crashed and the win went to Guthrie on a camshaft AJS. The Dutch TT was run at Assen just six days later – too soon for Simpson to recover from his injuries, and when Hunt fell ill the Norton team was reduced to just Stanley Woods.

Luckily the Dubliner was a very fit man. First he did 16 laps of the old circuit, a total of 172 miles, in the 350 cc race in which he finished third to winner Digger Simcock (AJS). Then, in the afternoon, he turned out on the 500 for another 18 laps (193 miles). Walker (Rudge) repeated his German GP win, averaging 77.50 mph, but Woods was second, less than a minute astern.

Incidentally 1930 was the first year since his novice days that Woods had used a full set of leathers. After finding that the poor leather used in the 1920s would tear like cardboard, he had switched first to cord breeches and then, in 1928 and 1929, to a complete green corduroy suit made for him by 'the finest tailor in Dublin'. Then American horse-hide became available – just at the time the ACU were insisting on leathers and 'field boots' for the 1930 TT.

Eight days after the Dutch TT the Rudge team scored another double in the Belgian Grand Prix at Spa. This time Tyrell Smith won the 500 cc class from team-mate Walker and Duncan on a Raleigh, with Woods a close fourth and a recovering Simpson fifth. The Nortons were reliable but not quite fast enough to win.

ABOVE This rather fanciful aerial view of the Norton works appeared in the 1930 Norton catalogue. It includes the neighbouring works of the parent company, R. T. Shelley, who made a wide range of goods in addition to Norton components.

RIGHT Italian Piero Taruffi on the 490 cc Norton on which he set a lap record at 112 mph in the 1931 Italian GP at Monza.

There was a six-week gap before practising for the Ulster, and Craig went back to Bracebridge Street confident that they were on the right track but still searching for those extra few horsepower. Stanley Woods remembers: 'When we met again in Ireland, Joe said to me,"I think I've found the trouble. It was the new test-bed. It was giving false readings."'

At the Ulster Craig was proved right. He had found the trouble. In the 500 cc race Walker set the pace but Woods was able to stay with him and when rain came and put the Rudge out with water in the magneto, Woods took over to win at 80.56 mph – his first Ulster success. Adding to Norton joy, Simpson set a lap record at 84.63 mph – and then nipped over to Sweden to win the 500 cc class of the grand prix there before travelling right across Europe to rejoin the Norton team at Pau for the French Grand Prix.

There he was involved in an accident when a boy on a bicycle, ignoring the orders of a gendarme, rode across the course during practice and was hit by Simpson. The lad was killed and Simpson suffered a broken leg which, with Hunt a non-starter, reduced the team to a single entry – Woods on a prototype which included many of the lessons that Craig had learned that year. Most noticeable were a down-draught carburettor, a four-speed gearbox and a shorter frame without the third, central chain stay. Reverting to his green corduroy riding suit, Woods ended the year on a high note by winning the 500 cc race with ease – but the opposition was too poor really to test the new machine.

On the home front Graham Goodman and Dennis Mansell had been keeping the Norton flag flying in trials – Goodman winning the Bemrose, Colmore, and Sunbeam events on a camshaft model. At Brooklands Bill Lacey, who had assisted Joe Craig in the Isle of Man throughout the TT, had been working hard on camshaft 490 cc and 596 cc machines and in October he set the pace. 'All eyes were on Lacey and his immaculate Norton – easily the fastest thing on the track that afternoon' reported *The Motor Cycle.* He won the 500 cc race at 99.01 mph and then the 750 cc at 108.27 mph with a lap at 112.42 mph – the fastest ever by a single-cylinder bike and not far short of the outright motorcycle lap record at that time.

Back in June Norton had launched a speedway model powered by a 490 cc OHV engine running on alcohol. It was a nice-looking machine but it was too heavy – and too late. Priced at £85, it is doubtful if more than a handful were sold for by that time Rudge had taken over from Douglas, and JAP were already thinking in terms of a purpose-built dirt-track engine.

Of more interest to the man in the street was the fact that in July Nortons advertised: 'Deliveries of the new camshaft Norton are now being effected.' At that time they were still catalogued as the CJ (£72) and the CS1 (£77.50)) although, at the very least, the 500 should have been the CS2. The picture actually shows the hybrid with Walter Moore top half that appeared at the Show but, because the model numbers remained the same, it is impossible to say how many of these 'mongrel' camshaft models were sold.

Writing of Moore reminds me that his single-cylinder NSU racer made its debut at a minor international at the Solitude circuit near Stuttgart in August 1930. Ridden by Englishman Tommy Bullus, the NSU won the race. The engine was almost identical to the CS1 and *The Motor Cycle* commented:

> A pronounced tendency towards British methods of design is evident in the machine; perhaps this is not altogether surprising, for on the NSU staff is an Englishman who was formerly on the technical staff of a well known British factory. The makers claim the engine to be a wholly German design.

ABOVE **Tim Hunt comes home to win the 1931 Junior (350 cc) TT for Norton at a speed of 73.94 mph. It was the first leg of the Junior/Senior double he scored that year.**

RIGHT **Jimmy Guthrie is congratulated by Dennis Mansell after finishing second in the 1931 Senior TT – beaten by team-mate Tim Hunt. On the right is mechanic Frank Sharratt.**

BELOW RIGHT **One of Norton's few failures – the 490 cc speedway model with twin-port head. Produced in 1930 it looked good but was no match for the lighter Rudge and JAP models.**

In the rather coy style of the time neither Moore nor Norton was mentioned by name! The NSU had a bore and stroke of 80 × 99 mm to give a capacity of 498 cc. Moore later said that he was able to use his Norton design with only minor alterations because the original had been conceived in his own time and not while he was actually working at Bracebridge Street. This seems a dubious claim, but wisely Nortons did not contest the matter in the courts – the factory preferred to let their riders prove the superiority of the Carroll–Craig engine on the circuits.

In September 1930 *The Motor Cycle* announced the Norton range for 1931 under the heading 'Still Neater Nortons'. Edgar Franks was the man responsible for both updating the range and introducing sensible economies whereby previously 'bought-in' components were replaced by ones designed and built within the Norton/Shelley group. Notable among these were hubs, brakes and a Webb-type front fork.

Franks also designed new, lower frames which dropped the riding position to a knees-full-bend posture with a saddle height of only 26½ inches. At the same time an ugly tank with lining that was totally different to the racing machines was adopted, losing the 'corporate image' of the previous few years.

But at long last twist-grip throttles, used by Hunt and Simpson for years, were standard on all models (but curiously enough, the catalogue for 1931 shows the complete range fitted with lever throttles – though the descriptions underneath all talk of 'twistgrip control'). And an improvement on the two side-valve machines was the adoption of detachable heads – a useful move in the days when it was necessary to de-coke engines at least every few thousand miles.

Times were very hard indeed and to keep the list-price down Nortons continued to offer things that we now consider essential as optional extras. These included Lucas magdyno lighting for £5.50, a neat fork-top instrument panel with speedometer for £2.25 and a four-speed gearbox for £2. The most expensive bike in the range, at £79.50 (plus the extras), was the 490 cc super-sports CS1 which by this time boasted the complete Carroll–Craig engine.

The public saw the models for the first time at the Olympia Show which opened on Monday 10 November and on that very day Bill Lacey, assisted by speedway star Wal Phillips, was at Montlhéry with a camshaft 490 cc attacking world records.

Lacey did the first hour at 112 mph (just missing the classic hour record) and they went on to take the 200-mile record at 104.18 mph, the 3-hour at 102.14 mph and the 500-kilometre at 102.07 mph before heavy rain

Norton

Graham Goodman was the star trials rider of the early thirties. He won the Bemrose, Colmore and Sunbeam trials, in 1930; pictured with his camshaft Norton at the 1931 Scottish Six Days Trial.

stopped play. The Norton was immediately rushed to London to take a place of honour on the Norton stand.

On 1 January 1931 a new Road Traffic Act came into force. The old blanket 20 mph speed limit that was still on the statute books (though totally ignored) was at last repealed. From then, until the present overall limits were imposed, you could go as fast as your bike could carry you once you were on the open road. At the same time the age limit was raised from 14 to 16 and third-party insurance became obligatory.

To promote the sales at the end of the winter, Nortons organised 'National Norton Week' in March 1931 and backed the sales drive with two-page advertisements in the two weeklies that listed all their dealers – 38 in the London area alone and over 200 all told. The slogan adopted for the campaign read: 'No other motor-cycle in the world has been so vastly improved in any one season. The value is phenomenal.'

It was in March that Hunt got a telegram from Craig summoning him to Pendine Sands to try the 1931 works racers. The Welsh beach was a known speed venue, the sands left hard and level at low tide, and Tim remembers that the bikes flew: 'Joe reckoned that the best run on the 500 was 118 mph but I'd say the true top speed was more like 110 mph.'

The changes tried by Woods at Pau the preceding September had all been adopted. Additionally plug size was reduced from 18 to 14 mm, an engine shock absorber fitted, the rear stand replaced by a centre stand and the Webb forks and Enfield brakes replaced by components of Norton manufacture. At first the new four-speed gearbox, with fully enclosed positive stop mechanism, gave trouble and Hunt remembers that Craig instructed Sturmey-Archer to make no less than 24 modifications: 'He was a hard, decisive man and knew exactly what he wanted. He stood no nonsense but I always got on well with him,' said Hunt, who went on to recall that when they were having trouble with Lucas magnetos Joe had at first delighted and then humbled the firm's representative by saying that there were three good things about the Lucas magnetos – the box they came in, the paper the package was wrapped in and the string it was tied with!

Alone among the Norton team, Simpson took a 500 down to Monza for the Italian Grand Prix which was run in April that year. There he was dicing for the lead with Bullus (NSU) and Hicks (AJS) when he came off on the very last corner while trying to sweep around his rivals on a track made treacherous by heavy rain.

1931 Gallery

The 1931 350 cc camshaft Model CJ with revised frame and lower riding position. Note the new pressed steel oil-bath primary chain-case. Price was £72 plus lights.

The 350 cc push-rod Model JE as it appeared in the 1931 Norton catalogue. It was supplied either with the tank-mounted hand-change as shown or with the more sporty foot operated change – but not yet with positive stop. Price £64.

For 1931 the 633 cc side-valve Big Four got a complete face-lift. At last the Druid fork was replaced by a Webb-type and this, combined with the new frame, primary chaincase and racing type tank gave the Big Four a thoroughly modern look. Price was a bargain £54.

LEFT **Stanley Woods in action in the 500 cc Belgian Grand Prix of 1931. He won the 250 mile race at an average of 71.15 mph – the race lasting over 3½ hours!**

RIGHT **Jimmy Guthrie prepares for the start of the 1932 Junior TT. The race was won by team-mate Stanley Woods and Guthrie retired after a spill.**

Hicks won the race from Bullus with a remounted Simpson third – the only time I can find that a Moore-NSU beat a works Norton in a major race.

Woods and Hunt tried out their 1931 TT machines in the Leinster and North West 200 where the bikes proved fast but did not, for one reason or another, win. At Leinster Woods rode his 350 and set the fastest lap, while in the North West he turned out in the bigger class and again clocked the fastest lap and led the race until a rear-wheel puncture slowed him.

Ernie Nott on the latest four-valve Rudge won the big class at the NW and some of the Rudges were fitted with an innovation – a rev-counter. Commented Stanley Woods: 'They seemed to be claiming astronomical revs – we called them "oxometers", they measured the bullshit!'

By this time Nortons were, for the first time, offering the public a positive-stop gearbox. It was the Sturmey-Archer three-speeder and could be obtained as an optional extra only on the top-of-the-range camshaft CS1. And Nortons switched the thrust of their advertising campaign from sport to touring, showing a clean-cut young married man studying a catalogue while relaxing in an armchair, with attentive spouse hovering in the background, under the banner heading 'Millie I'm going to get a Norton.'

Guthrie had rejoined Woods, Hunt and Simpson for the 1931 TT when vile weather kept practice speeds down until the final sessions when Woods bettered the existing 350 cc lap record and Hunt and Guthrie also put in fast laps.

In race week all Nortons' hopes were realised. Their silver-tanked machines completely dominated both events and equalled Rudge's score of the preceding year by taking five of the top six places. The pattern was set in the 350 cc race when Simpson streaked ahead pursued by Woods, Guthrie and Hunt who lost time on the first lap when his engine stopped. On coasting to a standstill he found that the screw-on plug terminal had come adrift. 'We had switched from KLG who used a clip to Lodge and when I'd changed from the warming-up to the race plug I obviously had not tightened it enough. I was a hopeless mechanic and after that Joe told me never to touch the bikes!'

At the end of the first lap Simpson led from Woods with Hunt down in eighth place. Simpson had broken the lap record from a standing start and he and Woods continued to dominate until Woods was slowed by a broken steering damper. As he slowed so Hunt, with a record lap at 75.27 mph, moved up, taking over second place on the fourth lap only 24 seconds behind the leader. On the fifth lap Hunt overtook Simpson, going on to win at a record 73.94 mph, close to the 500 cc speed of the previous year.

Reminiscing, Hunt said: 'I think it was the best race I ever rode. It was the only one I ever felt tired after. I just went as fast as I could like I always did.' Simpson's legendary bad luck struck on lap six when his engine cut out. Like Hunt he was a poor mechanic and it was only after he had smoked a cigarette that he decided to see if the bike would re-start. It did – the fault was nothing worse than dirt blocking the carburettor jet – and he eventually came home eighth.

When Simpson stopped, Guthrie came through to finish second while Nott (Rudge) spoiled the Norton clean sweep by finishing third ahead of Woods. Record speed, record lap, first, second, fourth and eighth and the team prize (Hunt, Woods and Simpson) – it could hardly be bettered. But it was – in the Senior TT just five days later.

Guthrie set the pace and led from Simpson, Woods and Hunt at the end of the opening lap. Simpson was flying and on the third lap he pushed the record over the 80 mark for the first time by getting round at 80.82 mph, despite coasting the last quarter-mile when he ran out of petrol as he came in for his pit-stop. Then came disaster. His rear brake locked as he approached Ballaugh Bridge (some said he was simply going too fast) and Simpson crashed into the bridge railings, damaging his machine and injuring his wrist.

Hunt took over the lead and held it to complete the first ever Junior–Senior TT double – his average speed of 77.90 mph completely shattering the 74.24 mph achieved by Handley (Rudge) the previous year. Guthrie was second while Woods, again hampered by problems, made it a first ever 1–2–3 for Nortons by beating Nott (Rudge) by 54 seconds.

In spite of the successes, all was not well behind the scenes. If Nortons had paid out according to the terms of a contract Hunt had signed in 1929 he would have received £8000 – around £200,000 in 1990 terms. But when he went to see Bill Mansell at Bracebridge Street after the TT he was told that all he would get was £1000 for the Senior win and £750 for the Junior.

'You can imagine how I felt. I'd worked it out that I'd get £8000 and there was the gaffer telling me I was going to get less than a quarter of that!' Mansell pointed out that Hunt had no contract for 1931 (he simply had not got around to asking for one) and they finally settled for £2000.

Soon the team were on their way to the French Grand Prix which was also the European Grand Prix that year. They used to travel by train – first from Birmingham to London, then across from Euston to Victoria with the bikes in a van, and at Victoria they would pick up the boat-train and on to their continental venue. 'The machines would travel as registered personal luggage. We carried very few spares with us. We didn't need them,' Stanley Woods remembers.

The French that year was at Montlhéry and Hunt won the 500 cc class but Woods was narrowly beaten in the 350 cc race by Nott (Rudge). At the German Grand Prix at the Nürburgring a week later, Craig insisted on team orders for the first time. 'The bikes were going so well that the orders were to take it easy until the last lap and then to fight it out,' said Woods. 'Hunt and I were in the 500 race and that is what we did. We started the last lap side by side and then the race was on. I finally beat him by half a wheel and I just said to myself, "Right, I'll not be beaten again. If I can beat Hunt I can beat anyone."'

Both had hectic moments on that final round – Hunt when he was caught out by the new four-speed gearbox, changing from third to second and locking the rear wheel when he meant to swop from top to third, and Woods when he went into a corner too fast and ended up fighting for control on the track-side grass. And when Craig stripped Hunt's engine in preparation for the Dutch TT (held six days later) he found the piston of Hunt's machine on the point of collapse, a fault that had almost certainly cost him the race in the hectic sprint to the finish.

In Holland Nortons did the double with Hunt winning the 500 cc class at 82.07 mph – the fastest ever speed for a major road race. Hunt also achieved a 'world record' lap at 84.99 mph as he scratched his way through the field after losing time with a blocked jet early in the race – finally beating Nott (Rudge) by just 8 seconds with Woods, slowed by a broken clutch lever, third.

Woods won the 350 cc class in Holland and from there the team made the short trip to Spa for the Belgian Grand Prix the following Sunday. It proved a wet and miserable affair but the result was another double. Woods won the 500 cc, covering the 250 miles at 71.15 mph in a race that lasted over three and a half hours, while Guthrie, at that time the junior member of the team, broke a run of bad luck by winning the 350 cc, run at the same time. Hunt's hopes of success were dashed on the first lap of the 500 cc event when a nail in the rear tyre put him out.

After this run of four classics the Norton team made their way back to Birmingham to prepare for the Swiss Grand Prix at Berne in mid August. There the 350 cc race was on the Saturday and Hunt won, with Woods second. The next day Woods won the big class at the record average of 73.41 mph and clocked a record lap at 77.74 mph. Again Hunt was out of luck and he was forced to pull out of the 44-lap, 205-mile race with engine trouble.

The coil valve springs of the time were still giving trouble and Woods remembers that Craig used to carry two pairs for each engine and switched them at alternate races. 'The idea was to give them a rest. It seemed to work,' said Woods, who also recalled the Norton race routine of the early 1930s.

> After the finish Craig and I would whip the heads off so that the officials could measure the engines. Then we'd put them together and they would be ready for the first practice session at the next meeting. During practising we would take the heads off again and Joe would have a look at the valves, check

Tim Hunt seen winning the 1931 Senior TT to complete the first ever Junior/Senior double.

BELOW The famous International 350 cc and 500 cc camshaft models were introduced in September 1931 and went on sale as part of the 1932 Norton range.

the pistons and change the springs. The engines ran on a fuel mixture of half petrol and half benzole – we seldom had any trouble, the bikes were very reliable.'

When Guthrie joined the team he too used to assist but neither Hunt nor Simpson was mechanically minded and, as Woods put it: 'They used to look after the social side of things. You could say they were the playboys and we did the work.' Asked how he got on with Craig, who had a reputation as a difficult man, Woods replied: 'One hundred per cent. I never found him difficult. He was used to perfection – maybe he was difficult when he didn't get it. I always tried to give a hundred per cent and we always got on well.'

For the Ulster Grand Prix on 5 September, Simpson was back in action having recovered from his TT injury, teaming with Woods and Hunt in the 500 cc race while Guthrie and Leo Davenport spearheaded the Norton effort in the 350 cc class.

Despite clutch problems Woods won the big class at the record average of 86.43 mph with a record lap at 89.67 mph – speeds which regained the title of 'the world's fastest road race' for the Irish classic. Nott on his Rudge was second with Hunt third and Simpson fifth, and it is worth noting that this was no sprint – the race distance was 246 miles.

Guthrie had an unscheduled pit stop in the 350 cc event to sort out a steering damper problem and after setting a record lap at 83.29 mph he finished second to Davenport who, because he was under contract to Mobiloil, was not a member of the official Norton team. To round off a superb year, Jock Muir (Norton) won the Senior Manx Grand Prix.

Sporting hearts beat faster when, in mid September, the Norton range for 1932 was announced. For there were two superb new models – the Model 30 490 cc International and the Model 40 348 cc International priced at £90 and £82.50 respectively. Both were road-going replicas of the camshaft machines on which the factory riders had dominated the classic races that year.

The name International was chosen to reflect the truly global run of Norton road-racing successes. Commented *The Motor Cycle*: 'These really are genuine replicas of the Nortons raced during the year.' The specification included the down-draught carburettor, the beautifully styled petrol tank, the massive oil tank and the Sturmey-Archer four-speed gearbox with positive stop.

For the sports tourist the CJ and CS camshaft models were kept in the range with three-speed hand-change gearboxes (costing £10 less than their International counterparts). The other models were continued much as before but all were now fitted with quickly detachable wheels, while a four-speed gearbox was available as an optional extra for just under £2.

Ramming the Norton message home, record breaker Bill Lacey took his very special 490 cc camshaft model to Montlhéry at the end of September and broke the classic hour record with a speed of 110.80 mph – which also took the 750 cc and 1000 cc records.

The 1932 season started with a welcome but unexpected win in the European Grand Prix, the title that year going to the Italians who ran the race at Littorio near Rome. It was run in April and with the all-important TT looming, Nortons did not send factory riders nor machines. But Piero Taruffi, later team manager with Gilera and the man who tempted Geoff Duke away from Nortons in 1953, had a very fast Norton which he had carefully tuned and lightened. At Monza the preceding year he had lapped at an impressive 112 mph, and at Littorio he outfought and outlasted the new four-cylinder Guzzis ridden by Bandini and Fumagelli – much to the chagrin of the partisan Italian crowd.

During the winter Craig had concentrated on weight saving. The 1932 TT Nortons were basically the same as the 1931 models but wherever lighter materials could be used they were. The biggest step was to cast the crank-cases in magnesium alloy (Elektron) – a move confirmed by the *Motor Cycle* technical review of the season which describes the 1932 works crank-case as 'a very fine and rigid piece of work . . . now bears heavy radial stiffening webs and is cast from a special alloy combining lightness with the highest dissipating qualities'. Probably the gearbox casing was also magnesium alloy – Rudges had used this material as early as 1930. Craig also used light alloy for the centre stand, mudguards and handlebar levers, which all helped to cut the weight of the 350 cc to 298 lb and the 500 cc to 312 lb.

'Early in 1932 Norton sent for me. They had a new front fork with extensions on the fork links and the damper springs. There was no friction damping and they were perfection, a great improvement,' said Woods. Another improvement was the fitting of even bigger tanks so that they could get through a seven-lap TT with a single stop. And for 1932 even Woods switched to a twist-grip throttle.

It was in 1932 that Nortons introduced team orders for the Isle of Man. Explained Woods: 'Bill Mansell decided that we would race for three laps and then hold that order. Now I think he did that because he thought that Simpson would win. He was always red-hot off the starting line and he was also very popular.'

This meant that Woods had to change his tactics. His normal inclination was to take things easily, to save his engine until things sorted themselves out. Now he had to go flat out from the word go, and to assist him he set up his own signalling stations which Nortons knew nothing about. He had one by the public telephone box in Sulby and another in a garden near the top of Bray Hill – just out of sight of the pit area.

It cost me practically nothing. I bribed the telephone operators with boxes of chocolates to answer the Sulby phone as soon as it was raised and not to look for money; I'd settle

up later. I also got on to the exchange in Douglas and arranged more or less instant clearance for the calls. This meant that I was given my exact position twice a lap by people I knew I could trust – but it was split-second work.

It was Stanley Woods' year. His luck held, he rode brilliantly and his signalling system worked perfectly. He shattered Hunt's average of the preceding year to win the Junior TT at 77.17 mph, pushing up the lap record by over 3 mph to 78.63 mph. There could be no question of orders, for Woods led from the start and, at the end, was the sole surviving Norton. Hunt went out with a broken rocker, Simpson with engine trouble and Guthrie after a crash.

The 1932 Senior TT quickly developed into a Woods/Simpson duel – and with boss's son Dennis Mansell acting as pit attendant to Simpson, Stanley was convinced that the factory wanted Simpson to win. The pace was fast and furious – Hunt crashed at Braddan Bridge and at the end of the first lap Simpson led Woods by just 3 seconds. On the next round he gained another 2. But on the all-important third lap Woods got ahead, finishing the lap 15 seconds up.

At his pit-stop Simpson, who had pushed up the lap record to 81.50 mph, complained of a slipping clutch and as Woods pulled away to win at a record average of 79.38 mph so Guthrie, riding with the handicap of a leg injured in his Junior TT spill, closed the gap. The Scot went into the last lap just 14 seconds behind Simpson and snatched second place from him by the same amount.

It was another Norton 1–2–3 and it was the first time that one make had achieved a clean sweep of both Junior and Senior races – and the first time that a factory had scored a double-double by winning both events in consecutive years. There to see the race and to present the trophies in the Villa Marina, packed by 8000 enthusiasts, was Prince George who, within a few years, became King George VI. At the prize-giving Woods remarked how proud he was to have won the first royal TT.

Many of the spectators stayed in the Cunningham Holiday Camp, close to the start–finish area and overlooking Douglas Bay. Accommodation was in bungalows or tents and the advertisement in *The Motor Cycle* claimed that it was 'select, sociable, comfortable, delightful and inexpensive'. The new dining room provided seating for 3000 'campers' and there was a free cinema show nightly before 'lights out'. The military note was reinforced by another telling line: 'Annually visited by thousands of young men' – members of the opposite sex were forbidden. What a very different world it was in 1932!

The superiority of the Norton team was such that on the Continent that year they took it in turns to win.

The first classic was the Dutch TT where Woods won the 350 cc race from Hunt, while Hunt took the 500 cc honours at 81.94 mph with a record lap at 84.41 mph. Woods finished a bike's length astern, and both had covered 365 miles in a single day.

Simpson joined them for the French Grand Prix, held on a short triangular circuit near Rheims in an area still scarred by war damage. The races were run concurrently and in the 500 cc over 224 miles Woods won at 79.40 mph with Hunt alongside, both credited with the same time. Simpson dominated the smaller class to win at 75.26 mph.

There was no German Grand Prix that year. The depression had hit so hard the German manufacturers would not support the event and the organisers cancelled it. So after the French the next Grand Prix was the Belgian and there Charlie Dodson, on a very fast JAP-powered Excelsior, battled hard with the Nortons of Woods and Hunt.

Dodson actually set a record lap at 81.49 mph before he got off-line at the flat-out, downhill curve at Burnenville, hit a bump and dislocated his shoulder while fighting to regain control. Hunt was eliminated by an equally unusual incident. Just a lap after Dodson had been forced to quit, Hunt pulled in to refuel. Unlike Woods he always pulled up his goggles while coming in to stop and as he accelerated away he took both hands off the 'bars to pull down his goggles, got into a wobble and crashed, breaking a collarbone. Woods went on to win at 77.66 mph.

LEFT **Guests assemble outside a Douglas boarding house in September 1932 to record a highly successful Manx Grand Prix. The machine on the right is the Norton on which Norman Gledhill (sitting behind main trophy) won the Senior. On his left is J. H. Carr who won the Junior riding the New Imperial pictured left.**

BELOW **Jimmie Simpson (Norton) leaps Ballig Bridge on his way to third place in the 1932 Senior TT.**

The full four-man team was at Spa and Simpson won the 350 cc race from Guthrie who, obeying team orders, slowed on the last lap to let his team-mate, who had lost time changing a plug, through to win at 72.94 mph. The team then split up. Hunt went home to nurse his injury while Guthrie travelled back to Scotland to dominate a major sand meeting at St Andrews – winning the 20-mile main event on a very fast beach course.

Only Woods went to Berne for the Swiss Grand Prix at the end of August, winning the 44-lap 350 cc race on the Saturday at 73.61 mph and the 500 cc event the following day at 76.44 mph with the record lap at 80.42 mph in the bag. Simpson went up to Saxtorp near Malmö for the Swedish Grand Prix where he had won the 500 cc class in both 1930 and 1931, but he was out of luck. His tank sprang a leak while leading and he ran out of petrol on the far side of the circuit.

After that Simpson dashed back for the Ulster which was held six days later, 3 September, over the Clady circuit, and there Nortons suffered a rare defeat. They dominated the 500 cc race, which Woods won at 85.15 mph with a fastest lap at 87.65 mph in a race slowed by rain. But things went wrong in the 350 cc class. First Guthrie's bike refused to start and he lost time changing a plug. Then, after a marvellous ride in which he actually broke the lap record at 84.25 mph despite rain, he took the lead only to crash. This left Davenport leading on the second works Norton, until water in the magneto eliminated him and let Tyrell Smith (Rudge) through to win.

It had been an incredible year for Bracebridge Street. Out of the 12 races Nortons contested at the six main classics, they won 11! But from Nortons' point of view the fact that Woods had won no less than eight while Simpson had scored twice, with Hunt gaining a single win, was not ideal. Mansell would have preferred the honours spread more equally so that the name Norton was the more prominent. Stanley Woods was achieving superstar status and stealing the limelight.

The racing year finished with Norman Gledhill (Norton) winning the Senior Manx Grand Prix from a short, tubby Londoner by the name of Harold Daniell (Norton) whose sight was so bad that he raced in thick pebble glasses. He had won a free entry to the Isle of Man races at a meeting at Syston and despite his ungainly appearance he was to figure prominently in the Norton story.

By now the International models were the top-selling sports roadsters and no less than 20 out of the 48 starters in the Senior Manx that year rode Internationals which could be ordered from the factory in full racing trim. About this time *The Motor Cycle* road tested the 'Inter': 'To make a getaway from rest through bottom gear and up to full throttle in second was to experience exhilaration in its highest form'.

CHAPTER 12

'Marvellous man! Marvellous mount! Marvellous organization!' 1933–1935

Nortons announced their range for 1933 in a double-page advertisement in *The Motor Cycle*. The heading proclaimed: 'The World's most successful motor-cycle offers YOU finest value for 1933.' The important news was the addition of two push-rod overhead-valve 350 cc sports roadsters – the Model 50 and the Model 55 which was identical except that it had a twin port head and twin exhaust systems.

The 50 cost only £53, little more than the dear old side-valve 490 cc 16H which was priced at a budget £49.75. The twin-port version cost £2 more. Bore and stroke were 71 × 88 mm, the same as the earlier push-rod 350 and the camshafts models. And a hand-change four-speed gearbox was standard, as it was on all except the side-valve 16H and Big Four models. Foot-change was extra.

Other modifications included new hubs, built-in pillion footrest lugs, racing forks with check springs on the International models (the price of which remained unchanged) and improved silencers on all models. Lights remained an optional extra but a new extra was a large tank-top instrument panel with speedometer, ammeter and switches.

One old favourite had disappeared. The 588 cc OHV engine had been replaced in the Model 19 by a 596 cc unit, the new engine having a bore and stroke of 82 × 113 mm as against the 79 × 120 mm engine first used in the Sidecar TT of 1923. The 596 cc capacity was not entirely new. Both Bill Lacey and sidecar exponent Kim Collett had successfully used enlarged camshaft engines of this capacity with the same 82 × 113 mm dimensions.

On the road-test front, *Motor Cycling* put a Model 18, the factory's best-selling OHV model, through its paces in January 1933 and the tester, bulkily clad in poncho and waders, recorded that 'the highest speed reached was exactly 80 mph . . . on a dead-level road, and neither helped nor hindered by wind'. Fuel consumption was 76 mpg and the Norton would cruise happily at 60 mph.

The basic price was £59.50 but the list of extras was formidable: magdyno lights £5.50, speedometer £2.50, instrument panel 50p, stop light 25p, three-gallon tank £1, petroflex fuel piping £1, air-cleaner 40p, pillion footrests 30p and central stand £1.

Early in 1933 a lot of talk centred on the ACU's decision to reintroduce the Sidecar TT after a lapse of eight years. The journalists of the day were in support and in April *Motor Cycling* commented: 'It is hoped that both Simpson and Woods will drive 600 cc Norton outfits and that Dennis Mansell will pilot a 350 cc combination.' But the Norton entries did not materialise and when only 10 entries were received the ACU had no option but to cancel the event.

The Norton team for the TT was the same as the preceding year: Woods, Hunt, Simpson and Guthrie. Woods and Hunt, the established stars, tried out the 1933 TT machines in the North West 200, with Woods winning the 500 cc and Hunt the 350 cc races.

Reporters at the meeting spotted that the cylinder heads were cast from a special alloy, but we are not told what this was. Almost certainly the heads used that year were made of an aluminium–bronze alloy – heavy but able to dissipate heat more readily than cast iron. Other improvements included a wider front brake drum and steel brake and clutch levers that replaced the fragile duralumin used in 1932. Woods went to Dublin to contest the Leinster and set the fastest lap at 81 mph before retiring with unspecified engine problems, and then the whole team met on the Isle of Man.

There the Bracebridge Street machines were truly 'unapproachable'. Woods set the pace by bettering the Senior lap record during practice with a lap at over 82 mph. 'How this beaming Irishman, always the picture of physical fitness, can ride! And how these world beating Nortons can motor!' commented one reporter.

In the Junior TT Woods led all the way but both Hunt and Simpson put in tremendous challenges. Hunt finished second, beaten by only 7 seconds after 264 miles of racing, but Simpson retired on the last lap with piston trouble. Guthrie was close behind and took over to complete the Norton 1–2–3. Summing up, *Motor Cycling* said: 'It was a titanic struggle but never was the Norton lead seriously in danger.'

Woods' speed was a record 78.08 mph and he also clocked the record lap at 79.22 mph. Nortons were eager for Simpson to win the Senior and he put in a great ride. At the end of lap one he trailed Woods by a single second but the Irishman was determined to complete the double for the second year in succession and, aided by his 'secret' signalling stations, he pressed relentlessly on, upping the lap record to 82.74 mph, to start the last lap over a minute ahead.

Then came an announcement over the loudspeaker

P. HUNT
3RD
SPEED 80·16 M.P.H

S. WOODS
WINNER OF THE 1933 SENIOR TOURIST TROPHY RACE, AT RECORD SPEED OF 81·04 M.P.H. RECORD LAP... 82·74 M.P.H

J.H. SIMPSON
2ND
SPEED 80·41 M.P.H

NORTON TEAM ALSO AWARDED MANUFACTURERS & CLUB TEAM PRIZES

ABOVE The winning Norton team after the 1933 Senior TT. – the riders are identified by the caption on the picture.

LEFT Formation riding at the French Grand Prix, Dieppe in 1933 with Stanley Woods leading Tim Hunt, who won the race.

system. Woods had stopped near Ramsey and Simpson, who had started ahead of Woods on the road and had already finished, was the winner! But a mistake had been made, Woods finished on schedule at a record 81.04 mph to beat Simpson by 1 minute 32 seconds with Hunt, who had lost time changing a plug at the start, third and Guthrie, hampered by a steering damper problem, fourth. The Norton clean sweep was complete and for the first time in the history of the TT a manufacturer had taken the first three places in both Junior and Senior races.

For Woods the TT had been a personal triumph. He had won four consecutive races and had set the record lap in three of them. As *Motor Cycling* succinctly said: 'Marvellous man! Marvellous mount! Marvellous organisation!' The specification of his winning Nortons in 1933 included four-speed Sturmey-Archer gearboxes, Amal carburettors, Lodge plugs, BTH magnetos, Pratts petrol-benzole, Castrol oil, Dunlop saddles and tyres, Norton forks and brakes, Ferodo brake linings and clutch plates, Renold chains and Nortons' own steering dampers.

Immediately after the TT Woods and Hunt went to Assen for the Dutch TT. Woods won the 350 cc race from Hunt in the morning, as agreed, but things went wrong for Hunt in the afternoon's 500 cc event. It was his turn to win and he started the last lap ahead of Woods, only to have his machine fail in the final few miles. This left the Irishman to win at 84.07 mph from Ragnar Sunnqvist on a works Husqvarna V-twin.

At the Swiss Grand Prix in Berne the following weekend the Norton domination continued. Hunt won the 350 cc from Woods and in the 500 cc race Woods won from Hunt, the Norton stars toying with the opposition. This domination continued at the French Grand Prix at Dieppe. There the races were run concurrently and while Hunt won the big class ahead of Woods, Simpson took the 350 cc honours by a length from Guthrie.

'Nothing in the 500 cc and 350 cc categories can beat this year's Nortons' commented *Motor Cycling*, adding: 'The winners are chosen not on the course, but

RIGHT Dennis Mansell in action on his camshaft Norton in the Streatham Trophy Trial in October 1934. Race mechanic Bill Mewis is in the sidecar.

LEFT Jack Williams, who took over from Graham Goodman as Norton's trials ace, with the camshaft Norton he used so successfully in 1933.

in the board-room of the manufacturer concerned.' The victory parade continued. At the Belgian Grand Prix Hunt won the 500 cc class from Woods by 1 second, Woods pushing up the lap record to 82.37 mph, while Guthrie took the 350 cc honours from Simpson. But behind the scenes those boardroom decisions about who would win caused a major problem when the team travelled over to Belfast for the Ulster Grand Prix. Stanley Woods takes up the story.

When Craig met me in Belfast he said, 'I've bad news for you – you're not to win. Hunt is to win.' I said, to hell with that. Mansell and I agreed in the spring that I was to have a free hand at the Ulster. Joe phoned Mansell and told him that I didn't agree.

Originally Mansell had not planned to attend the Ulster but when Woods came down to breakfast on the morning of the race there was the Norton boss in the dining room.

I said Hello and then went and had my breakfast with the riders – the staff did not mix with the bosses in those days! When I got up Mansell called me over and said that he'd heard I was being awkward. I said, What do you mean? and reminded him that we had agreed I was to win this race – my home grand prix – and as far as I was concerned that went. He replied that if I did this would be the last race that I would ride for Nortons.

Stanley was nonplussed. He finally decided to go as fast as he could in the early stages, break his own lap record, and then ease up and make it obvious that he was riding to orders. However, things did not work out as planned, neither for Woods nor Mansell. He shot ahead from the start then clipped the straw mattresses that covered the wall at Rectory Corner.

We used to use the pavement there to get the best line but I was going so fast that I grazed the sacking. I thought that I'd got away with it, gave the bike the gas, waved to the crowd and went to change into second – no gear lever! I looked down and saw that it had been bent back to the footrest. I threw out the anchors, slid the bike into the side of the road, jumped off and lay down so that I could force the lever back into place with my foot. Luckily it did not break and I was up and away before anyone caught me!

Hunt, however, did catch Woods and the two of them were neck and neck, sharing the fastest lap at 89.64 mph before Hunt was slowed by a broken steering damper. With Ernie Nott challenging on a Rudge, Hunt's bad luck meant that Woods was free to win with a clear conscience – which he did at a record 87.43 mph. Behind him Walter Rusk, called into the Norton team for the first time, finished a close second ahead of Nott and Hunt. 'When I came in for my pit-stop Joe said to me, "Keep it as you are, Tim's in trouble." So I won the race, but it had left a nasty taste in my mouth,' recalls Woods.

The Norton domination was broken in the 350 cc race. Things had looked good when Simpson took the lead from Guthrie but then Wal Handley on the latest Velocette got cracking and with a record lap at 85.91 mph he took the lead. 'For once the invincible Nortons were being fairly and squarely beaten,' reported *Motor Cycling*.

Simpson went out with magneto trouble leaving Guthrie to finish second and to receive a sympathetic pat on the back from *Motor Cycling*: '... poor Jim fought against hopeless odds magnificently; at the finish his hands were blistered in a horrible manner'.

From Ireland the team travelled to Scandinavia for the Swedish Grand Prix at Saxtorp which was also the

The 1933 Belgian Grand Prix, with Tim Hunt hot on the heels of Stanley Woods.

European Grand Prix. It was a tough nine-mile circuit, part of it dirt road, and it proved a disaster for Nortons and particularly for poor Tim Hunt.

He and Woods contested the 500 cc class and knew that the fast V-twin Husqvarnas would be hard to beat on home ground. One of the problems was that the Swedish machines would have to make only one pit-stop, while the Nortons made two. This meant that they had to go out and build up a lead – which they did. But when they came in to refuel for the first time Ragnar Sunnqvist (Husqvarna) got ahead. The Norton men caught the leader and the three of them were slipstreaming down the straight when a rider they were lapping suddenly and disastrously slowed.

Sunnqvist and Woods managed to miss him but Hunt, tucked flat on the tank, crashed into him. The rider was killed and Hunt received such severe injuries that he never raced again. Talking about the accident, he said: 'The last thing I remember was that Stanley suddenly veered to the right. I woke up in hospital two days later with concussion and a badly broken left

thigh.' After three months in Malmö hospital he was flown back to Croydon in a Swedish Airforce plane. Bill Mansell was there to meet him and he was taken by ambulance to Euston where he was put on a train to Manchester. He spent the next five years in and out of Bury Hospital.

After the crash Woods passed Sunnqvist and had built up a winning lead of over two minutes when his engine failed, something that hadn't happended in a major race for a long time. Sunnqvist retired with a broken chain and it was team-mate Gunnar Kalen who won. In the 350 cc class it was business as usual, with Simpson winning from Guthrie. From Sweden Guthrie and Craig flew down to Bilbao for the Spanish TT where the 350 cc was held on a circuit in the town on the Friday. The Scot, the only Norton rider there, won the race and the 500 cc on the Sunday.

Back home Harold Daniell headed a clean sweep for Nortons in the Senior Manx Grand Prix and although Austin Munks won the Junior on a Velocette, Norton riders, headed by Freddie Frith, took the next four places. On the rough stuff Nortons continued to impress, with two members of the six-man British Trophy team in the International Six Days Trial (held in Wales that year) riding Nortons.

The Norton range for 1934 was announced in late September. Four-speed hand-change gearboxes replaced the three-speeders as a standard fitting on all machines, with the TT-style positive-stop foot-change available as an extra (except on the International models where it was already standard). All models now had the Norton fork with race-developed rebound springs, and all were fitted with a very simple yet effective oil-bath primary chain-case designed by Edgar Franks together with a new clutch with built-in rubber shock absorber.

The aluminium–bronze heads had proved so successful that they were offered as an optional extra on the International models for £3.50 – about a week's wages for most workers in those days. All these models, together with a display of the trophies won, were on the Nortons' stand at Olympia that November, and it was at the Show that Stanley Woods finally split with Nortons.

The Vacuum Oil Company, whose brand name was Mobiloil, had approached him to see if he would ride for them in 1934 – which would mean racing the works Husqvarnas because they had the Swedish factory under contract. Woods had said he would – for a £2500 retainer. After some friendly haggling he agreed a fee of £1500 but left options open until the day the Show opened.

I went straight to Castrol who had Norton under contract and asked them how much they would pay me. Andy [the Castrol oil baron] said, 'You're fixed with Nortons.' I said, 'Never mind Nortons, it's Woods you're talking to. How much am I going to get?' He said, 'Don't be silly, you can't leave Nortons.' I asked, 'Is that your last word? Right-oh, it's been nice knowing you.' Then I went round to Nortons and told Mansell I was leaving. He wished me the best of luck. Mind you, he didn't think I had a hope in hell!

This meant that within three months Nortons had lost both Hunt and Woods, their two star riders – and Simpson was on the verge of quitting to join Shell as their racing manager, leaving only Guthrie as a certain starter. Within a few days Wal Handley was signed and later a deal whereby Simpson raced a works machine but used Shell oil was worked out – which must have hurt Castrol, who provided much of the finance needed to run the Norton racing set-up.

ABOVE LEFT **The 490 cc Norton on which Jimmy Guthrie broke the classic hour record at Montlhéry in October 1935 at a speed of 114.09 mph.**

LEFT **Jimmie Simpson in action in the 1934 Junior TT.**

RIGHT **Norton team in the 1934 Senior TT. Guthrie (left) won the race from Simpson (centre) with trials rider Vic Brittain (right) fifth.**

The Motor Cycle did a riding stunt with Wood's Senior TT-winning Norton in January 1934 when Arthur Bourne (Torrens) reported that: 'The honest to goodness speed is probably very little over 105 mph' and talked of a 0 to 60 mph time of 8.6 seconds. Earlier it had been reported that the 490 cc racing engine developed 34 bhp at 5500 rpm with a compression ratio of 7.1 to 1 – indicating that despite using half benzole the fuel had a modern-day octane rating of about 70.

Soon after this Nortons ran an advertisement with the slogan 'The manufacturer that put British motorcycle supremacy on the map and kept it there', superimposed on a map of the world. The Norton trials team of Vic Brittain, Jack Williams and Dennis Mansell continued to dominate and by April 1934 Nortons were seeking to take advantage of this by offering to supply any model to trials specification for just £5 over the normal list price. The spec included a frame with more ground clearance, narrower forks, a high-level exhaust system and trials tyres.

The 1934 Nortons had a first outing in the Leinster 200 in early May. Guthrie won the 350 cc race but although Handley was there and should have made his debut on the 500 he was a non-starter, which puzzled the *Motor Cycle* reporter. Guthrie then had a winning outing on the bigger bike at the North West 200 during which he pushed up the lap record to 82.16 mph. This time Handley did start and held second place until clutch trouble put him out.

Eventually the 1934 works Nortons were officially unveiled during TT practice – and they were substantially modified. The aluminium–bronze alloy head had been replaced by one with a bronze 'skull' on to which was cast an aluminium finned head with hairpin valve springs replacing the coil springs. Additionally there were twin plugs fired by a twin-spark BTH magneto. The second was positioned opposite the normal one and could be changed only when the cambox was removed.

The cylinder also had aluminium fins shrunk on to a cast-iron liner. The piston, too, was altered. Still made of Hiduminium, it now carried an oil-control ring in addition to two compression rings instead of the three compression rings previously used. Both petrol and oil tank were now fabricated from aluminium and were of the bolt-through type – secured by long studs which ran through tunnels welded into the tanks and insulated by rubber so that there was no metal-to-metal contact. These aluminium tanks were welded and

proved a great success, being both lighter and less prone to splitting than the soldered steel ones they replaced.

Husqvarna plans to mount a full-scale challenge headed by Woods in the Senior TT and Ernie Nott in the Junior were hard hit when the lorry carrying the machines slipped out of the rope slings as it was being craned aboard a ferry at Gothenberg. The canvas-top lorry turned over as it fell and the precious cargo of V-twins crashed on to the concrete quay. All the bikes were damaged and one engine completely wrecked. The team went back to the factory and worked day and night to build bikes for Woods and Nott to race.

By the time these arrived on the island, Guthrie was setting the pace. After serving his apprenticeship under the shadow of Woods, Hunt and Simpson he was determined to prove that he was now number one in the team. Writing about practice, the *Motor Cycle* reporter said of Guthrie:

> . . . as soon as he gets astride a motor bicycle he goes all crackers. This morning he gave a display of fireworks that rarely can have been equalled. His performance on Bray Hill was really frightening and how he held the model is a mystery . . . altogether his performance was a staggering one.

Guthrie won the Junior TT at the record speed of 79.16 mph with a record lap at 80.11 mph, but at the end he was only 9 seconds ahead of Simpson on a second Norton. Hopes of a 1–2–3 were dashed when Handley crashed at Governors' Bridge on the sixth lap and sustained a nose injury that put him out of the Senior TT.

Nortons had tried out small megaphone exhaust systems on the 500 cc during training and the machines raced by Guthrie and Simpson in the Friday race, run in rain and mist, sported 'loudspeakers'. Guthrie led from start to finish to score another Norton double – their fourth in five years – but Woods on a V-twin Husqvarna set the fastest lap at 80.49 mph and looked set to take second place until he ran out of fuel on the last lap. This let Simpson, suffering from cramp in his right hand, through to finish second.

That year the Dutch TT was the European Grand Prix, the equivalent of today's World Championships, and it started well for Nortons when Simpson won the 350 cc class at 81.79 mph. With Handley still out of action, Guthrie's team-mate for the 500 cc race was local hero Piet van Wijngaarden. Guthrie set the pace and looked to have the race won when he crashed.

While he was being stretchered round to the first-aid tent on a trailer towed by a motorcycle, the little Belgian Pol Demeuter crossed the line to win the 500 cc race and the European title. His mount was a beautifully engineered unit-construction single-cylinder FN. At hospital Guthrie was found to have a broken arm, and with the German Grand Prix at the Sachsenring the next weekend Nortons had to act fast.

Walter Rusk, who had ridden for them in the 1933 Ulster, was recruited and the factory fielded him in the 500 cc class and Simpson in the 350 cc. Simpson duly won the 50-lap, 270-mile event though Nott on the smaller Husqvarna was only 18 seconds behind at the flag, but things again went wrong in the 500 cc division. Rusk set off at a tremendous pace and was well ahead when he crashed after a few laps. Otto Ley on one of the new twin-cylinder, two-stroke DKW racers kept going to win at a speed fractionally faster than Simpson on the 350 cc Norton.

The following weekend it was business as usual at the Swiss Grand Prix at Berne. Simpson won the 350 cc, with Rusk third, on the Saturday and then on Sunday Simpson won the 500 cc class at 82.12 mph while Rusk set a new lap record at 87.31 mph before crashing – his second spill in the big class in consecutive grands prix. Stanley Woods, unlucky in the Isle of Man, was out of action at this time. He had come off the 500 cc Husqvarana at the Dutch TT and had damaged his left hand.

Handley was fit for the Belgian Grand Prix, a week after the Swiss, joining Simpson, while Joe Craig, never impressed by riders falling off his precious machines, ended the tie-up with Rusk who went back to racing factory Velocettes – a move Joe was to regret within a few weeks!

He almost regretted it straight away, for the blond Irishman set the lap record in the 350 cc Belgian at 83.96 mph (but could not catch Simpson who won at 82.03 mph). And it was just like old times when Nortons dominated the 500 cc class with Handley winning by a second from Charlie Dodson, who had replaced Rusk, at 84.08 mph.

Jimmie Simpson's career ended with a win when he took the 350 cc honours at the Ulster Grand Prix at a record 84.93 mph, but Guthrie came off his 500 while leading on the first lap and the dashing riding of Rusk

ABOVE Vic Brittain, cap reversed, with his 350 cc International Norton at a check in the 1935 International Six Days Trials.

LEFT The 1935 TT Norton engine with Norton (built by Burman) gearbox. Both head and barrel had light alloy fins and the crankcase was magnesium alloy.

on the big Velocette proved too much for Norton veterans Dodson and Handley. After stopping to change a plug Rusk upped the lap record to 92.13 mph to win by over a minute from Dodson, while Handley retired on the last lap.

Nortons did not go to Sweden in 1934 (where Sunnqvist on a Husqvarna won the 500 cc class from Rusk), but Guthrie took two works bikes down to Bilbao where the Spanish TT was run on a shorter two-mile circuit in early September. There the Scot won 350 cc and 500 cc races, beating Rusk (Velocettes) in both contests.

During the year Nortons had used megaphone exhaust systems in the majority of 500 cc races (though Guthrie reverted to the old-style set-up for the short Bilbao course where maximum acceleration out of slow corners was preferred to flat-out speed) and in some 350 cc events, including the Ulster. The 1934 megaphones were small, only 4 in in diameter at the 'mouth'.

Competitors for that year's Manx Grand Prix were able to use the recently opened Mersey Tunnel for the first time, and Crasher White came within a lap of competing a double on Nortons – living up to his nickname at close to 100 mph at Union Mills on the last lap of the Senior when well ahead. Freddie Frith (Norton) then took over, only to run out of petrol at Ramsey, and the win finally went to Doug Pirie on yet another Norton.

White had won the Junior MPG at a record 75.59 mph and set lap records in both races: 76.97 mph

ABOVE **A delighted Walter Rusk after winning the 350 cc class of the German Grand Prix at the Sachsenring in 1935.**

for the 350 cc and 81.74 mph – only 20 seconds outside the TT lap record. Although the factories had agreed not to support the Manx, his machines in both races were out-and-out works racers supplied by Nortons and tended by a factory mechanic.

A Cambridge graduate, John White, had been spotted by Norton talent scouts who had been impressed by his performances – notably his record lap on a Velocette in the 1933 Junior Manx at 75.64 mph. Speaking to me at his Oxfordshire home in 1990 he explained the set-up.

> Nortons offered to lend me TT machines for the 1934 Manx. It was of course contrary to all the agreements they had signed but that is what they were like – the ink wasn't dry before they started to break it. Mind you, they were not the only ones. In fact the 350 factory Norton was only slightly faster than my KTT Velocette. Well, I won the Junior Manx and was invited by Bill Mansell to join the team for 1935. At the time I was a biology master at Lydney Grammar School near Chepstow but luckily for me the headmaster agreed to me taking unpaid leave so that I could do the TT and then the classic races.

It was at this time that there was something of a crisis on the gearbox front. Sturmey-Archer of Nottingham, part of the Raleigh group, had supplied Nortons with gearboxes for 20 years but in 1934, when Raleigh stopped making motorcycles, they decided to quit. Nortons much preferred the S-A gearbox to the ones made by Burman and Albion, so the problem was neatly solved by Nortons obtaining the rights to the design, making some minor improvements and getting Burman to manufacture the gearboxes for them.

The Norton range for 1935 was announced in September 1934 and the big change concerned the gearboxes. All models would now be fitted with positive-stop four-speeders with foot-change – although buyers who preferred the older set-up could still be supplied with hand-change models to special order.

New tubular silencers of improved looks were adopted and from 1935 all machines with a single port would have the exhaust system on the right-hand side of the machine – until then the 18, 19 and ES2 had had the pipe on the left-hand side. The rubber-mounted handlebars, developed on the racers that year, were made a standard fitting and centre stands were fitted – though curiously the massive old rear stands were retained. And, as usual, improvements to the works racers were offered as optional extras on the two International models – in this case an aluminium finned bronze head with hairpin valve springs for £5.

Just before the Olympia Show Joe Craig and Jimmy Guthrie took a 490 cc racer, converted to run on alcohol, to Montlhéry. The obvious intention was to attack the classic one-hour record, for the machine was fitted with a massive seven-gallon tank. They claimed the 50 km and 50-mile records at 113.23 mph and 113.39 mph, but after that all was silence. The attempt was covered by 'Ambleside' of *The Motor Cycle* who flew over from Croydon to Paris. He wrote a two-page article but, as was so often the case in those days, said nothing at all about the bike and precious little about the records.

The big news early in 1935 was the introduction of the 30 mph speed limit in built-up areas. Since the repeal of the original Motor Car Act in 1930 there had been no speed limits at all, but a rise in road accidents forced the government into action. The 30 mph limit came into force on 18 March 1935. Later in the year, driving tests were introduced.

Nortons were still a dominant force in off-road sport. The Bemrose Trophy Trial of early 1935 was won by Vic Brittain on a 490 cc Norton while Dennis Mansell took the sidecar honours, and with Jack Williams doing well the Bracebridge Street trio won the team prize.

With Simpson retiring there was a complete reorganisation of the racing team. Guthrie was retained as the clear number one but veterans Handley and Dodson were replaced by a back-in-favour Walter Rusk and by MGP winner Crasher White. However, things went wrong for White when he made his works debut at the Leinster 200 in early May.

I got off on the wrong foot. Nortons didn't send the bike over in time for me to practise on it. Obviously I was keen to do well, tried too hard, fell off and damaged the bike. Joe Craig was pretty nasty about it. He said he thought they should have a more experienced rider and wanted to drop me for the TT. I pointed out that if they had sent the new

BELOW **Jimmy Guthrie in the 1935 Senior TT. Note the fully enclosed sohc rocker box.**

John Crasher White (right) with the winner's garland for the 350 cc class of the 1935 Belgian Grand Prix. Guthrie (left) won the 500 cc race with Rusk (centre) second, so the team had plenty to smile about.

500 over in time for practice I wouldn't have crashed. It wasn't a very promising start.

Nortons then signed a Scot, Johnny Duncan, and initially dropped White from their TT plans. The choice of Duncan now seems odd. He was experienced, having ridden for Raleigh, Cotton and New Imperial, but he had achieved no real successes. White protested and eventually Nortons agreed that he could ride in the Junior TT only, and even then not as a member of the team.

Both Guthrie and Rusk started the season well by winning the 500 cc and 350 cc classes of the North West 200, but when the factory Nortons arrived on the Isle of Man the *Motor Cycle* reporter commented enigmatically: 'There is no difference in the camshaft drive, and the rocker gear is completely enclosed.' At first sight that brief sentence suggests 'no change' – but wait a minute: 'rocker gear completely enclosed'. In all previous Nortons the rockers had been exposed. Did the reporter mean what he said? And if so, why did he not explain the layout of the new design and why it had not been adopted?

I can only assume that Nortons had asked the reporter not to say too much. For the change was a major one and was very obvious to anyone who looked under the tank. The old box with exposed rockers (retained for the International models until production ceased in the 1950s) had been replaced by an elongated rocker box that totally enclosed the rockers which now acted on the valve stems via short, solid tappets. This eliminated the 'wiping' movement of the rocker on the valve stem and also made for a much more oil-tight set-up.

Neither of the weeklies enlarged on this major change. In their technical follow-up article after the TT, *The Motor Cycle* reported, rather coyly: 'Two makers employed entirely enclosed rocker gear with short tappets between the rockers and valve stem.' But incredibly it does not say who the two were! No photograph appeared and the first drawing of the elongated rocker box was not published until May the following year.

Other changes for 1935 included increased finning on both the head and barrel, and the hairpin valve springs were of a modified type. Compression ratio of the 500 cc had been raised to 7.4 to 1 and that of the smaller engine to 7.75. Petrol-tank size had been increased to 4 gallons and the oil tank capacity increased to 7 pints.

The gearboxes were of the new type (built by Burman to the original Sturmey-Archer design but with Norton modifications) with fully enclosed positive-stop mechanism. This proved to be one of the best motorcycle gearboxes of all time and was retained, with minor changes, until the AMC box was adopted towards the end of the 1950s. Braking was improved with a wider, stiffer front drum with shrunk-on alloy cooling fins.

No records were broken in the Junior TT, which was run in poor weather. The race was another triumph for Nortons with Guthrie winning from Rusk with White in third place – well ahead of Duncan who crashed at Quarter Bridge but remounted to finish seventh to give Nortons the team prize. It was Norton's fifth Junior TT win in succession.

The Senior TT, postponed from Friday to Saturday because of appalling weather, was arguably the most sensational of all time. Guthrie, starting number one, shot ahead and led the race until the final mile. The Scot went into the last lap leading Stanley Woods on a V-twin works Guzzi by 26 seconds – a seemingly impossible margin for even the brilliant Irishman, who had hardly won a race the preceding year, to make up.

But Woods, ever a master tactician, still had two cards to play. First, he decided not to make a precautionary last-lap pit-stop (as Guthrie had done), gambling on there being enough fuel in the tank to get him home; second, he decided to use maximum revs of 7700 in all the gears and to over-rev in top gear.

'The bike was geared to do about 112 mph at 7700 rpm in top. I was pretty confident that I could go higher than that without blowing the engine because in practice I'd inadvertently revved her to 9000 in second gear and when they stripped her there was not a sign of any trouble,' Woods remembered. Having started 14½ minutes behind Guthrie (competitors started at 30-second intervals in those days) and with his signalling system working well, he knew exactly what he had to do.

Even so, he would not have won had Nortons not played into his hands by telling Guthrie, when he came into his pit at the start of the last lap, that the race was as good as won and that he could ease up. Imagine their faces when Woods streaked through to start his final lap without stopping! Despite this Woods still trailed Guthrie on corrected time at Ramsey – and when Guthrie crossed the line the BBC announced that he was the winner.

Over the Mountain Woods gave the Guzzi everything: 'We had rear springing that year and that had cured the handling problems – she was absolutely grand. Down the Mountain I just held her wide open and the revs went up to 8200 which works out to about 120 mph – it was win or bust!' And win he did – by just 4 seconds after 264 miles of racing at the record average speed of 84.68 mph – and on that last lap he pushed up the lap record to 86.53 mph. It completed a Guzzi double, for Woods had earlier won the 250 cc TT for the Italian company.

Consolation for Nortons was that they won the team prize with Guthrie, Rusk and Duncan finishing in the next three places. Within days Guthrie and Rusk were on their way to Berne for the Swiss Grand Prix. That year both races were on the Sunday – and both were dominated by the Norton duo with Rusk winning the 350 cc by a second from Guthrie while the Scot beat the Irishman by 4 seconds in the 500 cc class, both obviously riding to orders and covering a staggering 408 miles in a single day!

At this time a rumour was going around that the Norton racing engines were neither designed nor built at the grubby little factory in Bracebridge Street. Reacting furiously, Nortons ran a full-page advertisement under the heading 'Disclaimer' which read:

> Rumour is current that the Norton company are not responsible for the manufacture of the engines used in the machines entered in the Tourist Trophy races. The facts are that the design of every detail has been evolved by Norton staff; every Norton engine is made throughout in the Norton factory at Bracebridge Street . . . and with a factor of reliability that is unknown in any other make of machine.'

Six days after the Swiss the whole team were at the Dutch TT where White set the pace in the 350 cc race and looked to have the race won when the front fork spring broke, team-mate Rusk taking over to win. Guthrie won the 500 cc class at 86.37 mph to complete yet another Norton double.

From Holland the team travelled by the efficient European rail system to Chemnitz for the German Grand Prix at the Sachsenring. Commented the *Motor Cycle* reporter: 'Hands are constantly being raised in cheery Heil Hitler greetings – one no longer says Good Morning in Germany.' Only Guthrie and Rusk had made the trip and despite a strong German entry they scored the third double of the year for Nortons, Rusk taking the 350 cc honours at 74.06 mph and Guthrie the 500 cc at 78.79 mph.

A few days later the four-man team assembled for the Belgian Grand Prix and there Craig's instructions were that Duncan was to win the 350 cc class ahead of White while Guthrie should win the 500 cc race from Rusk. But in practice it became obvious that Duncan was not fast enough and eventually Joe realised this and gave White a free hand. He duly won the race at 81.64 mph and with a record lap of 84.82 mph, and from then on the relationship with Craig improved.

'I can't say we ever got on terribly well. He was mad keen on winning and got a bonus for every success. If you didn't win when you should have he got rather cross with you,' said White. Asked about Craig's mechanical ability, he replied: 'Joe was ignorant of any real mechanical knowledge but he was a genius at taking pains. He had no fundamental or theoretical training

1934–35 Gallery

The 1934 490 cc Model 20 with overhead-valve engine – identical to the Model 18 except for the twin port head and twin exhaust systems.

The 1934 348 cc Model 55 – the twin port version of the Model 50.

The 1934 348 cc Model 40 – the smaller of the two International models and a real thoroughbred.

The 1934 348 cc Model 55 with twin-ports and shown here with high level exhaust systems.

The 1934 633 cc side-valve Big Four – a favourite with the many sidecar enthusiasts.

The 348 cc camshaft Model CJ as it appeared in the 1935 catalogue. The price was £67.50.

The 490 cc overhead-valve Model 18 of 1935 was Norton's second best seller that year, beaten only by the cheaper 16H.

The 1935 Norton catalogue captures the spirit of the times. Nearly a quarter of all motorcycles in Britain had a sidecar attached.

but he did take an enormous amount of trouble to get things right.' Talking of the Norton people, White continued:

> The people I really disliked were the Mansells. Bill, who was the boss at the time, was a typical Birmingham businessman while his son Dennis, who also worked at Nortons though no one seemed to know exactly what he did, was a very boorish type. Gilbert Smith who I think looked after the financial side of things was a bit of a poor relation – he was not accepted by the Mansells.

This is contrary to the view taken by Stanley Woods who, despite his differences with Nortons, described Bill Mansell as 'a darling man' who had once helped him by lending him £1000 without security of any kind.

Guthrie won the 500 cc class in the Belgian at 88.12 mph with a record lap of 90.84 mph – a fourth double in succession – and with Rusk in second place Nortons were very much in control.

The Swedish was held in mid August that year. White had hoped to go but Nortons decided against it, preferring to concentrate on preparations for the Ulster Grand Prix. Woods travelled to Saxtorp, at his own expense he remembers, and won the 500 cc class for Husqvarna, his only major success for the Swedish factory.

In Ulster Guthrie rode an incredible race to win the 500 cc class. Rusk jumped into the lead from the start but then crashed, bringing down his team-mate who was unable to avoid the mêlée of man and machine. Rusk had damaged his wrist but Guthrie jumped up, kicked his machine as straight as possible, re-started and in spite of bent footrest, gear-change, handlebar and front wheel rim, set off in the pursuit of the leading group of Ted Mellors (FN), Stanley Woods (Guzzi) and Tyrell Smith who was racing a V-twin New Imperial.

Pushing the lap record up to 95.35 mph Guthrie passed all three to win at a record 90.98 mph, the first classic to be won at over the 90 mph mark. The pace proved too fast for the pursuing trio and all retired, with Rene Milhoux on a second works FN the eventual second-placed finisher. The run of Nortons doubles came to an end in the 350 cc race in which the Velocettes of Wal Handley and Ernie Thomas proved just too fast – Handley winning at 86.65 mph.

It was at the Ulster, that year the European Grand Prix, that *The Motor Cycle* first mentioned that the works Nortons were fitted with alloy rims. These had in fact been introduced for the TT but were fitted to the front wheels only, and were painted black. Steel rims were retained at the rear, probably because Joe Craig feared that the weaker alloy ones would not stand the hammering of the rigid framed machines on the rough roads of the day.

The Ulster was the last big race of 1935 but Guthrie went down to Bilbao in September to win the 350 cc and 500 cc races at the Spanish TT, held on an even shorter circuit of only 1½ miles that year. And in the Manx Grand Prix Nortons reigned supreme, Frith winning the Junior (in which Nortons took the first four places) and leading the Senior until clutch trouble dropped him to second place behind Jim Swanston – Nortons taking the first six places.

By the time the racing season ended Arthur Carroll, chief designer and the brilliant draughtsman who, together with Craig, was responsible for the incredibly successful camshaft Norton engine, was dead. He had been killed in a road accident while riding a 588 cc Norton and sidecar. 'As I understand it he had been gonged by the police and was trying to get away from them. It was completely against his character for he was a quiet, shy man,' said Woods. Many said that this would be the end of Craig – that Carroll was the man responsible for the Norton successes and now he was gone Joe would be 'found out'.

In October, just before the Olympia Show, Craig and Jimmy Guthrie went back to Montlhéry to complete the unfinished business of the preceding year – to break the classic hour record. The 490 cc Norton looked much the same as in 1934, sporting the seven-gallon tank and small megaphone but this time without the nose fairing.

Guthrie set off and put in a lap at 118.26 mph before a leaking tank slowed him. Despite fuel getting on to his goggles, he kept going to beat Bill Lacey's old Norton record of 110.80 mph with a new figure of 114.09 mph. Guthrie also took the intermediate records (50 km, 50 m, 100 km, 100 m) at over 114 mph and all five also beat the existing figures for the 750 cc and 1000 cc class.

Our old friend 'Ambleside' of *The Motor Cycle* was there again and wrote a lot about his own adventures, but told us precious little about the machine. However, you will be pleased to hear that on the return Imperial Airways flight from Paris to London he was served hot roast duck,' the first occasion on which a hot meal had been served on the Paris route'. The date was 22 October 1935. What 'Ambleside' could have told us was that the Norton was running on alcohol with a compression ratio of 13 to 1 and to cope with this a one-off stronger connecting rod had been fitted (details revealed by Craig in a wartime article that appeared in *Motor Cycling*).

The bike was then rushed to the Norton stand at Olympia where the 1936 range was on display. *The Motor Cycle*, in its Norton write-up, commented: 'No radical changes in a well-proven range'. Appearance had been improved by the adoption of larger petrol tanks (now $2\frac{3}{4}$ gallons) and buyers of the International models could get an alloy finned barrel as well as head, but otherwise there was little change.

Thanks to the work put in by Norton enthusiast Peter Roydhouse, a successful trial competitor on Nortons in the 1950s and 1960s, we have accurate production figures for the year from October 1934 to October 1935 – the figures running from October to October because everything centred around the Olympia Show held annually in November. The top-selling model that year was the 490 cc side-valve 16H, of which 823 were built. Second came the 490 cc push-rod 18 with 741, followed by the 350 cc OHV Model 50 (574), the cradle-frame 490 cc OHV ES2(568), the 596 cc OHV Model 19 (271), the twin-port 490 cc OHV Model 20 (226), the 633 cc side-valve Big Four (215), the twin-port 350 cc Model 55 (191), the 490 cc International Model 30 (172), the 490 cc overhead-camshaft CS1 (94), the 348 cc International Model 40 (83), the 348 cc overhead-camshaft CJ (32) and the built-to-order 596 cc overhead-camshaft of which seven were produced.

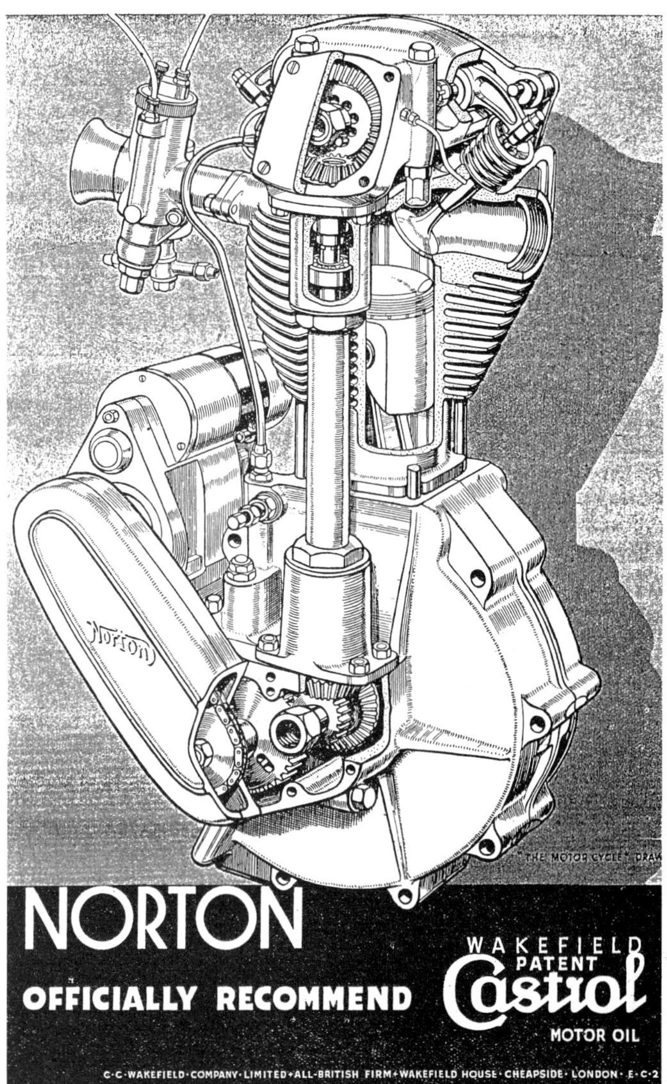

Castrol provided most of the money that financed Norton racing – so it made sense to use a drawing of the ohc engine in this 1936 advertisement.

This totals 3997 for the year – and to put this into perspective it is half the number Yamaha were building in a single day in 1980 and a third of the Honda production. How Nortons managed to sustain a highly successful racing programme on such a meagre financial base is a mystery. If each machine sold made a profit of £10 (which is doubtful given the cut-throat nature of the competition) this gives a profit for the year of just under £40,000 which, after paying a dividend to the shareholders, leaves precious little for the development of future models, improvements to the factory and racing.

In fact the racing was largely self-sufficient. Castrol put in a lump sum and also paid the riders their annual retainers of a few hundred pounds. Nortons paid their travelling and hotel expenses and they split the prize money between them, taking it in turns to win. Crasher White reckoned to make between £400 and £500 a year.

> We looked upon it as a paying sport. We didn't do it for the money. Nortons in fact were a thoroughly mean lot but you must remember that £500 was a lot of money in those days – it was the annual salary for a well-paid job.

CHAPTER 13

Jimmy Guthrie 1936–1937

Early in 1936 Nortons were awarded their first contract to supply the British armed forces with motorcycles. Unhappy with the performance of the 500 cc BSA machines, powered by a heavy V-twin engine, that were 'army issue' in the early 1930s, several leading manufacturers had been asked to submit machines for evaluation tests. Historian Peter Roydhouse takes up the story.

Norton responded by constructing, during May 1935, a 16H to quasi trials specification. Features included increased ground clearance, sports tyres, carrier, speedo and electric horn. The Army report of December 1935 said that the Norton proved to be the most outstanding machine.

After minor changes, the first contract for 300 bikes was placed in February. Further contracts followed and by the end of the year 900 of the military models, finished in khaki green, had been delivered – lifting 16H production to 1916 to put it well ahead in the model 'league' followed by the Model 18 (901), the 350 cc Model 50 (853) and the ES2 (736), with total production for 1936 rising to 5728, some 40 per cent up on the preceding year.

In February *Motor Cycling* road tested the 490 cc OHV Model 18 and commented: 'It looks what it is, a robust and powerful go-anywhere mount.' Speaking of performance, the tester said: 'On several occasions 80 mph was reached with a fully clad rider sitting up in a normal riding position.' He went on to give maximum speeds in the gears, with revs in brackets, as 68 mph in third (4700) and 52 in second (4840).

Fuel consumption worked out at 73 mph overall and 78 mph on long runs, which would be good by 1990 standards, but oil consumption was very heavy at 200 mile per pint. Incidentally, Nortons advised changing the oil every 2000 miles – there were no detergent additives in those days.

Despite the fact that 'Torrens' (Arthur Bourne) of *The Motor Cycle* had been to Scotland to interview Jimmy Guthrie only a few months earlier, 'Cyclops' (Harvey Pascal) of *Motor Cycling* went to Hawick in March 1936 to do the same job – and did it rather better. Like 'Torrens' he tells us that Guthrie was a partner with his brother Archie in a motor-repair business and that he was a technically minded man who worked long hours at lathe or bench, but he also told us that the Norton superstar was married and had a daughter of two. 'Torrens' seldom mentioned women – perhaps because they clashed with his Olympian view of motor-cycling.

While at Hawick 'Cyclops' got Guthrie to write an article about the future of racing in which he made two prophecies which showed the way Nortons were thinking at that time. First, he said: 'I am of the opinion that the majority of racing machines will continue to be powered by single-cylinder engines for some time to come'; secondly: 'Blowers will, I think, be conspicuous by their absence. Supercharged singles may be made to go faster, but they are not so reliable as a rule.'

The very next month the overhead-camshaft, supercharged, 500 cc flat-twin BMW works machines put on an impressive display at the Eilenriede races at Hanover. They were ridden by Karl Gall and Otto Ley and were rumoured to have a top speed of 125 mph – which was probably fairly accurate.

The Norton team for 1936 was Guthrie and White plus Frith. Duncan had been quietly dropped and Rusk was still handicapped by his arm injury. The first task for Frith was to assist White with the testing of a new frame with rear springing at Brooklands. They used a 490 cc racing engine running on alcohol which had a top speed of 110 mph, swopping the same engine from a standard rigid frame to the new 'springer' so that direct comparisons could be made.

The rear suspension was of a simple plunger design. The rear axle slotted into carriers which slid up and down in tubes with the movement controlled by springs. At first there was talk of Nortons having two types – one incorporating hydraulic damping. If this is true, it was soon abandoned in favour of a layout in which both suspension and rebound were taken care of by springs.

Crasher White was impressed: 'It certainly made for a more comfortable ride and improved the road holding.' Stanley Woods, by that time riding for the rival Velocette factory, was not: 'Why Joe Craig went to plungers I'll never know. The Guzzi on which I won the Senior in 1935 had a good swinging fork rear suspension and Velocettes came out with a swinging fork in 1936 the same time as Norton. To my mind the Nortons with plungers never handled very well.'

The first hint of the spring-frame Norton to appear in print was in TT Notes and News in *Motor Cycling*:

'The third manufacturer who, it is rumoured, had been building spring frames is "Mr Norton" – at any rate, a Norton fitted with a spring frame was seen at Brooklands a little while ago. After several fast laps the model was whisked off to Bracebridge Street.'

The very next week all was revealed. In 1936 the Swiss Grand Prix was held t Berne early in the year – on 3 May. *Motor Cycling* sent a reporter and the headline ran 'Jimmy Guthrie wins 500 and 350 cc Classes on Spring Frame Nortons!' Part of the report read: '. . . with a brand new spring-frame 499 cc Norton – mark well the engine size – matched against Stanley Woods on the new spring-frame Velocette. . . .'

To wring the last ounce of power out of the bigger engine the capacity had been enlarged from 490 to 499 cc by increasing the bore size from 79 to 79.7 mm. Unbeknown to the reporter, the smaller engine had received far more radical treatment, for instead of the 71 × 88 mm bore and stroke used since the first 350 cc Norton appeared in 1928, the 1936 racing engine had dimensions of 73.4 × 82.5 mm, 349 cc. The heads and barrels of both engines had increased finning and the size of the front brakes had been increased from 7 to 8 inches and they were fitted with deeper cooling fins.

RIGHT Jimmy Guthrie, motorcycle racing superstar of the mid-thirties, leader of the Norton team and 500 cc European Champion in 1935, 1936 and 1937.

BELOW A 1936 factory machine with the rear springing used for the first time. It ran in the Swiss Grand Prix where Jimmy Guthrie scored a 350 cc/500 cc double.

LEFT Close up of the Norton plunger rear suspension. Note the black-painted alloy rear rim and the Bowden carburettor, used only during the 1936 season.

RIGHT Jimmy Guthrie after winning the 500 cc class of the German Grand Prix at the Sachsenring in July 1936. Hermann Muller (centre) finished second on a DKW with Crasher White (right) third.

BELOW Freddie Frith hard at work at 100 mph during the 1936 Senior TT.

Guthrie had a busy day at the Swiss Grand Prix. First he led the 350 cc race, which started at 8 a.m., all the way, averaging over 80 mph for the 30-lap, 136-mile race. Then in the afternoon he completed another 30 laps to win the 500 cc race with a record lap at 91.7 mph. Among his rivals was Otto Ley on a supercharged BMW flat-twin racer, making a first appearance in a major race, and it was Ley who finished second.

After the Swiss Guthrie made his way to Ulster for the North West 200 where he joined team-mates Frith and White. In Ireland they proved unbeatable with Guthrie winning the 500 cc and White the 350 cc. But practising for the TT opened with a shock when Guthrie crashed, badly damaging the bike he was riding and putting himself into hospital. Fortunately nothing was broken and he was discharged after a short stay with a very stiff neck.

Despite this mishap Guthrie shot away at the start of the 1936 Junior TT with 'newboy' Frith, riding in his first major event as a member of the Norton team, in pursuit. After four laps Frith was only 33 seconds astern when the rear chain of Guthrie's machine jumped the sprockets at Hillberry. The Scot pulled in, replaced the chain and set off again.

A rumour spread that Guthrie had been helped by a marshal to re-start his machine – strictly forbidden by the rules. He was black-flagged at Ramsey and the *Motor Cycling* reporter was agog: 'Then came the most startling announcement that has ever been made to a crowd gathered to watch a TT race. Jim Guthrie, that beloved, clever, hard-headed Scotsman, had, or so they said, earned disqualification for a breach of the rules.'

Norton boss Bill Mansell was outraged and immediately protested. He said that the marshal had helped Guthrie to re-start but that this had happened off the course – from a point on the back road to Onchan to which Guthrie had pulled in when he realised his chain was off. This meant that when he rejoined the race the engine was running and he had not received 'outside assistance' while on the course. After a meeting of the stewards Guthrie, who had completed the course after

A spread of pictures of the Norton factory, taken from the 1936 catalogue. Clockwise from the top they show clutch sprockets being machined, a grinder at work on a cylinder head, gudgeon pins being examined, a multi-spindle drilling machine in the aluminium casting shop, a bay in the drilling section and part of the machine shop.

being stopped, was credited with fifth place – which gave Nortons the team prize – and was paid as though he had finished second.

The winner was Frith at a record average of 80.14 mph and with a record lap at 81.94 mph. Crasher White came through to snatch second place by passing Ted Mellors (Velocette) on the very last lap to pip him

by just 9 seconds for the runner-up spot. 'Cyclops' of *Motor Cycling* rode the winning Norton: 'The Norton spring frame smoothes the bumps and ruts out like magic – there were no jars to the spine, I seemed to float along rather than ride.'

The Senior was another Guthrie versus Woods duel. For 1936 Stanley had switched from Guzzi to the new Velocette with swinging-fork rear oleo-pneumatic suspension. It turned out to be another titanic struggle but this time Guthrie held on to win at a record 85.80 mph, beating Woods by just 18 seconds – the Irishman setting a new lap record at 86.98 mph. Frith and White came home third and fourth to give Nortons the team prize.

In the technical follow-up article in *Motor Cycling* it was noted that the Nortons were fitted with Bowden carburettors (in place of Amal) and that these had flexibly mounted float chambers. The writer also commented on the 'extended rocker boxes containing short thrust tappets to relieve the valve stems of side thrust'.

The next big race was the German Grand Prix at the Sachsenring on 5 July which was also the European Grand Prix. Frith won the 350 cc race at 73.25 mph with ease and Guthrie took the 500 cc honours. H.-P. Müller on a two-stroke twin DKW was only 34 seconds astern – and hard pressed by White who made a heroic effort to pass the German on the last corner, went up the slip road but scrambled round to finish third. This was the same Müller who raced Auto-Union cars and won the 250 cc World Championship on an NSU in 1955.

To ram home the importance of this double, Nortons ran the following advertisement: 'All that stood between Great Britain and defeat in both the Senior and Junior classes of the Grand Prix de l'Europe [German GP] was "The Roadholder". GP de l'Europe won for the fifth time in succession.'

Six days later the Norton boys did it again, at the Dutch TT. In the morning White and Frith played follow my leader to finish first and second in the 350 cc race and then in the afternoon, Guthrie beat Ley (BMW) to win the 500 cc class with Ginger Wood, having a one-off ride on a works Norton, in third place.

Two weeks later at the Belgian Grand Prix the Norton victory parade was interrupted. That year (1936) the race was held on the narrow, bumpy Floreffe circuit near Namur and Frith, the lone Norton in the 350 cc class, steamed away into a winning lead only to crash when his rear tyre punctured. This let Ted Mellors (Velocette) through to win. In the poorly supported 500 cc class it was very much business as usual, with Guthrie winning from White.

It was at this time that the Minister of Transport, Hore-Belisha (of Belisha beacon fame), made, to quote *Motor Cycling*, 'an astounding speedometer proposal'. The editorial continued: 'Our minister of Transport has really surpassed himself. Draft regulations that he has just issued propose that all motor vehicles, including motorcycles, should be required by law to be fitted with speedometers!'

From the wording and the exclamation mark it is clear that this was considered absurd. The editorial went on to point out the hardships this would lead to as the hard-up workers were forced to spend £2 on

Extras available as follows :—

	£	s.	d.
Special Tuning	5	0	0
Aluminium Alloy Cylinder Head and Barrel ...	5	0	0
Dull-plated Petrol Tank, with quick lift filler cap. (Capacity approx. 4¼ gallons in the case of the 490 c.c. model, approx. 3¾ gallons in the case of 348 c.c. model) ...	3	10	0
Large Dull-plated Oil Tank, with quick-lift filler cap		10	0
Straight-through Exhaust Pipe and Muffler, with lock nut (as spare) ...	1	15	0
Racing Tyres		8	0
Long type Clutch Lever		3	6
Chin Pad		5	0
Central Oil Feed to Rocker Box		15	0

Short Front Mudguard ... ...
Clip-up Rear Stand ... ...
B.T.H. Magneto ... ...
Open Front Chainguard ...
Racing Gearbox (no kick-starter) ... ...
Racing Pattern (3-plate) Clutch ... ...
T.T. Needle Carburetter ...

NO EXTRA CHARGE IS MADE FOR THESE ITEMS

(See page 27 for complete specification). Owing to the considerable demand for a machine for use under actual racing conditions, these details are provided as the recommended specification.

Page Thirty-three

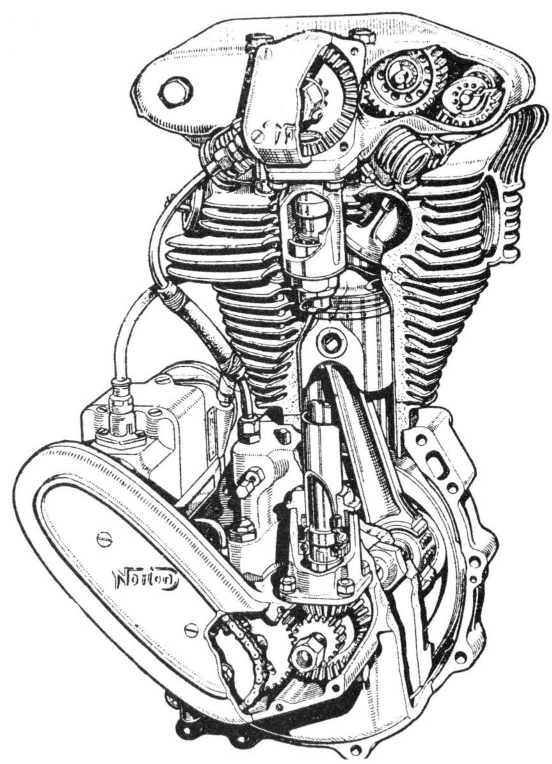

LEFT In pre-war days, racing machines were catalogued as the International to Racing Specification. Listed on the right are the extras offered in 1937.

RIGHT The factory engines for 1937 were fitted with the double overhead camshaft valve gear shown here.

BELOW LEFT Jimmy Guthrie winning the 500 cc Belgian Grand Prix in 1936. That year the race was held at Floreffe.

BELOW Jimmy Guthrie receives congratulations on winning the 1936 Senior TT.

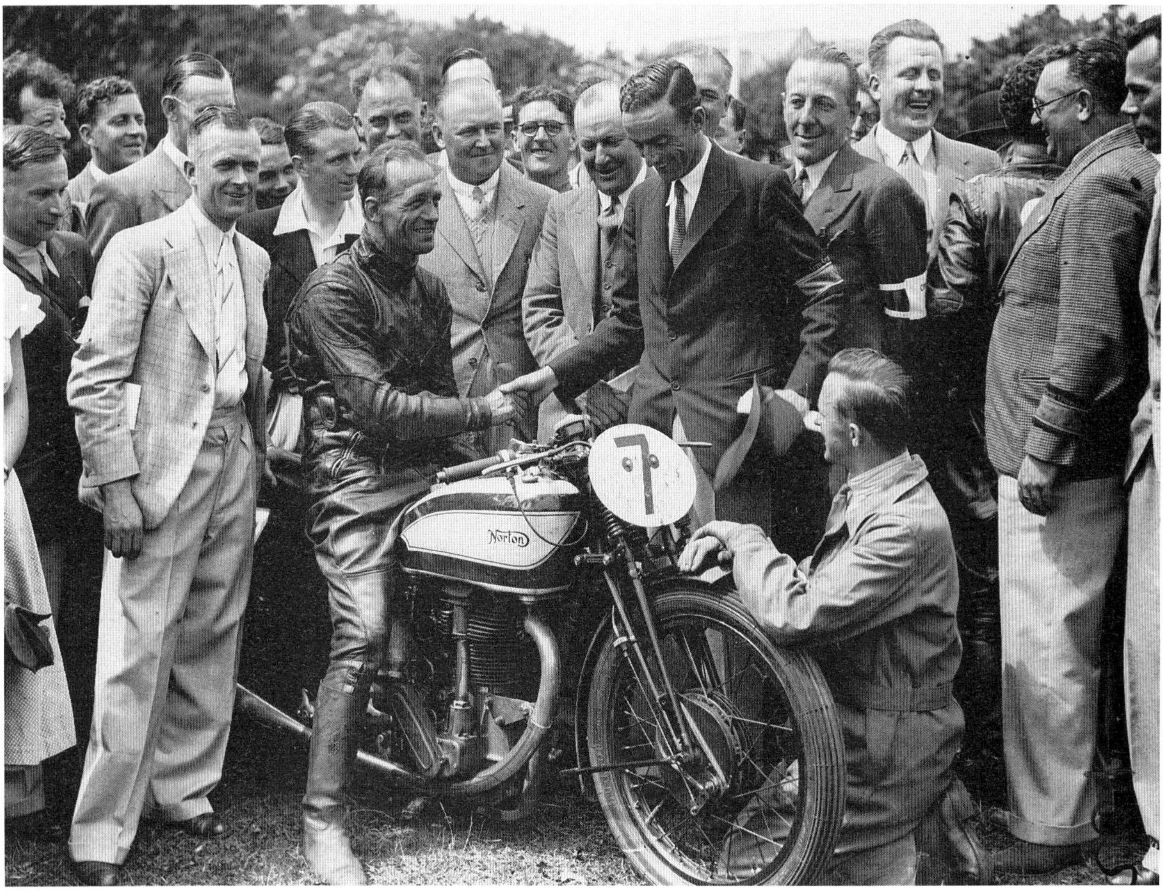

equipping their machines. At first the objections seem petty, but it then makes you realise what a a very different world it was in the mid 1930s. The wage for the 'man in the street' was around £5 a week, there was mass unemployment and many lived in grinding poverty.

Nortons gave the French Grand Prix a miss (Sunnqvist won the 500 cc for Husqvarna, Mellors the 350 cc for Velocette) to concentrate on the Ulster. Rusk was still not fit and his 350 cc entry was taken by Harold Daniell. It proved an unhappy works debut for the stocky Londoner for he retired on the first lap leaving White to battle it out with Mellors – the pair of them dead-heating at the end of the opening lap. White upped the lap record to 92.13 mph but then crashed, while Mellors was forced to stop to replace a chain, letting Ernie Thomas (Velocette) through to win.

In the 500 cc class, run concurrently, Guthrie made a slow start and then retired with engine trouble, but by this time Frith was just about as fast as the Norton 'captain' and he took over to win at a record 92.00 mph and with a record lap at 95.23 mph – indicating that the true top speed of the big Norton at that time must have been around the 115 mph mark.

The last big race of the season was the Swedish Grand Prix at Saxtorp, and there Nortons got a good hiding. In practice Guthrie and Ley (BMW) shared the fastest lap but in the race the supercharged flat-twin BMWs ran faultlessly and Ley romped away to win from team-mate Gall with Guthrie a well-beaten third, while White, in fourth place, was actually lapped. Ley's speed was 91.79 mph and he upped the lap record to 93.70 mph.

Frith had won the 350 cc, beating Mellors (Velocette), but it was clear to Craig that he would have to do a lot of work during the winter if the 500 was to remain competitive. Nevertheless, we should not lose sight of the fact that at the seven classic events they went to in 1936 Nortons won six of the 500 cc races and five of the 350 cc, only Velocette with two successes and BMW with one getting in on the act. And when it comes to individual honours, Guthrie had won five 500 cc races and one 350 cc and remained the undisputed champion.

The racing year ended with Norton riders, led by Austin Munks, dominating the Senior Manx Grand Prix and taking the first six places – though earlier in the week Munks had taken the Junior on a Velocette. In trials Nortons continued to do well, with Vic Brittain on a camshaft model a member of the winning three-man British team in the International Six Days Trial (held in Germany) and late in the year winning the British Experts Trial, an event in which he had been four times runner-up.

Just before the Show, the last one to be held at Olympia, Craig and Guthrie went to Montlhéry for their annual record outing. This time they took a 350 as well as 500 and Guthrie broke four 350 cc records, including the hour at 107.43 mph, and looked set to push his own 500 cc figure over 117 mph until he ran out of fuel with just a few minutes to go. The reason for the unexpectedly high fuel consumption was traced to a punctured float, and Nortons had the consolation of three records – the 50 km, 50 m and 100 km all at over 117 mph. Certainly the big Norton, on alcohol, was capable of over 120 mph.

The Norton roadster range for 1937 was practically unaltered. All the overhead-valve machines were fitted with 14 mm plugs and if you ordered your bike with the still 'optional extra' Lucas lighting set it now came with automatic voltage control. Prices of all models, except the camshaft machines, had been increased by £1.50 and although the spring frame had proved successful and had been used throughout the season by the racing team it was not offered as an optional extra.

Throughout the winter Craig worked on the engines and in particular perfecting the double-overhead-camshaft system which had been tested, but not raced, at the 1936 TT. There were rumours, but the first hard news came in May 1937 when *The Motor Cycle* reported: 'The TT Norton has a new cylinder head and two camshafts are now employed' – but nothing more! The next week there was another maddeningly brief mention: 'The massive overhead camshaft casing contains two camshafts instead of the usual one.' Full stop.

At last, in the 3 June issue of 1937, the first photograph of the double-overhead-camshaft engine appeared plus a description: 'A train of gears is used to drive the camshafts, which, together with the gears are housed in a cast aluminium box . . . short hollow push-rods project into the box and while one end bears against the cam the other bears on the valve stem . . . the springs and valves are exposed.'

In other words, the new set-up was a logical development of the single camshaft, with the rockers concealed within an elongated rocker box that had been introduced in 1935. The short push-rods (tappets) were retained but were now hollow and of larger diameter, but the rockers were replaced by a train of five gears – a design retained until the demise of the Manx Norton in the 1960s.

The finning of both the cylinder heads and barrels had been increased and the heads now had a distinctly square look. The improved cooling allowed the use of higher compression ratios – 8 to 1 for the 499 cc and 8.4 for the 349 cc. Bore and stroke of both engines was unchanged, which was a surprise, for the radically altered 349 cc unit had proved outstandingly successful and many thought that Craig would follow the same path with the bigger unit – a move which would allow bigger valves and higher revs.

One very noticeable innovation was that the Nortons

ABOVE LEFT Berne, 1937: Jimmy Guthrie (left) and Freddie Frith prepare their factory Nortons for the 350 cc race. Guthrie won the race from Frith and they went on to score a second 1-2 in the 500 cc class.

RIGHT Freddie Frith (left) swoops around Jack Williams (Norton) at the Ramsey Hairpin during his winning ride in the 1937 Senior TT.

ABOVE Jimmy Guthrie leads the supercharged BMWs of Karl Gall and Otto Ley in the 500 cc 1937 Dutch TT, – but Gall went on to win the race.

were at last fitted with rev-counters. Even so, Bill Mansell was dismissive and said he doubted that they would be kept on for the actual TT races. He was wrong. They were used and Nortons began TT week well by completey dominating the 350 cc Junior TT. Guthrie won at 84.43 mph – over 4 mph faster than the old record and quicker even than the old lap record. Guthrie and Frith, who finished second, shared the lap record at 85.18 mph. White was third to make it a clean sweep.

After the race it was noted that the Bowden carburettors of 1936 had been replaced by Amals, and while Guthrie had used a Lucas magneto both Frith and White stuck to BTH. Curiously *The Motor Cycle* headlined their report 'Spring-frame Nortons Score a 1, 2, 3 Victory', ignoring the fact that a spring-frame Norton had won the Junior the preceding year and failing to point out that the radical change from 1936 was the adoption of double overhead chamshafts.

The first ever 90 mph lap was achieved in the 1937 Senior TT – but not by Guthrie or Woods (Velocette) who disputed the lead in the early stages. Just as in 1935 and 1936 it was Guthrie who set the pace, with Woods in pursuit. But the Norton eventually failed on the Mountain climb – the engine still running but all compression gone.

Craig then gave Frith the 'flat-out' signal. The Grimsby rider caught Woods and the two of them started the last lap dead level. Shattering the lap record with a round at 90.27 mph, Frith took the lead to win at the record average of 88.21 mph. Despite a spill on the sixth lap White came third, with Norton's trials expert Jack Williams tenth on a 350 cc Norton.

There were stories that he raced an experimental machine with a single-overhead-camshaft engine with rockers and coil springs – all totally enclosed by an aluminium rocker box that bolted flush to a modified cylinder head. This had been designed by Edgar Franks and William later confirmed that he tried it during practising but did not race it because the valve springs kept breaking. Said *The Motor Cycle*: 'It is a development of the Norton Manx Grand Prix type and is something in the nature of an experiment.'

The use of the word Manx is interesting. Charlie Edwards, who started at Nortons as a boy in 1933 and later worked in the racing department under Craig, tells me the racing machines built for sale in the 1930s were called Manx models by the people at the factory, though catalogued as the 'International to racing specification'. The name was coined because the majority of the early race-prepared 'Inters' were built for the Manx Grand Prix and were labelled 'Manx' to differentiate them from the standard roadster Internationals being built at the same time. The name Manx was not used in the Norton catalogue until after the Second World War.

Charlie Edwards still has vivid memories of the factory at Bracebridge Street on race days.

They used to put a radio on the shop floor and we all gathered round. The firm supplied lemonade and if we won they gave us the rest of the day off. There was a great atmosphere at Nortons in those days. Many of the workers had been there for years – it was like a family; a happy family at that because we were better paid than most.

The fact that Nortons used four different rocker boxes within a short space of time has naturally led to some confusion but the sequence, upon investigation, is clear. In 1934 the works machines used the International type with exposed rockers. For 1935 these were replaced by the elongated box which completely enclosed the rockers which operated the valves through short, small-diameter solid tappets. These were used again in 1936 but were replaced for the 1937 season by the double-overhead-camshaft design in which gears replaced the rockers with the cams bearing on larger-diameter hollow tappets. Additionally the factory tried the Edgar Franks single camshaft layout with coil springs and total enclosure in 1937.

The existence of the elongated rocker box seems to have escaped the notice of some who have written about Nortons, and one article that appeared in *Motorcycle Sport* suggested that it was a lash-up to which Nortons reverted when the first of their DOHC designs did not work. What actually happened was that Craig was keen to replace the enclosed single-camshaft set-up with a double-overhead-camshaft layout for the 1936 season but the prototype boxes (which differed from the 1937 version by retaining the small diameter solid tappets) were ready only just before the TT. Craig, a great believer in 'making haste slowly', decided to stick with the proven single-camshaft layout for 1936 rather than gamble on the relatively untried new design.

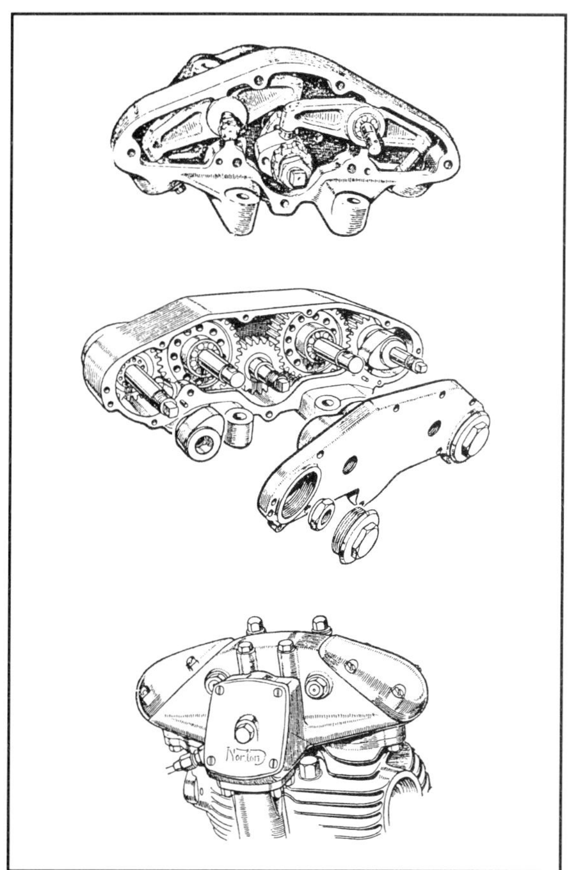

TOP **The single overhead camshaft layout with enclosed rockers used on the works machines in 1935 and 1936.** MIDDLE **The double overhead camshaft adopted in 1937.** BOTTOM **The experimental fully enclosed, coil spring design tried at the 1937 TT.**

This in turn led, in later years when memories were becoming confused, to stories that the works Nortons used a single-camshaft layout when they were said to have double-overhead-camshaft engines. If any confusion arises, the year was 1936, and Craig himself makes this clear in an article entitled 'Development and the Time Factor' which he wrote for *Motor Cycling* in October 1943.

In this he confirms that double-overhead-camshaft engines were taken to the island in 1936 but that Guthrie and Frith reverted to single-overhead-camshaft engines to win the Senior and Junior respectively. Says Craig:

A double overhead camshaft was accordingly designed and made to replace the existing gear, but due to the late start and the amount of work and time necessary to produce a rather complicated sub-assembly of this nature the engine did not reach the brake-testing stage until the practising period for the 1936 TT races was looming unpleasantly close. . . .

As explained, the new engine was not raced that year but the new valve gear was steadily developed and larger-diameter hollow tappets adopted. Craig continued:

As a result the engines which came to the starting line in the latter year [1937], instead of being practically unknown quantities, especially as regards the valve gear, as they would certainly have been the previous year, proved to be as reliable as their predecessors and considerably faster . . . the real benefit derived from the double overhead camshaft was much more marked on the 500 cc engine than on the 350 cc power unit, although the latter ran at appreciably higher rpm.

Crasher White remembers that the 350 cc revved to 7000 and the bigger engine to 6200 or 6500 when pressed. And he has fond memories of those days: 'When Frith came into the team it was a very happy set-up. We got on well and used to travel together'.

The next race was the Dutch TT and there Crasher again won the 350 cc race, pushing up the lap record to 91.20 mph to finish less than a second ahead of Frith. For the 500 cc class Nortons had 'called up' Harold Daniell who had ridden his own Nortons, tuned by

brother-in-law Steve Lancefield, in the TT, finishing fifth in both races. But Harold missed the boat from Harwich and eventually arrived in time to do only seven practice laps. It seems strange that Nortons gave the second 500 to him – Frith was the more logical choice to partner Guthrie in the hotly contested 500 cc class which would have left Daniell free to ride in the 350 cc where the Nortons were markedly superior.

The long straights of the old 10-mile Dutch TT circuit suited the supercharged BMWs of Gall and Ley, and in an attempt to keep the Norton engines cool Craig fitted an extra ribbed aluminium tank which not only increased the amount of oil circulating but also acted as an oil cooler. This was mounted behind the rider's right leg on the rear wheel stays.

Guthrie held the BMWs for the first few laps but they began to pull away with Gall in the lead. After 10 laps Guthrie's Norton lost compression on the long straight down to Hooghalen and the Scot disappeared from the race – riding straight on to his hotel. Daniell moved up to third and when Ley's BMW quit the Londoner inherited second place. Gall averaged 92.27 mph and pushed up the lap record to 95 mph.

The next race was the Swiss Grand Prix at Berne which was also the European Grand Prix – the most important race of the year. The 500 cc entry reflected this with works entries form Norton, BMW, Guzzi, DKW and Gilera who fielded improved versions of the Rondine supercharged, water-cooled four-cylinder machines.

Because the 350 cc race was on the Saturday, Nortons sent only Guthrie and Frith and they got in some useful extra practice with Guthrie winning the 45-lap, 204-mile race at a record 82.78 mph. He finished a split second ahead of Frith and they shared the lap record at 86.24 mph. The start of Sunday's 500 cc race was eventful – and painful for poor Joe Craig. Giordano Aldrighetti's Gilera started so well that he hit the back of Noel Pope's Norton, which cannoned into Craig who was standing alongside the starting grid.

Craig was knocked flying and quite severely cut but he stuck to his post at the Norton pit and saw the Norton pair gain revenge for the Dutch defeat. Gall shot ahead from the start but on the twisty Bremgarten circuit, handling counted for more than sheer speed and the Nortons soon passed him. Gall retired, leaving the British riders to put on another high-speed display with Guthrie winning another 45-lapper at a record 88.39 mph by 2.4 seconds from Frith, who upped the lap record to 92.46 mph, with Omobono Tenni, on a Guzzi V-twin, way behind in third place.

ABOVE LEFT **For some races in 1937 the 500 cc Nortons were fitted with a supplementary finned aluminium oil tank which doubled as a cooler. It can be seen here mounted between the normal oil tank and the plunger rear suspension unit. This is the machine used by Guthrie to win the 500 cc Swiss Grand Prix.**

ABOVE **A classic shot of Crasher White in action in the 350 cc class of the 1937 German Grand Prix. Riding to team orders he finished second to Harold Daniell.**

Both of the BMWs had given trouble in Switzerland and the Munich factory did not contest the Belgian Grand Prix. There were no such problems for the reliable Nortons. Crasher White rejoined the team and won the 350 cc Belgian at 79.21 mph with a record lap at 84.82 mph; and Guthrie won the 500 cc from Frith, despite sliding off on oil dropped by a crashed competitor at Eau Rouge. His average for the 28-lap, 259-mile race was 86.68 mph and he set a new lap record of 93.93 mph – phenomenal speeds considering the machinery and the circuit.

As the teams journeyed to the Sachsenring for the German Grand Prix, scheduled for 8 August 1937, the scores in the major races stood at four wins out of four in the 350 cc class for Nortons and three out of four in the 500 cc – the only defeat being by Gall (BMW) at the Dutch TT. The German started well for the Bracebridge Street boys. Daniell had again been called in and this time Craig did the logical thing and teamed him with White in the 350 cc. There were no problems and Daniell won his first major race for Nortons, covering the 40 laps, 213 miles at 76.9 mph, setting a new lap record at 81.15 mph and finishing one second ahead of White.

Initially things went well in the 500 cc class too. On lap four Guthrie took the lead from Ley and pulled away while Frith held third place ahead of Gall and Tenni. Then Ley retired with gearbox trouble while Frith was slowed by a misfire. Guthrie increased his lead but lost it when he came in for his scheduled fuel stop. But BMW hopes seemed to be dashed when Gall pulled in for petrol and lost time making adjustments to his gear pedal.

This gave Guthrie a lead of $1\frac{1}{2}$ minutes and Craig signalled him to ease off. The Scot had no trouble holding his position and went into the last lap with nearly two minutes in hand. The Swastika arm-banded officials were ready to hoist the Union Jack for the second time that day and *The Motor Cycle* reported:

The vast crowd stood up preparatory to cheering the winner. The minutes passed. There was no sign of the Scot. At last Gall could be seen approaching . . . when the winner Gall came in he was scarcely cheered. The silence of the vast

throng of people as they waited anxiously for news of Guthrie was eloquent of their fine sporting spirit.

When the news did come it was bad. Guthrie had crashed and been seriously injured, and was on his way to hospital. Unfortunately the 500 cc was the last race of the day and by the time the ambulance got to Guthrie and started the journey to Chemnitz the roads were jammed with 300,000 spectators. What caused the accident? Stanley Woods has no doubts.

He was fouled. As an intelligent, interested eye-witness I am prepared to take an oath that he was the victim of foul riding. I saw the accident because I was coasting to a standstill with a broken petrol pipe when two riders passed me – a German and Guthrie. It was just before a very fast downhill right-hander which Jimmy took flat out – he didn't let up at all. The German rider had been with Guthrie for some time and definitely knew he was there – but he couldn't take that bend flat out and he pulled across and forced Jimmy into the right-hand gutter.

Unfortunately there was a line of saplings right by the road. The handlebar of Jimmy's Norton rattled along them like rattling a stick along railings. He came off the bike and finished up in the ditch on the outside of the bend. I was the first to reach him and I could see that he was completely and utterly shattered – both legs were broken and an arm. But he had no head injuries and was conscious – he had no idea he was dying. The stretcher bearers arrived and I went with him in the ambulance to hospital. The roads were completely jammed and it took two hours. He lapsed into unconsciousness just before we arrived. They rushed him straight into the operating theatre but after 20 minutes or so the surgeon came out and told me that although they had revived him momentarily, he had died. You can imagine how I felt. We had been team-mates and rivals for ten years and I looked upon him as one of my best friends. I was shattered.

Neither of the weeklies gave a definite reason for the crash. The accident happened right at the end of the meeting, they had deadlines to meet and no one at the time realised that Stanley Woods had been an eye-witness. Three rumours circulated. The first was that he had been forced off the road by a rider he was lapping. The second was that the rear spindle had broken, locking the rear wheel. The third was that the con-rod had failed, possibly because the engine had run low on oil and had seized, locking the engine solid and throwing the bike into a 100 mph skid.

Craig believed the last theory correct. The Norton engines did use a lot of oil and the level would have been low. Crasher White confirms Craig's belief and Daniell told brother-in-law Steve Lancefield the same story. However, Woods remains adamant: 'The connecting rod may have broken during the accident. Possibly the throttle jammed flat out after the bike hit the trees and this caused the con-rod to break. But as I said, I am sure that Guthrie was fouled.'

Austrian motorcycle historian Helmut Krackowizer has investigated the mystery.

The lapped rider was Kurt Mansfeld on a works DKW. They had been together for some time because Guthrie had slowed a little knowing that he was well ahead of Gall. Mansfeld was an emotional man and he was certainly trying to keep ahead of Guthrie to show that although he had lost a lap he was just as fast. But I spoke to Mansfeld about this and I cannot believe he deliberately pushed Guthrie off . . .

However, the German public, like Woods, believed that Mansfeld was the guilty party.

Gall won the race from Mansfeld with fellow DKW

rider Karl Bodmer third. Poor Guthrie was accorded full military honours. He lay in honour, guarded by storm troopers, until he was transported to his home in Scotland – the hearse packed with huge wreaths in the German colours of the time, black, red and white.

Craig was stunned by the death of his number one rider, the reigning European Champion and his closest friend for several years. The Norton team pulled out of the Ulster Grand Prix as a mark of respect and the team attended the funeral in Hawick. There Craig, Frith, Simpson and Woods were among the pall-bearers and the coffin was draped in the Union Jack that the German officials had been waiting to raise when Guthrie crossed the line.

LEFT One of the last pictures taken of Jimmy Guthrie shows him leading the 1937 500 cc German Grand Prix. He has just lapped the other rider in the picture, Kurt Mansfeld (DKW) who was involved in Guthrie's fatal crash.

RIGHT This news agency picture from Germany shows the tree that Guthrie's machine struck (black arrow) before ricocheting across the circuit and into a tree on the far side (white arrow) during the last lap.

BELOW A guard of honour in the hospital in Chemnitz where he died.

EXCLUSIVE PICTURES FROM GERMANY

Germans do Honour to Jimmy Guthrie

Our picture shows the late Jimmy Guthrie lying in state in the hospital at Chemnitz, where he was removed after his terrible accident. Doctors fought to save his life, but he had raced his last race.

It was in this room, as Jimmy Guthrie lay dying, that the deputation from Herr Hulnlein brought the special trophy which was originally intended for the fastest German rider in the Grand Prix, and laid it down reverently by his bed-side. No words were spoken; it was too late.

After his death, a guard of honour from the N.S.K.K. was posted in the room, and past the still, silent figure filed many hundreds of people who had watched the Hawick rider that day to pay their last homage.

CHAPTER 14

The Challenge from BMW, Gilera, and the Third Reich 1937–1941

The death of Jimmy Guthrie marked the end of a significant chapter in the history of Nortons – and it is worthwhile pausing for a moment to review the successes achieved by the factory team from the time Guthrie rejoined the squad for the 1931 season. During the next seven seasons Nortons won no less than 78 out of the 100 major 350 cc and 500 cc races held – and of these they did not contest eight!

To put this astonishing record of superiority into perspective, the next most successful factory was Velocette with eight wins followed by BMW with five and Husqvarna with three. Guthrie himself was the superstar of the era, winning 26 TT and grand prix races, all on Nortons. Stanley Woods ran him close with 20 wins, 18 achieved on Nortons. Two more Norton riders come third and fourth in the table – Simpson with 11 victories and Hunt with nine.

The tricky Bremgarten circuit in Berne where the Swiss Grand Prix was held was Norton's happiest hunting ground, for although it was usually hotly contested by the Italian and German factories, Joe Craig's Bracebridge Street brigade won both the 350 cc and 500 cc races seven years in succession – a stunning achievement.

Every worker at the Norton factory was given a framed photograph of Guthrie and a fund was set up by *The Motor Cycle* which raised over £1500 (some £60,000 in 1990 terms), used to build the Guthrie Memorial in the Isle of Man – at the spot on the Mountain climb where he retired from his last TT race, the 1937 Senior – and to finance beds in Nobles Hospital in Douglas and the Ramsey Cottage Hospital. Additionally the people of Hawick raised money and a bronze statue of Guthrie in his leathers was later unveiled in Wilton Lodge Park in that town.

But life must go on. In September 1937 Norton machines took the first 12 places in the Senior Manx Grand Prix and the first eight in the Junior, and that same month the 1938 range was announced. Basically the models remained the same but there were cosmetic changes. Most noticeable of these was the introduction of a large, slab-sided silencer with twin outlets – known, rather unkindly, by Norton workers as the cow's udder – and the adoption of push-rods that were inclined towards one another at the top rather than parallel as they had been since Pa Norton built the first experimental OHV engine in 1921. This was done to give the engines a more 'modern' appearance. More usefully, the overhead-valve gear was fully enclosed in an oil-tight rocker box.

After two years of testing on the works bikes, the plunger rear suspension was now offered as an optional extra on the Internationals for £15. This meant that the price for the International to racing specification had risen to around the £120 mark – six months' wages for a manual worker. The price of the basic 16H had crept up to £55 and lights and speedometer were still extra.

Production for the year from October 1936 to October 1937 was 6487 machines – a rise of 659 over the preceding 12 months which was accounted for totally by the increase in the numbers of 16H machines built to fulfil War Department contracts. The actual number of 16H models made was 2532 while the Model 18 was selling well and output jumped from 901 to 1429. But the ES2 dropped back from 736 to 639, the Model 50 350 cc from 853 to 705 and the Big Four 633 cc from 263 to 222.

Totals for other models were 490 cc International 214, Model 19 596 cc OHV 177, Model 20 490 cc twin-port 161, Model 55 350 cc twin-port 150, 348 cc International 116, CS1 490 cc touring camshaft 83, CJ 348 cc touring camshaft 50, plus nine 596 cc OHC machines built to order for sidecar racing which was becoming increasingly popular. Of the 330 Internationals built, 122 were to racing/Manx specification.

Trials were very much Dennis Mansell's domain. As the son of the boss he appears to have had no definite job but there is no doubt that he worked hard on his own successful sidecar trials career and on making sure that Nortons had a strong team. He also took a tremendous interest in racing and in particular the TT and the Manx Grand Prix, spending six weeks of every year at the Castle Mona Hotel in Douglas covering the lengthy practice periods and race weeks.

While on the island he seldom missed a practice period, watching from different places, stopwatch in hand, to spot new talent. He was also Nortons' link-man with the Army and from the time the contracts for the 16H WD model first came 'on stream' he spent an increasing amount of time liaising with the forces – a very pleasant task in those days of splendid officers' messes and one which, as the boss's son, he was well equipped to do.

ABOVE The Norton trials team at the Stroud Team Trial, October 1937; (from left to right) Harold Flook with sidecar, Jack Williams and Vic Brittain.

LEFT Harold Daniell winning the 1938 Senior TT.

Later Gilbert Smith tried to take the credit for winning the military contracts for Nortons, claiming to have constantly pestered the War Department until they gave in. But it seems far more likely that the War Department trials of 1935 were the deciding factor and that Dennis Mansell should be given the credit, first for Nortons being so heavily involved in trials that they could supply a suitable machine, and second for constant lobbying for the factory at military events.

At the end of April 1938 came sensational news – and as was so often the case it was tucked away in a small paragraph. In TT Notes and News in *The Motor Cycle* (confusingly, both of the weeklies used the same title at this time) of 28 April appeared the following: 'The Junior (Norton) engine will have a bore of 75.9 and a stroke of 77 mm while the corresponding dimensions of the Senior engine will be 82 × 94.3 mm.'

The item continued: '. . . both machines will have stiffer crankcases, and the crankcase of the Senior engine is carried higher up to give increased support to the cylinder barrel.' In other words, both engines had been extensively changed and the 79 × 100 mm dimensions for the 500 cc unit that had been introduced by Pa Norton in 1911 had at last been abandoned.

In fact, the whole design of the racing machines had been revamped. When Frith appeared on the prototype at the North West 200 in May 1938 it was seen that a telescopic front fork replaced the old girders, the rear plunger suspension had been lightened and cleaned up, the old cradle frame replaced by one in which tubes ran back under the engine and gearbox, massive magnesium conical hubs were fitted both front and rear (a conical front hub had been adopted the year before), while the size and shape of the oil tank had been changed.

Frith, the only works rider at the NW 200, shot ahead in the 500 cc class but then slid off when he hit a wet patch in a race plagued by showers. But, reported *The Motor Cycle*, Craig left a happy man having 'learned all he wanted to know in practice'. Commenting on the performance, the reporter said:

> . . . braking was simply astonishing . . . the new front forks make all the difference to the road holding on corners. The most impressive thing about the new Norton was the complete absence of fork chatter – the front end of the machine just rose and fell like a ship in a heavy swell. . . . Freddie Frith was full of praise, and remarked that there was no sign of the front end hopping out on the very fast corners.

The telescopic fork was of a very simple design. It used springs for both suspension and damping without any hydraulic assistance, and the movement was limited to two inches – half that of the wartime Teledraulic developed by AMC and of the post-war hydraulically damped Norton 'Roadholder' fork.

Both of the engines were 'squarer' than they had ever been – a step taken to reduce piston speeds and to allow the use of larger valves. The double-overhead-camshaft layout adopted the preceding year was retained but the finning of the cylinder heads was increased and given a very square look. Cylinder finning was also increased but the actual construction remained the same – light alloy fins shrunk on to an aluminium–bronze alloy skull for the head and on to a cast-iron barrel.

The lower bevel housing was modified so that the exhaust pipe which ran under it would have more ground clearance when cornering, and larger bore Amal racing carburettors with remote needles were adopted. Craig said, at the time, that the compression ratios were 8.3 for the 500 cc engine and 8.6 for the smaller unit – yet he contradicts this when writing a wartime article for *Motor Cycling* when he speaks of using ratios of 10 to 1 and over in 1938 and 1939.

Possibly he gave the lower figures in 1938 to confuse the opposition. Nortons had abandoned the twin-plug set-up (first used when the megaphone exhaust system was introduced on the 500 cc engine in 1934) when Craig adopted the double-overhead-camshaft layout in 1937, and the new engines had only a single sparking plug. Over the years the megaphone exhaust systems had grown bigger and bigger. The original outlet had been four inches in diameter. By 1936 it was some six inches and the 'trumpets' fitted in 1938 were enormous – in the region of eight inches. A refinement which was later abandoned was the fitting of a cylindrical oil filter mounted above the gearbox.

The team for the TT was Frith, White and Daniell, now on a full contract to replace Guthrie. But the factory bikes were delayed and the trio started the two-week practice period on old bikes – which was just as well, for Daniell suffered a near flat-out prang on Lancefield's 500 cc Norton near Ballig. The machine was completely wrecked, even the main shaft was bent,

LEFT Daniell's TT-winning 500 cc; a complete revamp with telescopic front forks and a 'squarer' engine.

RIGHT Harold Daniell cools off after winning the 1938 Senior TT at a record 89.11 mph and with a record lap at 91 mph. Note the fly encrusted number plate and fly-screen, the telescopic fork and the front-brake air-scoop. With Daniell are Bill Mewis (left) and Frank Sharratt.

ABOVE **The works 500 cc Norton on which Freddie Frith (whose head can be seen above the tank) set a record lap at 98.90 mph in the 1938 Ulster Grand Prix.**

LEFT **Ouch! Freddie Frith lands at 100 mph at the top of Bray Hill during the 1938 Senior TT. He finished third – less than two seconds behind Stanley Woods.**

but Daniell was incredibly lucky. He escaped with minor injuries which prevented him from practising until the end of the second week.

When the works machines did eventually arrive on the island they certainly looked the part. In an article 'Light Metals and the Motorcycle' which Craig wrote during the war, he lists the components and what they were made of. Magnesium alloy, considerably lighter than aluminium, had been used increasingly by Nortons since 1932 and in 1938 this material was used for the crank-cases, cambox and bevel housings, front and rear hubs, brake shoes and plates, steering damper adjuster, magneto chain cover and magneto casing.

Parts cast in aluminium alloy included the cylinder head and barrel (with cast-iron liner), carburettor, front fork head clip, gearbox shell, petrol tank filler cap, clutch outer plate and contact breaker housing. Additionally light alloy was used in bar, sheet and extruded forms for the piston, engine plates, front fork legs, wheel rims and the petrol and oil tanks.

The bad weather that had plagued the practice cleared for the Junior, but despite the good conditions speeds were down. Disappointingly the new Nortons proved no match for the latest Velocettes which, ridden by Woods and Mellors, romped to a 1–2 success. Woods' winning speed was 84.08 mph, slower than Guthrie the preceding year, though he did beat the Norton lap record by just 2 seconds with a lap at 85.30 mph.

Woods would argue, quite rightly, that he had no need to go any faster. Frith could make no such excuse. He could get nowhere near his times of the year before and although he rode as hard as he could to try and catch Mellors, who beat him by only 7 seconds, his average was 82.35 mph compared with the 83.29 mph he had achieved in 1937 – hardly an impressive first TT for the new look telescopic fork racer!

Daniell was certainly not impressed. It was his first TT as a works Norton rider and because of his crash early in practice he had been unable to do more than just qualify in a single practice session. When he came in for his pit-stop he shouted to Craig, 'By God, you must have had some ruddy good riders to have won seven years running with one of these!' He eventually finished fifth and with White fourth Nortons did win the team prize.

The Norton run of seven successive Junior TT wins had come to an end – what would the bigger machines do against the challenge of Woods on the 500 cc Velocette and the works supercharged BMWs of the formidable Georg Meier and the experienced Jock West in Friday's Senior TT?

It turned out to be another sensationally close race – and yet again Stanley Woods was to figure large in the proceedings, just as he had in 1935, 1936 and 1937. Frith led for the first two laps but when Woods got his nose in front and after four laps led by a single second from Frith, with Daniell third, 12 seconds covering the three of them. On lap five Woods increased his advantage to 3 seconds over Frith and Daniell who now dead-heated for second place.

By this time Daniell was flying. His speed for the sixth lap was a record 90.75 mph and he went into the last lap leading by 5 seconds from Woods and Frith who dead-heated for second place. The chips were down and the south Londoner responded with a final lap at a record 91.00 mph to beat Woods by 15.2 seconds, who got the better of Frith by just 1.6 seconds – now that really was racing!

White came home fourth to give Nortons yet another team prize and West was the best BMW in fifth spot. Meier had retired on the first lap, while Gall was a non-starter having done himself a serious mischief when he dropped his BMW while riding in the reverse direction of the course on open roads near Ramsey.

Within hours 'Paton' of *The Motor Cycle* was riding the winning machine.

At 4000 rpm there was little power at all. At 'four-five' it started to come in – quite gradually. At 5000 rpm the acceleration began to be really lively, but it was not until 6000 rpm had been reached that the engine began to develop full power. When it did the power was stupendous . . . at 7000 rpm I slipped into second gear – the gear change of course is magnificent, and almost instantaneous. Again the rev-counter needle dropped back, and again there was the marvellous, breath-taking surge of power as the revs built up . . . yes, that ride on that record breaking Norton is the most thrilling experience that I have ever had. . . .

The next big race was the Belgian Grand Prix. There White proved that the smaller Norton was a match for the Velocette by winning the 350 cc race at 84.54 mph after a long dice with Mellors (Velocette). White also clocked a record lap at 86.59 mph. But in the 500 cc class Meier and his BMW were just too fast and won the race at 90.39 mph from Frith who pushed up the lap record to 96.94 mph, which at that time was the fastest ever lap in a classic road race and proved that there was still life in the Norton, even on such a fast circuit as Spa-Francorchamps.

West on the second BMW was third, well behind Frith and only 14 seconds ahead of Daniell. Stanley Woods remembers the race well.

At first I did battle with Harold Daniell and Jock West. I finally wore them down and I then caught and eventually passed Frith down the Masta straight. But coming out of Stavelot he went by me like the shot out of a gun and steadily drew away from me. I realised then the power the Norton had compared to my poor Velocette was fantastic.

That year the Swiss Grand Prix moved to a short circuit around the League of Nations buildings in Geneva – and Nortons won the three main races. First Daniell won the 350 cc class from Frith, who crashed but remounted, and then Arthur Horton with a 596 cc camshaft Norton took the sidecar honours – the lone British competitor in the class. The Gilera team were expected to challenge in the 500 cc event and sure enough, Dorino Serafini and Aldrighetti shot ahead from the start – then Aldrighetti crashed and Serafini punctured and Daniell, Frith and local ace Georges Cordey made it a 1–2–3 for Nortons. It was the eighth year in succession that Nortons had scored the 350 cc and 500 cc double in Switzerland, and Frith set the lap record for the two-mile circuit at 67.53 mph to prove that it was no fluke.

Nortons gave the Dutch TT a miss in 1938, probably because the long straights and acute corners made it a perfect circuit for the supercharged BMWs and Gileras. Ted Mellors won the 350 cc race for Velocette and Meier the 500 cc for BMW.

That year the German was the European Grand Prix and the riders wore speedway-style helmet covers in the colours of their national federation – white for Germany, red for Italy, green for Great Britain and so on. Walter Rusk was at last fit again and he partnered White in the 350 cc event but crashed when holding second place to Crasher who went on to win the 40-lap, 213-mile race at 79.78 mph with a record lap at 81.71 mph. Meier won the 500 cc class for BMW but Daniell and Frith kept the Norton flag flying by taking second and third places. From four starts the Norton team had scored a win, a second and third plus a lap record.

But things went awry in the final big race of the year, the Ulster Grand Prix. First White came off his 350 cc Norton while dicing with Mellors (Velocette) who went on to win from Rusk on the second Norton. Then in the 500 cc class Frith shot ahead, built up a big lead and put in a record lap at 98.80 mph only to slide off when a shower swept across the circuit leaving damp patches. All was not lost, for team-mate Daniell had established himself in second place and took over the lead. Then a wheel failed and West came through to win for BMW. What a sickener for Craig – to have had victory twice snatched from his grasp in the world's fastest road race.

Nortons continued to dominate the Manx in which Ken Bills scored a double and fellow Norton riders took

LEFT Sidecar racing increased in popularity during the thirties. Here Arthur Horton and passenger Les Seals show their style on their 596 cc camshaft Norton at the Crystal Palace track in June 1938. Within weeks they crossed the channel to win their class at the Swiss Grand Prix.

RIGHT In 1938 the Swiss Grand Prix moved from Berne to Geneva – but this did not stop Nortons winning. Harold Daniell, who scored a 350 cc/500 cc double, is garlanded after one of his wins. This was the eighth year in succession that Nortons had scored a Swiss double.

ABOVE Freddie Frith is congratulated by pit-attendant Dennis Mansell after finishing third in the 1939 Senior TT. The Norton was exactly as raced the previous year.

LEFT These are the two types of camshaft engine you could buy in 1939. On the left is what the Press described as 'the latest type of Manx Grand Prix engine' with works type square cylinder head but still with the old single overhead camshaft valve gear – on the right is the standard International engine.

ABOVE RIGHT Charles Mortimer aboard the 350 cc Norton with sidecar on which he set British records at Brooklands in July 1939 – the last to be broken by a Norton at the Surrey track before it closed at the outbreak of war. With him are John Rowlands and Francis Beart who prepared the machine.

the first four places in the Senior and the top six in the Junior. Earlier in the year there had been two Nortons in Great Britain's winning team of four in the International Six Days Trial (held in Wales) – both Williams and Brittain riding overhead-camshaft 348 cc Internationals.

At the Earls Court Show the *Motor Cycle* reporter commented: 'the sleek looking Manx Grand Prix Nortons – but alas without the new plunger forks.' However, the price of the optional extra rear suspension had been halved, from £15 to £7.10s, and was now on offer for the push-rod ES2 as well as on the Internationals – though not, curiously enough, listed for the camshaft CS1 and CJ models.

The 'udder' twin-outlet silencer was gone after only a year, replaced for 1939 by a conventional cylindrical one, and the appearance of the timing side of the engines had been improved by fitting a smooth, highly polished cover to the magdyno drive chain. Prices were up but at last lighting and horn were standard fittings which meant that the actual 'on the road' prices remained virtually the same – the 16H costing £61, the Model 18 £71 and the basic 490 cc International £100. As before, any machine could be supplied in trials trim for an extra £5, and records show that during the late 1930s there was a steady trickle of orders for trials Nortons – 114 in 1935, 95 the next year and then 74, 48 and 49 up to the outbreak of war in September 1939.

Then in December 1938 came the bombshell. The editors of both motor-cycling weeklies were telephoned and invited to meet the directors of Norton Motors at the Bracebridge Street factory the following morning. Neither knew why, but when they arrived they were told that Nortons had decided to 'refrain from racing, officially and unofficially, for one year'. It was explained that the factory had been working flat out to fulfil WD orders for the 16H and that even with day and night shifts they were hard pressed.

To take men off the production line to work on new racing machines was out of the question. Commented former Norton, Sunbeam and Rudge racer Graham Walker, who had taken over as editor of *Motor Cycling* early in 1938: 'Faced with the alternatives of racing, with consequent delay in execution of standard and WD deliveries, or of keeping faith with their customers, the Directors have decided that racing must be dispensed with for the time being.'

Walker had been through a similar situation when Rudge quit in 1933. Then he formed the Rudge Syndicate and raced the works machines for a further two seasons. He suggested that Nortons might do the same, but at the time gaffer Bill Mansell appeared to reject the idea

The production figures for the year to October 1938 (before the night shift was fully operational) were, surprisingly, slightly down on those for the preceding year at 6219 compared with 6487. Production of the 16H had shot up to 3310 but had been compensated for by falling figures for the Model 18 (down from 1429 to 838), the Model 50 (from 705 to 483) and the ES2 (from 639 to 585) and so on throughout the range, though sales of the 'Inters' remained static at around 200 for the 490 cc and 100 for the 348 cc.

An interesting newcomer in the production chart is the 633 cc Model 1 to WD specification. A pilot batch of 15 had been built complete with sidecars and with sidecar wheel drive. This was of a crude type used by Dennis Mansell in trials in the early 1930s. It had proved so successful that it had been outlawed, but it was an essential for a three-wheeler built for military service. There was no differential. The rider simply engaged a dog-clutch that coupled the live rear axle to the sidecar wheel and disengaged the drive as soon as the hazard had been surmounted.

The 'no racing' bombshell was followed by another sensation when Joe Craig left Nortons and joined BSA in January 1939. Commented *Motor Cycling*: 'An able designer, Joe possesses an unrivalled knowledge of development and tuning work, whilst his experience as a racing man has proved invaluable in team management.'

Craig, who had been in charge of the Norton racing effort since he took over from Walter Moore in 1929, was by this time regarded by many, and particularly the public, with an awe that bordered on reverence. To Norton fans throughout the world his defection to BSA was a shattering blow. Exactly why BSA, at that time Britain's largest motorcycle manufacturer, wanted Craig is not clear. It seems they had plans to go racing and Joe himself later hinted at a major BSA racing effort – but the war put a stop to all that.

Despite pulling out of racing, Nortons remained very active in trials. Dennis Mansell had won the sidecar class of the British Experts Trial late in 1938 and he continued winning in 1939. For example, the team dominated the Colmore Cup Trial which Vic Brittain won while Mansell took the sidecar class, and the two of them plus Flook won the team prize.

Rumours abounded on the racing front. One was that Meier was to switch to driving the Auto Union grand prix cars full time (he had already had outings as a reserve driver) and that Frith was to take his place in the BMW team; another (which proved true) was that Crasher White was to race one of the new supercharged twin-cylinder NSUs in the Junior TT.

Despite the looming war clouds, entries for the Isle of Man were well up on previous years and with AJS fielding two of their revamped four-cylinder machines, now water-cooled as well as supercharged, there was no lack of interest. Possibly this state of affairs was not to Bill Mansell's liking. In any event he relented and at the very last minute agreed to let Frith and Daniell race the 1938 machines. *Motor Cycling* was elated.

> Here is a bit of really 'hot' TT news – Frith and Daniell will be riding the same machines in the Junior and Senior races as they used in 1938! Originally 'Mr Norton' had no intention of loaning the machines to anyone; in fact, Frith and Daniell actually entered ordinary Manx Grand Prix machines, but last week the two riders visited the Norton works together and after considerable discussion it was agreed to loan them a 350 cc and a 500 cc apiece provided the machines were accepted just as they stood . . . not a nut or bolt has been changed since last year.

In the same issue (24 May) appeared a picture of a Norton racing engine with the caption: 'The latest Manx Grand Prix type of Norton engine which will be fitted to some of the machines for the TT'. This had a factory-type square head and deeply finned barrel but was still sohc with exposed rockers.

The Junior TT of 1939 was dominated by a battle between Stanley Woods (Velocette) and the Norton riders. Frith led for the first three laps, then Woods overtook him and a lap later Frith's Norton stopped near Kirkmichael. Daniell took up the challenge and put in the fastest lap at 85.05 mph, failing to catch

An Indian military policeman on a Norton in Egypt during the war.

ABOVE Freddie Frith airborne again, this time at the 1939 TT.

RIGHT With apologies for poor quality, the racing International as shown in the 1940 Norton catalogue (not issued in the UK). Note the telescopic fork.

Woods by just 8 seconds.

But despite the various improvements to bikes and course, Guthrie's race record of 1937 of 84.43 mph was unbeaten, and was to remain so until the advent of the 'featherbed' in 1950. Crasher White, who remembers that NSU paid him a retainer of £250, did not complete a single lap at racing speeds. After a stop at Kirkmichael he toured in to retire.

He had done all his Senior practising on Ron Harris's standard Norton racer but he then asked Nortons if he could borrow the spare 500 for the Senior and, as *Motor Cycling* put it, 'permission was quickly granted'. The BMW camp were under a cloud because Gall, who had not long recovered from his Isle of Man crash of the preceding year, had been fatally injured when he came off at Ballaugh Bridge during practising. But after some discussion it was agreed that Meier, the favourite, and West should start.

Meier led all the way to win at a record 89.38 mph but he was never pushed and did not break the Norton lap record of 91.00 mph set by Daniell in 1938. Daniell's plan was to go as fast as possible straight from the start but it backfired when the Norton 'nipped up' – something which was prone to happen if the engines were given absolutely maximum revs from the word go rather than being allowed gradually to reach working temperatures before being hammered.

Frith and White were doing their best but as they started the last lap it looked as though there would not be a Norton among the first three for the first time since 1929. Meier led from West with Stanley Woods (Velocette) in third place ahead of Frith. Then the Lincolnshire rider put in a storming last lap to beat the Irishman by 6 seconds to finish only 32 seconds behind West.

In 1939 the ACU provided facilities for weighing the machines – something that had not been done for a number of years. It was not compulsory and was slightly hit or miss in that some of the bikes had half-empty tanks, but the officials tried to compensate for this by deducting the estimated weight of the fuel and oil from the weighbridge figures to give a 'dry' weight.

Lightest of the 500 cc machines were the BMWs. Meier's winning bike scaled only 302 lb, while West's was 307. Frith's Norton tipped the scales at 336, Woods' Velocette was 338 and the heaviest machine was Rusk's works supercharged four-cylinder AJS at 404. Curiously the 350 cc Nortons, seemingly identical to the bigger machines, were far lighter; Daniell's weighed in at 306 lb and Frith's at 309. Following the disappointing performance of the 75.9 × 77 mm, 349 cc engine in the 1938 race, Frith reverted to a 1937 73.4 × 82.5 mm engine in 1939.

Nortons would not let Frith and Daniell take the works machines to the Continent, and Meier won the big class at the Dutch TT and the Belgian, where he put in the first lap at over the 'ton' ever recorded in a grand prix run on a road circuit (100.63 mph) before he came unstuck in the Swedish Grand Prix at Saxtorp. There Serafini (Gilera) set the pace and although Meier raised the lap record to 100.83 mph, he crashed attempting to catch the Italian and injured his back so badly that he was not able to contest the German Grand Prix.

At the Sachsenring Serafini won again before travelling to Ireland to win the 500 cc Ulster Grand Prix at a record 97.85 mph. It was in this race that Walter Rusk (AJS) did the first lap at over 100 mph on a British road circuit before retiring with a broken fork link. Serafini then topped that lap with a round at 100.03 mph. Frith, allowed to use the works Norton, finished second at the impressive average of 96.83 mph, though he admitted that the Norton was completely outpaced by the Gilera. In fact he told a story of how he was flat out, chin buried in the sponge-rubber on the tank top, maximum revs on the clock and travelling down the seven-mile straight on the old Clady circuit at 120 mph when Serafini pulled alongside sitting up, grinned across at him, opened the throttle and pulled away.

Daniell, who had not travelled to Ulster, and Frith had a last outing on the factory Nortons at Donington on 26 August 1939. Frith took both 350 cc and 500 cc races and Arthur Horton won the sidecar event to make it a clean sweep.

When the German army massed on the Polish border in the week after Donington, a British contingent was in Germany competing in the International Six Days Trial – and again there were two Nortons in the four-machine British Trophy team: Vic Brittain on a 490 cc International and Harold Flook with a 596 cc camshaft-powered sidecar outfit.

Korpsführer Huhnlein, the German motor-sport supremo, guaranteed the British party safe conduct to Switzerland whatever happened, but as the situation worsened the telegrams began to fly and after much heart-searching the entire contingent pulled out and rode for the Swiss border.

One of the first casualties of the war was the 1940 Norton catalogue. An initial batch was produced with spaces left where the prices could be over-printed when the political and economic situation settled down. When war was declared the bulk of these were pulped and very few have survived, but thanks to the kindness of Austrian colleague Helmut Krackowizer I have one before me as I write. On the front is the rubber-stamp of Norton's pre-war Stuttgart agents, the Hermann brothers Fritz and Willie, and it was presumably posted to them just days before the war began.

And pretty sensational it is too, for it reveals that far from sitting back and merely concentrating on churning out the military models, Nortons planned a number of important changes. From a sporting point of view the most significant was that in 1940 they intended to offer, for the first time, a batch of out-and-out racing machines – not just the 'International to racing specification' as in previous years.

This first genuine 'over the counter' racer since the demise of the Brookland Special of the 1920s was still not called the Manx. It was catalogued as the 'Racing International' and was to be supplied with the telescopic front forks first used on the factory bikes in 1938. Rear-plunger springing was also standard, as was an Elektron (magnesium alloy) crank-case – the first time I can trace that this material had been specified on a Norton to be sold to the public, though some of the earlier models supplied to special customers may have been similarly equipped.

The size of the bigger engine had been increased from 490 to 499 cc (as the factory engines had been for the 1936 season) and an exhaust system with megaphone was standard on both models. The front brake was of conical racing pattern and although the petrol and oil tanks were still of sheet steel (with the soldered, deckle-edged lower joint so beloved of enthusiasts) they were fitted with quick-filler caps (petrol capacities were 4¼ gallons for the 499 cc and 3¾ for the 348 cc).

Commenting on the adoption of the telescopic front forks, the brochure says: 'Plunger type fork, provisional patent 13638, giving all the advantages of reduced

1939 Gallery

The 1939 models had a sleeker look with a revised silencer and polished magneto chain case. This is the 348 cc Model 50 and at last the lights were standard equipment and not listed as an optional extra.

Cost of the 1939 OHV 596 cc Model 19 was just over £70 ready for the road. This lusty big single was popular with sporting sidecar riders.

For 1939 any machine in the range could be supplied in trials trim for an extra £5. The picture shows the 490 cc Model 18 to trials specification with high level exhaust, extra ground clearance and competition tyres.

Classic lines. The 1939 490 cc Model 30 International was the top sports machine of its day and cost exactly £100 – 20 weeks pay for the average worker.

LEFT The stamp on the back of this photograph, taken in 1940, certifies that it has been passed by the censors. A lieutenant of the Royal Montreal regiment aboard a WD 16H Norton.

ABOVE RIGHT Norton at war – the crew of a 633 cc combination with sidecar wheel drive take aim for a propaganda picture in November 1940.

RIGHT Into battle. Norton mounted troops on manoeuvres in October 1941.

C4185189

Two Norton advertisements in *Motor Cycling* and *The Motor Cycle*, both from 1941.

unsprung weight, improved braking and more positive steering.' Obviously Nortons felt this type of fork had a bright future for they were offered as optional extras not only on the standard Internationals but also on their top-of-the-range overhead-valve model, the ES2. Additionally the ES2 could be supplied with the racing-style International tank.

The theme of building special competition models rather than listing optional extras designed to upgrade roadster machines was carried through to the trials field. In previous years any model could be supplied in trials trim but the intention for 1940 was to sell two fully equipped trials machines, both powered by push-rod engines with aluminium heads and barrels (348 cc and 496 cc), high ground clearance ($5\frac{1}{4}$ in), short wheelbase, trials ratio gearbox, high-level exhaust system . . . in fact, according to the catalogue, 'similar to machines used so successfully by the Norton works team of reliability trial riders'.

Other changes listed but because of the war either delayed or never made, included alloy cylinder heads for the side-valve engines, cradle frames for all models and, surprisingly, to change the bore and stroke of the 500 cc engines (except camshaft) from 79 × 100 mm (490 cc) to 82 × 94 mm (496 cc) – reverting to the dimensions used by Pa Norton before he switched to 79 × 100 mm for the 1911 TT! The catalogue claimed this would result in 'enhanced performance and smoother power output' but the planned switch was never made and the 79 × 100 mm soldiered on for the best part of another quarter-century.

Unlike in 1914, petrol rationing was imposed almost immediately though motor sport was allowed to continue for a while – competitors using their meagre ration – and Nortons made a clean sweep in the British Experts trial in December 1939 when factory solo riders Jack Williams and Vic Brittain actually tied for first place while Flook won the sidecar class.

By this time Nortons had stopped production of all except the 490 cc side-valve WD 16H model and the 633 cc side-valve WD Model 1 sidecar machine – and with night-shift working, allied to building just two near-identical models, production rose to a peak of over 400 a week. Harold Daniell, holder of the Isle of Man lap record, was rejected for military service because his eyesight was too bad but Frith and White were soon in uniform, initially serving as sergeant instructors at a Motor Transport depot.

The Norton advertisements had taken a warlike turn. One showed an artist's impression of machine gunners firing from the sidecars of two 633 cc sidecar outfits and shooting down a Heinkel 111 bomber; another (shown above) featured a smiling despatch rider on a Norton passing a column of surly looking captured Italians outside Tobruk with the cryptic slogan: 'Mobile units played an important part.'

CHAPTER 15

Trying to win the peace 1943–1949

The Norton advertisements of 1943 featured a series of humorous sketches in which the riders were mounted on push-rod models with telescopic forks – all ending with the slogan: 'Holds the roads, the records, and the reputation'. Clearly Nortons were convinced of the superiority of this type of front suspension and, behind the scenes, development work was going on.

In January 1944 Nortons took out a number of patents on a completely new design of telescopic fork. This included hydraulic damping and was the basis for the very successful 'Roadholder' fork which became a standard fitting on all Nortons in September 1946. According to Charlie Edwards, this was designed by Jackie Moore (no relation to Walter Moore), who had taken over the prototype work from Edgar Franks as the years went by. Said Edwards:

> Jackie Moore used to do a lot of work during the night while he was at the factory on fire-watching duty. Obviously when there were no air-raids there was nothing to do and he could work without interruption. he also designed a very neat unit-construction 350 cc twin and a prototype was built but I don't know what happened to that.

Joe Craig, still working at AMC, continued to write articles for the weeklies which also published the texts of papers he read to members of the Institute of Automobile Engineers. In these he reveals a deep knowledge of the workings of single-cylinder racing engines and even in those days he was talking of 'squish' in connection with the combustion chamber – a factor which came very much to the fore after the war.

The talks and articles make it clear that Craig had thought long and hard over every aspect of the development of the Norton racing engines. Commenting on the twin-plug set-up used in conjunction with the early megaphone exhaust, he said that this gave better acceleration and improved low down power but gave no more at the top end and had the disadvantage of being very critical on ignition timing. He also said that the piston rather than the valve gear was the limiting factor in the Norton engines. Another aspect emphasised by Craig was the important part played by oil in cooling the racing engines. In the 1938 design the pump circulated oil at the rate of 35 gallons an hour (at 6000 rpm) and 80 per cent of this went to the big-end and was then flung out to cool the underside of the piston crown and lubricate the small-end and cylinder walls.

By early 1945 the end of the war was in sight and Triumph stole a march by announcing their post-war range. Said *Motor Cycling*: 'Triumphs of tomorrow. Famous Coventry concern first in the field with an attractive post-war programme.' The original Triumph works in Coventry had been destroyed by bombing and a completely new factory had been built at Meriden.

RIGHT **This war-time *Motor Cycling* front page advertisement (April 1943) shows the ES2 with telescopic front fork as shown in the 1940 catalogue.**

ABOVE LEFT June 1943. Why Bert has a civilian prototype 1940 ES2 with telescopic fork instead of a WD 16H is not explained.

ABOVE A stylish success advertisement used following the Norton 1–2 in the 1947 Senior TT.

RIGHT Artie Bell rounds Keppel Gate on his way to second place in the 1947 Senior TT, won by team-mate Harold Daniell.

These new Triumphs, with long-travel telescopic forks, neat vertical twin engines and modern styling, were an attractive proposition – especially the sports 500 cc Tiger 100. And when the war did finally end Triumph were far better placed to capture the market than Norton, who were still building military models.

It was not until August 1945 that there was definite news from Bracebridge Street. Then an advertisement appeared: '1946 Norton programme. At the end of August we complete our contracts for the services. Remember that one in every four was a Norton.' This referred to the fact that of the 400,000 motorcycles built for the services 100,000 were Nortons – an impressive output for a small factory.

There were to be just two models for 1946 – a civilian version of the side-valve 16H plus a slightly revamped 490 cc OHV Model 18. Both would have a cradle frame but there was no rear-springing and, even worse, no telescopic forks which made the Nortons look positively antiquated alongside the new models from rivals' factories. Fortunately this did not cost them sales – there simply were not enough new bikes to go round and every machine was sold before it got to the showrooms.

It is difficult in these days of plenty to imagine just how tough things were in post-war Britain. A basic petrol ration had been restored in 1945 but it was pitifully small – about a gallon a week depending on engine size. Food was still very strictly rationed and was to remain so for several years; coal was short, there was nothing in the shops and if you wanted a car or motorcycle you ordered it and waited . . . and waited.

The sport creaked back into action and attracted enormous crowds. The first post-war race was held in the grounds of Bangor Castle in Northern Ireland in July 1945, even before the end of hostilities with Japan. There were just 35 entries but significantly Ernie Lyons on a Triumph twin fitted with McCandless swinging fork rear suspension won the Experts class while among the entry were the two McCandless brothers, Rex and Cromie, both riding Triumph-powered specials with a twin-tube frame designed by Rex – the forerunner of the soon to be famous 'featherbed' frame.

First genuine road race was the Ulster 100 run on a new circuit near Lisburn, Co Antrim in September 1945 where the 500 cc class was won by a thoughtful, forceful Ulsterman named Artie Bell. A close friend of the McCandless brothers, he had started to make a name for himself pre-war and he won the 1945 race on his 1938 Norton with plunger springing and girder forks.

The first post-war event to be held over the Isle of Man TT circuit was the 1946 Manx Grand Prix. For this Nortons built a small batch of updated racers. The engines were 1939 pattern, built mainly from a stock of spares that had been sent to the island in 1939 and left there during the war. The frames with plunger springing were also of pre-war type but were improved by the fitting of the new Roadholder forks.

Ken Bills had scored a double for Nortons in the last pre-war Manx in 1938 but thought he had retired from racing until Steve Lancefield and Harold Daniell visited him in mid 1946. Speaking in 1990 Bills recalled: 'They wanted me to ride Nortons, which Steve would prepare, in the Manx. I hadn't been on a motorcycle for seven years, weighed over 14 stone and was by that time a married man with a son. It seemed a daft idea, but in the end I agreed.'

He won the Junior and set the fastest lap but lashing rain and winds made the Senior a miserable affair. And, explained Bills, that was not the only problem.

> Lancefield was so confident that I'd win that he set the mixture on the rich side. In the conditions it was far too rich and simply didn't perform. I wasn't prepared to stick my neck out and when they signalled that Ernie Lyons was well ahead I decided to let him go.

Lyons won the race on a factory Triumph and Bills finished second.

In April that year there was talk of Nortons being made under licence in Spain, but nothing came of this, and the same month English short-circuit racing restarted with a meeting at Cadwell Park – quickly followed by the first meeting to be staged on one of the many surplus wartime airfields. This was at Gransden Lodge near Caxton on the Royston to Huntingdon road and was organised by the Cambridge University AC. There Syd Barnett (Norton) won two major races, beating George Brown (HRD) who had won at Cadwell.

Jock West took the mighty four-cylinder, supercharged AJS to Chimay in Belgium and won the 500 cc class there in June, and later that month Harold Daniell had his first post-war outing at North Weald airfield where, riding an alcohol-burning Lancefield Norton, he won the main event. Things were coming back to life and in July 1946 the authorities helped by increasing the basic petrol ration to six gallons a month for bikes up to 250 cc and to seven for larger machines.

At last, in late September 1946, the Norton post-war range was launched. The Roadholder forks were standard and there were six roadster models: the 16H and Big Four side-valves at £158 and £163; the 490 cc OHV Model 18 and ES2 (with spring frame) at £165 and £180; and the two Internationals with unchanged

ABOVE **British superstar of the era George Formby and wife Beryl are cheered by Norton workers as they take delivery of an International outside the Bracebridge Street works, July 1947.**

RIGHT **The first major Grand Prix to be held after the war was the 1947 Dutch TT. Harold Daniell leads (500 cc) but retired with a puncture. Team-mate Artie Bell won.**

camshaft engines at £221 and £230. The near doubling of the prices compared with 1939 is explained partly by the 25 per cent purchase tax levied.

In addition, purpose-built road-racing and trials bikes were catalogued, and for the first time the factory used the name 'Manx Norton' for the racers. These were available as 348 cc (71 × 88 mm) or 499 cc (79.62 × 100 mm), both priced at £298. The engines were of the single-overhead-camshaft type with exposed rockers and to cope with the 70 octane 'pool' petrol (different brands were not available; all petrol was 'pooled' – hence the name), the compression ratios had been dropped to just over the 7 to 1 mark. The trials bikes were push-rod 350 and 500 cc models both priced at £171.

Crasher White, who finished the war with a commission, was by this time married and he decided not to resume racing. But Freddie Frith was back and had his only post-war outing on a works Norton at the Shelsley Walsh hill-climb in October 1946. But the winner was that man Lyons on a Triumph.

In December the FICM, the sport's international governing body, met in Paris and decided to ban superchargers and to insist that all machines ran on normally available pump petrol. Curiously the Italians backed the supercharger ban while the British delegation were in favour of the fuel decision – though both seemed to be against the interests of their home factories.

At this time there was an upheaval at Nortons. First Craig rejoined the firm on the first day of 1947 and then, at the end of the month, the Mansells pulled out and took Bill Mewis with them. Bill Mansell had joined the firm in 1912 and had taken over as managing director in 1927. He had handed over to Gilbert Smith in 1945 but both he and his son Dennis had stayed on the board. Just what triggered the exodus is not clear. Possibly majority shareholder Tony Vandervell (of CAV fame) had decided that it was time for a reorganisation. Certainly it pleased Gilbert Smith and Craig, neither of whom had got on well with the Mansells in recent years.

Although the usual polite words were spoken, Dennis Mansell made his feelings plain when he immediately switched to a BSA for trials. The Norton changes came at a time of national crisis. The dockers were on strike, the transport system in turmoil, it was the worst winter for years, food rations were cut back to wartime levels and the country teetered on the edge of bankruptcy. It was a situation similar to the one facing Russia in 1991.

Secondary strike action in support of the dockers put the power stations out of action and stopped production at the Norton factory in March 1947 – and also stopped publication of the two weeklies, something that not even Hitler had managed! As the grip of winter eased so did the strike, and in late March the Norton team for the first post-war TT was announced – veteran Harold Daniell was retained and was to be joined by two Irishmen, Artie Bell and MGP winner Ernie Lyons, plus Ken Bills, tempted out of retirement for another year.

Riding his own Norton, Bell won the North West 200, the traditional TT 'warm-up', but Daniell on a works 500 crashed while chasing Bell. The factory racers for 1947 were the 1938 machines with modifications. The short-movement original telescopic forks were replaced by the new Roadholders, the rear-plunger suspension was improved by fitting small external hydraulic dampers and the compression ratio was dropped from around 10 to 1 right down to 7.2 for the 500 cc, which reduced the power output from close to 50 bhp at 6800 rpm to little over 40 bhp.

The 1947 Junior TT – the first post-war TT – proved a disaster for Nortons. Bell went out with a broken chain, Lyons crashed at Waterworks and Bills was never in the reckoning after sliding off on wet tar at Glen Helen. Only Daniell challenged for the lead. He held second place until the engine quit on the fourth lap. Even he had been completely outpaced by Bob

LEFT Charles Markham of *Motor Cycling* aboard a Norton International, Isle of Man 1947. The riding gear is typical – flat cap, Mark VIII RAF goggles, a towel around the neck, one piece tank-suit and wellington boots.

BELOW The 1948 factory Nortons retained the pre-war 'garden gate' frames but were fitted with a comprehensive primary chain guard. The massive alloy oil tank was prone to splitting.

RIGHT Brothers-in-law Harold Daniell (right) and Steve Lancefield inspect the latest 490 cc side-valve Model 16H Norton outside Daniell's showroom in Forest Hill, South London in May 1948.

Foster (Velocette) and when he retired Velocettes took the first four places, their engines reacting more favourably to the low-octane diet.

For the Senior Frith switched to a V-twin Guzzi but was eliminated by a crash during practice, and the main opposition to the Nortons were the new AJS 'Porcupine' twins. Their challenge soon faded, leaving team-mates Daniell and Bell to battle it out ahead of Bills. Eventually Daniell won the race by 22 seconds at a speed of 82.81 mph – compared with his 1938 petrol-benzole winning average of 89.11 mph.

To encourage the less well off to go racing the ACU instigated the Clubman's TT in 1947. This was for riders without international experience riding standard catalogue sports machines. Both Junior (350 cc) and Senior (500 cc) races were won by Nortons – by Eric Briggs and Denis Parkinson respectively. Both rode 1939 Internationals with girder forks, preferring the old machines because the pre-war specification allowed them to use alloy heads and barrels.

The first classic to be run after the war with anything like a full-scale international entry was the Dutch TT of 1947. Nortons sent the TT team of four with Bills and Lyons riding the 350s and Daniell and Bell on the bigger machines. Peter Goodman (Velocette) won the 350 cc but Bills pushed him hard, recording the fastest lap at 82.12 mph and finishing only 5 seconds astern. Daniell looked set to repeat his TT win when he romped away and set the fastest lap at 86.90 mph – only to retire with a punctured rear tyre. This let team-mate Bell through to win.

Eight days later Nortons won the three main classes at the Belgian Grand Prix at Spa-Francorchamps. Said the *Motor Cycling* reporter: 'It has been a great day all round for Nortons. Kenneth Bills won the 350 race with such graceful ease that one felt prompted to remark, "It's a shame to take the money."' Surprisingly Bills on his Norton had easily outpaced the Velocettes, winning at 85.19 mph and clocking the fastest lap at 86.02 mph – but Lyons, who had crashed again in Holland, was again out of luck and retired with engine trouble.

Short of entries, the organisers invited Nortons to field all four riders in the 500 cc class and Craig obliged by lending Bills the spare 500 while Lyons switched to Bill's still hot 350 cc winning bike. With little opposition the race was a Norton parade, with Daniell winning from Bell and Bills, a second covering the three of them.

It was the sidecar race that really excited the crowd and the *Motor Cycling* reporter. Local hero Frans Vanderschrick (Norton) battled it out with Switzerland's Hans Haldemann (Norton).

> They alternate with a regularity which drives the crowd hysterical. It is a truly amazing spectacle; these chair dicers pull every trick from the sidecarist's repertoire . . . fork blades whip and sway like rushes in a high wind, third wheels rise and fall, and passengers leap and dive with incredible activity.

Eventually Vanderschrick won at 71.39 mph, with Haldemann second after hitting a straw bale.

In July *Motor Cycling* road tested the 490 cc International and claimed a stop speed of 97 mph. This sounds wildly optimistic. The works road racer with double overhead camshafts, huge carburettor and megaphone exhaust had a level-road maximum on pool petrol of about 110 mph at that time. It was at least 50 lb lighter and did not have to drive the magdyno which was said to knock around 7 mph off the top speed of any machine!

Nevertheless the 'Inter' was a very desirable sports machine and George Formby (of 'No Limit' and 'When I'm Cleaning Windows' fame) was pictured taking delivery of one of these camshaft Nortons in July that year. The country was still in a shocking financial state and the petrol ration was first reduced and then, in August, it was announced that when the basic ration coupons ran out at the end of November they would not be replaced. There was to be no petrol except for 'essential' users and a complete ban on what the government termed 'pleasure motoring'.

Despite the gloom Nortons entered five bikes for the first post-war Ulster Grand Prix – held on a shortened Clady circuit that still included the incredible, bumpy seven-mile straight. There was no foreign opposition but the Velocettes were going well and Bob Foster took an early lead in the 500 cc class before his engine dropped a valve. Daniell suffered his usual Ulster luck when his rear wheel punctured – just as it had in Holland – but Bell and Lyons kept going to finish first and second in the marathon 15-lap, 247-mile event.

In the 350 cc race, run concurrently, Nortons fielded Bills and to assist him recruited Johnny Lockett who had made his name pre-war on Beart-prepared Nortons before switching to Lancefield-tuned machines. Frith (Velocette) set the early pace but Lockett had caught him when the Velo, like its bigger brother, dropped a valve. Lockett went on to win at 84.77 mph (compared with Bell's 91.25 mph) but team-mate Bills retired.

Soon after the Ulster Craig, Daniell and Bell set off

This was the scene at the Villa Marina, Douglas, as Artie Bell stepped up to receive the trophy after winning the 1948 Senior TT. On the right is Norton MD Gilbert Smith.

TOP John Cobb, famous for his attempts on the land speed record, tries Artie Bell's Senior TT winning Norton in June 1948.

ABOVE For the private owner – the 1948 Manx Norton in full racing trim but with single overhead camshaft engine. 348 cc and 499 cc cost the same – £315.

LEFT Britain's winning Trophy Team at the 1948 International Six Days Trial. In the centre is Jack Williams on his International Norton. Others (left to right) are Charlie Rogers (Royal Enfield), Allan Jefferies (Triumph), Hugh Viney (AJS) and former Norton teamster Vic Brittain (Royal Enfield).

BELOW Artie Bell on his 350 cc Norton crosses the tramlines at the Swiss Grand Prix in Geneva in 1948. He won the class – and team-mate Harold Daniell the 500 cc, despite strong Italian opposition.

ABOVE The 1948 version of the Norton International – available with either 348 cc or 490 cc camshaft engine – the larger machine capable of around 100 mph.

ABOVE RIGHT It poured throughout the 1948 TT week – and it's still raining as Artie Bell wheels a factory Norton off the boat at the start of 1949 TT week.

RIGHT Artie Bell on one of his Nortons at the 1949 TT, illustrating the small frontal area of the racing single-cylinder machine.

for the Italian Grand Prix, held that year on a short road circuit on the outskirts of Milan. It was the first time that Nortons had been officially represented in Italy since Simpson had taken a works bike to Monza in 1931, because in the 1930s it was impossible for Nortons to sell machines in Mussolini's Italy and the factory declined to race where they could not sell. It proved a disappointing outing. Bell retired with a fuel problem, later traced to an air lock, while Daniell was involved in a pile-up but remounted to finish third behind Arciso Artesiani (Gilera) and Enrico Lorenzetti (Guzzi), both riding light single-cylinder machines.

At home Nortons did magnificently in the Manx Grand Prix where Clubman's winner Eric Briggs did the double on Lancefield-tuned machines, with Nortons taking seven out of the first 10 places in the Junior and filling the top 11 places in the Senior – convincing proof that the Bracebridge Street machines were the best racing bikes money could buy.

Ken Bills left the team at the end of the year: 'I was on good terms with everyone. But I felt I wasn't able to give Nortons what they wanted . . . with a wife and son and two businesses to run I just had too many responsibilities to ride flat out all the time.' Of Craig he said: 'He was an exceptionally painstaking tuner. He knew an awful lot – he came up the trial and error way.' Bills in fact did not retire – he made another comeback to race Velocettes for Nigel Spring in 1948.

It was a gloomy winter and not surprisingly there was little new in the Norton range for 1948. An official statement read: 'We shall continue with the same range of models.' There were however, numerous engine modifications including new pistons of low-expansion aluminium alloy with longer skirts, heavier flywheels and one-piece rocker boxes for the OHV engines, while the cam followers had been eliminated by the adoption of new valve gear with rotating, mushroom-based tappets. Prices were up slightly – the Manx models to £315.

At the end of the year came welcome news that the authorities were going to allow fuel to be used for competitions and that coupons would be issued both to competitors and officials. In January 1948 Triumph launched their 500 cc twin-cylinder Grand Prix racer. Modelled on Ernie Lyons MGP winner, this came complete with Edward Turner's sprung rear hub and was priced at £337.

In the same issue of *The Motor Cycle* Norton announced their new trials model, the 500T, with 490 cc OHV engine (with alloy head and barrel) mounted in a modified 16H frame with 52 in wheelbase and 7½ in ground clearance. The complete machine was claimed to weigh only 300 lb and cost under £200. It was a good time for new models, for the following week AMC launched the 350 cc single-cylinder, overhead-camshaft 7R AJS racer.

While all this was going on, Lancefield was on his way to Daytona in Florida. The United States was then a popular export market for British motorcycles and

Gilbert Smith was eager to build on Norton racing successes there. Part of the plan was to send the famous south London tuner to Daytona to assist all those riding Nortons – and in particular Canadian Bill Mathews, a previous winner of the main event on a Norton, plus up-and-coming Dick Klamfoth and Dons Evans in the supporting amateur race.

The machines used in American Motorcycle Association events had to be catalogue models, which let the Manx in, but they also had to be fitted with a kick-starter and the maximum compression ratio allowed was 7.5 to 1. Norton got round the first proviso by fitting International gearboxes. The compression problem was another matter. The excellent pump fuel provided had an octane rating of about 85 and the correct ratio for the Manx would have been 9 to 1.

Things went well initially when Evans and Klamfoth took the first two places in the 100-mile race, but in the more important 200-miler Mathews was beaten by just 18 seconds by Floyd Emde on an Indian. Lancefield was far from happy about the lap scoring but he had learned a lot about Daytona, run in those days on a four-mile circuit, one straight of which was the famous beach and the other a narrow tarmac road behind the dunes.

Spirits were raised in the spring of 1948 when the government announced that the basic fuel ration was to be restored on 1 June – riders with under 250 cc bikes were to be allowed 9 gallons for six months while those with bigger machines could get 13 gallons for the half-year.

The first classic of 1948 was the Swiss at Geneva and, as in pre-war days, Switzerland proved a happy hunting ground for Nortons who sent Daniell and Bell to contest both races despite the proximity of TT practice. Bell won the 350 cc race from David Whitworth (Velocette), with Daniell third despite sliding off on oil. Daniell won the 500 cc from Bell, the Nortons getting the better of the strong Italian contingent which included Tenni and Lyons on Guzzi V-twins. And there was a third success for Nortons when Haldemann won the sidecar race from fellow Swiss Ferdi Aubert.

The 1948 TT Nortons were still the pre-war models with modifications. There were new and stiffer crankcases with a larger sump, increased finning on the cylinder heads and comprehensive primary chain guards. Most of the changes were aimed at improving performance on the low-octane fuel, but Craig was experimenting with two leading shoe front brakes. The team was Daniell, Bell and Lockett who had replaced Ken Bills, with MGP double winner Eric Briggs taking the place of Ernie Lyons. One change from 1938 was that Craig had followed Frith's lead of 1939 and reverted to 73.4 × 82.5 mm bore and stroke for the 350 cc engines.

In the Junior TT Frith and Foster on the best Velocettes were just too fast. Daniell held third place until a split tank put him out on lap four; Bell came through

LEFT **A 1949 works Norton – the last year of the 'garden gate' frames. They were reliable but slow and only won when the opposition faded as in the Senior TT when Harold Daniell kept going as his rivals retired. Note the complex mounting of the float bowl for the Amal carburettor.**

ABOVE RIGHT **Ireland's Artie Bell is congratulated by Norton's boss Gilbert Smith after winning the 1948 Senior TT. On the left is Joe Craig and on the right Rex McCandless who later designed the featherbed frame.**

RIGHT **The Duke of Edinburgh flags Artie Bell away at the start of the 1949 Senior TT.**

to finish third, complaining that his bike was over-geared, and Lockett was fourth. The Senior looked like being a disaster too as Tenni (Guzzi) and Les Graham (AJS) set the early pace. Then the Italian was slowed by valve-spring failure and when Graham stopped at Ballig, Nortons were left in control with Bell coming home to win at 84.97 mph. Daniell was in second place when he was forced out by gearbox trouble on the last lap and it was Bill Doran and Jock Weddell on standard Manx models who made it a 1–2–3 for Nortons.

Despite the increasing opposition of the AJS and Guzzi twins, Nortons continued their winning ways on the continent. In Holland Bell won the 500 cc class at 82.75 mph with the fastest lap at 87.75 mph, and only a split oil tank prevented Daniell from finishing second. They could not match the speed of Ken Bills on a Nigel Spring Velocette (a works machine) in the 350 cc race in which the former Norton rider beat Frith on a second Velocette ahead of Briggs – Bell losing any chance when a plug oiled at the start, and Lockett being forced out with yet another tank failure.

In Belgium the following weekend a carburettor problem put paid to Bell's chances of making it three 500 cc classics in a row, but Lockett rode a splendid race to win for Nortons at 91.82 mph from Jock West (AJS) and Daniell. Again the Nortons could not hold the Velocettes in the 350 cc race, won by Bob Foster, but Frans Vanderschrick made it two wins for Norton when he beat Eric Oliver in the sidecar race.

The 1948 Ulster was the wettest on record. Daniell's Irish luck struck even before the race started when he went down with 'flu and in a last-minute switch Lockett took over his machine. He and Bell fought a great battle with Lorenzetti on a single-cylinder Guzzi but the

Italian got the better of them to win at 85.55 mph with the fastest lap at 88.57 mph – incredible speeds considering the conditions.

Bell went out when he tried to pass Lorenzetti at the end of the seven-mile straight, got into difficulties, hit the bank and broke the frame, but Lockett kept going to finish second. Out of a total race entry of 93 only 28 finished the course. All things considered, it had not been a bad year. Out of the five classics contested Nortons won four of the 500 cc races and one of the 350 cc, while Velocette had four victories and Guzzi one.

There was again bad weather for the Manx Grand Prix. The Junior was postponed for a day and was then won by Denis Parkinson on a Beart Norton, but only after he had been given a shock by a newcomer having his first Isle of Man outing – a certain G. E. Duke on a very standard Manx who had no idea that he was doing so well until he retired on the fourth lap with a split oil tank! Charlie Edwards remembers that he helped Duke to build the bike from bits and pieces scrounged from the factory: 'Geoff was a fanatic about weight and we lightened everything we could and he had managed to get hold of one of the pre-war alloy oil tanks which split and put him out.'

The part that chance plays in life is well illustrated by Duke's career. After serving as a motorcycle sergeant instructor in the Royal Signals (where he was also a member of the motorcycle display team) Duke joined BSA as a factory trials rider in 1947. Purely by chance he was spotted by Artie Bell at the Scott Trial in Yorkshire. Artie was impressed and suggested to Nortons that Duke be employed to ride and help develop the new 500T trials Norton which his partner Rex McCandless had designed for the Birmingham factory.

Unknown to Nortons, Duke was already in contact with AMC. He had been in the Army with Hugh Viney who was, by this time, in charge of the AJS/Matchless trials team. Duke wrote to Viney and went down to Woolwich where he was offered a job which he, to use his own words, 'virtually accepted'. Only one thing rankled: it had been made clear that his ambition to go road racing would be discouraged.

When he got back to his lodgings in Birmingham a letter from Nortons was waiting for him. They wanted him to run his own small competition department where he would develop the 500T, riding it in trials at the weekends. The clincher came when Duke met Gilbert Smith for a final interview. When the question of riding in the Clubman's TT was mentioned the Norton boss's reaction was one of positive encouragement. Duke started work at Bracebridge Street in January 1948 but his entry for the Clubman's TT was turned down because he had no road-racing experience and the event was over-subscribed – which was why he made his Isle of Man debut as a raw novice in September that year.

In November 1948 came news of the first really new Norton since the introduction of the camshaft models back in 1927. The headline in *The Motor Cycle* read: 'Norton vertical-twin announced'. Bracebridge Street had at last given in to popular demand and had followed the trend originated by Triumph and taken up by BSA, Ariel, Royal Enfield and AJS/Matchless.

The Model 7, soon named the Dominator, was designed by Bert Hopwood who had served under Edward Turner at Triumph before joining Nortons in April 1947, and was first shown to the public at Earls Court in late November 1948, the first show for ten years. It was a handsome machine with a 497 cc push-rod overhead-valve engine with 66 × 72.6 mm bore and stroke. This was mounted in a normal Norton frame with telescopic forks and plunger rear suspension and was priced at £216 – more expensive than the push-rod single ES2 (£193) but cheaper than the 490cc International (£247) which both used the same chassis.

The weeklies were full of praise for the new twin but in reality it was no match for the already well-established Triumph Tiger 100. The Norton was overweight at 440 lb – no less than 75 lb heavier than the standard Triumph 500 cc twins! True the Norton had rear springing, but the Triumph was available with the sprung hub and this added less than 20 lb to the weight. Moreover the Norton twin had a disappointing performance. It was fast but lacked the mid-range torque that the other twins had and which was where the twins were supposed to score over the singles.

ABOVE **Flat out! Geoff Duke heads for victory in the 1949 Senior Manx Grand Prix.**

RIGHT **Just over three months before winning the Manx, Geoff Duke had won the 1949 Senior Clubmans' TT on an International Norton carrying the same number 23. He rounds Governors Bridge in that race.**

The sporting year ended with Nortons winning the team prize at the gruelling Scott Trial. Jim Alves won for Triumph but Norton teamsters Rex Young, Geoff Duke and Ted Ogden packed the places – just a year after Duke had caught Artie Bell's eye and set in motion the train of events that led to him joining Nortons.

The year 1949 opened with news that the FICM had decided to instigate the road-racing World Championships based on the results of the major grands prix, but early in the year the interest of British enthusiasts centred on Daytona. It was at this time that Nortons were thinking in terms of replacing the single-cylinder works racers with a four-cylinder design. It was thought that Joe Craig would be busy liaising with BRM who were to design the unit, and to take the weight off his shoulders Lancefield joined Nortons to run the works team for a season. This meant that he was too busy to go to America and Francis Beart went instead.

The two were great rivals and not on particularly friendly terms but on this occasion Lancefield cooperated to the full and gave Beart a thorough briefing on what to expect. The trip proved a great success. The Beart-prepared Manx Nortons, with International kick-start gearboxes, ridden by Klamfoth and Mathews, finished first and second in the 200-miler in which Tex Luse on another Norton made it a 1–2–3 for Britain.

Klamfoth's speed was a record 85.31 mph and completing a perfect weekend Don Evans (Norton) won the amateur 100-miler from Ted Totoraitis on an old, but very fast, International Norton. Following the refuelling problems of the preceding year, new gravity quick-fillers had been designed and these proved capable of dumping four gallons of petrol in just 11 seconds.

Two test impressions appeared in *Motor Cycling* early in 1949. The first was of the new Dominator twin and in a typical piece of 'read between the lines' journalese the road tester said: 'The Dominator is not light at 438 lb, but the weight is well distributed. . . .' Top speed was given as 95 mph with a quarter-mile speed of 92 mph – curiously these were virtually the same as the test figures for the very much lighter and slightly more powerful Triumph Tiger 100.

The other impression was of the trials 500T, designed by Rex McCandless and refined by Geoff Duke. Cyril Quantrill, then sports editor of *Motor Cycling*, took the machine through the woods and found it to be 'one of the most lusty, cut-and-shut, easy to navigate competition 500s you've ever set your eyes on; a jolly nice bicycle'.

Duke meanwhile was continuing to startle the stars on an alcohol-burning 350 cc Manx. At Bemsee's meeting at Haddenham he beat Les Graham on the brand-

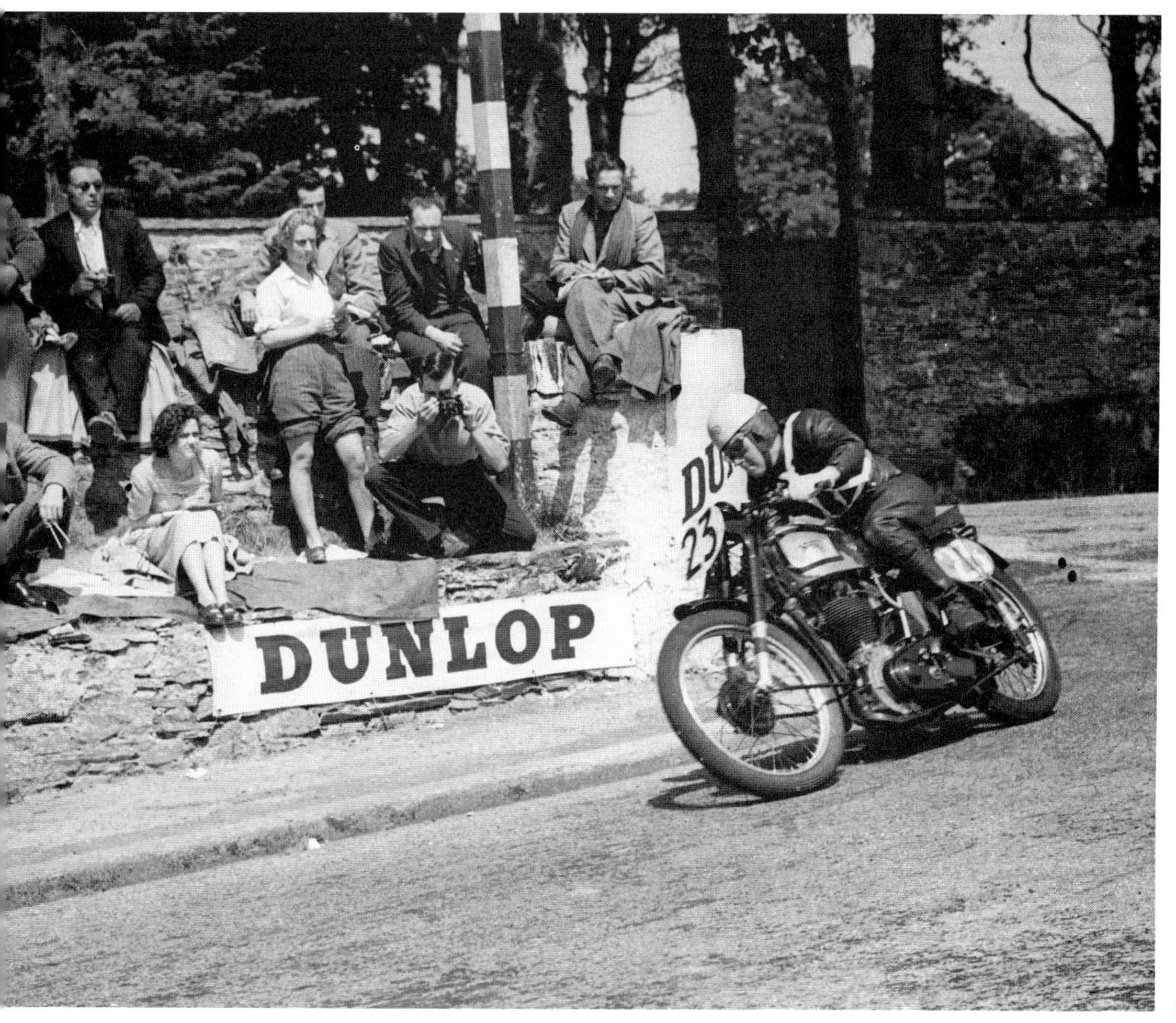

ABOVE **Veteran Harold Daniell wins the 1949 Senior TT. Les Graham (AJS) led until the armature shaft of his magneto broke two miles from the finish.**

RIGHT **Geoff Duke in the paddock after winning the 1949 Senior Manx Grand Prix after a hard fought battle with Cromie McCandless (on Duke's left).**

new 7R AJS in the 350 cc class and later in April he won the Non-experts class at Blandford competing against bikes up to 1000 cc – and also finished second in the Open 350 cc class, narrowly beaten by Graham. It was at Blandford that the 1949 works machines made a first appearance, with Lockett and Daniell contesting the 350 cc class only. The bikes were basically the preceding year's updated but one very noticeable modification was the adoption of a completely new front fork. This had a very large-diameter spindle carried in clamps which jutted forward from the fork legs.

They did not do well at Blandford but things went better at the North West 200 in May where Bell won the 500 cc class from Lockett and Daniell took the 350 cc honours, beating Frith (Velocette) by a split second. Duke, fresh from the Scottish Six Days Trial where he had been a member of the Norton squad which won the team prize (with Jack Blackwell and Rex Young), rode his own Manx into third place. He certainly was not a works rider – Lancefield made this abundantly clear by throwing him out of the garage the factory were using!

When the team arrived on the island it was seen that all the bikes were fitted with normal forks. The new ones had proved a failure. None of the riders liked them, complaining of a pendulum effect which made the bikes difficult to control at high speeds. Some blame Hopwood for the design but Doug Hele, who had joined Nortons from Douglas (where he had worked under Walter Moore of early Norton and NSU fame), explains the situation:

> Basically the fork was Craig's idea. He thought the more upright the legs were the better the fork would work. This was right up to a point but over 100 mph other forces came into play. I did the detail drawings and I can remember some very embarrassing moments at the drawing board with Craig on one side and Hopwood on the other arguing about the details and the cost. It made it very difficult for me – I got on well with both of them.

Edwards also remembers the clash of personalities: 'Hopwood and Craig never got on. I don't think they

could stand each other. In many ways they were too much alike.'

Of the two, Edwards preferred Craig.

He was a hard man but if you were doing things right he was all right. But you had to stand up to him. When it came to engines he got results. He was no designer, mind you. He had been left with a very good engine and he patiently and logically developed it.

Talking of Hopwood, Edwards continued:

He was a man who couldn't bear criticism of any kind. In the winter when we were not racing I used to go out testing the prototypes – putting mileage on them. He hated it if I came back and criticised the bike – he only wanted praise. He was a very difficult man.

Hopwood's brief when he joined Nortons was to design a twin-cylinder machine and to improve the roadsters. He soon found he was fighting a constant battle with Craig, who had his own racing empire within the factory. Hopwood felt that Nortons should devote more of the available finance to roadster projects – even if the racing had to suffer. Such talk was heresy to Craig, especially as his salary was augmented by a generous bonus scheme based on racing successes. Gilbert Smith sided with Craig and things came to a head when the production line had to be stopped because of a surge of warranty claims when the valve gear of the Hopwood modified OHV engines wore out within a few hundred miles.

As far as Gilbert was concerned this was the last straw. Hopwood was sacked early in 1949 and soon after he left Craig was injured and his wife killed when he was involved in an accident while riding a Dominator twin. Hele, who had been recruited by Craig, recalls: 'At the time Joe was working to improve the performance of the twin and he was riding the bike to evaluate progress.' Hopwood went to BSA in May 1949 and in August Hele left Nortons to join him.

That year (1949) Velocette switched to double overhead camshafts and Frith won the Junior TT – but only after poor Bill Doran on the simple, single-overhead-cam 7R AJS retired on the last lap with gearbox trouble. Lyons (Velocette) was second ahead of Bell and Daniell, and with Lockett seventh Nortons took the team prize. AJS were even unluckier in the Senior, for that was the year Les Graham on a Porcupine twin led until the magneto drive sheared just two miles from the finish.

Daniell came home to win his third Senior ahead of Lockett and with Bell fourth Nortons won another team

ABOVE The first twin-cylinder Norton of the modern era was the 497 cc Dominator Model 7 designed by Bert Hopwood and announced in November 1948.

BELOW The successful Norton team at Daytona in 1949 when Canadian Bill Mathews (left) came second in the classic 200-miler behind Dick Klamforth from Ohio.

Joe Craig in the test-house working on a roadster OHV engine in 1949 when production was stopped following problems with a new design of cam-followers.

prize. Reliability had paid off, for at the halfway mark there was not a Norton in the first three places. On the Continent the Nortons were no match for their rivals. In the Swiss at Berne, Frith (Velocette) won the 350 cc class and Graham (AJS) took the 500 cc though Eric Oliver with Denis Jenkinson in the sidecar did win the sidecar class for Norton.

At the Dutch TT Frith won again and Nello Pagani proved just how fast the new four-cylinder Gilera was by playing cat and mouse to beat Graham (AJS) with a last-lap surge. In Belgium it was Frith again and Doran rode a brilliant race to win the 500 cc class for AJS, passing Artesiani (Gilera) and Lorenzetti (Guzzi) on the last bend.

The tale of Norton woe continued at the Ulster. There Nortons fielded a record seven works riders. Daniell, Bell, Lockett and Australian George Morrison rode in the 500 cc race while Dickie Dale, Australian Harry Hinton and local star Louis Carter were lent factory bikes for the 350 cc. In the big race only Bell finished – in second place, a fine ride and beaten only by Graham who clinched the first 500 cc World Championship. The 350s were reliable but woefully slow, finishing sixth, seventh and eighth.

There was no point in going to Monza for the Italian Grand Prix in September and the only real success was that achieved by Oliver/Jenkinson who finished the year as sidecar World Champions. But there was encouragement for Nortons at the Manx Grand Prix. In June Duke had won the Senior Clubman's TT on an International Norton at record speed and with a record lap. And in September he fought two great duels with Cromie McCandless (brother of designer Rex) who was riding Beart's Nortons. The Ulsterman won the Junior from Duke who lost time when he slid off when leading at Ramsey on the fifth lap, but Duke turned the tables to win the Senior – breaking all MGP records and getting very close to the June TT speeds.

Works team race mechanic Charlie Edwards confirms that both of Duke's machines were standard single-overhead-camshaft Manx models, but adds: 'Mind you, they were put together right.' And Charlie was on the island to assist. Soon afterwards he was on his way to Montlhéry with Craig, Bell, Oliver and Duke. The plan was to beat world records in the 350, 500 cc and Sidecar classes just before the Earls Court Show opened in November. The engines were modified to run on a special high-octane brew supplied by Monsieur Garreau, the French importer, and a total of 21 records were broken – but it was quantity rather than quality and none was very impressive.

Back at Earls Court Nortons unveiled the 1950 range. The roadsters were little changed but racing enthusiasts were delighted with the latest Manx models which had double-overhead-camshaft valve gear for the first time. This was modelled on the design first used on the works machines in 1937. The price of the Manx had risen to £347, a year's wages for most workers.

Behind the scenes Craig's liaison with Raymond Mays and BRM on the design of a water-cooled four-cylinder 500 cc racer was not going well. BRM were having all sorts of problems and although they did eventually produce a 125 cc single-cylinder slave unit (one cylinder of the projected design) a complete engine was never built, and Craig's own inclination was further to develop both the frames and the engines of his beloved singles.

CHAPTER 16

Geoff Duke and the Featherbed 1950–1952

The new decade began well for Nortons. Duke won the Victory Cup Trial in Shropshire with Arthur Humphries top in the Sidecar class and the same February weekend Nortons finished 1, 2 and 4 in the 200-miler at Daytona with Canadian veteran Billy Mathews winning from Dick Klamfoth, both riding Manx Nortons prepared by Francis Beart.

But the real activity was taking place behind the scenes where completely new racing machines were being built and tested. These had double-loop welded frames designed and made by Ulsterman Rex McCandless in his Belfast workshop. Rex and Norton teamster Artie Bell were old friends and had worked together for several years on various projects. The new frame with swinging-fork rear suspension was a direct development of one built by McCandless in 1944, powered by a Triumph Tiger 100 engine. By July 1945 when racing in Ireland resumed with the meeting at Bangor, two bikes had been built and were raced by Rex and brother Cromie. Rex then built a number of similar frames for grass tracking but it was not until 1949 that he managed to persuade Gilbert Smith that Nortons should try one of his frames, fitted with a works engine, against a factory racer with plunger suspension.

Gilbert probably did not need much encouragement. The old 'garden gate' frames were heavy, did not handle well and were constantly breaking. The first test was held on the Isle of Man late in 1949 when Artie Bell on the McCandless-framed machine proved considerably faster than Geoff Duke on the 1949 works 500 on the Windy Corner, Keppel Gate and Kate's Cottage section– the roads temporarily closed by the cooperative local chief of police who by lucky chance happened to be a relative of brother Cromie's Manx wife.

Having passed that test the prototype 'featherbed' was taken to Montlhéry near Paris where the entire Norton team thrashed it round the bumpy French circuit to see if they could break it. They wore out two engines but no serious frame faults developed and both Gilbert Smith and Joe Craig were sold on the idea – not to mention the riders.

RIGHT **New man, new machine. Geoff Duke joined the Norton team for 1950, here winning the 500 cc race at Blandford on 29 April that year – the first public appearance of the famous featherbed racing Norton.**

BELOW **Eric Oliver won the sidecar class of the Belgian Grand Prix six years in succession for Nortons. Here he leads Belgian Frans Vanderschrick (Norton) in 1950.**

By happy coincidence a lot of work was being done on the engines – particularly the 500. The man behind this was a former Polish fighter pilot named Leo Kuzmicki who in pre-war days had been a lecturer on internal combustion engines at Warsaw University. After the war he had decided to stay in England and had got a job at Nortons – as a sweeper-up!

Charlie Edwards remembers their first meeting:

When I came in one morning he was sweeping the experimental department and we got talking. It was soon obvious this man was no ordinary sweeper-up and we were chatting away when Joe Craig came in. He was like a bear with a sore head most mornings and he gave Leo a right dressing-down for standing talking and not getting on with it – and then I got one! But I told Joe that this guy might be able to help, and that he should have a talk with him. Well, it wasn't long before Leo was in the drawing office and in my opinion it was he who vastly improved first the 500 and then the 350. He was brilliant on cam profiles, combustion chamber shapes, valve timing, porting – the lot.

The new racers were not ready for the first major British meeting of 1950 – Silverstone Saturday, sponsored by *Motor Cycling*. Duke and Daniell turned out on the old models and dominated the meeting. Said the *Motor Cycling* report: 'That irrepressible young man G.E. Duke, riding 350 and 500 cc Nortons, dominated the race meeting. . . .' He was too fast for Daniell who fell off trying to pass him and injured a hand.

A week later the prototype 'featherbed' was ready and Duke wheeled it out for the 500 cc race at Blandford in Dorset on 30 April 1950. Commented *Motor Cycling*: 'At Blandford the cat metaphorically jumped out of the bag when Joe Craig lifted the all enveloping cover from Geoff Duke's 500 cc model.' Duke won at record speed and with a record lap – and the next week a long description of the McCandless frame appeared in both magazines. Curiously there was little information about the new engine despite the fact that it looked different. For the first time the fins of the cylinder head enclosed the top bevel housing.

A week after Blandford, Duke's team-mates Bell and Lockett made winning debuts on works 'featherbeds' at the Leinster – Artie winning the 500 cc class and Johnny the 350 cc in which he went so fast that he actually beat all the 500s except Bell, all classes starting together. The team met for the North West 200 where Bell and Lockett took the first two places in the 500 cc race while Duke, the junior member of the squad, won the 350 cc.

News of the engines was finally released in mid May. Reported *Motor Cycling*: 'The cylinder head is entirely

Norton
Norton

LEFT The Norton equipe at the Swiss Grand Prix in 1950. Railway transport, used pre-war, had given way to a van painted in two tones of grey. Following tyre troubles at the Belgian Grand Prix and Dutch TT the bikes are fitted with Italian Pirelli tyres but these were soon replaced by Avons.

BELOW LEFT Norton mechanics work on the factory bikes in the garage under the Castle Mona Hotel, Douglas in 1950. Note the streamlined tails and the rear suspension legs with extra oil reservoirs. Standing (wearing glasses) is Ivor Smith, nearest camera is Bill Clarke.

RIGHT The two men responsible for the race winning featherbed. On the left Joe Craig who led the team who built revised and more powerful 350 cc and 500 cc engines – on the right Rex McCandless the brilliant Belfast engineer who developed the twin loop featherbed frame.

new and is a beautiful piece of foundry work. It is unusual in that it has the bevel housing cast integrally with it. Close pitched fins run diagonally across the head, from drive side to timing side.' The old aluminium bronze 'skull' with bonded fins was gone - the new head was aluminium with inserted steel valve seats.

The bore and stroke of both units remained the same. After the war the factory had reverted to a relatively long stroke for the 350 cc – 73.4 × 82.5 mm, 349 cc. This had been tried successfully in 1936 and retained in 1937 before a switch to 75.9 × 77 mm in 1938, but Frith reverted to one of the older engines in 1939. The 500 cc retained the 82 × 94.3 mm, 498 cc dimensions adopted in 1938.

A new Amal carburettor (which became the GP) was fitted and the petrol tanks for the TT held nearly six gallons – but because they sat on the twin frame tubes and had no upper frame member running through a tunnel they looked no bigger than the old, smaller-capacity tanks.

On the Isle of Man the Nortons were sensational. Bell won the Junior TT at a record 86.32 mph with a record lap at 87.31 mph with Duke second and veteran Daniell third, passing Les Graham (AJS) on the last lap. At the prize-giving Bell paid tribute to Rex McCandless for designing the frame and to Joe Craig whom he described as 'the Maestro of poke'. Daniell too praised the new frame and suspension and commented that it was so comfortable that one could fall asleep while riding it; and it was Harold who coined the nickname 'featherbed'.

In practice Duke had been the first to lap the TT circuit at over 90 mph since the war – getting round at 90.27 mph. And it was the new member of the team who led the Senior from start to finish to win at an astounding 92.27 mph – an average faster than the old lap record which he pushed up to 93.33 mph. Bell finished second and Lockett took third place ahead of Graham (AJS), with Daniell fifth. It was another Norton 1–2–3 and once again Nortons had swept the board in both Junior and Senior races – a feat achieved only once before, in 1933 by Nortons!

ABOVE LEFT **Johnny Lockett in action at Ballaugh Bridge on his works featherbed during the 1950 Junior TT.**

ABOVE **Geoff Duke rounds Quarter Bridge in the 1950 Junior TT. He finished second to team-mate Artie Bell.**

ABOVE RIGHT **Artie Bell airborne at Ballaugh Bridge as he heads for victory in the 1950 Junior TT.**

The next classic was the Belgian Grand Prix. There Foster's Velocette proved too fast on the ultra-quick Francorchamps circuit and he won the 350 cc race from Bell and Duke. Then came a crushing blow for the team in the 500 cc race. Les Graham's AJS twin was fitted with a massive 10 in front brake and it locked when he braked hard to avoid Carlo Bandirola who was leading on a Gilera. Graham went down on a 100 mph curve and took Bell, in his slipstream, with him. They finished up under a track-side marshal's post and although Graham escaped unscathed, Bell was seriously injured and never raced again.

Duke, close behind just avoided the mêlée, took the lead and had established a winning gap of 30 seconds, when, on the twelfth lap of the 14-lap race, the tread peeled off his rear tyre. Umberto Masetti (Gilera) took over to win at 101.18 mph, though Duke had set a new lap record at 103.89 mph. Lockett had also been forced to pull out with tyre trouble and it was an irate Craig who confronted Dunlop's Dickie Davis after the race. He was assured that it was a freak happening, a faulty batch, and that all would be well for the Dutch TT the following weekend.

At the 350 cc Dutch TT six days later Foster (Velocette) again got the better of Duke to prove that the 'featherbed' frame and a brilliant rider were not the complete answer – you also needed a good engine. The batch of new Dunlop tyres had given no trouble during practice but in the 500 cc race, in which Dickie Dale took the place of Bell, disaster struck early. On only the second lap, while slipstreaming the leader Masetti (Gilera) at 125 mph, the tread peeled off the rear tyre of Duke's Norton, locked the rear wheel and flung him down the road. As luck would have it Duke had just emerged from a long avenue of trees and he bounced down the track-side grass verge, escaping with severe bruising. A few seconds earlier and he would have hit

the trees and been killed. Realising what had happened, Craig signalled the other riders into the pits.

Masetti went on to win from team-mate Pagani, with Hinton on a Manx Norton third. For the Swiss Grand Prix at Geneva two weeks later Nortons switched to Italian Pirelli tyres but found these gave nothing like the grip of the Dunlops – and they were not helped by torrential rain. In addition Duke was still suffering from his Dutch crash. Again lack of power meant he had no real chance in the 350 cc in which he finished third, beaten by Graham (AJS) and Foster (Velocette), and in the 500 cc race Duke battled home in fourth place.

The season which had started so brilliantly at the TT was crumbling about Nortons' ears. Luckily there was time to get things sorted out before the Ulster in mid-August. Craig decided to switch to Avon tyres. These had been well proven by, among others, George Brown on the mighty 998 cc Vincent V-twin Black Shadow racer which was capable of 140 mph. They proved the complete answer and from then on were standard wear on the factory Nortons.

In Ulster the races were still run concurrently and the factory fielded six riders: Duke, Lockett and Dale in the big class and Daniell, Hinton and Louis Carter in the 350 cc. Duke pulverised the opposition in the 500 cc race, averaging a record 99.56 mph and pushing up the lap figure to 101.77 mph to beat Graham (AJS) easily, with Lockett and Dale third and fourth. But it was the old story in the 350 cc in which Foster and Reg Armstrong (Velocettes) took a 1–2 ahead of Hinton.

Behind the scenes Kuzmicki had been working hard on the 350 cc engine and at the Italian Grand Prix at Monza in September, where the final World Championship round was held, his efforts paid off. Duke won the class, beating Graham (AJS) by a second with Hinton third, 2 seconds covering the three of them! Nortons scored a second win when Oliver got the better of great rival Ercole Frigerio (Gilera) on the very last lap of the sidecar race.

The situation in the 500 cc class was interesting. Despite retiring from the Belgian and Dutch races Duke could still win the title, but he had to finish first at Monza with Masetti no higher than third. It proved a tremendous battle. Duke gradually wore down his opponet, the road-holding of the Norton proving of more benefit than the extra power of the Gilera in the long and gruelling race. Eventually Duke won by nearly a minute and Masetti was so fatigued that he had to be lifted from his machine – but second place was enough to win him the 500 cc World Championship by a single point!

Obviously, but for the tyre problems Duke would have been the champion by a wide margin. He had been well ahead in Belgium and a win there would have been enough to reverse the final placings. As it was Duke finished second in both 350 cc and 500 cc classes but Nortons did have the consolation of taking the 500 cc Manufacturers' title, scoring 32 points to Gilera's 29. Additionally Oliver won the Sidecar title for a second year, overcoming the opposition of Frigerio and his four-cylinder Gilera.

At a time when enthusiasts were talking in terms of multi-cylinder racers, Fergus Anderson, a respected racer and journalist who went on to win two World Championships for Moto Guzzi, took the opposite view. In a provocative article in *The Motor Cycle* at the end of 1950 he posed the question 'Have racing multis had it?' and wrote:

> As the multis could not win at Monza the question arises – can they win anywhere? Personally I do not think they can, and my opinion can be backed up by facts. But for the unlucky tyre trouble . . . it is likely that Nortons would have won every race in the 500 cc class in which they started, excepting the Swiss Grand Prix.

After writing of the various characteristics of the rival types, including useable power, frontal area and handling, he concluded by saying: 'If, today I was given the pick of all the 500 cc racing machines . . . I should have no hesitation in choosing a Norton.'

57

So it was not only Craig who still had faith in the single – there were others who realised that the extra weight, bulk and power of the best of the multis was not perhaps the easy way to success. Certainly for the private owner the single was to be the answer for a long time to come and in November 1950 Nortons made the important announcement that they would be building and selling a batch of Manx racers with the 'featherbed' frame – replicas of the works machines though still powered by the old-style long-stroke double-overhead-camshaft engines. The price was £346 including tax.

The roadster models were unchanged apart from new petrol tanks on the ES2, 18, Big Four and 16H. The country was still struggling to recover from the war, materials were short and strikes were a major problem – both weekly journals losing several issues in the autumn of 1950. During the winter Harold Daniell, one of the few whose career successfully spanned the war, retired to concentrate on his motorcycle business in south London while Duke continued to ride with success in trials, creating a lot of interest when he turned out for the Colmore on a prototype with push-rod engine in a featherbed frame. That was in February 1951 and two overseas riders who were soon to star for Nortons arrived – Ray Amm and Ken Kavanagh.

At the end of February Beart was in Daytona to mastermind another Norton double – Klamfoth winning the 200-miler at a record 92.81 mph and Bob Michael the amateur 100-mile race at 82.54 mph. In Europe the World Championship series opened with the Spanish Grand Prix in Barcelona where Masetti started his defence of the 500 cc title with a win. Nortons had decided to stay at home, though Oliver went to Spain and beat the Gilera opposition despite the fact that the capacity limit had been reduced from 600 to 500 cc. This move slightly favoured the Italians who, unlike Oliver, did not have 600 cc engines. Notably Oliver's outfit used the Hopwood fork, tried briefly by the solo team in 1949.

At home Duke did the double at the *Motor Cycling* sponsored Goodwood meeting, the only motorcycle race ever held at the Sussex circuit (and incidentally the first I ever went to). He then went over to Belgium to win the 500 cc race at Mettet and to try one of the new Manx featherbed frames, fitted with a works engine, in the 350 cc class, finishing third beaten by Doran (AJS) and Graham who had left AJS and rode a Velocette (he had signed to race MV Agusta in the big class but was free to race what he liked in the 350 cc division).

In the North West 200, the traditional May try-out for the TT bikes, Duke led the 350 cc class using the

Geoff Duke takes the chequered flag ahead of Artie Bell to win the 1950 Senior TT at the record average speed of 92.27 mph and with a record lap at 93.33 mph.

49
57
41

LEFT The winning Norton line-up after the 1950 Senior TT. Left to right: Johnny Lockett, Geoff Duke and Artie Bell.

BELOW LEFT This was the scene at the 1950 Belgian Grand Prix after Les Graham and Artie Bell had collided in the 500 cc race. Graham's works AJS Porcupine is upside down under the marshal's post with Bell's mangled Norton in the foreground. Graham was unhurt but Bell never raced again.

RIGHT Eric Oliver and passenger Lorenzo Dobelli sliding across the cobbled track at Monza on their way to winning the sidecar class of the 1950 Italian Grand Prix – a win that clinched the World Championship.

BELOW Nortons again dominated America's most important race, the Daytona 200, in 1950. Here Francis Beart (dark glasses) poses with the team on the famous beach. Canadian Bill Mathews (left) had again won the big race from Dick Klamfoth (centre) with Bill Tuman (right) in fourth place.

BIERE FLAD
D 69
MONPLAISIR

ABOVE **The 1951 Manx Norton had the new featherbed frame but the engines were unchanged from the long-stroke double knocker units first offered in 1949.**

LEFT **Real road racing! Eric Oliver leads his great rival Ercole Frigerio on a four-cylinder Gilera during the 1951 French Grand Prix at Albi. Oliver won the race.**

latest Kuzmicki engine and set a lap record at 89.19 mph which beat the old 500 cc figure! When he was eliminated by magneto failure, team-mate Dale took over to win from Lockett. Duke won the 500 cc race easily, with a record lap of 92.27 mph, from Lockett and Dale, the former on a standard Manx.

The 1951 works machines had been quite radically altered. The bore and stroke of both engines had been changed – the 350 cc from 73.4 × 82.5 mm to virtually square at 75.9 × 77 mm to give 348 cc. Peak revs were up to 8000 and a smaller megaphone exhaust with reverse cone was fitted which made the engine more flexible. Power, thanks to Kuzmicki, had been increased from around 30 to close to 36 bhp in the space of a year. Dimensions of the bigger engine changed from 82 × 94.3 mm to 84 × 90 mm, 498 cc. Maximum revs rose slightly from 6800 to 7000.

Both were mounted in modified featherbed frames made from lighter-gauge tubing and with new rear-suspension legs without the external oil reservoirs of the preceding year. The streamlined 'tail' was gone and the 19 in rear wheel was replaced by an 18 in one. But

perhaps the most noticeable change was that of the exhaust pipes of both models now swept out and over the lower bevel housing to give a shorter pipe and increased cornering clearance. Technically the engines were improved by mounting the cambox on platforms machined on the cylinder head rather than on spacers to give a more stable base.

Although the 'Swiss' was back in Berne, a happy hunting ground for Nortons, it proved a disaster for Duke when he and Craig went over for the meeting which clashed with the start of the TT practice – taking extra machines for local star Georges Cordey. Duke bettered both lap records during training and led the 350 cc until the magneto failed again. Masetti had crashed in practice and was a non-starter in the 500 cc class having hurt a foot, but Duke retired early. Again his ignition failed, just after he had taken the lead, leaving Fergus Anderson to win on a Guzzi V-twin. Cordey, a fine rider, held second place until ignition trouble also put him out, just as it had in the 350 cc class.

Four starts – and four retirements. What was at first thought to be plug trouble was traced to magneto failures due to internal arcing. This was caused by the greater resistance at the plug gap from higher compression ratios and increased revs – a case of one thing leading to another and typical of the problems faced by engineers as they attempt to get the last ounce of power out of an engine. Every cloud has a silver lining, for Duke and Craig arrived at the TT knowing it was the magnetos and not plugs that were the problem.

ABOVE **One of the first featherbed Manx models to be built for sale. The price was £346 including tax.**

RIGHT **Geoff Duke in action in the wet 500 cc Ulster Grand Prix of 1951. He won the race to clinch the World Championship.**

When they reached the Isle of Man they found that Dale was ill with pleurisy. His place was taken by Jack Brett and the team scored a 1–2–3 in the Junior TT with Duke averaging a record 89.09 mph and putting in a record lap at 91.38 mph. Duke completed the double in the Senior in which his average speed of 93.83 mph actually bettered his own lap record of the preceding year. He also set the new lap record at 95.22 mph and became the fourth rider in TT history to score the Junior/Senior double – the others being Tim Hunt, Stanley Wood and Jimmy Guthrie, all riding Nortons.

Team-mates Brett and Lockett were out of luck. Brett crashed early in the race and Lockett retired when holding second place after a chain broke on the last lap, letting Bill Doran (AJS) through to take the runner-up spot. Nortons took 13 out of the top 14 places and also did well in the Clubmans' races – Ivor Arber winning the Senior on an International and Norton riders finishing second, third and fourth in the Junior.

In Belgium Duke scored another double. In the

350 cc he averaged a record 100.52 mph, the first time a classic 350 cc race had been won at over the ton, with a record lap at 101.30 mph. On paper the 500 looked a far tougher task. Ranged against the Nortons were teams from Gilera, AJS, Guzzi and MV Agusta. Masetti got away first but Duke was in brilliant form. He took the lead within half a mile and pulled away to win at 106.6 mph, putting in the fastest lap at 107.8 mph – both records. He won by 25 seconds and later said that it was the hardest race of his whole career. Oliver won the Sidecar class to make it a clean sweep for Nortons, beating Frigerio on his four-cylinder Gilera by 22 seconds.

Six days later at the Dutch TT any chance of another double was spoilt when Duke came off at the start of the second lap of the 350 cc race. Fearing wet weather he had modified the front tyre with a series of saw cuts and this, coupled with the speed of the 350 aided by a strong tail wind, caught him out at the 115 mph flat-out S bend just beyond the start. Down he went – and possibly for the only time in the history of the team both the other members came off too, Brett crashing on the first lap and Lockett on lap nine when he hit Reg Armstrong's AJS.

Battered and bruised, Duke fought and won a great battle with the Gileras and Guzzis in the 500 cc race. Duke's plan was simply to go as fast as he could and trust that the multis would fade if forced to use full throttle all the time. It worked – both Masetti and Pagani retired and Duke cruised home ahead of Alfredo Milani (Gilera), Lorenzetti (Guzzi), Lockett and Brett.

The team had a tough schedule that year for the French Grand Prix was run the following weekend at Albi in the South of France, and the mechanics were stretched to the limit when poor fuel wrecked several engines in the early practice periods. The Nortons were critical on fuel and pre-detonation, undetectable by the rider at racing speeds, burned cylinder heads, valves and pistons and meant that engines had to be stripped, compression ratios lowered and new parts fitted.

This did not matter so much in the smaller class where the Nortons had the edge, Duke winning easily from Brett, but in the 500 cc race it was a different matter – more so because the triangular five-mile course called for good acceleration out of the three slow corners and little else. On that type of going the Nortons could not match the multis and Milani (Gilera) won from Doran (AJS), Pagani (Gilera) and Masetti (Gilera) who beat Duke by a wheel for fourth place. Oliver too was up against it in the sidecar race but by dint of hard riding on the corners he harried Frigerio until the Gilera slowed and then took over to win.

In late July a picture of a prototype Norton roadster with a twin-cylinder Dominator engine in a featherbed frame appeared in *Motor Cycling* with a caption which read: '. . . there is no little speculation as to the possibility of a similar production model appearing later in the year'. Nortons had realised that the new frame was a winner and the sooner they could get it into production and on sale the better. And the Norton team for the International Six Days Trial in Italy were mounted on Dominator twins with featherbed frames – all finishing without loss of marks.

The Ulster Grand Prix got off to a horrific start when Guzzi teamsters Sante Geminani and Gianni Leoni collided head on while riding their race machines on open roads before a practice session. It seems that they had set out to ride to the start together, had lost touch and that one had turned back to find the other, and the 'drive on the left' rule had caught one of them out with fatal results to both.

For the first time the 'Ulster' was run on normal grand prix lines with separate races at different times so that riders could compete in more than one class. Nortons had added Australian Ken Kavanagh to their line-up and while Duke romped away to win the 350 cc race at a record 96.85 mph, with a record lap at 98.40 mph, Kavanagh enjoyed himself and finished second ahead of Lockett. This success clinched the World Championship for Norton and for Duke.

Hours later Duke made sure of the 500 cc crown when he overcame wet conditions to win the big class, and Kavanagh made sure of keeping his place in the team by taking second place ahead of the deposed champion Masetti (Gilera) and his team-mate Milani. At the end of August the Norton team flew to Stuttgart to take part in the first major race to be held in Germany since the war – the German Grand Prix at the Solitude circuit near Stuttgart. It was a non-championship event but the Germans were determined that Nortons should be there and laid on a special reception with the BMW and NSU teams at the airport to meet them – plus Mercedes who arranged transport and lent Craig a car.

An estimated half-million spectators turned up to see the fun and completely overwhelmed the marshals, crowding 20 deep right to the edge of the circuit. Despite this racing went ahead and Duke led the Norton team to a 1–2–3 in the 350 cc class and a 1–2–3–4 in the 500 cc in which 1939 Senior TT winner Georg Meier finished a fine fifth, a split second behind Lockett, on a BMW.

The classic racing year ended at Monza. There Nortons swept the board in the 350 cc class with Duke winning from Kavanagh and Brett, but it was very different in the 500 cc race where Gileras finished 1–2–3 ahead of Duke. And this time not even Oliver could beat the power of the multis. Despite a last-bend effort he was beaten by Albino Milani by a wheel. But with Frigerio retiring, Oliver took the World Championship for a third year and made it three titles for Nortons. In the Sidecar class Pip Harris, Hans Haldemann, Jacques Drion and Jean Murit packed the places and underlined the fact that for the private owner Norton power was tops in the Sidecar class as well in the 350 cc and 500 cc divisions.

Despite those wet cobbles, Duke has a smile for the photographer before the start of the 1951 Swiss Grand Prix at Berne. Magneto trouble put him out of the race.

At home Dave Bennett, who like Duke worked for Nortons, won the Senior Manx Grand Prix with Nortons finishing in seven of the first eight places, though they were not so successful in the Junior which was won by Robin Sherry (AJS). Then at long last came the news that enthusiasts were waiting for – Norton were to market a featherbed roadster, the Dominator de Luxe with 497 cc twin-cylinder engine.

ABOVE **500 cc class of the 1951 Dutch TT. Fergus Anderson leads on a vee-twin Moto Guzzi chased by Nello Pagani on a four-cylinder Gilera but Geoff Duke on his single cylinder Norton is closing fast.**

RIGHT **This prototype Norton twin cylinder roadster with featherbed frame was spotted in the paddock at a Continental grand prix in 1951.**

The newcomer was on display at the Earls Court Show in November 1951. The weight had been pared to a reasonable 380 lb and the price was £260. The snag was that it was for export only. The balance of trade deficit was still so bad that many goods made at this time went for export – you simply could not buy them in the UK. This was a tragedy, for at last Nortons had a roadster that was in advance of anything the opposition could offer yet the British enthusiast had to make do with the existing range which was continued virtually unchanged. Prices had crept up – the plunger-sprung Dominator to £245, Manx models to £429 and the 490 cc International to £269.

Duke continued to ride in trials during the winter, appearing with a 490 cc side-valve-engined model on a couple of occasions, but the factory's most successful trials exponent at that time was Rex Young who finished runner-up to Billy Nicholson (BSA) in the 1951 Trials Championship, while Arthur Humphries kept the Norton flag flying in the Sidecar class, also finishing second.

In February 1952 things began to stir. First there was yet another 'national financial crisis'. This was followed by new restrictions on hire purchase, a cut in the money that those going abroad could take with them to £25 a year and the rationing of steel in an attempt to force manufacturers to export all they could.

There were bright spots. Duke was voted 'Sportsman of the Year' by the readers of *Sporting Record*, the first and at that time the most prestigious sporting poll, and Nortons won the Daytona 200 again despite a ban on the featherbed Manx imposed by the American Motorcycle Association. Klamfoth won for the third time from Red Farwell (Norton) but the weather was so bad that the 100-miler was at first postponed and then abandoned.

Duke had agreed to stay with Nortons for another year, provided that they allowed him to race in the lucrative non-championship events and to drive an Aston Martin in sports car races, and his season opened with a hectic weekend. First he practised at San Remo, then flew home to practise and race at Silverstone where he won both 350 and 500 cc classes and pushed the lap record up to 92.10 mph before flying back overnight to ride at San Remo on the Sunday. There he won again, beating Pagani (Gilera), so it had been a successful if tiring weekend.

The next Sunday Duke won again at Codogno near Milan – a nasty blow to Italian prestige for Gilera, MV Agusta and Guzzi all had their factories within a few miles of the circuit. Duke's bike in Italy was a 1952 prototype works racer and the bore and stroke of the 500 had been altered yet again. The 84 × 90 mm dimensions adopted the preceding year had been superseded by a virtually 'square' engine of 85.93 × 86 mm, 499 cc. The finning of the barrel had been increased and now enclosed the vertical shaft of the bevel drive, and the length of the carburettor intake had been increased as had the size of the inlet 'trumpet'. The frame rear subassembly was now welded and not bolted to the main frame and a 16 in rear wheel with 4 in section tyre replaced the 18 in with 3.50 section cover while, to keep the heat of brake away from the sprocket, the drum had been moved to the offside of the wheel and was operated by cable.

The team underwent a shuffle for the 1952 season. Kavanagh was retained but out went Brett, replaced by Reg Armstrong, while Lockett retired and with Dale still not recovered from his pleurisy young Dave Bennett became the fourth man. Armstrong got the feel of the Nortons by winning both classes at the Leinster and then joined the team in Berne for the Swiss Grand Prix. There fate took a hand. Problems in the Near East, centred on Iran, coupled with the Korean War, had created another fuel crisis and the organisers of the Swiss substituted leaded petrol of 80 octane for the unleaded stipulated by the FIM. Before Craig realised this, three 500 engines had been wrecked!

Working overnight the mechanics stripped and rebuilt the engines. Duke won the 350 cc at a record

The first twins with the featherbed frame were used by the Norton team in the 1951 International Six Days Trial in Italy. This is the near identical 1952 version.

ABOVE Cyril Smith and passenger Bob Clements in action on their Norton-Watsonian at the Swiss Grand Prix, Berne in 1952. They finished second.

BELOW The works Norton on which Geoff Duke won the 1952 Junior (350 cc) TT. Note the finned lower bevel housing and the reverse cone megaphone exhaust system.

91.54 mph with a record lap at 93.2 mph, and after 19 laps of the 28-lap 500 cc race he was leading by a minute when an exhaust valve dropped in – a failure almost certainly caused by the poor fuel. Ironically Brett, who had switched to the rival AJS team, won the race.

Tragically Bennett died when he crashed while dicing with Doran (AJS) for second place. Oliver had been injured, breaking a leg when he crashed at a minor meeting at Bordeaux early in May, but Cyril Smith, who worked at the Norton factory as a tester, took up the sidecar challenge. Despite having crashed heavily at Mettet just a couple of weeks earlier, he split the Gileras and finished a close second to Albino Milani. Frigerio, well behind in third place, crashed on the last lap and was killed.

TT week started well when Duke won the Junior at a record 90.29 mph from team-mate Reg Armstrong. Duke looked set to complete the double when he shot ahead from the start of the Senior and, despite a slight misfire, established a lead of over a minute from Les Graham on a works four-cylinder MV Agusta. Then at the end of four laps Duke pulled into his pit and after inspecting the clutch, retired.

Duke said that the clutch had packed up towards the end of the lap and that it was dangerous to continue even if he had been able to re-start the machine. Additionally the primary chain had been running dry and was in bad condition. But mechanic Charlie Edwards is still puzzled: 'I couldn't understand it. He was miles ahead and there was nothing wrong with the bike. Even if he did have problems he could have continued at reduced speed and still won the race – he was a minute and a half ahead with only three laps to go.'

With Duke out Graham took the lead, but Armstrong was gaining ground and he passed the MV Agusta to win by 27 seconds – the primary chain of his Norton breaking and falling into the road as he crossed the line! Graham was runner-up but Ray Amm, who had been lent a works Norton following good rides in Switzerland, finished only 36 seconds behind him in third place and well ahead of Rod Coleman on a works AJS twin.

The riders were not happy with the handling of the 500 cc with the wide rear tyre on a 16 in rim. They complained of a 'jellied eel feel' but they persevered with them at the Dutch TT where Craig fielded a four-

man team in both races: Duke, Armstrong, Kavanagh (out of luck at the TT) and Amm. Duke opened by winning the 350 cc and at last broke Crasher White's lap record of 91.20 mph set in 1937. Duke's speed was 94.64 mph, with Amm second ahead of Coleman on the triple-knocker AJS.

The 500 cc race had the 100,000 spectators screaming with excitement as Masetti (Gilera) and Duke battled it out. The long straights and slow corners of the old van Drenthe circuit suited the Italian multis but Duke hung on, hoping that Masetti would be forced to over-rev the Gilera. However, the Italian kept his cool and, timing his effort to perfection, crossed the line to win by just 1.2 seconds. Kavanagh and Armstrong were third and fourth; out of the first ten places in the two classes factory Nortons had taken seven.

Eight days later at the Belgian Grand Prix Nortons scored a clean sweep in the 350 cc race, Duke beating Amm by 7 seconds with Armstrong third – with Duke clocking an impressive lap record at 103.13 mph. For the 500 cc race Nortons reverted to 18 in rear wheels shod with 3.50 tyres and it proved an even more exciting race than the Dutch. This time it was a three-sided battle with Amm joining Duke and Masetti up front. But again the speed and acceleration of the Gilera told, with Masetti pushing up the lap record to 109.34 mph to win by 2 seconds from Duke with Rhodesian-born Amm just 1 second behind his team leader.

The sidecar race was even closer with Oliver, his leg still in plaster from his Bordeaux crash and with a stand-in passenger, beating Albino Milani (Gilera) by a second with Cyril Smith (Norton) third.

Then came disaster. Duke had signed to ride in a lucrative international at the Schotten circuit in Germany which was run just before the first World Championship German Grand Prix at Solitude. The idea was to make a bit of money but the plan backfired when Duke, having established a lead of over 2 minutes in the 350 cc race, lost concentration, mixed up two similar-looking corners and crashed at 90 mph. He was in fact amazingly lucky for the Schotten circuit was extremely dangerous – narrow, slippery and tree-lined. Duke's Norton hit a tree and was totally wrecked; he went between two trees and escaped with a broken ankle. He was out for the rest of the season and his chance of retaining the 500 cc championship was gone – though fortunately the four wins he had already scored assured him of the 350 cc title for a second year.

More misfortune came Nortons' way at Solitude when Amm was injured practising. His place was taken by Syd Lawton who teamed with Kavanagh and Armstrong. This trio then had a brilliant weekend. First they finished 1–2–4 in the 350 cc race in which Armstrong beat Kavanagh with Bill Lomas (AJS) third. Then they trounced the multis by taking the first three places in the 500 cc class. Again Armstrong was the winner ahead of Kavanagh and Lawton. It was a stunning victory and it put Armstrong ahead of Masetti in the all-important World Championship table. Completing Nortons' day, Smith pulled out of the slipstream of Ernesto Merlo's works Gilera to win the sidecar race, Oliver retiring with a broken sidecar axle while leading on the last lap.

At the Ulster Armstrong looked set to extend his championship advantage when he established a winning lead in the 500 cc class only to retire with a broken chain with less than two laps to cover. His misfortune let Cromie McCandless through to win on a Gilera at a record 99.79 mph but with Masetti failing to score,

FAR LEFT Rhodesian Ray Amm scored his first major success when he was promoted into the Norton squad for the 1952 TT and finished third in the Senior TT.

LEFT The 500 cc class of the 1952 Belgian Grand Prix with Geoff Duke and Ray Amm on Nortons leading the Gilera fours of Alfredo Milani and Umberto Masetti.

Armstrong still led the title chase. Earlier Kavanagh had won the 350 cc class from Armstrong.

Amm was back in action for the Italian Grand Prix at Monza in September and won the 350 cc class, his first win for Norton in a World Championship race. This promoted him to third place in the final 350 cc table in which Nortons scored a clean sweep – Duke winning from Armstrong and Amm. Kavanagh had crashed and was a non-starter in the 500 cc race and with Amm soon out with engine trouble, Armstrong was left to battle alone against the multis. The race was won by Graham (MV Agusta) but Masetti took second place, and with Armstrong finishing only sixth the Italian took the lead in the championship table with one round, the Spanish Grand Prix, to go.

In Barcelona there was no 350 cc race and Nortons fielded five works bikes in the 500 cc class: Armstrong, Kavanagh, Amm, Lawton and Belgian Auguste Goffin. In fact Craig and his men were busy for they also provided 'Joe Motors' for Oliver, Smith and Jacques Drion in the Sidecar class. Surprisingly the multis proved a far better bet around the twists and turns of Montjuich Park. Graham won again and Masetti took second place to clinch the 500 cc title for a second time, with Kavanagh the best Norton in third spot.

Things went better in the Sidecar class. Oliver won from Drion but Smith, who struggled round with a broken frame for most of the race, came home third to clinch the championship. By Nortons' standards losing the 500 cc crown was a disappointment but they were still far and away the most successful factory in racing with two championships in the bag.

That September Nortons failed to win a Manx Grand Prix for the first time since 1930. Then in October came important news. The plunger rear springing for the roadster models was to be replaced for 1953 by a swinging-fork set-up grafted on to the standard frame – the featherbed was still reserved for the export-only Dominator de Luxe, though later in the year came the news that the 1953 Internationals would also be fitted with the featherbed frame. Additionally the 'Inters' would have alloy heads and barrels as standard – and all for no extra cost, Nortons keeping the price at £279.

Off-road Nortons were doing well. Jeff Smith, later to star with BSA, won the Reliance Trial on a 500T while John Draper took the Scott Trial for Nortons in November, and it was announced that Les Archer and Eric Cheney would race featherbed-framed motocrossers in the big events in 1953. But on the road-racing front there were signs of defection. Reg Armstrong left to join Gilera, while Duke kept everyone guessing. At first he said he would concentrate on driving Aston Martins with occasional outings on a mystery British 250, but enthusiasts hoped that he might still be persuaded to stay with Nortons. And on that note 1952 ended.

BELOW **Umberto Masetti on his four-cylinder Gilera leads Geoff Duke (Norton) in the 500 cc class of the 1952 Dutch TT. Masetti won from Duke, with Nortons also third and fourth.**

CHAPTER 17

Ray Amm and the 'fish' 1953–1955

If Duke's car-racing career had gone well he would probably never have raced a motorcycle again. But it did not. He was fast on four wheels but prone to crash, and things came to a head early in 1953 when he collided with a slower car at Sebring in Florida when well ahead. Co-driver Peter Collins, star of the Aston Martin team who had built up the early lead was not impressed – and made his feelings known.

Duke returned home in depressed mood and not sure what to do. Then Graham Walker telephoned him with a request that he race Nortons at the *Motor Cycling* Silverstone Saturday meeting in April. Walker said that Gilbert Smith had promised to supply works Nortons for Duke to ride. This surprised him because the preceding year, while recovering from his Schotten injuries, Duke had had a long talk with the Norton boss during which he had declined to sign for the Bracebridge Street team for the 1953 season. In his book *In Pursuit of Perfection* Duke makes it clear that he would have stayed with Nortons if there had been any prospect of the long-awaited four-cylinder racer being ready to compete, or at least test, in 1953.

Speaking to me at the TT in 1990 Duke confirmed this:

The prospect of the four had been dangled in front of me like a carrot and by 1952 it was taking shape. BRM had made a number of basic errors in the original design. For a start where was no provision for mounting it in a motorcycle frame! Eventually Nortons got fed up with them and took the project over and in 1952 a lot of work was done on it in the Norton drawing office. I was very excited by the prospect – particularly as Leo Kuzmicki was involved. After the way he had transformed the singles, particularly the 350 cc, I had great respect for him.

Why, then, was Gilbert Smith unable to confirm that Nortons would press ahead with the 'four'? Said Duke:

I think by that time they were running out of money. Norton was a small firm. They only employed 100 or so people and produced about 200 bikes a week – and the market was beginning to collapse as small, cheap cars became available. They needed sponsorship – but in those days there were no big commercial backers as there are today and by the end of 1952

LEFT **Impressive line-up. A detachment of the Calcutta police with their Norton sidecars on parade in 1953.**

Gilbert Smith had obviously decided to knock the project on the head.

Asked for his opinion of the top men at Nortons, Duke replied:

Gilbert Smith was a typical hard-headed business man – not a very approachable character. Joe Craig was a first-class racing manager and did a damn good job. I always got on well with him. Technically I would call him a trial and error man rather than a brilliant technician. He had been in racing a long time and there was very little he had not tried.

RIGHT **Joe Craig (left) fastens Ray Amm's helmet during the record breaking spree at Montlhéry, October 1953.**

BELOW **Busy scene at Montlhéry during the Norton record attempts as Ray Amm hands over to Eric Oliver (left). Using the 350 cc engine they covered 1,000 km (621 miles) at an average of just under 120 mph.**

If Nortons had honoured the promise to provide works machines for Silverstone the rift might still have been healed. But when they sent a standard 350 cc Manx instead of a brace of factory racers Duke was naturally incensed; matters were made worse by the fact that it was brand new and down on power. Most would have told Nortons what to do with their racer, but Duke stuck to his part of the bargain with Graham Walker and battled home in eighth place.

Despite this Duke was interested when Graham Walker later passed on the news that Gilbert Smith wanted him to ride factory bikes in the TT. He had still not made up his mind what to do and felt that although the Nortons would be outpaced in the grands prix they would still be competitive in the Isle of Man, and he actually went to see Gilbert Smith to find out what the offer was. To his amazement the subject of the TT was never broached. He was determined not to ask for machines – it was up to Gilbert to make the offer. It never came, and within hours the *Birmingham Mail* carried a story to the effect that Duke had pleaded for Nortons for the TT but Gilbert Smith had replied: 'There is no place for Duke in the Norton team.'

The following day, after the clutch of his Aston Martin had failed during a race at Silverstone, Duke telephoned Austin Munks who was in contact with Gileras and said that if an offer the Italian factory had made in September still stood, he would like to join them for 1953. The next day, 11 May, Duke received a telegram from Giuseppe Gilera welcoming him into the team and asking him to fly to Italy to test the machine. I trace the events in detail to make it clear that Duke certainly did not abandon Nortons simply because of a big-money offer – it was only after he knew that the four-cylinder project had been abandoned and after two clear rebuffs that he joined Gilera.

Meanwhile, a lot had been going on. Duke had received the OBE in the New Year's Honours list, 'For services to British Motor Cycle Racing' (the first racer to be honoured was Freddie Frith in 1950). Pool petrol had at last been replaced by brands with more than one grade available (though the best was still around 80 octane), and the first trial, a team event, had been shown on BBC Television. More seriously, the Associated Motor Cycles group had swallowed up Norton Motors Ltd so that Nortons were now in the same financial stable as AJS, Matchless, Francis-Barnett and James. Gilbert Smith issued a statement saying that he envisaged his company continuing as a separate entity with the same management and the same keen competition in the racing sphere. But as a Norton enthusiast at that time, this announcement, coupled with Duke leaving the team, filled me with foreboding.

A road test of the face-lifted Model 7 Dominator with swinging-fork rear suspension did little to lift spirits. The top speed, given as an optimistic 95 when the original twin was introduced, was down to a more realistic 87 mph while the weight was still an unwieldy 413 lb. But the racing department did have a new machine – the low-profile 'Flying Fish' with kneeler riding position. This was the brainchild of Artie Bell and Rex McCandless with the prototype built by Oliver Nelson in Belfast. The idea was simple – to create a fully streamlined machine of small frontal area.

At that time the regulations did not restrict the amount of streamlining that could be used. If you wanted fully to enclose the machine you could, provided that the rider could push-start it and get aboard when the flag dropped. Again the Ulstermen were ahead in their thinking for even at the fastest circuits none of the teams had used anything more than the very briefest of streamlining in 1952.

The first hint to enthusiasts about the 'Fish' was when a photograph appeared in *Motor Cycling* in February 1953. This had been taken by a French photographer who had spotted the new Norton undergoing tests at Montlhéry. It showed Kavanagh trying the prototype, but did not mention that the little Australian had fallen off! 'He was testing it on the road circuit and I think he was showing off because Georges Monneret, the old French rider, was watching. Anyway he came off in a big way and I had to go out and get the bike because he couldn't ride it back to the pits,' remembers Charlie Edwards.

Nortons then took the Fish to the Isle of Man in March and ran tests over the Mountain section of the course with Kavanagh and Amm riding and with Artie Bell, Oliver Nelson and Gilbert Smith in attendance. The Rhodesian was the faster of the two on the Fish and it was he who rode it the only time it was used in a race – the 350 cc class of the North West 200 in May. After making a very bad start, leaving the grid absolutely last, he was up to fourth place at the end of the first lap and then had only McIntyre (AJS) to pass when the Norton slowed and stopped, suffering from overheating. Despite this Amm set the fastest lap of the race at 87.72 mph. In the 500 cc class Armstrong and Dale made their debuts on four-cylinder Gileras and were well beaten by the Norton boys, Lawton winning, with a record lap at 96.20 mph, from Kavanagh with Armstrong third – there was still life in the old singles!

The team had tried various things at Floreffe in Belgium before the NW 200. There Amm rode a 500 with an odd-looking trailing link front fork and clocked a record lap at 94.02 mph while finishing second to team-mate Kavanagh with Lawton third. Earlier Lawton had won the 350 cc race from Kavanagh and Amm who again set the lap record, this time at 89.95 mph.

The 14 May issue of *Motor Cycling* carried a report about the Fish headed: 'First description of aerodynamic racing model with extremely low centre of gravity'. The frame was described as 'a depressed featherbed'. Wheels were 19 in and the fuel, carried in pannier tanks each side of the engine, was lifted to the carburettor by a pump driven by a face cam on the end of the inlet camshaft. The rider's arms and legs were supported by rubber-lined troughs in the streamlined body.

When Amm took the fish to the machine examiners at the TT they were dubious about his ability to start in the conventional run-and-bump way – but he put

BELOW **Ray Amm in action on the Norton streamliner in road racing trim.**

BELOW RIGHT **The Norton streamliner as used at Montlhéry to break world records (including the one hour at 133.7 mph) in October 1953.**

on an impressive demonstration and Nortons were allowed to use it during practice, though the powers that be still had reservations about letting it actually enter the race.

The secrets of the conventional works machines for 1953 were then revealed. The bore and stroke of the bigger engine had been changed yet again – from 85.93 × 86 mm to well 'oversquare' at 88 × 82 mm, 499 cc, but the dimensions of the successful 350 cc had been left alone. Provision for cooling the sodium exhaust valve by circulating oil around the valve guide was increased and this oil was taken back to the crankcase via a simple oil cooler mounted on the offside front downtube. The oil tank was painted matt black to help dissipate heat. The Amal GP carburettor was fitted with a more sophisticated weir system with a pump, mechanically driven from the inlet camshaft, to return excess fuel to the tank – a reversal of the role played by the pump fitted to the fish.

And wheel sizes had changed again. For 1953 19 in rims were fitted front and rear. Practice ended badly for Nortons when Lawton riding close behind Amm on the Fish, ran wide and clipped a gate-post accelerating away from Creg-ny-Baa. He was badly injured and spent several months in hospital. Meanwhile Amm, who knew nothing of the accident, completed his lap on the Fish at 90.33 mph, bettered only by Les Graham on a works four-cylinder MV Agusta.

Amm's speed was very close to Duke's Norton lap record and again proved the potential of the unorthodox machine, but Nortons decided not to race it. According to Charlie Edwards the ACU were not keen: 'I don't think we could have got it past Vic Anstice who was the chief scrutineer. He was a stickler for the rules and nearly threw the featherbed out the first time we used it at the TT. He said the Fish was unsafe and that was that.'

Changing machines made no difference to Amm. He won the race at a record 90.52 mph and pushed up the lap record to 91.82 mph, but beat Kavanagh by only 9 seconds, with Fergus Anderson on a 325 cc Guzzi back in third.

BSA won the Junior Clubman's but Nortons' morale was boosted when the new featherbed Internationals swept the board in the Senior production machine race – Bob Keeler leading a 1–2–3 for the Bracebridge Street sports models. In Friday's Senior TT Duke made his debut on the big Gilera and after three laps had established a lead of a minute. Then came disaster. He gave the Italian multi just a shade too much throttle as he accelerated away from Quarter Bridge, the rear wheel spun and off he came.

Amm took over, and having hoisted the record lap to 97.41 mph (over 2 mph faster than Duke's Norton

record), won at 93.95 mph, just beating Armstrong's record average of the preceding year. Brett, back in the team, came home second, only 12 second behind Amm and ahead of Armstrong (Gilera). It was another double for Nortons and Amm joined Hunt, Woods, Guthrie and Duke as the only riders to have achieved the Junior/Senior double. Yet the race will be remembered as the one in which Les Graham, a charming and typically British sportsman, lost his life when his bulky four-cylinder MV Agusta with its odd-looking Earles forks got out of control and crashed at the bottom of Bray Hill at over 100 mph.

The previous year I had ridden my 1938 Model 50 to the Swiss Grand Prix and in 1953 I paid my first visit to the Dutch TT and Belgian Grand Prix – by this time riding a marvellous 1936 350 cc International – and I remember watching the Norton team at Hooghalen where they set up an informal pit area during training. New Zealander Ken Mudford had taken the place of Lawton and although Amm tried the Fish during practice he again reverted to the orthodox machine for the 350 cc race.

In that event Nortons got a nasty shock. After the successful showing of the 325 cc ridden into third place in the Junior TT by Anderson, Guzzis built two 345 cc engines for Anderson and Lorenzetti to use in Holland. These did not produce as much power as the British singles but they were partly streamlined and far lighter. Anderson went out with clutch trouble but Lorenzetti won easily from Amm, Kavanagh and Brett. The line-up for the 500 cc race was formidable with six works Gileras, four Nortons, three AJS twins, two four-cylinder Guzzis and one BMW – 16 factory machines of five very different types despite the absence of MV Agusta. Duke eventually won the race at a record 99.92 mph but Amm, after a gallant effort, retired on the last lap when holding a secure second place as he ran out of petrol. He had the consolation of a record lap at 100.91 mph but his retirement let Armstrong

ABOVE Montlhéry 1953: Joe Craig signals to Ray Amm that he is maintaining the planned 124 mph during the attempt on the one hour record.

RIGHT The 1953 works 499 cc Norton racing machine ready for action. With Ray Amm the bike set a new TT lap record at 97.41 mph.

through with Kavanagh and Brett taking third and fifth for Nortons, Mudford retiring with a broken chain.

The Belgian that year was the 'fastest ever' grand prix. Anderson and Lorenzetti dominated the 350 cc which the British rider won at 103.32 mph though Amm, in third place, again clocked the record lap, at 105.93 mph. Duke looked set to win the 500 cc class until a throttle cable broke, leaving team-mate Milani to win by 25 seconds from Amm with Armstrong third and Kavanagh fourth. Again only Gileras had got the better of the Nortons – Milani averaging 109.94 mph and Duke pushing up the lap record to 112.33 mph. Only in the Sidecar class were Norton successful. After trying a brand-new fully streamlined Watsonian outfit, modelled on the solo Fish, Oliver reverted to his battered, oil-stained, naked outfit and won at 90.55 mph with a record lap at 92.03 mph.

According to the FIM calendar the next classic should have been the German Grand Prix. In a seemingly absurd move, this had been switched from the lovely Solitude circuit to the incredibly dangerous Schotten course where Duke had had his lucky escape the year before. Piet Nortier, leading FIM official and editor of the Dutch *Motor* magazine, inspected the course and passed it, but the leading riders and teams made their own inspection, refused to compete and the meeting was downgraded.

The teams met again at Rouen in early August for the French Grand Prix. On the twisty, demanding circuit Amm's riding skill made up for any lack of speed and with 28 of the 30 laps covered he led Anderson in the 350 cc race by 12 seconds. Determined to hold his advantage Amm overdid it on a difficult, adversely cambered hairpin, crashed and broke a collarbone. Duke led a Gilera 1–2–3 in the big class with Kavanagh fourth; again the Nortons had beaten all other works machines including two Gileras. At Rouen Oliver beat Smith to win the sidecar race.

With Amm out, Nortons concentrated on a three-man team in Ulster: Kavanagh, Brett and Mudford. That year the race had switched from the Clady circuit to Dundrod, another genuine road course. It proved a good move so far as Nortons were concerned for they won the three main classes. First Mudford took the 350 cc honours with a record lap at 88.11 mph, beating Bob McIntyre on a works AJS. Then Smith won the sidecar race after Oliver had retired with a seized engine, and finally Kavanagh beat Duke in the rain-swept 500 cc race. Both shared the fastest lap at 91.74 mph, Duke slowing towards the end with clutch trouble. Behind him Brett won another Norton–Gilera battle to beat Armstrong.

Hopes that Amm would be fit to race in the Swiss at Berne just three weeks after his crash were dashed when he found during practice, that you need two good collarbones to wrestle a works Norton around the Bremgarten circuit. Anderson again won the 350 cc for Guzzi and Oliver came back to win the Sidecar class from Smith, with Willi Noll on a BMW third – the first top-three placing by a BMW outfit in a World

Championship race. Gilera had again entered six in the 500 cc class and the Italian fours dominated, taking the first four places with Duke the winner. Kavanagh, who had finished second in the 350 cc class, was never in the hunt and retired.

With the solo titles settled, Nortons did not make the trip to Monza for the Italian Grand Prix. But both Oliver and Smith used works engines as they battled it out for sidecar honours. Oliver won the closest race of the year, beating Smith by a wheel, to regain the World Championship – the two British stars sharing the record lap at 91.16 mph. At home Manx Nortons again dominated the Manx Grand Prix with Frank Fox winning the Junior and Denis Parkinson the Senior from young Bob Keeler.

There were few changes in the Norton range for 1954. Commented *The Motor Cycle*: 'Consolidation is the keynote of Bracebridge Street plans.' The only real changes was that all models now had an 8 in front brake in place of the 7 in unit. The featherbed Internationals introduced for 1953 were continued unchanged and the Dominator de Luxe with the McCandless frame was still for export only.

But very real changes were made to the two Manx racers for 1954. Out went the time-honoured long-stroke 71 × 88 mm and 79 × 100 mm units to be replaced by 'square' engines of 76 × 76.85 mm and 86 × 85.8 mm – based on the works engines of recent years. It is interesting to note that all 500 cc camshaft engines sold by the factory since the introduction of Walter Moore's CS1 in 1927 had been 79 × 100 mm – a lifespan of 26 years. Like the factory racers the new Manx models had the top bevel housing integral with the cylinder head and the cylinder finning surrounding the vertical bevel drive. The prices of the roadsters remained about the same but the Manx went up to £418.

At home Kavanagh gave Norton fans something to shout about when he won the two main classes at the Hutchinson 100 meeting at Silverstone in late September, Oliver making is debut on the fully streamlined outfit to beat Smith in the Sidecar class.

Then, just in time for the Earls Court Show, Craig took the Fish to Montlhéry and with Amm and Oliver in the saddle captured no less than 61 world records! The most important were the 350 cc and 500 cc one-hour records which Amm took at 124.30 and 133.7 mph respectively – handsomely beating the old figures. The 500 cc, an outright record which beat the 750 cc and 1000 cc figures, was especially pleasing because it broke the record of 127.50 mph set by Piero Taruffi on a supercharged, streamlined four-cylinder Gilera. Oliver teamed with Amm for the distance records, the longest of which was 1000 km (621 miles), on the 350 cc at a shade under 120 mph! The fastest record was 137.60 mph for the ten miles on the 500 cc and Amm recorded laps at close to 140 mph around the bumpy French bowl. It was a stunning demonstration of speed and reliability by the British team.

ABOVE **Real sidecar racing! Eric Oliver/Stan Dibben (Norton) lead Cyril Smith/Les Nutt (Norton) with Willi Faust/Karl Remmert (BMW) in pursuit at Malmedy during the 1953 Belgian Grand Prix. Oliver went on to win.**

RIGHT **The 1954 works Norton – with outside flywheel – which marked the culmination of Joe Craig's development work at Bracebridge Street.**

There was more good news for Norton fans early in 1954 when the intensely patriotic Ray Amm signed for another year, and in February he went to Brazil. There in two meetings at the Interlagos complex in Sao Paulo, marred by typically South American financial chicanery, he started in four races and won all four (two 350 cc and two 500 cc), beating Lorenzetti (Guzzi) and Milani (Gilera) in the process.

Back from Brazil Amm was beaten by Duke at Silverstone and then went out to Imola where he was

Norton
Norton

The 1954 works Norton single engine. The normal internal flywheels have been replaced by bob-weights and an outside flywheel – and the bore/stroke dimensions changed again – the 350 cc to 78 × 73 mm and the 500 cc to 90 × 78.4 mm.

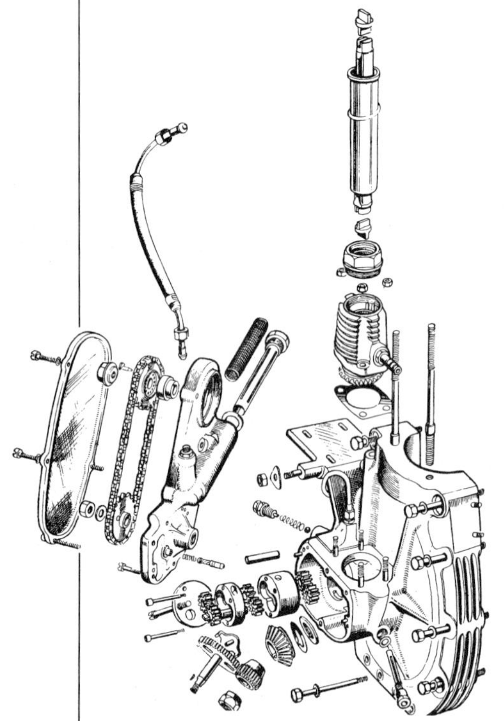

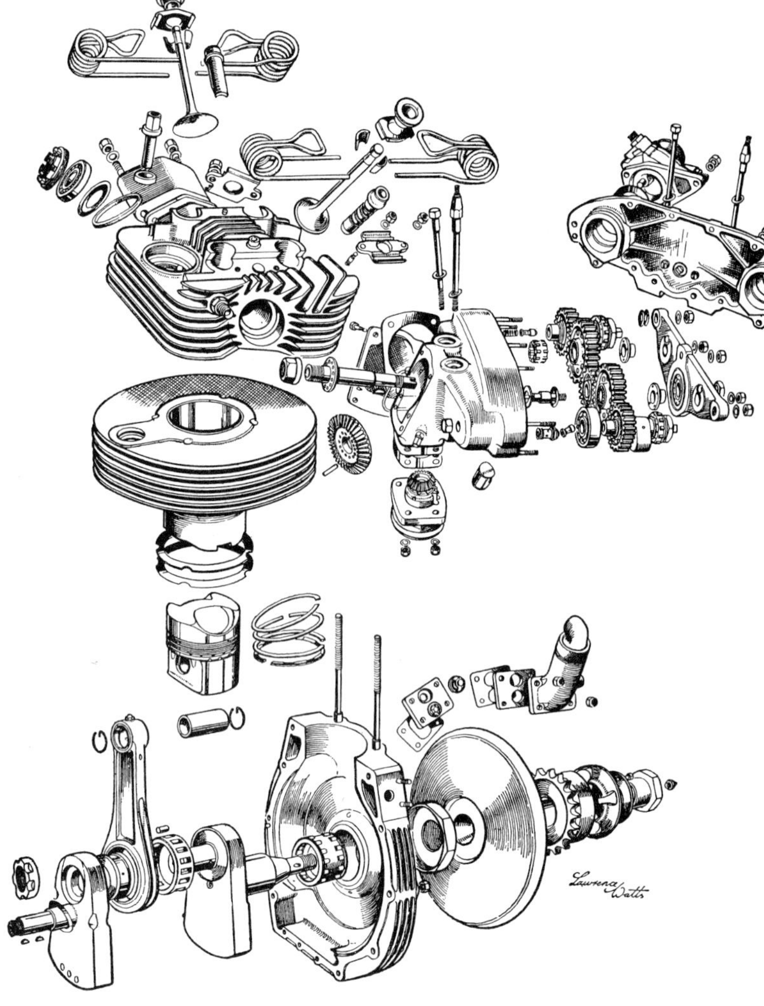

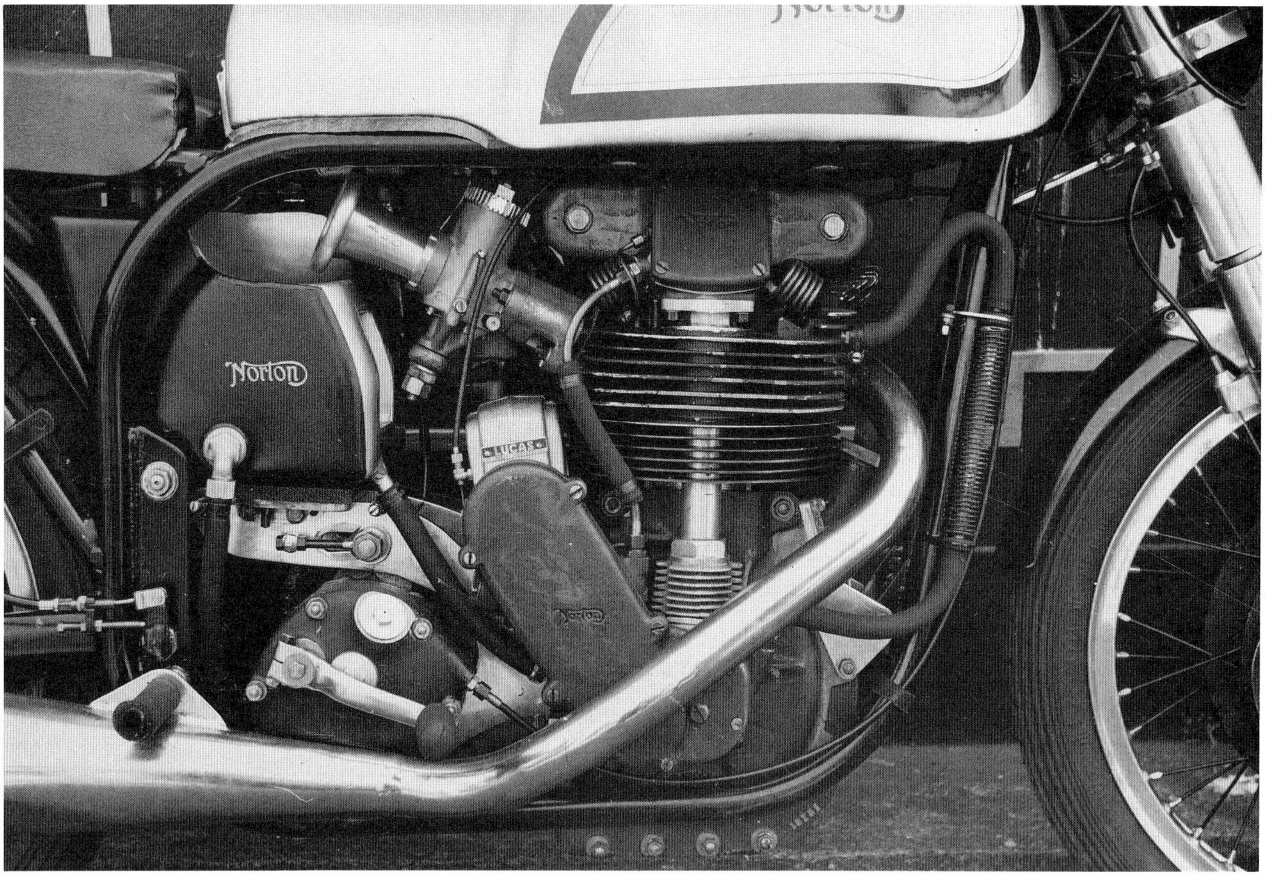

ABOVE The 350 cc 1954 factory engine. Note the oil cooler fixed to the offside front downtube, the massive carburettor, the finned lower bevel housing and the five-speed Burman gearbox.

LEFT Ray Amm in action on his works Norton with proboscis streamlining during the 500 cc class of the 1954 Belgian Grand Prix.

RIGHT Ray Amm rounds Ginger Hall during his winning ride in the shortened 1954 Senior TT – bad weather forced officials to stop the race after four laps.

again second, beaten by Masetti (Gilera). In Italy Guzzi continued to develop their single-cylinder 500 as well as the in-line four, and their new 'one lunger' for 1954 had a bore and stroke of 88 × 82 mm, bevel-driven overhead camshafts and twin-plug ignition.

The new works Nortons were wheeled out by Amm for a pre-TT try-out at Floreffe in Belgium. They were radically different and represent the pinnacle of Craig's achievements at Nortons. All racing motorcycles have a certain beauty but for many the 1954 factory Nortons are the most handsome ever built – starkly functional, almost brutish and yet balanced and elegant. In short, a work of art.

Bore and stroke had been changed yet again – the 350 cc from 75.9 × 77 to 78 × 73 mm, 349 cc, and the 500 from 88 × 82 to 90 × 78.4 mm, 499 cc. Internal flywheels become an increasing problem as strokes shorten and at last Nortons followed Guzzi giving both capacities a large-diameter outside flywheel mounted on the drive-side main shaft inboard of the engine sprocket. Explained *The Motor Cycle*: 'The outside flywheels . . . minimize crankcase size and oil drag . . . save weight . . . and the larger the diameter the lighter it can be for a given flywheel effect.' The new, more compact crank-case was fitted with a large, flap-type breather mounted at the front just below the cylinder barrel. Excess oil from this was used to lubricate the primary chain, in addition to a supply carried in the top nearside frame tube. Cooling of the front brake was assisted by a vane type muff designed to 'throw' air out of the drum by centrifugal force, and another radical departure was the adoption of a five-speed Burman gearbox.

Unlike Amm, Kavanagh had left Nortons to join Guzzi and it was the little Australian who won the 350 cc class at Floreffe with the Rhodesian second. Streamlining was beginning to creep in and Kavanagh's Guzzie was comprehensively faired while Amm's Norton was partly streamlined. Dale, who had switched from Gilera to MV Agusta, won the 500 cc race but again Amm was second. For the TT Nortons replaced Kavanagh with Bob Keeler, who teamed with Brett and Amm. Realising the advantage of streamlining, Amm had been carrying out tests with a layout that had a

RIGHT During the fifties Les Archer kept the Norton flag flying in moto-cross worldwide. This shot was taken at the Moto Cross des Nations in Holland in 1954.

BELOW Eric Oliver/Les Nutt (left) with the fully streamlined Norton/ Watsonian battle it out with Cyril Smith/Stan Dibben on their more orthodox Norton/ Watsonian, Silverstone 1954.

TOP LEFT **In 1955 the factory riders used virtually standard Manx models. This is the 350 cc with reverse cone megaphone.**

LEFT **The three riders who won world championships on Nortons. On the left, Cyril Smith, centre Eric Oliver and right Geoff Duke.**

RIGHT **The F-type engine that Norton were preparing for 1955. It was abandoned when Norton decided to use standard Manx machines only.**

long 'nose' projecting out over the front wheel and, for the TT, pannier tanks on each side of the engine. These doubled as streamlining and, using a normal TT tank, increased total fuel capacity to just over nine gallons – enough to complete a seven-lap race without a pit-stop.

In the Junior TT Amm proved sensationally fast. That year the race distance was reduced from seven to five laps because of the crowded race programme, and the Norton star slaughtered his own lap record of 91.82 mph with an astounding lap at 94.61 mph. Amm had a seemingly unbeatable advantage of 1 minute 16 seconds when a broken inlet tappet put him out at Kirkmichael on the last lap and let Rod Coleman (AJS) through to win from team-mate Derek Farrant, with Keeler on a 'naked' Norton a very close third, Brett having retired with magneto trouble.

Because of problems with gear selection, Nortons had reverted to the old four-speed gearboxes for both races and following his record lap in the Junior Amm decided to use the 'proboscis' streamlining with side tanks and to attempt to cover the seven laps of the Senior TT without a stop. The race started in foul conditions of rain and wind yet despite the handicap of setting off with a 65 lb fuel load Amm held second place only 14 seconds behind Duke (Gilera) at the end of the first lap. On the second Amm cut Duke's advantage to 2 seconds and on the third he took the lead and went into the fourth lap 28 seconds ahead of Duke, who lost a few seconds slowing to pull into his pit.

Torrential rain and mist on the Mountain had not cleared as quickly as the organisers had hoped. A meeting of the stewards decided to stop the race after four laps. Unfortunately this decision was made too late for signals to be made to the riders and when Amm was flagged home the winner, 1 minute 6 seconds ahead of Duke, controversey erupted. Many claimed that Duke and Gilera had been robbed by the organisers whom they accused of stopping the race when the British machine was ahead. Norton fans countered by pointing out that Duke would have had to gain 22 seconds a lap on Amm to have caught him, and with the Norton going faster as it used fuel and got lighter this simply was not on; after all, Duke had led by only 2 seconds after two laps. Obviously it is an argument no one can win. But the record book shows that Amm won the race, put in the fastest lap at 89.82 mph, gained eight World Championship points and led Nortons to yet another team prize with Brett a gallant third ahead of Armstrong (Gilera) and Keeler eighth.

Charlie Edwards, who worked with both riders during his time with Nortons, had no doubts: 'There is no way that Duke would have won if Amm's bike had kept going. It's true that the weather improved as the race finished but in those wet and dry conditions around the TT course no one could beat Ray Amm.'

At the prize-giving at the Villa Marina that evening Duke was not exactly magnanimous in defeat, saying: 'Amm's win was 99 per cent due to Ray and 1 per cent due to Nortons', which must have offended his former mentor Craig who masterminded the building of such a competitive TT machine.

It was the second Norton TT win of the week, for earlier Oliver had won the first Sidecar TT to be held since 1925. The race was run on the new Clypse circuit that incorporated parts of the Mountain course, including the start–finish area, linked by narrow country lanes.

That year the Ulster was held the week after the TT, the idea being to cut down travelling, but Gilera did not compete and Amm scored a double in yet another wet and windy meeting. In the 350 cc he beat team-mate Brett and in the 500 cc he outpaced Colemen (AJS), with Australian Gordon Laing on a works Norton third. Originally Craig had intended that South African Rudy Allison should take over from Keeler but when Allison crashed in practice the ride passed to Laing. In the Sidecar class Oliver made his classic debut on the Watsonian streamliner and won from Smith with Noll third.

In Belgium Nortons fielded only Amm and Laing and the team was tragically reduced to one when Laing crashed at a flat-out bend and was killed instantly – the 2nd Norton works rider to die in an accident since Guthrie 17 years earlier. At the time Amm was battling with Kavanagh for the 350 cc lead but on the sixth lap the Norton's clutch failed. The same component broke in the 500 cc class in which Amm was holding second place to Duke, who went on to win.

In the Sidecar class Oliver scored his fifth Belgian win in succession to beat Noll, with Smith third. Oliver again used his streamlined outfit with kneeler riding position and with three wins from three starts looked certain to win the six-event Sidecar Championship. But a crash at a hill-climb in Germany put him into hospital with a broken arm and although he gallantly came back to race in the final round in Italy, that accident cost him the title.

Six days after the Belgian Amm was the only Norton works rider at the Dutch TT. He retired with engine trouble while holding third place in the 350 cc but in the 500 cc class only Duke and his Gilera were ahead of the Norton rider when his petrol tank split on lap 13 of the 16-lap race. At the German Grand Prix at Solitude, a true riders' circuit, Amm fought and won a great battle with the Guzzi team to win the 350 cc race, despite sliding off on wet tar and wiping off a foot-rest midway through the race! In the big class Duke rode a canny race to win by 4 seconds. Realising that he could not shake off the Rhodesian, Duke sat in the slipstream of the Norton until the closing stages and then pulled ahead to win. In the Sidecar class Noll, with passenger Fritz Cron, scored the first of many BMW wins ahead of Walter Schneider (BMW) and Smith.

The next big clash came in the Swiss Grand Prix at Berne – and it turned out to be the third rain-swept meeting of the year. Anderson and Kavanagh finished first and second in the 350 cc race ahead of Amm and Brett. Then in the 500 cc, Kavanagh on a single-cylinder Guzzi led from Amm and Duke until 'water in the works' eliminated the Italian machine. Amm took over, only to be passed by Duke. Armstrong took third place but with Brett fourth Nortons again out-paced and out-lasted the Guzzi, AJS, MV Agusta and BMW entries.

Smith did his best in the sidecar race and took a fine second place but with Noll the winner the outcome of the three-wheeler title depended on the result of the Italian Grand Prix at Monza in September. There Oliver rode despite his arm injury – and finished in fifth place – but Noll won to take the title, the first non-British rider to win the Sidecar World Championship. It was a disastrous meeting for Nortons, for Guzzis took the first four places in the 350 cc race ahead of Amm and Brett while Italian bikes completely dominated the 500 cc event which Duke won to clinch the World Championship, with Amm struggling home in seventh place lapped by the Gilera. Although we did not know it at the time, it was to be the last grand prix in which Nortons fielded pukka works racers.

The problems for the British factories that supported racing, Norton and AJS/Matchless, were mounting. Basically they wanted to race machines that could be produced for sale – the factory bikes being used to test new ideas that, if successful, would be incorporated into their production racers. This was the path taken by Nortons since the inception of the CS1 camshaft model in 1927 and by the end of 1954 the Manx Norton was the best racing machine that money could buy for the 500 cc class and was on a par with the 7R AJS for the smaller class. Additionally the British factories did not agree with the ever-increasing use of all-enveloping streamlining (which went unchecked by the FIM until the end of 1957), and in any event money was getting tight as motorcycle sales were hit by the increasing competition of cheap cars.

Also feeling the pinch were NSU of Germany whose brilliant lightweight machines had dominated the 125 cc and 250 cc classes in 1953 and 1954. They announced their withdrawal from grand prix racing in October 1954 and there were soon rumours that Norton and AJS/Matchless were to follow suit. Charlie Edwards remembers that he and Ray Amm heard the news when they returned from a test session at the MIRA track near Birmingham late in November:

Ironically Ray had been testing the prototype 1955 works Norton with horizontal Guzzi-style cylinder and five-speed gearbox in unit. Joe Craig was very keen on the idea and it had gone really well that day in a lash-up frame. When we got back to the factory we were told that there would be no works racing the next year and I remember Ray went straight in and phoned MV Agusta from the Norton factory!

The new Norton racer with horizontal engine which Amm had been testing was known as the F (for flat engine) type. The 350 cc and 500 cc engines retained the bore and stroke of the 1954 units as well as the crank-case layout and the outside flywheel. But to take advantage of the new engine position, radial cylinder-head finning was adopted. Tackling the gearbox problem (the five-speed Burman adopted for 1954 had never been trouble free) a completely new three-shaft five-speeder had been designed and although in a separate casing was bolted to the rear of the crank-case to give a semi-unit-contruction layout with gear primary drive.

The design work had been done by Ernie Walsh and only one 500 cc engine was completed – now in Sammy Miller's excellent museum in New Milton. 'But the bike we took to MIRA didn't look anything like that,' says Charlie Edwards.

It was real lash-up and I remember that Craig was not there to see the bike ridden at racing speeds for the first time. He was ill with shingles. Because of the gear primary drive the engine ran backwards and there hadn't been time to get the

ABOVE **The F-type, fired in anger only once – when Ray Amm took it to MIRA late in 1954. Engine was basically a 1954 with new cylinder head and a new five-speed gearbox.**

LEFT **Ray Amm scored his last win for Norton at the 1954 German Grand Prix at Solitude where he won the 350 cc race.**

cams right — yet it gave more power straight away than the old engine. I've no doubt it would have been a winner but as far as I know it never fired again in anger.

Motor Cycling broke the news of Amm's departure on 9 December 1954 when Cyril Quantrill wrote in his Sports Gossip column: 'And – a real bombshell this – from Italy news that Amm will be riding MV next year.' The sporting year closed with Les Archer on his camshaft moto-cross Norton winning the first ever BBC television scramble, screened at peak viewing time on a December Saturday afternoon.

As part of the belt-tightening act the Norton range was trimmed for 1955. Out went the plodding side valves which traced their ancestry back to Pa Norton's design of 1908, and the Model 18 was also dropped. Replacing these as a sidecar machine the Model 19 with 596 cc single-cylinder overhead-valve engine was reintroduced – the 19R with rigid frame while the 19S had the old-type frame with swinging-fork suspension. Prices were £190 and £208 respectively. The Model 7 Dominator was continued at £223 and the Model 88, the Dominator de Luxe with featherbed frame, was at last available on the home market at £259. The International and Manx models continued unchanged but the trials 500T was not selling and was axed.

For a while Nortons' racing plans were unclear. Then in February 1955 Gilbert Smith announed that because the FIM had not banned streamlining and because the big races were switching from true road circuits to purpose-built tracks, Nortons would not support the World Championship series that year. However, they would contest the TT and the factory riders would race machines which could be sold to private owners – the works bikes incorporating ideas which could be used on future Manx models. The riders were to be two talented 21-year-olds – John Surtees and John Hartle – plus the veteran Jack Brett. The Model F was scrapped.

Poor Ray Amm was killed at Imola early in April on his debut on a works four-cylinder MV Agusta. He crashed in the 350 cc race while chasing Kavanagh (Guzzi), his head striking a metal fence post just below the rim of the pudding-basin helmet which was standard wear at that time. The new Norton team, still with Craig in charge, had a pre-TT outing at Mettet in Belgium and in both 350 cc and 500 cc classes Surtees finished second to Fergus Anderson on works Guzzis – and in both Hartle and Brett were third and fourth.

The team machines were carefully prepared Manx models with larger valves, rotating magnet magnetos and with electronic rev-counters replacing the old mechanical ones. Strikes were still part of the British way of life and one by railway workers caused *Motor Cycling* to cancel their TT excursion that year when the 'naked' Nortons were completely out-paced in both races. The best they could do was fourth (Surtees) in the Junior and fourth (Brett) in the Senior, though they did win the team prize in the latter in which Hartle and Surtees both pushed in after running out of fuel on the last lap.

Surtees went under his own steam to the German Grand Prix, back at the Nürburgring for the first time since the early 1930s, and finished a close third in the 350 cc race beaten only by Lomas (Guzzi) and Hobl (DKW) and ahead of a pack of works machines including Sandford and Kavanagh on Guzzis.

In the sidecar races Oliver and Smith battled on, using the outside flywheel 1954 works engines. These were fast, as Smith proved when he led the Belgian and set a lap record at 98.43, only to miss a gear and bend a valve; with Oliver out BMWs took 1–2–3. It was a similar story in Holland a week later. There Smith was well ahead when the con-rod broke.

Later in July the Norton team had an outing to the non-championship Swedish Grand Prix at Hedemora and took a 1–2–3 in the 350 cc race, Hartle beating Surtees and Brett ahead of the works three-cylinder DKWs. In the 500 cc class Duke (Gilera) was the winner but Surtees, Brett and Hartle were next home, the Nortons again proving fast and reliable. The team then contested the Ulster Grand Prix and despite strong factory opposition Hartle finished second in both classes, beaten in both races by Lomas on fully streamlined Guzzis.

On the Isle of Man, Londoner Geoff Tanner scored a Norton double in the Manx Grand Prix and then, in a series of top-class home meetings, enthusiasts saw memorable battles between Duke (Gilera) and Surtees (Norton) in the 500 cc classes at Scarborough, Aintree, Silverstone and Brands Hatch. Duke won the opening two rounds but Surtees beat him fair and square at Silverstone, where they shared the lap record at 96.28 mph, and again at Brands where Alan Trow relegated the Gilera rider to third place much to the delight of a partisan crowd. Surtees won the 350 cc class at all four meetings, then left Nortons to join the MV Agusta team in October.

As the season closed came the long-awaited news that Nortons were to market a bigger twin in 1956, following the trend set by Triumph, BSA and Royal Enfield. But instead of enlarging the Dominator engine to 650 cc or 700 cc, as their rivals had, Nortons increased the capacity from 497 cc (66 × 72.6 mm) by just 100 cc to 597 cc (68 × 82 mm). The new model with featherbed frame was catalogued as the Dominator 99 de Luxe and was priced at £259, only £7 more than the 88 de Luxe.

Broadening the capacity range, the Model 50 with 348 cc overhead-valve engine, dropped in 1939, was reintroduced. The engine, with pre-war bore and stroke of 71 × 88 mm, was mounted in the older-style frame with swinging-fork rear suspension and the price was £209: the cheapest bike in the range. One model was dropped and another quietly sidelined. The standard Domintor Model 7 with non-featherbed frame got the chop while the marvellous 348 and 490 cc Internationals were simply left out of the catalogue. They were still available to special order but no work had been done on them – if you did order one it could be supplied to 1955 specification. The 'Inters' had been outpaced by the new BSA Gold Stars and rather than uprate them in an attempt to win back this lucrative corner of the market, Nortons had thrown in the towel.

Then, on 1 December 1955, came a bombshell when Joe Craig announced his retirement. Aged 58 and associated with Nortons since 1925, he had obviously tired of trying to compete with virtually standard Manx machines. On 20 December he married Nellie van Wijngaarden, widow of Dutch rider Piet van Wijngaarden, and went to live in Rotterdam. In was the end of the Craig era – one in which the Norton racing team had flourished and become the most famous and successful in the history of the sport. During Craig's reign as race manager and technical director, Nortons won 27 TT races, scores of grands prix and nine Manufacturers World Championships – a score no one else could get near.

Budget-priced machine for the sidecar enthusiast – the 596 cc Model 19R of 1955 cost £190. The 19S with swinging fork rear springing cost £18 more.

CHAPTER 18

AMC and the slow decline 1956–1962

Bert Hopwood, sacked by Gilbert Smith in 1949, returned to Nortons in May 1956. He had started well at BSA refining the 500 cc twin and designing a 'bigger brother', the excellent 650 cc which powered the Golden Flash and later, in up-rated form, the Super Rocket and Rocket Gold Star. He had also designed, in conjunction with his right-hand man Doug Hele, the four-valve, overhead-camshaft 250 cc racing engine that, but for a fit of cold feet by the BSA management, Geoff Duke would have raced in 1955.

However, towards the end of his time at BSA things had not gone so well and two of the designs he was associated with, the Dandy lightweight and the Beeza scooter, proved costly disasters. Despite these setbacks Donald Heather, managing director of Associated Motor Cycles, invited Hopwood to join the company as a director at Nortons.

The 26 April 1956 issue of *Motor Cycling* reported: 'Norton Motors Ltd announce that Mr Herbert Hopwood has been invited to join the board of the company and is expected to take up his full time duties towards the end of May when he will become responsible for all matters appertaining to design and production.' Gilbert Smith was still the boss at Bracebridge Street but he was at loggerheads with Heather and this move by AMC was an obvious snub to the Norton MD. I stress the date of the move because in his book *Whatever Happened to the British Motorcycle Industry* Hopwood gives the date as April 1955, but the two weeklies both confirm that he actually did move one year later.

The Norton advertising had taken a definite turn for the worse: drawings of men in flat caps, ties, tweed sports jackets, slacks and walking shoes with their wives/girlfriends equally unsuitably clad on the pillion. The dashing, sporting image was fading though the factory continued to field an official team on Manx development models. The riders for 1956 were Hartle, Brett and Trow – but no form of streamlining was allowed on the works machines.

Alan Wilson had taken over as team manager and he took the squad to Floreffe for the usual pre-TT try-out. There Lomas and Dale dominated the 350 cc race on streamlined Guzzis but Hartle and Brett finished third and fourth. Surtees (MV Agusta) took the 500 cc honours from Lomas with Brett and Trow third and fourth. I played a small part in the sidecar race that day for I had joined Cyril Smith as his passenger. We were using a two-year-old Craig engine with outside flywheel and one of the five-speed Burman gearboxes, and although we were only third round the first bend we led the race before we got to the next corner – the ease with which the single-cylinder Norton outpaced the factory twin-cylinder BMWs of Walter Schneider and Fritz Hillebrand on the long straight, which included a hill, confirming the amazing slogging power of the old single.

LEFT **Flat out in the Clubmans' TT. Alan Shepherd on a Norton International in the 1956 Junior Clubmans' in which he came third. The 'Inter' had already been dropped from the Norton catalogue.**

Earlier that year we had won againt lesser opposition at Mettet in Belgium but we were out of luck at Floreffe. After building up a 12-second lead the clutch withdrawal mechanism failed and Schneider took over to win. A week later we finished second to World Champion Willi Noll at the then ultra-fast Hockenheim circuit where the Norton averaged 97.93 mph. On the way home to the TT we won again at Chimay in Belgium but in the Isle of Man parted company because I simply did not have the experience to master the difficult Clypse circuit in three short practice periods.

Tragically Fergus Anderson, that great defender of the single-cylinder racing engine, died in a crash at Floreffe. Angered because Moto Guzzi wanted him to retire at the age of 47, he had switched to a factory BMW and incredibly set a lap record faster than winner John Surtees (MV Agusta) just before he died. Significantly Guzzi relied on a single for the 350 cc class and continued to develop a single for the 500 cc division although early in 1956 they had unveiled their V-8 500, still the most complex motorcycle ever raced.

At the TT Kavanagh (Guzzi) won the Junior from Derek Ennett (AJS) with Hartle third ahead of Cecil Sandford on a works three-cylinder DKW. The Senior that year was emasculated by the absence of Duke and

ABOVE **John Surtees on his 500 cc Manx Norton at Brands Hatch, October 1957. Although he joined the MV Agusta team for 1956, Surtees continued to race his own Nortons when his contract allowed.**

ABOVE RIGHT **The 1957 Manx Norton engine. This is the 499 cc unit – an update of the factory engine of 1937. Bore and stroke were almost square at 86 × 85.5 mm, power output around 51 bhp and peak revs 7,200.**

Armstrong on their Gileras – both had been suspended for supporting the riders' strike for more starting money at the preceding year's Dutch TT. They had not taken any strike action themselves and, in an act of pure malice that would not be tolerated today, the FIM had banned them from racing for six months. Surtees won the race, the first Senior TT win by MV Agusta, and it was a good day for Nortons with Hartle and Brett second and third ahead of Walter Zeller on a works BMW with Lomas, on the only Guzzi that finished the race, down in fifth place.

Like Guzzis only one of the factory BMWs kept going in the Sidecar TT, ex-Luftwaffe pilot Hillebrand winning ahead of a pack of Nortons led by Pip Harris, Bill Boddice and Australian Bob Mitchell. There was no real Norton interest in the solo classes in Holland

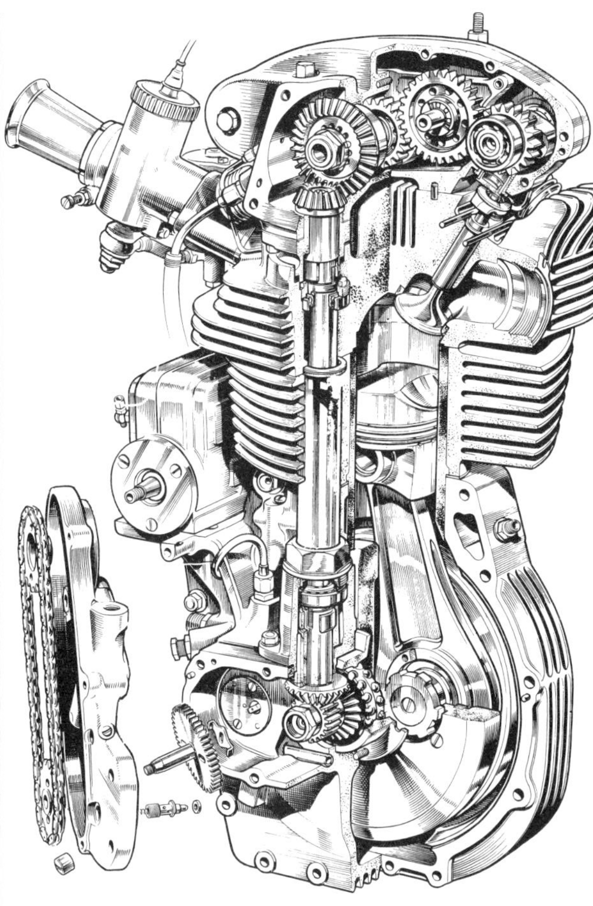

and Belgium but the sidecar boys kept slugging it out with the BMW team. At the Dutch, Hillebrand won from Noll with Smith and Mitchell third and fourth, and in Belgium Smith, with Stan Dibben in the sidecar, took the lead, set up a record lap at 99.30 mph but then missed a gear and bent the valves. This let Noll through to win with Harris and Mitchell second and third. Despite factory backing, superb streamlining, a reliable five-speed gearbox and tremendous acceleration, the German twins still had to battle to beat the Nortons.

The Norton team had their next outing at the non-championship Swedish Grand Prix. There the suspended riders were back and Campbell, on his streamlined Nortons, won the 350 cc race and finished second to Duke (Gilera) in the 500 cc. In both he beat Hartle and Brett on their naked factory bikes. Then in August came a morale-boosting success when Hartle outlasted all the Italian factory riders and bikes to win the 500 cc Ulster. He also took third place in the 350 cc behind Lomas and Dale on Guzzis and ahead of the AJS and DKW teams.

In the Manx Grand Prix Nortons took the first ten places in the Senior and the first four in the Junior – Scotland's Jimmy Buchan doing the double. And the sporting year finished on a high note when Aldershot's Les Archer clinched the 500 cc European Moto Cross Championship – the forerunner of the World Championship. Archer, son of a famous road racer, rode a bike with frame and engine built by his mechanic Ron Hankin. The power-unit was a long-stroke Manx crank-case with an International single-overhead-camshaft top half grafted on to it, mounted in a duplex frame with single top tube. During the season Archer won five of the nine rounds (The French, British, Belgian, Swedish and Danish Grands Prix) to beat Johnny Draper (BSA) and Nic Jansen (Matchless) to the title.

The British road-racing season ended with the Hutchinson 100 at Silverstone where Norton riders took the first three places in the three main classes. Brett won the 350 cc from Bob McIntyre and Hartle, who later won the 500 cc from McIntyre and Brett. Previously McIntyre had achieved most of his successes on AJS machines but for 1956 he had switched to a pair of Nortons prepared by his Glasgow sponsor Joe Potts. In the Sidecar class Harris won from Smith and Jackie Beeton.

Within days McIntyre had joined Gilera to team with Duke and to take the place of Armstrong who had retired. The German DKW factory had decided to follow the lead of Norton, AJS and NSU and to pull out of racing. Nortons too were reconsidering their situation and in November the factory issued a statement: 'It has been decided that the company will not enter an official works team in next season's racing events. It is however, the Company's intention to continue to make, and sell, racing machines.' In a way it was a blessing in disguise for it meant that in future the development machines would be entered by dealers and that the riders would be able to use streamlining – worth 10 mph on the faster circuits.

The Norton roadsters for 1957 were slightly restyled and the advertisements focused on a new 'smooth look' with the line 'Now we proudly introduce from racing experience the new smooth look.' The tanks and silencers were more streamlined and the cylinder heads and barrels changed – but to the horror of Norton enthusiasts these now had a definite AMC look about them. The three single-cylinder models were continued plus the two twins with featherbed frames and there was a new machine of sorts – the 597 cc twin-cylinder engine in the old frame with swinging-fork rear suspension. This had been introduced to cater for those who wanted a twin for sidecar work, for at that time the factory did not recommend the featherbed as a sidecar machine. Catalogued as the Model 77, this was priced at £260 including tax – the same as the Model 88 and £7 cheaper than the 99.

The two Manx racers were further improved. The most important change was the adoption of coarser teeth on the bevel drive. This strengthened the gears and eliminated some of the problems suffered with the

old set-up which had been increasingly over-stressed as the revs increased over the years. Other modifications included redesigned con-rods, big-ends and crankpins, bigger-bore carburettors and the adoption of a sodium-cooled inlet valve as well as a sodium-cooled exhaust valve. The frames were also improved with a shorter, stiffer sub-frame and built-in streamlining mounts. The price was £481.

That was the winter of the Suez crisis. Petrol rationing was again imposed on the long-suffering British public and this, allied to continuing strikes, did little to help the motorcycle makers. *Motor Cycling* carried a road test of the new 597 cc Model 77 which, fitted with a Swallow Jet 80 sports sidecar, recorded a top speed of 70 mph and cost a total of £354, as much as a family car.

In March 1957 Joe Craig was killed in a car accident near Landeck in Austria. Joe and his wife had been touring and were on their way home to Rotterdam when the accident occurred. While the news came as a shock, it was not totally unexpected for Joe had a reputation as a reckless driver – Artie Bell was one of many who much preferred sitting in the back if Joe was driving.

The Norton trio to ride the works development Manx machines in 1957 was again Hartle (riding for Eric Bowers), Brett (Lord Montagu) and Alan Trow (Reg Dearden) and in May Hartle put in an amazing ride in the German Grand Prix at Hockenheim to finish second in the rain-swept 350 cc race, beaten only by Liberati (Gilera). In the Junior TT the smaller Norton again proved competitive in Hartle's hands and after three laps he held second place only 31 seconds behind the leader Dale (Guzzi) and 24 seconds ahead of McIntyre (Gilera). Then on the fourth lap both Dale and

ABOVE The 1957–8 version of the Model 99 with 600 cc vertical twin engine and featherbed frame.

ABOVE RIGHT John Surtees heads for victory in the 350 cc race at Silverstone in 1957 on his Norton with MV Agusta style streamlining. Surtees set a class lap record at 92.87 mph.

Hartle crashed on oil at Quarry Bends. This double mishap let McIntyre through to win ahead of Campbell, who had been promoted into the Guzzi team, Bob Brown, who had replaced the injured Duke in the Gilera line-up, and John Surtees (MV Agusta).

For the Senior TT Nortons sprang a surprise. Brett, Trow and Jackie Woods, riding in place of the injured Hartle, turned out on 90-bore machines. These had a stroke of 76.48 mm to give a capacity of 499 cc but unlike the Joe Motors of 1954 they did not have outside flywheels. This engine had been designed by Doug Hele, who had rejoined Hopwood at Nortons. Jack Brett lapped at 97.5 mph and was holding fourth place on the last lap, ahead of the Guzzis of Dale and Campbell, when he crashed at Sulby. Ironically the race that year was extended from seven to eight laps as part of the fiftieth anniversary of the races – any other year and Brett would have been fourth. The race was won by Bob McIntyre (Gilera) and during it he became the first to lap at over 100 mph.

There were rumours of Nortons with desmodromic valve gear. This system (the valves closed as well as opened mechanically) was tried during practice but not in either of the races.

At the Dutch TT Brett kept going to finish fourth

in both races and once again Cyril Smith proved his Norton could match the BMWs by setting the fastest lap and leading until slowed by clutch trouble. Hillebrand won from Beeton (Norton). By this time I was working as a road-racing reporter with Cyril Quantrill's infant *Motorcycle News* and at the Dutch that year had the first of many enjoyable rides with the Swiss Edgar Strub. He was, at that time, racing a Norton and we finished fourth – my best placing with Norton power in a World Championship race.

In Belgium a week later the Strub Norton blew up in a big way on full revs down the Masta straight and the sidecar race was a clean sweep for BMWs with Schneider winning from Swiss Florian Camathias with Hillebrand third. All the Nortons were completely outpaced in the 350 cc race (won by Campbell on a Guzzi) but at the end of an amazing 500 cc race the single-cylinder machines from Bracebridge Street were placed 1–2–3! Duke, Dale, McIntyre and Lomas were all out with injuries and Gilera strength was reduced to one when Liberati's bike failed during the warm-up and he took over Bob Brown's works machine. Zeller (BMW), Surtees and Campbell were soon out and although Liberati crossed the line in first place he was disqualified because the machine switch had not been authorised. Brett (Norton) was the winner from Australian Keith Bryens (Norton) with 'King of Brands' Derek Minter (Norton) third.

Hartle was back for the Swedish Grand Prix at Hedemora, again a non-championship event. There Campbell won both big races on single-cylinder Guzzis – the 500 cc class on a 352 cc version. And in the big class Hartle rode a 90-bore Norton into second place after getting the better of Geoff Duke who was making a comeback ride on his works Gilera. Back home Nortons had no luck in the Ulster Grand Prix. Hartle was the best placed, finishing fourth in the 350 cc class, while Geoff Tanner was the top Norton in the 500 cc race, again finishing fourth.

Alan Holmes scored a Norton double in the Manx Grand Prix and Cyril Smith took second place at the Italian, beaten only by Albino Milani who had persuaded Gilera to let him have a works four-cylinder machine for the race. Cyril fought and won a tremendous dice with Camathias, beating the Swiss BMW rider across the line by a wheel. Sadly Hillebrand, who had clinched the world title, was absent – he had been killed practising for a minor meeting at Bilbao in Spain.

Hartle was the most successful Norton rider at Monza, finishing sixth in the 350 cc class and ninth in

ABOVE **Jack Brett finished second in the 1957 500 cc Belgian Grand Prix, but was promoted to first when Libero Liberati (Gilera) was disqualified.**

RIGHT **Start of the 1957 500 cc Belgian Grand Prix, with Australians Keith Campbell (Guzzi) and Keith Bryens (Guzzi) leading from Libero Liberati (Gilera), John Surtees (MV Agusta) and Jack Brett (Norton).**

the 500 cc, and back in England he turned out at Scarborough in late September on an interesting lightweight 350 cc Norton. This had the oil carried in a separate compartment at the rear of the petrol tank and was fitted with one of the old works five-speed gearboxes, but it was Brett (Norton) who won the race from Peter Murphy (AJS) with Hartle third. Surtees rode a Norton to win the 500 cc race from Hartle and Brett with Duke, who switched his entry from a Gilera to a Norton (his first Norton ride for five years), out of the reckoning.

I remember that Scarborough meeting for two reasons. Firstly because Strub arrived with an immaculate ex-works BMW with right-hand sidecar which he had bought from a German rider who had lost a leg in a racing accident – and we finished third on it. Second because in that week's *MCN* our Italian correspondent Carlo Perelli had reported the scoop news that Gilera, Guzzi and Mondial were pulling out of racing – and Geoff Duke did not believe it! It seems that the Italians had not told Duke or McIntyre and I, as the representative of *MCN*, got the full blast of their anger.

Norton production at this time was still in the region of 200 machines a week of which the majority were twins, and the range for 1958 was virtually unchanged – three twins (77, 88 and 99) and three push-rod singles

GULF
BP
BP
BP
CASTROL
LUCAS
ENGLEBERT

ABOVE The author on a Dunstall racing Norton twin at Brands Hatch, October 1958, before a track-test. Fettling the machine is owner Paul Dunstall.

(50, ES2 and 19S). The Manx was continued unchanged except for the adoption of the racing AMC/Burman gearbox. This replaced the Norton/Burman unit but because of the common ancestry the effect of the change was minimal. The price was £496.

The camshaft International models had finally been axed – and in February 1958 poor Gilbert Smith got the chop too. He had joined the company as an office boy in 1916, had been made a director when he was 26 and promoted to MD in 1945. But his days were numbered when AMC bought Nortons; when his contract came up for renewal he was 'invited' to resign. A hard-headed, hard-drinking Birmingham businessman, he was an unsympathetic character used to getting his own way – especially with the pliant motorcycle press of the day.

On the credit side there is no doubt that for many years he did a good job at Nortons, and he was a great racing enthusiast who took a tremendous interest in the TT and the Manx Grand Prix. His whole life revolved around the Bracebridge Street factory and there are those who say that having to leave broke his heart. Certainly he died within a few years.

That same February Slazengers decided to sponsor the Norton racing team. They were, as far as I know, the first big company outside the trade to put money into the sport as a form of publicity. Hartle, having completed his National Service, had decided to join Surtees at MV Agusta but Brett and Trow joined the Slazenger-Norton team and Mike O'Rourke was the third man. The bikes they would use would be the development Manx models, with Doug Hele directing operations back at the factory.

In March Nortons released news about a new model for the North American market. Named the Nomad, this consisted of an up-rated 597 cc twin in an old-style single-downtube chassis with increased ground clearance and was aimed at the growing enduro market. Later in March came the news that Duke would be Norton mounted for 1958 and he started his campaign on a pair of Reg Dearden bikes at Oulton Park where he twice finished second to Alastair King (Nortons). Later Duke had a brief flirtation with BMW who lent him bikes for the 500 cc class but he never looked happy on the Munich twin and by the end of July was back on a Norton for the 500 cc class.

Hopwood was appointed MD of Norton Motors and R.T. Shelley in April, and the 1958 batch of Manx racers earned high praise from the riders. For example, New Zealander John Hempleman picked up his new bikes, drove to Salzburg for the Austrian Grand Prix and raced his 500 'straight from the crate', clocking the fastest lap and finishing second to Ernst Hiller on a works BMW.

There was plenty of Norton activity at the TT. Duke tried an experimental ultra-short-stroke 350 cc (80 × 69.5 mm, 349 cc) during practice. He reverted to a 1953 works engine with a 1954 five-speed gearbox for the race but various problems put him out on the first lap. The Junior was won by Surtees (MV Agusta) but Nortons filled the next 12 places, which put the AJS supporters in their place.

For the Senior Hele produced two even bigger-bore engines which were raced by former Guzzi teamster Keith Campbell and double MGP winner Alan Holmes. These had bore and stroke dimensions of 93 × 73.5 mm, 499 cc but retained normal inside flywheels. Unfortunately both retired – Campbell with clutch and brake problems and Holmes when the clip holding the carburettor needle broke when he was lying fourth.

RIGHT The 490 cc ES2 as offered in 1958, but the next year all Norton roadsters had the featherbed frame.

The race was won by Surtees (MV Agusta) from Bob Anderson on a Bill Stuart-tuned standard Manx, with Bob Brown using a Hele 90-bore engine in third place. But the most outstanding lap (and strangely enough this has been largely ignored up to now) was put in by Bob McIntyre on his Joe Potts-prepared Manx Norton. For the tough Scot lapped at 99.98 mph and averaged 99.19 mph for the first two laps before bevel trouble put him out when holding second place on the third.

With only MV Agusta contesting the grands prix with pukka works machinery, Norton riders had a good time in the classics. And when the Italian factory decided not to contest the Swedish Grand Prix, upgraded to World Championship status that year, Duke won both classes to give the Bracebridge Street factory their first championship double since 1951. His 350 cc had a special Reynolds frame with a single large-diameter front downtube which doubled as the oil tank, built for him by Ken Sprayson. The engine was a Manx supplied by Dearden but the 500 was a complete factory bike with 93-bore engine flown out by Nortons for the meeting. Speaking to me about the 93-bore Hele said:

It was an exercise to find out if that was the way we should be going. Joe Craig had shortened the stroke and increased the bore – first from 79 to 82, then to 84 in 1951 and to 85.93 the next year. In 1953 it was up to 88 and in 1954 to 90 mm. We took it another stage with the 93-bore and it was a very smooth engine but to do the job properly it needed a new cylinder head with revised valve angles, different combustion-chamber shape, new cambox and so on and we simply ran out of time and money. You must remember that we were a very small team and had to work on a number of projects. The most pressing of them at that time was to develop the twins as sports models and the Manx was not top priority.

In mid September *MCN* carried the headline 'Top Secret 500 cc Norton' with a story which read: 'A new development 500 cc Norton racing engine made its debut at Scarborough on Saturday when it was ridden by Alan Holmes into fifth place in the 500 cc final. Alan lay second for several laps until slowed by gearbox trouble.' The engine was basically the Manx but the bevel drive had been redesigned in a bid to eliminate problems.

In the new design the bevels were splined to a larger-diameter vertical shaft which ran in needle roller bearings. This in turn required a larger-diameter vertical cover and with the lower bevel housing radically altered the new unit looked very different. The new engine proved a success and was immediately incorporated into the Manx models for 1959. Other alterations included a Nimonic inlet valve in place of the sodium valve and a modified clutch. Despite the very real improvements the price increased only a few pounds – to £496.

Far more radical changes were announced for the roadsters. Out went the two sidecar machines – the single-cylinder 596 cc Model 19S and the 597 cc Model 77 – while the two surviving singles, the 350 cc Model 50 and the 490 cc ES2, now appeared in featherbed frames and sporting alternators which had been introduced on the twins the preceding year. The 88 and 99 were continued, with larger inlet valves and higher compression ratios to take advantage of the better fuel

now available. Optional extras for the twins included a 'speed package' of twin carburettors, polished ports and even higher compression ratios plus total enclosure of the secondary chain, which was available for all models. Despite the improvements the prices were held, and in the case of the twins actually reduced slightly with the 88 listed at £280 and the 99 at £285. The standard colour was polychromatic grey but for £3 extra you could specify a red, black, silver or metallic blue finish.

But the real sensation of 1958 was the launch, at the Earls Court Show, of the twin-cylinder 250 cc Jubilee – so called to celebrate the sixtieth birthday of the founding of the Norton company. The engine was a neat vertical twin with 'over-square' bore and stroke of 60 × 44 mm, 249 cc, designed by Hopwood and Hele with Bill Pitcher doing the detailing. The four-speed gearbox was in unit, which was a step forward, but the valves were push-rod operated and the unit was slotted into what was obviously basically a Francis-Barnett rolling chassis with the addition of semi-enclosure of the rear wheel. It was the only 250 cc twin-cylinder four-stroke on the British market at that time but it was a touring mount, not a sporting one. The price was £216 and Hopwood's idea was to expand the range down into the utility/touring market.

Even at the time that seemed wrong. Norton was a prestige motorcycle with a hard-won reputation. What we Norton fans wanted was rip-snorting road-burners. Yet one after another the British factories fell for the utility line and semi-enclosure. First it was Velocette with the under-powered LE flat-twin, then Triumph and Norton with semi-enclosure of the rear wheel. All proved a disaster and were scrapped after a few years.

A young Londoner named Paul Dunstall had the right idea. He bought a 99, had the twin curburettor speed kit fitted, raised the compression ratio to 10 to 1, swopped the roadster forks for the shorter Manx ones, fitted Manx units at the rear, replaced the alternator and coil ignition with a magneto – and won the second race he ever contested at Brands Hatch, competing against pukka racing machines. The engine revved to 7000 and the bike would do 118 mph without a fairing.

In January 1959 came bad news for Nortons. The Dutch were starting to import machines from Japan and Gerhard Klomps, Dutch correspondent for *MCN*, wrote in glowing terms about a 250 cc parallel twin named the 'Dream' which the Honda factory were producing. The styling was reminiscent of NSU but the engine was technically superior to the Norton with a chain-driven overhead camshaft and an electric starter – surely a must for a new touring mount. He finished his report with a chilling line: 'The Honda company is now exploring the possibility of export markets.'

Leading up to the 1959 TT there were rumours about Hele persevering with desmo valve gear experiments plus a 350 cc with an outside flywheel and a 500 cc with a stronger crank. Terry Shepherd, Gary Hocking and Bob McIntyre tried the experimental engines during TT practice but reverted to Manx models for the races. Surtees (MV Agustas) scored another double to equal Stanley Woods' feat of 1932–33 and the most successful Norton rider was Alastair King who finished third in the Junior and second in the Senior.

The FIM introduced a class for catalogue racing machines in 1959. This was known as Formula One and grand prix organisers were invited to run either a 350 cc or a 500 cc F1 race in place of the grand prix class. Both the Dutch and Belgian held a 350 cc F1 and both were completely dominated by Manx Norton riders. Bob Brown won in Holland where Nortons took the first eight places, while Hocking beat him in Belgium where all 13 finishers were Manx mounted.

The unstoppable Surtees did yet another double at

RIGHT **Action at Aberdare Park in 1959 as a young Mike Hailwood hurls his Manx Norton to yet another win.**

FAR RIGHT **Rhodesian sensation Gary Hocking swings aboard a Reg Dearden Manx Norton in May 1959.**

the Ulster but Nortons took all the places with Brown and Duke second and third in the 350 cc and McIntyre and Duke filling the same positions in the 500 cc. Duke then went to the Italian Grand Prix at Monza where he finished third in the 500 cc class, beaten only by the MV Agustas of Surtees and Venturi, before finishing his two-wheeled career with three wins at Locarno – two on Nortons plus the 250 cc on a works Benelli. Nortons then scored a double in the Manx Grand Prix with Peter Middleton first in the Junior and Eddie Crooks the victor in the Senior.

In November Nortons launched what *MCN* dubbed the 'Futuristic Featherbeds'. These were de luxe versions of the 88 and 99 which had the Jubilee-style partial enclosure of the rear wheel. Additionally the engines of all the twins had impoved cylinder heads, bigger inlet valves, increased finning and, for the bigger twin, a new cylinder block.

The most expensive bike in the range for 1960 was the 99 de Luxe at £280, £5 more than the standard version. The 88 de Luxe cost £274 (standard model £268) while the ES2 and the Model 50 were £234 and £228 with the Jubilee reduced in price from £216 to £208 – a sure sign that it was not selling. Competition was hotting up in the 250 cc class and early in 1960 Ariel launched the completely new Arrow with an ultra modern pressed steel frame and two-stroke twin engine for £167 – £41 cheaper than the little Norton.

In February 1960 Nortons announced the specification for that year's Manx models. Compression ratio was increased to 11 to 1 for both 350 and 500 cc, the top piston ring was chrome plated and the large-diameter hollow tappets were Stellite faced to reduce wear. Glass fibre was used for the first time – for the seat base and the neat front number plate. According to the factory over 100 would be built, but a spokesman warned that 'demand exceeds supply'. If this were true, why not build more? Obviously the profit margin on the Manx models (now retailing at £497) was greater than on any other machine and so was the demand for spares, which were expensive and provided a regular secondary source of revenue.

The racing year opened with a surprise win for Nortons in the 500 cc class of the non-championship Spanish Grand Prix at Barcelona. There Jim Redman on a Manx beat similarly mounted Peter Ferbrache with Remo Venturi on a works MV Agusta a well-beaten third – Nortons taking 10 of the first 11 places! At home Mike Hailwood (Norton) celebrated his twentieth birthday by winning the 500 cc class at the pre-TT international at Silverstone when he became the first rider to lap the famous circuit at over 100 mph on a motorcycle. He also took the 125 cc and 250 cc honours on a pair of 'desmo' Ducatis, while Minter (Norton)

won the 350 cc class in which the first 10 were Norton mounted.

Originally Dave Chadwick and Eddie Crooks were to have ridden the works bikes in the 1960 TT but tragically Dave was killed when he collided with another rider at Mettet in May and it was Crooks who tried out what *MCN* described as a 'startling new Norton'. This was very low but unlike the Fish retained an orthodox riding position. To reduce height the forks were shortened and had no top yoke – only a massive lower yoke, bicycle style. To enable the rider to get even lower, the normal fuel tank had been eliminated and replaced by one situated behind the engine in a slightly longer featherbed frame. The fuel from this was lifted by a pump driven from the end of the inlet camshaft. The displaced oil tank was fitted behind and below the petrol tank. The engine was a 350 cc Manx, fitted to test the handling, with the exhaust running under the engine (the sump of which had been modified) and with a flattened megaphone located centrally and terminating 7 in ahead of the rear tyre. Crooks found it difficult to ride with too much weight carried by the arms and it was not used in the race.

Hele was still working on the 'desmo' idea. He took with him to the island a test engine – a 350 cc with massively 'over-square' dimensions (86 × 60 mm, 348.5 cc). This was a hybrid, a 500 cc head on a modified 350 cc bottom half, and the idea was to test the valves and valve gear of the bigger engine at far higher revs than a 500 would normally achieve. The engine had an outside flywheel but was never raced. Speaking of the 'desmo' project, Hele says:

> That engine revved to 9300 without any problems but we could never get a desmodromic engine to consistently give more power than a normal Manx and we finally dropped the idea because they were very difficult to set up. You have to remember that we were developing racing machines to be sold to private riders and the maintenance of a 'desmo' would have been a real problem. To make it worthwhile they would have to have produced more power – and they never did this.

At the 1960 TT Minter, riding a Manx prepared by Lancefield, became the first rider on a single-cylinder machine to lap the circuit at over 100 mph. He did in fact go one better, literally, by getting round at 101.05 mph before retiring with a split oil tank. Hailwood was the second to lap at over the 'ton' on a single (100.37 mph) and he finished third, beaten by the MV Agusta duo Surtees and Hartle. It is worth recording that of the 81 starters in the Senior that year 55 rode Nortons; the next most popular make was Matchless, which had recently launched the single-cylinder G50, with 14. In the Junior the figures were 97 starters: 57 Norton, 27 AJS.

In late November 1960 Nortons launched the Navigator – a 350 cc version of the twin-cylinder Jubilee. This was offered in two versions, a basic sports model

ABOVE **This 1954 Joe Craig outside flywheel 350 cc engine was brought out of retirement for practising at the 1959 TT.**

ABOVE RIGHT **Norton domination of the private rider market: the start of the Formula One 350 cc race at the 1959 Dutch TT – and all the riders are on Nortons.**

BELOW RIGHT **Another Norton line-up – this time at Aberdare Park in 1959. Left to right: Mike Hailwood, Alan Trow, Dan Shorey and Eric Hinton.**

at £230 and the de Luxe with Jubilee-style partial enclosure of the rear wheel for £238. A major improvement was that the new models had pukka Roadholder forks which replaced the flimsy Francis-Barnett component fitted to the Jubilee. The new engine had a bore and stroke of 63 × 56 mm, 349 cc and produced enough power to give the Navigator a top speed of 84 mph when road tested by Peter Howdle for *MCN*.

The following month the first picture of a 650 cc Norton twin appeared in the press. The bike was dubbed the Norton Manxman and while the 68 mm bore of the 600 cc engine was retained, the stroke had been lengthened to 89 mm to give an exact capacity of 646 cc. Compression ratio was 8.3 and twin down-draught carburettors were fitted; the unit slotted into a featherbed frame. Said the press release: 'The Manxman has been expressly developed for the American market and is strictly for export only.'

At the 1960 Earls Court Show it was revealed that the Manx models for 1961 would be little changed. The pistons would carry two rings instead of three (one compression and a scraper), the oil tanks would be of a new type, hinged at the top and held in place by rubber bands, while the megaphone exhaust systems were

24
19
2
7
25

ABOVE **The 1959 Manx Norton showing the modified clutch. The price was £496 including tax.**

BELOW **Les Archer with the camshaft 500 cc Norton he rode as a member of the winning British team at the Moto Cross des Nations in Belgium in 1959.**

LEFT A publicity shot of the 250 cc twin-cylinder Norton Jubilee launched at the 1958 Earls Court Show. Note riding gear!

BELOW The 350 cc twin Norton Navigator was introduced to the range in 1960. The picture shows MCN's Peter Howdle speed-testing at Silverstone in March 1961.

to be strengthened to stop splitting. And in December came the good news that Castrol were to sponsor MGP winner Phil Read on the works development models.

Early in April 1961 tester Dennis Greenfield appeared at Silverstone on a Manx fitted with a neat double front brake. This had two 7 in twin leading shoe units 'back to back' to give 45 per cent more lining area than the standard 8 in Manx brake which top-liners felt was not good enough. Hailwood had used an Italian Oldani the preceding year, as did Minter when he set the first 100 mph TT lap by a Norton in June 1960. The new brake was a success and was soon fitted as standard on the Manx models.

Then, in late April 1961, the SS (Sports Special) models were launched – the 600 cc 99SS with a claimed top speed of 107 mph for £297 and the 500 cc 88SS (101 mph) priced at £291. Both were upgraded Dominator models with sports camshafts, twin carburettors, siamesed exhaust pipes and all the 'go faster' bits and pieces previously listed as 'optional extras'. But behind the scenes the factory was in turmoil as rumours circulated. For while Nortons had been doing reasonably well the Associated Motor Cycles group as a whole had not. The shareholders were demanding changes, the board of directors were talking of a move to a new

ABOVE LEFT **Norton's Doug Hele with the twin-cylinder Domiracer that came third in the 1961 Senior TT. A lap at over 100 mph was the first by a push-rod engine and the first by a twin of any sort.**

ABOVE **Doug Hele's 350 cc unit used by Derek Minter in 1961. The magneto has been replaced by battery-powered coil ignition.**

factory in the Isle of Sheppey, and it was clear that the whole set-up was crumbling.

Tiring of the battle, Hopwood left Nortons at the end of May 1961 to rejoin Edward Turner at Triumphs. Alec Skinner, a chartered accountant who had been with Nortons since 1950, took over as MD. Things were also changing on the racing front and just before the TT *MCN* reported: 'Norton break with tradition – a twin for the TT.' The news item continued: 'The new machine is a works development project aimed at finding a replacement for the present single cylinder Manx.' Doug Hele, in charge of the project, takes up the story.

At the time we were doing a lot of work to improve the performance of the twins – initially with the 600 cc engine and then with the 500 cc. I remember that we prepared an 88 for Dennis Greenfield and Fred Swift to race in the Thruxton 500 in 1960. They won the 500 cc class and that encouraged us to take things a stage further and for the 1961 TT we built a really serious engine. This had short con-rods, thicker crankpins, full race cams with the camshaft running in needle roller bearings, hollow push-rods and hollow tappets, eccentric rocker adjustments and a separate pressurised oil supply to the rockers.

This gave 55 bhp on the bench and revved to 8000, but Hele knew that the crank was not really strong enough and this, combined with the flexing of the shaft, kept the revs down in the island. In a further attempt to shed weight a new, lower and lighter frame had been designed at Nortons and this was made by Ken Sprayson at Reynolds Tubes (who built all the featherbed frames for Nortons after Rex McCandless and Oliver North returned to Belfast after making the initial batches). The complete machine weighed 280 lb dry – 35 lb less than a standard Manx.

As works development rider, Read tried the new twin in practice but slid off at Creg-ny-Baa. He remounted to finish the lap and confirmed the bike was fast, but he was obviously not impressed for he reverted to a Manx for the Senior TT. The Domiracer then passed to Australian Tom Phillis who did a standing-start lap at 93 mph first time out on the bike during the Thursday practice – a misfire on the second round putting paid to hopes of an even faster lap.

Read rode his own Bill Lacey-tuned Manx in the Junior TT, and took over to score Norton's final Junior TT success after Hailwood's AJS broke a crankpin on the last lap when he was well ahead. Hocking (MV Agusta) hit trouble in the Senior TT when a sticking throttle put him out. Hailwood took the lead and this time his machine, a Manx Norton also prepared by Bill Lacey, kept going to win at 100.60 mph – the first time a single had averaged over 100 mph for a complete TT. Bob McIntyre on another Manx finished second, with Phillis on the Domiracer a magnificent third at 98.78 mph and with a lap at over 100 mph – the first by a twin and the first by a push-rod engine. Fittingly Rem Fowler, the only man to win a TT on a twin-cylinder Norton, was at the finish to congratulate all three Norton riders.

Minter, who had recently split with Lancefield, took over from Read as the development rider and finished third in the 350 cc race at Brands Hatch in July riding a hybrid – a Manx engine in the lighter and lower frame

This is one of a small batch of 500 cc twins built by Nortons for the 1962 Daytona 200 race in Florida.

originally built for the Domiracer. Over on the continent Hailwood was building on his TT success, taking second place to Hocking in Holland, Belgium and East Germany before returning for the Ulster where he was again runner-up.

In Ireland Phillis had his second outing on the Domiracer. By this time Hele had the engine revving to 8000 on the road as well as on the test-bed and he remembers how pleased Phillis was at the end of practice: 'He was thrilled to bits. He found he could stay with the MV Agusta and he really felt he was in with a chance of winning. But rain started to fall on the second lap and he came off while well up. I often wonder what would have happened if it had stayed dry . . ..'

Nortons announced that there would be no Domiracers for sale in 1962. The Manx would be continued for at least another year. Towards the end of 1961 Hele concentrated on the 350 cc, Minter winning at Castle Combe and breaking the lap record at Oulton Park. This engine had battery-powered coil ignition, the engine shorn of the familiar chain-driven magneto. Bore and stroke were standard Manx but the con-rod was shorter and the crank-case smaller – and mounted lower in the Domiracer frame. At that time Hele also had a 500 cc Manx with larger valves and a needle roller small-end which gave a marked increase in power but wore very quickly. 'The small-end experiment was very interesting and gave a surprising increase in power. I would liked to have done more work on that,' remembers Hele.

In early September Hailwood joined Hocking in the MV Agusta team and promptly won the 500 cc class of the Italian Grand Prix in which Nortons took the next five places. Then Ned Minihan headed a Norton clean sweep of the first seven places in the Senior Manx Grand Prix, though the improved 7R AJS models got the better of the Manx in the Junior, Frank Reynolds heading a 1–2–3 for the Woolwich racers. And despite the decision to stick to the Manx for the 500 cc class, the factory continued to experiment with the Domiracer. Minter and Greenfield both appeared on the twins at the international meeting staged at Cadwell in September 1961.

One of the greatest mysteries surrounding the development of the racing Nortons centres on the failure to equip the machines with a five-speed gearbox. As speeds and power rose, so a gearbox with more than four speeds became ever more important – first so that the rider could make a good start and second so that the engine could be kept within the power band, which got progressively narrower as power increased.

Nortons had switched from a three- to a four-speed box for racing in 1931 when the then relatively low-powered engines had a lusty spread of power with no megaphone exhaust system to complicate the issue. It is true that works riders had used a Burman five-speeder occasionally in 1954 but the factory had then decided against a five-speeder for the Manx and privateers had to struggle on with four speeds. Harold Daniell had been one of the first to market a five-speed conversion in early 1960 but this was not a success. Hailwood tried an Italian-built box but this too was a failure and the first successful five-speeders were a conversion to the Manx box built by a Swede, Torsten Argaard. However, it was an Austrian farmer's son, Michael Schafleitner, who, early in 1961, really showed the way. Working in the basement of the family farm near Salzburg he built for his friend, the Austrian rider Rudi Thalhammer, a six-speed cluster which slotted into the standard Manx gearbox with the addition of a spacer less than an inch thick.

The gearbox was completed just before the Austrian Grand Prix. There Thalhammer used it in the 350 cc race and finished third. He was third again at the German Gand Prix at Hockenheim where he averaged 109.59 mph on his 350 cc Manx and was beaten only by the works Jawa twins of Stastny and Havel. Thalhammer then won at Tubbergen, Bolderberg and Chimay – and after that just about every serious racer of Manx Nortons was on his way to Austria!

Why had Nortons, who had spent thousands tinkering with desmodromic valve gear, cams, port shapes, pistons, exhausts, single and twin plug layouts and every facet of the engine that you can think of, stuck to the four-speeder when a five- or six-speed gearbox would have been of such obvious benefit? Doug Hele explains.

> With hindsight I agree. We should have persevered with the five-speeder. I think we were scared by the lack of reliability. We had several of these boxes in the stores and I can remember working all one night trying to get one to work properly – the selector mechanism was the problem. Certainly a good five-speeder would have been of benefit. There was no edict from above that forbade the use of such a gearbox – if we could have found a reliable one we would have used it.

On the marketing front the Norton export drive was going well. The Czech government had started to buy Nortons and in August 1961 placed a fifth order for the single-cylinder 490 cc ES2 model – around 150 machines with spares. And in America the aggressive Berliner brothers, who had taken over the distribution of Nortons in the late 1950s, were starting to sell the British machines in large numbers – something that had never happened before despite those wins at Daytona in the early post-war years.

For 1962 Nortons expanded the Dominator range to nine models – three different capacity engines offered in three guises. First there was the basic range with 500, 600, and 650 cc single-carburettor engines, then the de luxe models with single carburettors but with partial enclosure of the rear wheel, and finally the Sports Special trio with twin carburettors, sports camshafts and other 'go faster' extras. The most powerful,

ABOVE **Hectic moment as Derek Minter loses control during a 500 cc race at Brands Hatch September 1962. Minter recovered and went on to win.**

RIGHT **The 1962 Norton catalogue showing a Sports Special twin – available with 500 cc, 600 cc or 650 cc engine.**

with the 650 cc engine originally used only in the Manxman, gave a claimed 49 bhp at 6800 rpm – enough for a 120 mph performance.

Prices of the new 650 cc twins ranged from £293 to £311. The Jubilee and Navigator were continued in standard and de luxe trim plus the single-cylinder Model 50 and ES2. It was confirmed that the 1962 Manx models would have the twin front brake but were otherwise unchanged. The first road test report on the 650SS appeared in *Motor Cycling* in February 1962 and recorded a one-way speed of 119 mph with a mean average of 112 mph. During the next month came the first guarded mention of a 750 cc variant of the Dominator – for export only.

Despite the story that they were not going to market Domiracers in 1962, two in fact were built and sold

ABOVE **Les Archer finally retired after the 1961 season. Here he is seen in action in the Hants Grand National.**

– both to foreigners. Swiss former sidecar ace Hans Haldemann got one for Luigi Taveri to race, and Rudi Thalhammer bought the other one. Both fitted Schafleitner six-speeders and Taveri, who went on to star with Honda, finished fourth in the 500 cc class at Imola in April 1962 beaten only by Italian works machines. Thalhammer was not so lucky. He picked up his machine at the TT and wrecked it when he was involved in a crash while testing the bike on open roads.

Between these two incidents Minter had ridden a works 650 cc twin (described by Hele as a tuned roadster engine in a Manx frame) at Brands where he beat Hailwood on his very fast Manx. Then in May Nortons won the three main classes at the British Motor Cycle Racing Club's 1000 km production machine race at Silverstone. Phil Read and Brian Setchell took the Open class on a 650SS, Dennis Greenfield and Fred Swift the 500 cc class on an 88SS, while Hayward and Robinson won the 350 cc on a Navigator. Later in the year Read and Setchell were again outright winners at the Thruxton 500 Mile Race with Swift, teaming with Roy Ingram, on an 88SS second overall and best 500 cc machine. Impressive performances in the two most important production machine races in the British calendar.

During practice for the 1962 TT, Minter rode a works Domiracer fitted with a Schafleitner six-speeder which Thalhammer had dropped off at the factory when he picked up his Manx-framed Domiracer. Roy Ingram (sponsored by Reg Dearden) tried a second factory twin, his bike equipped with an Argaard five-speeder, and Read also tested one of the twins. But all reverted to their Manx models for the race and, with Thalhammer injured, not a single Domiracer started in the Senior TT that year. Hocking won for MV Agusta and Manx Nortons took the next seven places.

Then in late July came a shattering blow for all true Norton enthusiasts – Nortons were to leave Bracebridge Street! Commented *Motor Cycle*: 'It's almost as unthinkable as if Nelson were to desert his column!' AMC, who had survived a shareholders' revolt and had abandoned plans to move, were doing badly. They had decided to consolidate the business at Woolwich and the manufacture of Nortons was to be transferred over the next year. Managing director Alec Skinner resigned immediately.

CHAPTER 19

Dennis Poore 1963–1976

The resignation of Alec Skinner was the first of many. Doug Hele, the inspiration behind the racing effort, left in August 1962 and when the final move to Woolwich was made in February 1963 John Hudson remembers that he was one of a handful of Norton employees who made the transfer.

No one wanted to move. I'd been at Bracebridge Street since January 1955 and I thought it was a wonderful place to work. Everyone knew what they were doing and got on with it. There was a real Norton tradition there. When we got to Woolwich I felt the workers rather resented us Norton people, though I got on well enough.

Hudson's job was officially described as 'technical writer' which meant that he answered queries and dealt with technical questions. Not surprisingly, the Norton range for 1963 had been 'pruned'. Out went the 600 cc twins, made superfluous by the introduction of the 650 cc engine the preceding year, and the de luxe version of the 88, with partial enclosure of the rear wheel, was also axed. This still left a 10-model range (two Jubilee 250 cc, two Navigator 350 cc, two Dominator 88, two Dominator 650 cc and the Model 50 and ES2 singles) plus the Manx racers – and following requests from the go-ahead Berliner brothers in America, a 750 cc twin named the Atlas was shown for the first time at Earls Court late in 1962, just before Nortons moved.

Originally the 1963 Manx models had been listed at £528 but the Inland Revenue then decided that racing motorcycles should be exempt from purchase tax, and the price came down to £440. That was the good news. The bad news was that very few Manx racers were actually built that year. A full-scale batch had been made in 1961 with a smaller run the following year. A few

BELOW **Winning group after the 1972 Thruxton 500-mile race – left to right: Dave Croxford, Chairman Dennis Poore and Mick Grant.**

were built in 1963 from spares. The sad thing is that prepared by the right man and handled by the right rider the Manx was still a winner – as Derek Minter proved when he won the £1000 Race of the Year at Mallory Park in September 1962, beating a field that included Jim Redman on a works four-cylinder Honda.

The first new Norton to go into production at Woolwich was the Electra 400 twin. Built to fulfil a £500,000 order from the Berliners, this had an up-rated Navigator engine with 66 × 58 mm bore and stroke (compared with the 63 × 56 mm of the 350 cc engine), a stronger gearbox, bigger brakes and, most important of all, an electric starter – the first Norton to be equipped with a self-starter. It was in fact the first British-built four-stroke to be offered for sale with a piece of equipment that the car industry had taken for granted for over 30 years! The Electra 400 was launched in January 1963 while the transfer was taking place.

On the racing front there was tragedy at Brands Hatch when Minter, on a twin-plug, Petty-tuned Manx, crashed while battling for the lead with Dave Downer on a Dunstall 650 cc Dominator. Minter escaped with a back injury but Downer suffered a punctured lung and died on the way to hospital.

At the Blackpool Show in May Nortons displayed a 750 cc prototype police model and in June axed the de luxe models with partial rear wheel enclosure. This news was followed in September by the announcement that the single-cylinder Nortons were to be dropped.

ABOVE **The 750 cc Norton Atlas. At a 1964 price of £359, it was then the largest capacity vertical twin in the world.**

FAR RIGHT **Pre-war factory rider and post-war Norton agent Freddie Frith with the Norton Commando at Cadwell Park in May 1968.**

Reported *Motor Cycling*: 'Nortons will henceforth produce only twins and these will be retailored in accordance with an analysis by the sales staff of 1964 market requirements . . . accordingly the smaller models are available only in touring guise and the larger ones only in sports trim.'

This cut the range to five – the 250 cc Jubilee, 350 cc Navigator, 400 cc Electra, 500 cc Dominator 88SS and 650 cc Dominator 650SS with prices ranging from £244 to £351. The 750 cc Atlas was in production for export only. An improvement was that both the SS twins were fitted with 12-volt electrical systems. The Manx and the 7R AJS and G50 Matchless racers were officially finished – none would be built in 1964. Norman Sharpe, then editor of *Motor Cycling*, drew an excellent cartoon showing a hearse leaving the factory carrying the three famous racing machines with the words 'Woolwich Co-operative Society' on the side. This caused a stir not only at the factory but at the Co-op, who wrote a letter of protest!

In the spring of 1964 the 750cc Atlas came off the 'export only' list and was offered on the home market at £359. Powered by a 73 × 89 mm, 745 cc unit it was the largest vertical twin in the world and produced a thumping 49 bhp in touring tune. At the TT that year Roy Ingram on a Reg Dearden Manx clocked 136.7 mph through the *Motor Cycling* speed trap at the Highlander. This was an accurate electric-eye set-up operated by the National Sprint Association on one of the fastest sections of the course near Greeba Castle and reflects the true top speed of a well-tuned Manx with dolphin fairing. The best 350 cc Norton was Minter at 126.3 mph on his Petty Norton. For comparison, Hailwood clocked 144.6 mph on his 500 cc MV Agusta with Redman the top 350 cc at 143.4 mph on a works four-cylinder Honda.

Both at home and abroad the big-twin Atlas was proving popular. In addition to the standard machine the Berliners persuaded Woolwich to build the N15, a scrambler version with the Atlas engine in a Matchless frame. Nortons were selling well in the States but the sales figures for the AJS and Matchless models continued to fall. Norton morale was given a boost when Phil Read switched from a Tom Kirby Matchless to a Dearden Norton to win the 500 cc class of the Ulster Grand Prix – the first British 500 cc World Championship win for two years. And Jack Ahearn made it two when he won the big class in Finland on his Manx.

It was hard to keep pace with the hybrid machines now leaving Woolwich and in October 1964, when the factory announced their range for 1965, *Motor Cycling* headlined the story 'AMC Mix Marques for 1965'. No changes had been made to the Norton models but the 350 cc Matchless G3 and the 500 cc Matchless G80 singles were now built with Norton badges and were offered as the Model 50 Mark 2 and the ES2 Mark 2 – the same machines (except for the badges) continued to be catalogued by both Matchless and AJS. In a reverse move AMC put on sale models powered by the 750 cc Atlas engine – the AJS 33 and Matchless G15 twins.

This meant that for 1965 Nortons offered eight models – the 250 cc Jubilee, 350 cc Navigator, 350 cc 50 Mark 2, ES400, ES2 Mark 2, 88SS, 99SS and Atlas at prices ranging from £339 to £405. But the industry was in decline, hit by falling sales. Douglas went into liquidation, while Villiers were bought by E. & H.P. Smith, a Wolverhampton-based group who already controlled Royal Enfield and Albion. By the start of 1965 AMC were in debt to the tune of £1,534,216 – a staggering amount which equates to around £20,000,000 by 1990 standards.

On the racing side the aging Nortons continued to do well with Joe Dunphy second to Hailwood (MV Agusta) in the Senior TT and Dick Creith winning a wet 500 cc Ulster grand Prix on sponsor Joe Ryan's

ABOVE The Commando 750S with high level exhaust, chromed mudguards and headlamp, polished primary chain-case, small tank and sports seat.

LEFT Bob Trigg, who styled the original Commando models, astride a Commando S in 1969, with Malcolm Homer of Norton Villiers.

ABOVE RIGHT The 1968 Dunstall uprated sports model with 750 cc Atlas engine. The previous year Rex Butcher had taken the 750 cc one hour record at 126.7 mph at Monza.

RIGHT Handsome machine – a 1970 Norton Commando Fastback to Californian specifications in front of a warehouse of Commandos at Andover.

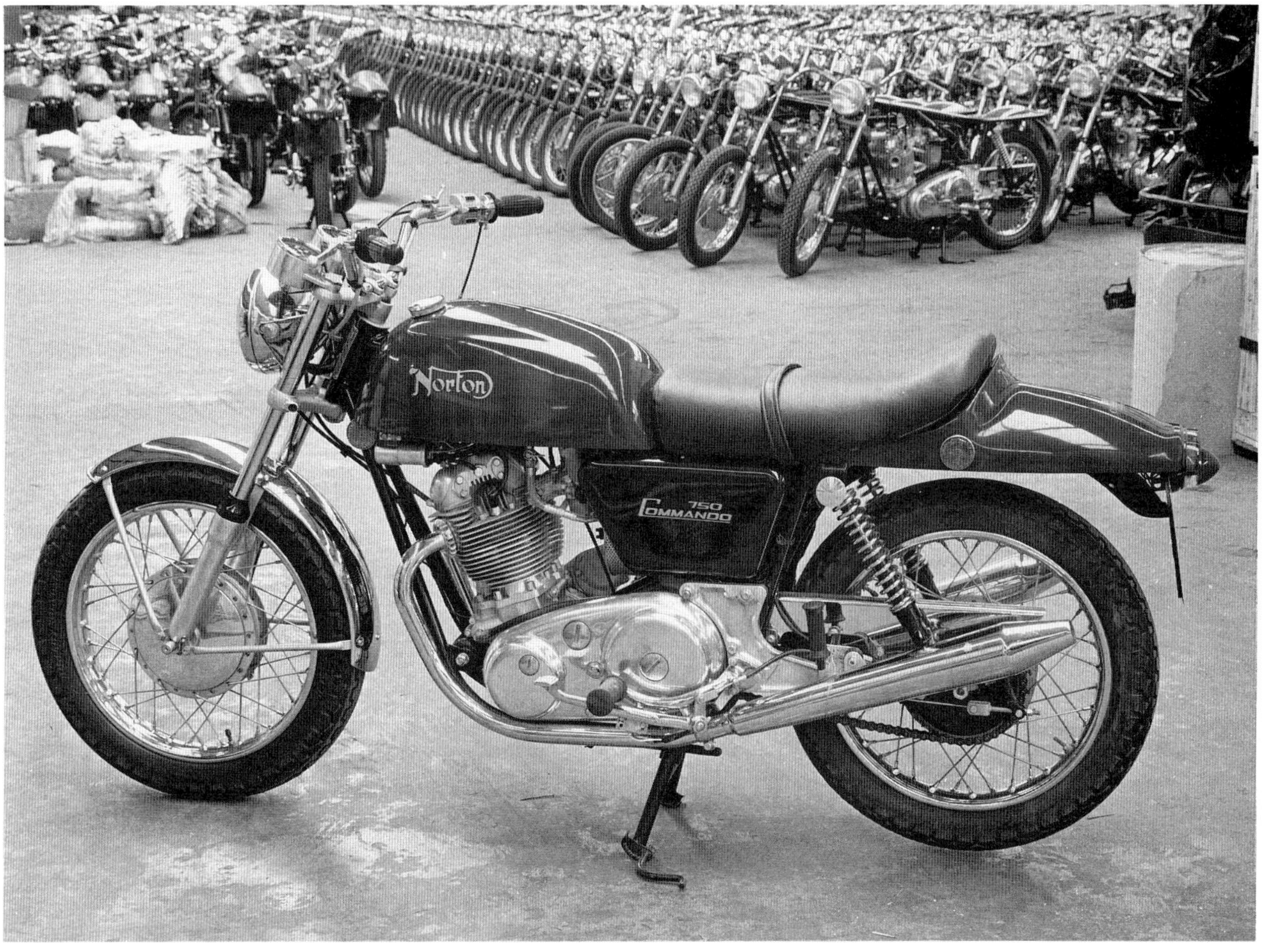

Manx, but there was more bad news for the tottering British industry when Honda unveiled the CB450 Black Bomber at the Brighton Show in September 1965 – the first direct challenge to British machines in the lucrative big bike market.

True, it was only 450 cc but it was neatly styled, fast and powerful and obviously well engineered with a double-overhead-camshaft engine which gave a top speed of over 100 mph – faster than all but the top sports British machines. The specification included an electric starter and the price was £349 – a few pounds cheaper than the 88SS.

The 350 cc Navigator was dropped for 1966 but all the other models were continued. Paul Dunstall continued to gain publicity, with Griff Jenkins scoring well on his twins and film star Steve McQueen buying a special Dunstall Dominator, a 650SS engine in a Manx frame. Star of *The Great Escape*, Steve was a genuine motorcyclist who had competed in the 1964 International Six Days Trial in Germany.

In April 1966 things came to a financial crunch. The *Sunday Times* reported that the AMC group was £2.2 million in debt. Because the Norton models were selling well in America the Berliners pumped in more money in an attempt to keep the ailing ship afloat, but in *Motor Cycling* dated 13 August 1966 came the news we had been dreading: 'Official receiver manager appointed by Barclays Bank'. The report went on to say that motorcycle production would continue while the receiver, Kenneth Cork, made a thorough survey of the problems. It was later revealed that no less than 80 per cent of the entire AMC production was going to Berliners in America – most of them Nortons. This makes it clear that AJS and Matchless output had slowed to a trickle and that AMC's share of the British market had shrunk to around 50 bikes a week.

AMC blamed 'the present national economic crisis' and Joe Berliner flew over to see if a rescue package could be worked out. Immediate economies were made by closing the retail spares counter at Woolwich and axing the Electra 400 twin. Then in September 1966 *Motor Cycling* carried the front-page headline 'AMC Saved'. The Woolwich company had been bought by Villiers which had recently been acquired by E. & H.P. Smith, part of the giant Manganese Bronze Holdings group. It was all getting too complicated for ordinary minds to understand.

Under the deal Villiers acquired the manufacturing and distribution rights of AMC, but not the factories at Greet (James and Francis-Barnett) and Woolwich (AJS, Matchless and Norton). It was reported that production of the surviving Norton models would continue at Woolwich, 'but only for the time being'.

In October 1966 Manganese Bronze formed a new company named Norton Matchless Ltd. Bill Smith, a likable Scot who had been in charge of the sales side at Woolwich, was to be sales director and the intention was to continue to produce all five makes – or that was

LEFT **This Commando was supplied to the French Garde Republicaine early in 1971. It had metallic blue finish, 4½ gallon tank and front disc brake.**

ABOVE **Catering for the American market this customised version of the Commando (the Hi-rider) went on sale in 1971.**

the story put about at the time. The Norton range was cut to just two models – the 650SS and the 750cc Atlas at £367 and £375. John Neville was then appointed MD of Nortons reporting to Dennis Poore, the chairman of Manganese Bronze.

In December yet another company was formed. This was named Norton Villiers and encompassed the Villiers Wolverhampton factory as well as the production of Norton, AJS, Matchless, James and Francis-Barnett machines. The way in which Norton was put foremost in the titles of the two new companies indicates the high esteem in which the famous old name was still held.

In July 1967 Hugh Palin left the Motor Cycle Industry Association where he was chief executive to join Norton Villiers as executive director with special responsibility for motorcycles, and the following month Norton Villiers ran a whole-page advertisement in *Motor Cycle* explaining the new set-up. Under the heading 'Norton Villiers' was a row of four circles containing the names Norton Villiers Matchless, Norton

ABOVE Peter Williams on a Commando during the 1970 Production Machine TT. He took the lead on the last lap but lost by 1.6 seconds when he ran short of petrol in the final mile.

Villiers Norton, Norton Villiers AJS and Norton Villiers Royal Enfield, followed by: 'At the Earls Court Show on September 16 Norton Villiers will be exhibiting, for the first time, their new models.' The idea, which was short-lived, was that all the models produced would have a similar tank badge, each with the company name of Norton Villiers at the top with the actual marque in larger letters across the centre.

Behind the scenes a brand-new machine the Commando, was taking shape. Dennis Poore, boss of Manganese Bronze Holdings, was a motoring enthusiast who had been a successful racing driver. He had the best interests of the motorcycle industry at heart and was determined to pump new life into it. On 1 January 1967 he appointed Dr Stefan Bauer, previously with Rolls Royce, to lead a new design team at Norton Villiers. His terms of reference were to create a new large-capacity sporting motorcycle, but as money and time were limited he would have to use the existing twin-cylinder engine.

A charming man who had been a lecturer at Eton and had worked on atomic energy projects, Dr Bauer was an 'egghead' rather than a practical engineer. Luckily he had working with him two down-to-earth motorcycle men – Bob Trigg, who was largely responsible for the styling, and Bernard Hooper, who turned the paper plans into metal. By June 1967 they had a prototype on the road and in September the Norton Commando was launched at the Earls Court Show.

To counter the inherent problem of vibration they cleverly mounted the 750 cc Atlas engine complete with AMC gearbox with final drive, swinging fork and wheel as a single, separate rubber-mounted unit. This system, patented under the name 'Isolastic', allowed the power unit to oscillate in a new single-top-tube frame – the rider insulated from the vibrations by the flexible mounting.

The question of styling had been carefully considered. The engine was inclined forward to give a 'go-faster' look and the lines of the tank, seat and rear mudguard – in fact, every part of the bike – had been styled to give the Commando a thoroughly modern look and was a tribute to the flair of Bob Trigg. The launch price at Earls Court was £397 but by the time the first models went on sale in April 1968 this had risen to £456.

Other models in the 1968 Norton range were the 650SS and 750 Atlas and two AMC hybrids also powered by the Atlas engine – the N15CS American 'Street Scrambler' and the more serious P11 in which the engine was mounted in the Matchless G85CS scrambles chassis – a very handsome machine. These were marketed with full road equipment, including lights, for £383 and £397 respectively.

Clint Eastwood was an early customer for the P11, taking delivery of the slightly improved P11A version in April 1968 while filming in the UK, but it was the Commando that was the focus of attention and in May 1968 Peter Fraser, chief road tester for *Motor Cycle*, reported: 'The Commando is a complete answer to those who accuse Britain's motorcycle manufacturers of stale conservatism. In some ways it embodies more original thought than any other post-war machine.' He continued:

Riding the Commando soon shows the result is no mere novelty but an entirely new motor-cycling experience. For engine vibration, bugbear of big parallel twins, has been completely tamed. Tamed – not eliminated. There is still some vibration in the engine. But once the bike is under way not a trace reaches the rider through handlebar, footrest or seat.

The 70 mph blanket speed limit had recently been introduced but Peter reported a top speed of 110 mph and said that the Commando would cruise at 100 mph.

At much the same time *Motor Cycle* rally reporter John Ebbrell was enthusing about the P11A Street Scrambler.

Here's a mettlesome beast, sure enough. It's a cross country machine with high ground clearance, high level exhaust and all the trimmings. This super potent trail bike is fundamentally a Norton Atlas engine grafted into the new Matchless G85CS scrambler frame; it was suggested by Bob Blair of ZDS Motors, the Norton Matchless West Coast distributors.

At this time Dunstall-prepared 750 cc Nortons were doing well. Late in 1967 Rex Butcher had taken the one-hour record for the class at 126.7 mph at Monza (it is worth noting that this compares with the 500 cc hour record of 133.6 mph set by Ray Amm on the Norton Fish at Montlhéry 14 years earlier) and in June 1968 Ray Pickrell won the 750 cc class of the Production Machine TT with a record lap at 99.39 mph. In July a Norton Atlas ridden by Ricardo Fargas and the Spanish importer who rode under the pseudonym 'Juanjo' won the Barcelona 24-hour race.

During 1968 the Atlas was phased out in favour of the Commando and at the end of the year the only model in the range with the famous featherbed frame was the Mercury, which took the place of the 650SS. Unlike its predecessors this had only a single carburettor and was described as a 'budget performance bike' selling for £399. The Commando continued at £457 while the American market P11A had been rechristened the Ranger.

By this time the decision had been made to move from Woolwich to Thruxton and it was Dennis Poore who cut the first sod on the site for the new Norton Villiers factory at Andover on 1 October 1968. While the factory was being built, production continued at Woolwich but a separate competition department was opened in a building alongside the racing circuit at Thruxton. This was called the Norton Villiers Performance Shop and work on the AJS scramblers as well as on Nortons was carried out there with Peter Inchley as head man.

One of the first to move was Peter Williams, a top road racer who earned money during the winter months by working as a design draughtsman at Woolwich. When I spoke to Peter at his Blisworth home in 1991, he remembered:

I just drifted into the job with Nortons. I went down to Thruxton early in 1969 and my first job was to prepare a Commando for that year's Production Machine TT. I was going to race it myself but I was injured in a crash and Paul Smart took over and finished second to Malcolm Uphill on the works Triumph.

Woolwich finally closed in July 1969 and the same month it was confirmed that Williams was to 'head a new road racing department'. Around this time there was a lot of press conjecture following the appointment of Alec Issigonis as the new 'technical overlord' at Norton Villiers following the departure of Dr Bauer, who had moved to BSA-Triumph. Issigonis was the brain behind the brilliant Austin/Morris Mini and his appointment naturally created a great deal of interest. Reported *Motor Cycle*: 'he is to have a completely free hand in designing new machines' and 'As design overlord, Issigonis will head a Norton Villiers team responsible for producing all the companies' new machines.' In fact nothing at all appears to have resulted from this liaison which it transpired was at best a 'consultancy' rather than a full-time job.

Things were going well at this time. In September Londoner Godfrey Nash won the 500 cc class of the Yugoslav Grand Prix riding a nine-year-old Manx, the final World Championship win by a Norton. More importantly the American market was booming and it was a confident Dennis Poore who hosted an open day at the Andover factory in October 1969. He said that output would increase substantially in 1970 and that the target for 1971 was to produce 10,000 machines.

To take advantage of the American market the Commando S had been launched during 1969. This was a sports model with high-level exhaust system, small tank, sporty seat and higher American-style handlebars. I was the first British journalist to ride the bike and the spread of power and lack of vibration impressed me – but I admitted in my report that as a Norton enthusiast I was biased.

In January 1970 a third Commando was launched – the Roadster. This was virtually identical to the S except that it had a more orthodox low-level exhaust system. To differentiate, the original Commando was by this time called the Fastback. The two new models were priced at £525 with the Fastback at £499, and the Mercury was still available, now at the cheaper price of £390.

The first news of a batch of Commandos being built for production machine racing came in February 1970. The engines had bigger valves, a sportier camshaft and increased compression ratio and were claimed to produce 68 bhp. For the first time a disc brake was fitted (front wheel only), rims were light alloy and a nose fairing was standard. The new Commando looked impressive with a striking yellow finish but the price was a hefty £795, over £100 more than the four-cylinder Honda CB750 roadster which had just been released on the British market.

In March 1970 Bob Trigg and Bernard Hooper were the joint winners of the Castrol Design Award for their work on the Commando, and especially on the Isolastic system, receiving the award at a ceremony at the RAC in Pall Mall – but only after a Commando finished in yellow had been replaced by one of a different hue. The original had been far too close to the colour of the rival AA for the comfort of the RAC!

The first real fruits of the new racing operation came in May 1970 when Williams teamed with Charlie Sanby to win the *Motor Cycle* 500 Mile Race at Thruxton – breaking a five-year domination by Triumph. And Williams came astonishingly close to winning the Production Machine TT:

I made a terrible start and spent the whole race catching Malcolm Uphill who was riding a factory three-cylinder Triumph. I finally caught him on the last lap and passed him at Creg-ny-Baa just three miles from the finish. Then at Hillberry the Norton coughed. I'd run short of petrol and Uphill passed me to win by 1.6 seconds!

It was at this time that Mike Jackson, who made his name at Greeves before joining AJS at Thruxton, switched to Nortons. He was appointed general manager of the Norton Villiers Corporation that had been set up in California to market Norton and AJS machines in the Western States – leaving Berliner to concentrate on the East. Mike, who now runs the autonomous Norton Andover company, remembers:

There had been a trail of disaster with NVC in California and Poore sent me out to try and sort things out. We controlled seven States to start with but in 1971 took over all the States west of the Mississippi, 24 in all. I had the wonderful task of going round all the Norton dealers in this territory – I was on the road for six or seven weeks.

During the two years he was in America, Jackson reckons that more than half of the Norton production was sold there: 'I would say that in 1971 when about 12,000 Commandos were produced, 7000 went to North America, 3000 to Europe with the remaining 2000 going to the UK market.' He remembers Poore with affection: 'I always got on well with him. He was an excellent businessman, a terrific negotiator and had a great sense of humour. He was a high flyer, a financial man who

understood situations but unfortunately not people – he was not good at communicating with the workers.'

The range for 1971 was expanded to five Commandos – the Fastback, S and Roadster were joined by the Hi-Rider and the Fastback LR. The Hi-Rider was a monstrosity with enormously high 'ape-hanger' handlebars and a curious seat which swept up steeply at the back and was sold only in America. The Fastback LR was the original model fitted with a big $5\frac{1}{2}$-gallon tank for long-range cruising – hence the LR. The price for all except the Hi-Rider was £595.

In April 1971 yet another company was formed – Norton Villiers Europe Ltd – to market Commandos in Europe. The same month Peter Williams took the racing a stage further when he turned out at Crystal Palace not on a Commando but on a prototype out-and-out racer: 'The idea was to find out if a Norton-powered machine could compete successfully in the Open class.' He went home happy after twice finishing a very close second and sharing the fastest lap of the day at 80.97 mph with Charlie Sanby (Gus Kuhn Norton).

At the TT that year Nortons did reasonably well with Williams finishing third in the new Formula 750 race and setting a lap record of 101.06 mph in the 750 cc Production Machine race, leading until ignition trouble put him out on the third lap.

ABOVE LEFT **Peter Williams produced his first racing Norton early in 1971. Here (standing) he discusses the machine with manufacturer Colin Seeley.**

ABOVE **Phil Read and Peter Williams, team-mates in the new John Player Norton squad, in action at Brands Hatch, March 1972.**

But it was not all fun and games in 1971. The BSA-Triumph group was in serious financial trouble. A number of projects (the Beagle, Dandy and Pixie lightweights and the Tina and Tigress scooters to name five) had all gone seriously awry and 850 of the 7000 work force were made redundant in July when a trading loss of £3 million was announced.

Nortons, on the other hand, were doing well. Poore's decision to market a single new large-capacity machine with a number of derivatives (all in the new 'superbike' bracket) was paying off – and two further steps were taken in December 1971 when the Interstate was launched and a tie-up with John Player announced. The Interstate was described by *Motor Cycle* as 'a long distance strider with the speed of a sprinter'. In 'optional extra' form it was powered by a new high-performance Combat engine with high-compression pistons and a claimed output of 65 bhp – 5 more than the previous best standard 750 cc unit. It also had a Lockheed disc front brake and the price was £734 in sports form or £694 in standard guise.

In fact the Combat engine proved a disaster. Poore had insisted on a higher performance engine despite the warnings of the technical men who said that the 10 to 1 compression ratio was simply too much for the current engine. 'Poore wanted a more powerful engine as part of the speed package together with the disc brake. But it proved a mistake,' remembers Mike Jackson.

The John Player Norton team was launched at a reception in London early in 1972. The riders were to be Peter Williams, Phil Read (then the reigning 250 cc World Champion) and Tony Rutter, a surprise selection who had no big-bike experience and who was soon dropped in favour of John Cooper. Former Suzuki works rider Frank Perris was signed to manage the team and at the time it was speculated that John Player's financial backing was £20,000. Looking back, Peter Williams thinks it was more like £30,000 – enough to get the team off to a good start.

John Player were not interested in production machine racing. The plan was to contest the 750 cc races at Daytona and Imola and other important big-bike events. The bikes were finished in light blue and white and at the first race, the Daytona 200 in March,

ABOVE Dave Croxford on a works Norton Commando during the Thruxton 500-mile race, 1972. Teaming with Mick Grant he won the race.

LEFT Dave Aldana in action at Ascot Park, California 1972. Aldana won the Ascot Championship that year on his Norton-powered dirt-tracker.

ABOVE RIGHT Norton dirt-trackers: three Ron Wood Nortons at Ascot Park in 1978.

they performed well. Despite being undergeared, Read clocked 152.54 mph through the speed trap and actually led the race for four laps at the midway stage before slowing slightly to finish fourth, the first four-stroke home.

Back in Europe Read was also fourth in the Imola 200 and Peter Williams took second place in the production machine TT despite gearbox trouble. He was beaten only by Ray Pickrell on a three-cylinder Triumph Trident and at 141.7 mph the Norton was 1.6 mph faster through the speed trap than the Triumph. For the more important Formula 750 TT Nortons fielded three bikes in the blue and white John Player livery – Williams, Read and Cooper. But all fell by the wayside. Williams, who clocked 148.8 mph through the trap, was going well until his gearbox failed; Read was eliminated by a binding rear brake; and Cooper was sidelined when the gear pedal fell off.

In the lesser races that followed, Williams was plagued by gearbox trouble.

The basic problem was that the main shaft used to bend. It was all right when we used a single-chain primary drive but the Commando had a wide triplex chain and this extra width put a bending force on the shaft. We knew what the problem was but we were stuck with what we had for that season. Phil Read was easier than I was on gearboxes – that was a great plus in his favour, he was easy on machinery.

Out in the States things were still going well and in the all-important Californian market the Norton name achieved regular and valuable publicity at Ascot where half-mile dirt-track and TT events were held on a weekly basis. In 1970 Jody Nicholas had been top dog on a Norton tuned by Harold Alison, and the performance of the British engine so impressed the legendary tuner C.R. Axtell (known to aficionados as 'CR') that he switched from Harley-Davidson to Norton in June that year. Nicholas won the Ascot championship again in 1971 but in 1972 was ousted by another Norton rider – Dave Aldana – and the little Mexican-American continued to dominate in 1973. At home Nortons finished first and second in the 1972 Thruxton 500 Mile Race for production bikes and then Read won the Race of the South at Brands Hatch. Peter Williams remembers:

That was a good day for us. I won the supporting race with Read well behind. I think he was surprised that I'd beaten Paul Smart on the three-cylinder Kawasaki because he certainly tried a lot harder in the main event and won from Paul with me in third place. That was right at the end of the season – a good time to prove to our sponsors that we were competitive.

ABOVE **Phil Read on a John Player Norton at Daytona in 1972. Read clocked 152.4 mph through the speed-trap and finished fourth.**

The promise of financial success had been fulfilled. When the accounts for the financial year were published in the autumn of 1972 they showed that turnover had increased by 58 per cent to £5,566,000 with home sales up from £290,000 to £1,578,000 and exports to the USA rising from £2,343,000 to £3,181,000. All very encouraging and a great credit to Dennis Poore who had mapped out the Norton road to recovery.

In December 1972 John Player confirmed their continued support for 1973 but with a change of colours. Out went the blue and white, replaced by black and red with gold lining on a white background – the colours of Player's No 10, the brand the tobacco giant wanted to push. And it was agreed that the Player's backing would extend to production machine events. On the rider front, Read had left to join Giacomo Agostini in the MV Agusta team and John Cooper had been signed to join Peter Williams on completely revamped F750 racers.

The engines were little changed but the frame, designd by Peter Williams, was unusual. *Motor Cycle* reported that the 1973 Norton racer 'features an unusual double-skin monocoque frame and is lighter, lower and better streamlined than last year's version'. Fabricated from stainless steel it was lower and better streamlined, but it was certainly not lighter.

The first machine was ready for Daytona in March 1973 and Williams rode it but suffered constant carburation and fuel problems. Cooper and Aldana raced the old models but were out-paced by the new wave of Japanese two-strokes. That same month Nortons launched the 850 Interstate – the first bike over 750 cc to be marketed under the Norton trademark. In fact the bigger engine was simply a modified version of the 750 with the bore increased from 73 to 77 mm to give dimensions of 77 × 89 mm and an exact capacity of 829 cc. This meant that Hopwood's original design had grown from 497 cc first to 597 cc then 646 cc and up to 745 cc before eventually being enlarged to 829 cc some 25 years after it first appeared.

With a modest 8.5 to 1 compression ratio the new engine produced 60 bhp at 6200 rpm and had a road-test top speed of 121 mph with, according to *Motor Cycle*, 'a cruising potential of 90 mph'. The launch price was £647, only £18 more than the similarly disc-braked Fastback and Roadster models. Completing the six-model range were drum-braked Fastback, Hi-Rider and Roadster at £599.

At the end of March came a shock announcement. Under the headling 'Triumph–Norton Merger'. *Motor Cycle* reported: 'A Government backed merger between the BSA-Triumph group and Norton Villiers received qualified approval at the weekend after crisis talks between the Department of Trade and Industry and Manganese Bronze Holdings, the parent company of Norton Villiers.' From a government standpoint it was a logical move. Dennis Poore with MBH backing had saved Nortons – surely he could do the same for the now bankrupt BSA-Triumph group?

Probably flattered by the government's faith in his ability, Poore took up the challenge and a new company, Norton Villiers Triumph, was set up in 1973 to run the new conglomerate with Manganese Bronze and the government both contributing £4.8 million. Poore's plan was to close Meriden and concentrate manufacturing at the old BSA factory at Small Heath, at Wolverhampton and at Andover. But it all went terribly wrong when the workers at Meriden occupied the factory and began a war of attrition that eventually led to the demise of Norton Villiers.

Mike Jackson, by this time back at Andover as European sales manager, comments:

On paper it was a good deal but when the gates clanged shut at Meriden it meant that Small Heath was left with nothing

ABOVE **John Cooper was in the 1973 Norton team at Daytona, but the four-stroke British twins were outpaced by the new wave of Japanese two-strokes.**

to do because a lot of the parts used to assemble machines in Birmingham came from Meriden. Poore had miscalculated the reaction of the Meriden work force and when he tried to push things through he was blocked by the government.

It was an astonishing situation in which the Meriden workers, who at the time could quite easily have got jobs elsewhere, played on public sympathy and held the motorcycle industry to ransom. A change of government, from Conservative to Labour, did not help – especially when left-wingers Tony Benn and Eric Heffer were put in charge. The whole set-up had become a nightmare – and Norton suffered.

To make matters worse, Nortons had their own problems. Following complaints about quality, a series of meetings was held and it was decided that instead of the engines and gearboxes being sent from Wolverhampton for final assembly at Andover, as from May 1973 the Commandos would be built at Wolverhampton. They would then be sent down to Andover for road testing and despatch. This decision led to redundancies at Andover, a strike and a sit-in, but unlike Meriden the situation was quickly cleared up and the new plan put into operation.

Williams' new frame was proving a success. Recovering from the disappointment of Daytona he was top scorer in the Easter Anglo-American series, winning three of the six races held at three circuits. The Norton team leader then won at Cadwell beating Barry Sheene (Suzuki) and Ray Pickrell (Triumph), but his greatest triumph came in the Isle of Man where, after retiring from the Production Machine Race when leading, he won the F750 event at a record 105.4 mph and with a record lap of 107.2 mph. This was the second-fastest race in the history of the TT, exceeded only by Mike Hailwood who had averaged 105.62 mph on a Honda while winning that epic battle with Agostini (MV Agusta) in 1967.

The figures for the financial year that ended in mid 1973 made sombre reading. The cost of producing the new 850 engine, allied to money lost by the strike at Andover, had turned the healthy profit of the preceding year into a shortfall of £275,000. And the outlook was not good. The collapse of BSA-Triumph had dumped several thousand of their 'superbikes' on the market at rock-bottom prices just at a time when the Japanese were moving into the big-bike market – Suzuki, Kawasaki and Yamaha all following the Honda lead.

The racing team continued to do well. Mick Grant had replaced Cooper and in September he won at Scarborough and set a new lap record of 73.64 mph. Phil Read, who had just won the 500 cc World Championship, brought his MV Agusta over to win the Race of the Year but Williams was a good second, and a works Commando in the hands of Rex Butcher and Norman White won the 500-miler at Thruxton. In America Tom Christenson was grabbing the drag headlines on his double-engined Norton-powered Hogslayer – so named because he had built it to beat the Harley-Davidson's. He succeeded brilliantly, winning the AMA Supernationals in November 1973 with a standing-start quarter-mile time of 8.45 seconds and a terminal speed of 167 mph (earlier in the year in more favourable conditions 'TC' had crossed the line at 180.13 mph).

In Britain the winter of 1973–74 was grim. The miners, railwaymen and power-station workers were on strike and the price of petrol rocketed when the Gulf states announced a price increase of 70 per cent as a protest against the US support of Israel in the Yom Kippur war. It was the 'Winter of Discontent' during which Prime Minister Edward Heath imposed the three-day working week in order to conserve energy – and when he went to the country in March 1974 the voters refused to back him and elected a Labour government headed by Harold Wilson. Hardly a good climate in which to sell luxury high-performance motorcycles!

John Player renewed their sponsorship for a third year. The team dropped production machine racing to concentrate on F750 – and, suprisingly in view of the successes achieved in 1973, the monocoque frame was dropped too. It was replaced by a curious-looking multi-tube frame which inspired the *Motor Cycle* reporter to comment: 'You never saw so many tubes in a frame.' Peter Williams was furious:

> I was very disappointed. Looking back I can only put the change town to jealousy. I was getting too much credit for the Norton success because I both designed and rode the bikes. The team resented this and a committee decision was made to replace the monocoque with the multi-tube. It had all got very political.

RIGHT **The Race of the Year at Mallory Park was the climax of the British season. Here, in the 1973 race, Percy Tait (Triumph) leads Peter Williams (Norton).**

One excuse put forward for abandoning the monocoque was that it made it hard to work on the engine without taking it out of the frame. Williams refutes this: 'In many ways it was more accessible. It's true it was heavy but we could have reduced this for 1974. As it was we were stuck with an inferior frame designed by a committee who were good mechanics but not frame designers.'

Matters were complicated by the team using a short-stroke engine. Williams, partnered by Dave Croxford, started the season with the old long-stroke motors but results were disappointing. Williams finished tenth at Daytona, the first four-stroke, but in the Anglo-American series in which he had stop-scored the preceding year he managed only 49 points, well behind Sheene (Suzuki), Stan Woods (Suzuki) and Barry Ditchburn (Kawasaki). The short-stroke engine, which had been 'rumoured' for a long time, finally appeared at the TT. Externally it looked little different but the bore and stroke were 77 × 80.4 mm, 749 cc – still in fact a long-stroke but offering more tuning scope than the 73 × 89 mm it replaced. Like the frame, it proved a disappointment. Said Williams:

> It only produced 78 bhp at 7200 – about the same as the old engine! The trouble was that we had to use the old crank-case and that was like a paper bag. It was just too weak. We tried to overcome this by making a one-piece crankshaft which would have been stiffer and placed less stress on the crank-case than the built-up cranks. As it turned out the short-stroke was a waste of time.

Despite the problems Williams led the F750 TT – but only as far as Ballaugh on the first lap when the engine seized. Croxford's mount expired on the second lap. The short-stroke engine undoubtedly suffered because it was intended only as an interim unit while Cosworth designed and developed a completely new high-tech twin which would be used both for racing and in a completely new sports model.

This project had begun as long ago as the autumn of 1971, at the same time as the original John Player sponsorship was agreed. At first most of the work was done at the Norton Villiers factory in Wolverhampton and various layouts were discussed – including a three-cylinder based on BRM technology and a twin, basically two cylinders of the race-winning Cosworth Formula One DFV unit. Peter Williams was very much against the idea of a triple.

I wanted a twin. I was convinced, and still am, that a twin is quite capable of producing enough power to make you go as fast as you want to on a racing bike – and facts are bearing me out. Look at the performance of the Ducatis in the 1990 World Superbike Championships, won by Raymond Roche competing against works four-cylinder machines from the Japanese factories. Tony Denniss then started work on the layout for a twin and went to Duckworth to do the cylinder head – and they eventually took the whole project over.

The Cosworth engine, which did not appear in public until 1975, was a complete and utter failure. How did Cosworth, who had succeeded so brilliantly with the DFV and with many subsequent car engines, fail so miserably? Ironically Peter Williams now works for the Northampton firm, and has done for eight years:

You could say that every company has a skeleton in the cupboard and the Challenge engine, as it was dubbed, is Cosworths! I partly blame Dr Bauer. He had rejoined Norton Villiers and had a bee in his bonnet about having a symmetrical engine – it had to look the same from either side. I know this sounds crazy but it is true. He also insisted on a tremendous safety factor. The outcome was design by committee and an enormously heavy engine with a massive balance shaft and huge gearbox.

Bore and stroke were 85.7 x 64.8 mm, 748 cc and the design output was 115-120 bhp at 10,500 rpm.

Peter Williams actually tried a prototype chassis with monoshock rear suspension at the John Player meeting at Silverstone in August 1974. This had been built for

The Dennis Manning twin-engined Norton record machine on the Utah salt flats in 1974. The engines, running on an alcohol mix, had been prepared by drag-race champion Tom Christenson. Piloted by Boris Murray, it hit 271 mph but was unable to beat the record.

ABOVE **Through Parliament Square in the 1973 Formula 750 TT – probably Peter Williams' finest race on a 750 cc John Player Norton. He won at a record 105.4 mph with a record lap at 107.2 mph.**

LEFT **Another shot of Peter Williams – this time flat out at Daytona in 1974.**

TOP RIGHT **Dave Croxford testing the ill-fated Cosworth-powered Norton Challenge at Brands Hatch at the end of 1975.**

the Cosworth Challenge but because this was not ready it was fitted with a Norton engine. In the big race both Williams and Croxford retired. Then later in August came the crash at Oulton Park which put him out of racing for good.

There was plenty of other Norton activity around this time. The 750 cc engine had been a favourite with sidecar moto-cross crews for several years and in September the Swiss Robert Grogg regained the European Championship which he had first won two years earlier – and Norton Wasp outfits took the first three places in the British round of the contest. Over in the States Dennis Manning had built a world motorcycle speed-record machine and in October took it to Bonneville for a crack at the 265.492 mph record set by Cal Rayborn in a Harley-Davidson-powered 'flying cigar' – which, incidentally, had also been built by Manning.

The two Norton engines had been prepared by Tom Christenson and the pilot, who sat ahead of the engines in the fully streamlined machine, was former drag star Boris Murray. As sports editor of *Motor Cycle* I flew to Salt Lake City to see the fun. Unfortunately the Norton attempt ran into all sorts of problems and although it eventually did one run at 271 mph it never did the two 'back to back' runs necessary to claim a record. In any case, by that time Don Vesco, using Yamaha power, had upped the record to 281.7 mph, his San Diego-based crew sharing Bonneville with Manning's Norton team.

The whole Norton set-up was in decline. John Player terminated the sponsorship agreement at the end of 1974 and in December Norton Villiers Triumph announced that despite increasing the turnover figure to £24,484,000 the group had suffered a loss of £3,670,000 for the financial year. This was almost entirely due to the continuing Meriden sit-in and it was history repeating itself – for just as the losses of AMC in the early 1960s had dragged down the profitable Norton side of business, so the actions of the Triumph workers were destroying the resurrected Norton company a decade later. Explains Mike Jackson:

The Meriden situation destroyed Norton. The time, energy and money that were spent trying to solve the problems created by the workers occupying the Triumph factory simply bled the new Norton Villiers Triumph company white. One example is that they refused to release patterns so that the three-cylinder Trident engines could be made at Small Heath. These had to be duplicated at a cost of £500,000 –

AJS STORMER
Norton
DUCATI
Norton
850
COMMANDO
Sensational New
NORTON 850 ROADSTER

LEFT **The massive Cosworth designed Challenge 750 cc twin cylinder engine of 1975 which Nortons never got to run properly.**

BELOW LEFT **The 850 Interstate Commando was launched in March 1973 with the Norton twin enlarged to 829 cc. The Roadster, shown here, followed later that year.**

RIGHT **Michael Heseltine (left) with Dennis Poore at a confidence-boosting Norton press conference in London in July 1975.**

BELOW **The 850 Commando Interpol police specification machine of 1975 that Neale Shilton sold to police forces around the world.**

and while they were being duplicated six months' production was lost.

Jackson is also bitter that the 'workers', said to have the best interests of the industry at heart, left several hundred virtually complete Triumph machines out in the open to deteriorate: 'They were so keen on motorcycles that they couldn't summon up the energy to push them inside the building.'

On the roadster side the first big-twin Norton with an electric starter was launched in April 1975. This was the Commando Mark 111 Electric Start. The price was £1161 and the starter was an American Prestolite. At the same time the gear pedal was moved from the traditional British right to the left side of the machine – as favoured by the continentals and the Japanese – and the drum rear brake was replaced by a disc. Other machines catalogued at this time include the simpler Mark 11A version, the Interstate, Roadster, Hi-Rider and the John Player Replica – a titivated sports bike with a flashy fairing rather than a serious racing machine. And a New Thruxton Club Racer was available to special order. With 74 bhp short-stroke engine and Quaife five-speed, this was priced at £1500 – more than the proven 250 cc Yamaha which had a similar performance.

Despite the withdrawal of Player sponsorship, Poore decided to press on with the Cosworth project. At first it was hoped to field a machine with the new engine at Daytona in March 1975; then at the TT in June. When it became obvious it would still not be ready, two 850 cc bikes were prepared and started in the new 'Classic TT'. Australian Jack Findlay got only a few miles before the ignition failed and team-mate Croxford also went out on the first lap with an oil leak.

The Cosworth engine made a first public appearance as a prop at a London press reception in late July 1975. This was a morale-boosting publicity exercise to show

the British press that Norton Villiers Triumph were alive and kicking. Michael Heseltine, then the Shadow Minister for Industry, was on hand to see not only the Cosworth Challenge 750 cc racing engine but also two new lightweights the group intended to produce – a 125 cc trail bike with Taiwan-built engine and a neat 50 cc moped (the Easyrider) designed by Bob Trigg and powered by an Italian Morini unit. Also at the reception was a prototype machine powered by a twin-rotor Wankel engine.

Even to Norton enthusiasts the Cosworth was becoming a joke. It finally appeared at the Race of the South meeting at Brands Hatch in October 1975. Croxford was the rider and ironically he was involved in a nine-rider pile-up just yards after the start of the main event. Truth to tell, the Challenge had not been impressive during practice. With Croxford injured Alex George took over the Challenge and rode it at Brands on the Sunday, the second day of the weekend

ABOVE The unsuccessful 750 cc Norton Thruxton Club racer claimed a power output of 74 bhp but the price was £1,500 – more than the 250 cc Yamaha two-stroke with similar performance.

LEFT American drag-racer Tom Christenson in action on his double-engined Hogslayer – claimed at the time to be the most successful drag bike ever.

meeting, but retired when the cooling system boiled over.

Incredibly the Labour government, following the advice of Minister of Trade Tony Benn, had decided to back the Meriden workers' cooperative, which had not made a motorcycle for some two years, and completely to undermine Norton Villiers Triumph by withdrawing vital export guarantee facilities. This in turn led to a lack of confidence by the banks, who started to call in loans made to the company.

This in effect bankrupted Norton Villiers Triumph. Mike Jackson outlines what happened:

> The government had appointed a London company, the Boston Consultancy, to look into the future of the motorcycle industry world-wide. They spent a lot of tax-payers' money flying all over the place and came up with the conclusion that there was no room for a high-priced, high-quality, traditionally built motorcycle – which completely ignored the place of Ducati, Guzzi and BMW in the market. We suspect that they had been primed by the government to rubbish the future of the industry – we called them the 'Boston Stranglers' for obvious reasons.

In a desperate effort to remain solvent, the company unloaded all complete machines at rock-bottom prices. Poore sent Mike Jackson to America with instructions to sell their stock of 1000 Triumph Tridents within a week at the best price he could get for them. 'I remember that if a dealer bought 25 we cut the price to half what he would normally have paid. We were in a distressed state; Benn had pulled the rug out from under our feet,' said Jackson.

Production of Tridents at Small Heath ended in September 1975 and the workers were laid off – bitter that they had lost their jobs at a time when the government were putting money back into Meriden. And in November, when Norton Villier Triumph's debts had risen to over £5 million, the company went into liquidation and an official receiver was appointed. At that time there were enough Commando components at the Wolverhampton factory to build 1500 machines. Poore stepped in with an offer to buy, from the liquidator, all these for an agreed price. This would allow the factory to be 'wound down' in an orderly manner and would keep dealers supplied with machines for the time being.

The liquidator accepted the offer and Poore set up a new company at Lynn Lane in Shenstone to handle the distribution of these Commandos. The original Andover factory was closed but soon reopened to handle Commando spares, both for existing machines and for those being built at Wolverhampton under the direction of the receiver. 'The dealers were naturally wary about buying the new Commandos unless they were assured of spares. This was why Andover Norton was was set up by Poore in the old Andover buildings. There were an enormous amount of spares transferred from Wolverhampton and initially they completely filled the old Norton complex,' remembers Mike Jackson.

Just before the financial collapse four Nortons were shown at Earls Court in September 1975 – the 850 Mark 111 Roadster, the Interstate, the Thruxton Club Racer and the Interpol, the police model which Neale Shilton had successfully sold around the world. After the collapse only the Mark 111 Roadster and the Interstate were built, both powered by the same 850 engine – the original 750 cc unit having been phased out in favour of the bigger engine by 1974, except to special order.

Incredibly the Cosworth project was continued, operating from the separate Norton Villiers Performance Shop premises at the Thruxton circuit. *Motor Cycle* editor Peter Kelly rode the machine on a bitterly cold and wet day at Silverstone in December 1975 and for a while there was talk of both Phil Read and Spaniard Victor Palomo racing the machine in 1976 – Palomo with cash backing from the Spanish motorcycle federation. A 'fighting fund' was set up and enthusiasts had contributed £4000 by April 1976 when Croxford took the bike to Italy for the Imola 200 and retired with gearbox trouble after setting the sixty-ninth fastest qualifying lap.

Man in charge Frank Perris had tried to drum up dealer support by staging a demonstration day at Mallory Park and offering Cosworth-Norton Challenge racers for sale at £5000 apiece. At the time you could buy the excellent Yamaha TZ750 four-cylinder two-stroke racer for far less and dealers were not impressed. Even so, several donated £800 a-piece to the 'fighting fund'. The final humiliation was when Croxford was forced out of the first leg of the 1976 Anglo-American series with gearbox trouble. He went home in disgust and his place in the team was taken by a youngster named Ron Haslam (Yamaha), the same man signed by the John Player team to race the rotary Norton in 1991. Perris struggled on at Thruxton, reduced to modifying sidecars to fit to the cheap Russian 600 cc flat-twin machines that were being imported at that time. He eventually quit in January 1977.

CHAPTER 20

Rotary 1977–present day

The last Norton Commandos were produced in 1977, and the next motorcycle with the famous old trademark on the tank to be offered to the public was the rotary-engined Classic in 1987. The fact that the company, reconstituted as Norton Motors (1978) Ltd, survived at all through those years is remarkable. Initially the marketing of the 'liquidated' Commandos and the sales of the Easyrider moped brought in the cash. Later the company made money by distributing the Triumph twins which were by that time being made at Meriden by the government-backed workers' cooperative. When Meriden folded Dennis Poore did everything in his power to keep Nortons going, confident that the rotary engine being patiently developed at Shenstone would be a commercial winner with a wide variety of applications – motorcycles, light aircraft, boats, pumps and as charging units for a new wave of electrically powered cars.

Incredibly the history of the Norton rotary goes back to 1969. David Garside, Norton's director of engineering who had been working on the project for 22 years when interviewed in 1991 explains: 'BSA advertised for staff to develop a new type of engine. Because I had worked on a rotary engine project at Rolls-Royce I applied and got the job.' Initially this was at the BSA Group Research Centre at Kitts Green. A couple of years later the project moved to the BSA-Triumph motorcycle reseach centre at Umberslade Hall. Said Garside:

> It seems incredible now but there were about 240 people at Umberslade Hall in the early 1970s all working on the design and development of new motorcycles for BSA-Triumph. But within six months of me moving to Umberslade BSA-Triumph were in financial difficulties. By the end of 1972 there were only nine of the 240 left – and the one project that survived was the rotary engine.

The history of the engine itself goes back to the 1930s when Dr Felix Wankel, a German engineer from Lindau near the Austrian and Swiss borders, schemed out an engine with a rotating piston rather than a reciprocating one. His work on the project stopped during the war when he was employed by the German Airforce to develop rotary valves for reciprocating engines – a form of valve gear that during the 1930s appeared to offer a great deal but never lived up to its promise.

After the war Dr Wankel resumed work on the rotary and joined the NSU company – the same firm that had employed Walter Moore of CS1 fame from 1929 until 1939. At first NSU, like the Luftwaffe, were more interested in rotary valves but eventually Dr Wankel persuaded them that the rotary piston had far more potential and in 1960 I remember being flown to Germany at NSU's expense for the press launch of the Wankel engine – mounted at that time in a 'bubble' car. I was impressed by the compact little single-cylinder unit and the smooth power it developed, but a lot of problems remained to be solved.

The object of the press launch was to gain publicity and generate interest which would lead to NSU selling the manufacturing rights around the world. BSA-Triumph took an option and in August 1972, after three years of promising development work by the team headed by Garside, the British group signed an agree-

RIGHT **An air-cooled twin rotor prototype Norton engine.**

ment with NSU-Audi to manufacture and sell motorcycles powered by Wankel rotary engines world-wide.

Others working on Wankel projects included Suzuki, Yamaha and DKW/Hercules. In November 1973 Suzuki launched their first rotary, the RX5 water-cooled single with a nominal capacity of 500 cc, at the Tokyo Show. Yamaha followed with a prototype. Neither was sold in the UK but in 1974 two Wankel-engined machines were marketed in Britain – the lightweight DKW W2000 (sold as a Hercules on the Continent) with fan-cooled single-rotor engine, and the super-sports Suzuki RE5 with water-cooled twin-rotor engine. Both were expensive and fast, but also extremely thirsty with the Suzuki guzzling fuel at around 22 mpg when ridden hard.

By this time BSA-Triumph had been taken over by Poore's Norton Villiers group. Umberslade Hall had been closed and Garside and his team moved back to Kitts Green. Said Garside:

> From 1969 to 1976 I only had from two to four people working on the project full time but I was convinced of the potential of the engine and when Poore took over in 1973 I wrote a technical report and gave it to him. I suggested that we should drop everything else to concentrate on the rotary. In my opinion it was useless to try to compete with the Japanese with a reciprocating engine – better to do something different and to try and leapfrog them.

Poore agreed and in 1974, in a bid to boost public confidence, a prototype machine with air-cooled twin rotor engine was shown to the press and was road tested by John Nutting of *Motor Cycle*. Under the heading 'Dynamite was never so silky' he enthused over the smooth, vibrationless power of the machine and wrote of a 'breakthrough in motorcycle design'.

A review by technical editor Vic Willoughby supported by a cutaway drawing by Lawrie Watts followed, and in November 1974 *Motor Cycle* reported: 'Green light for Wankel . . . it's all systems go for Norton's Wankel-engined bike.' Little did we realise that the plan would take 13 years to come to fruition!

RIGHT **Nortons returned to the Isle of Man in 1988 – here Trevor Nation accelerates away from the Gooseneck on his Duckhams sponsored air-cooled rotary.**

BELOW RIGHT **One of the very last Commandos to leave the Andover Norton works was this 850 Electric Start model, bought by Norton-tuner Ray Petty (left) for an anonymous collector.**

BELOW **American ace Kenny Roberts on one of the last 850 Commandos at a Goodyear function at the RAC in London in 1979.**

The sad fact is that Poore's Norton Villiers Triumph empire was crumbling. Said Garside:

> By 1975 the staff at Kitts Green had been cut to three – the caretaker, the company secretary and myself. I remember running engines on the test-bed so I must have been able to get money to buy petrol. I got a lot of work done then – there was no one to interrupt me and no time was wasted.

The following year Garside moved to Poore's new Norton premises at Shenstone to continue work on the rotary engine.

By this time the Japanese and the Germans had lost interest in Dr Wankel's brainchild as far as motorcycles were concerned. During the early 1970s oil was cheap and fuel consumption of secondary importance. But all that changed in 1973 when OPEC formed their cartel and forced up the price by 70 per cent – suddenly miles per gallon was important and the early engines developed by the Germans and the Japanese were far thirstier than reciprocating units of similar power.

As managing directors came and went Garside soldiered on and in 1978 design work on a production machine started. Garside remembers:

> Money was short and I remember that Poore sold land behind the factory to keep us going. He was very keen on the project and would visit us for a day once a week. He had done engineering at university but had never worked as an engineer. He was always coming up with fantastic ideas. It was good to have someone so enthusiastic but the problem was he expected us to do more than we possibly could.

ABOVE **The machine for the job: the Norton Commando Paramedic and the considerable amount of kit it was designed to carry.**

This new prototype retained the air-cooled twin-rotor engine and during the four-year span from 1979 to 1982 road and durability testing was carried on side by side with development. Freelance riders, mainly police motorcyclists earning a bit of pocket money in their spare time, put mileage on the bikes at the rate of 600 miles a day. 'We used to operate a two-shift system and riders would get paid at the rate of 10p a mile – so they would knock up £30 a shift which was good money in those days,' remembers Garside. That way a prototype would cover 30,000 miles in less than 10 weeks and the experienced police riders would 'feed back' information to supplement that gathered by Nortons' own testers.

That police contact led to the West Midlands force acquiring a Norton rotary in 1983, at first on loan. Explained Garside: 'It was not with the intention that it would be a police bike – more a way of getting a lot of miles on a machine that was being used under arduous conditions.' But the loan led to an order from the police and the first Norton rotaries were sold to the West Midlands force in 1983.

By that time another famous name, Doug Hele, had rejoined Nortons for the third time. Signed by Joe Craig in 1947, he had left to join BSA in 1949, returning with Hopwood in the mid 1950s only to leave again in 1962 when Nortons left Bracebridge Street. He then joined Triumphs and was largely responsible for the outstanding racing successes of the 750 cc three-cylinder Triumph and BSA racers of the 1970–72 period. After that Hele left the motorcycle industry for a spell, working on outboard boat engines. His brief at Nortons was to look after the motorcycle side while Garside concentrated on engine development for both motorcycles and light aircraft.

In 1983 Garside had made a prototype water-cooled engine for possible aircraft use but company policy at that time was to stick to air-cooling for the bikes. Said Garside:

> We had sold a licence to an American company to look into the use of the rotary for light aircraft, and that brought in quite a lot of much-needed cash – about $250,000. We also had a contract to convert our engine to liquid cooling and were making quite a lot of money selling one-off prototypes.

But just as the rocketing price of oil had torpedoed the early Wankel-engined machines, so the wave of public liability litigation in the USA at this time killed off the light aircraft industry – even such a famous firm as Cessna cutting right back.

All projects to use the Norton rotary in light passenger-carrying aircraft ceased, but Garside later developed a light, simple but powerful air-cooled single-rotor engine to power remotely controlled target-towing drones for military use. Code-named the NR731, this weighed only 23 lb yet produced 38 bhp. An initial batch of 75 was built at Shenstone and this remains one of the 'bread and butter' lines that have kept Nortons going.

By 1984 Nortons had a lash-up water-cooled model on the road and the air-cooled version was in production to fulfil police and, in 1986, RAC and RAF orders, 100 being supplied to the Air Force for despatch rider work in Germany. With hindsight Garside regrets that they did not opt for water-cooling at that time:

> We spent more money solving the problems of the air-cooled engine than it would have taken to put the liquid-cooled one into production. In the end we spent money both ways . . . we solved the problems of the air-cooled and put the liquid-cooled one into production.

It was taking Nortons so long to get machines to the production stage that by the time they were ready the fashion of the styling had changed – and so had the necessary power output. The original engines gave

ABOVE **Trevor Nation on the rotary in 1988 when he scored two wins in the ten-round British Formula One series.**

around 72 bhp but Poore insisted this be raised to 82 bhp. By 1985 Manganese Bronze were beginning to tire of the tremendous effort and time their chairman, Dennis Poore, was putting into Nortons. It was suggested that they sell the company. In the winter of 1986–87 things came to head when Poore fell terminally ill with cancer of the spine. He was in the final stages of negotiations to sell when he died in February 1987.

The new man at the helm was Philippe Le Roux, a 35-year-old South African-born financier who saw the potential of both the world-famous Norton name and the rotary-engine project. He took over as chief executive and, working full time at Shenstone, put a new sense of urgency into the little company. He immediately decided to market a limited-edition batch of 100 machines – the air-cooled, unfaired Classic which went on sale in December 1987 at the premium price of £6000 – and all were sold before the first models reached the showrooms.

He also gave Brian Crighton the go-ahead for the racing project that eventually grew into the highly successful, championship-winning John Player Norton team. Crighton, a former road racer and motorcycle dealer, originally joined Nortons in 1984 and worked in the service department before moving on to research and development. As a former competitor he quickly realised the enormous potential of the rotary.

> I wanted to go racing. But no one wanted to know. I was convinced that I could up the power from the 92 the best engines were giving to around 120 and eventually it was agreed that I could work on a racer provided I did so in my own time and at my own expense – working evenings and weekends.

Fed up with the lack of interest in his racing project, Crighton left Nortons in 1986 and went back to his original profession as an electronics expert in the computer industry. But when Le Roux took over, things changed. Crighton went to see him and the South African agreed to finance a pilot racing scheme. Crighton says:

> He let me have the kitchen in the caretaker's house as a race

LEFT Steve Spray took the 1989 British Formula One Championship. He left the team after a disappointing 1990 season.

BELOW The air-cooled limited-edition Classic released in December 1987. All 100 were snapped up.

RIGHT Ron Haslam on the new NRS588 Norton racer. Bad starts cost him championship points but he finished 1991 strongly with a lap record at Brands Hatch.

shop and we eventually took over the whole ground floor. I got hold of a police bike that had been written off in an accident and the air-cooled engine from that was the basis of the first rotary-engined Norton racer.

The engine was modified by Crighton, built into a Spondon frame and taken to MIRA (the motor industry's Midlands test track) where it clocked an impressive 170 mph. Six weeks later Malcolm Heath rode the Norton on its debut at Darley Moor in early September 1987, and finished third. Later that season Heath scored the rotary's first win in a 'Battle of the Twins' race at Snetterton. 'By that time the engine was giving 135 bhp at about 10,000 rpm. It had fulfilled its promise and Le Roux gave the go-ahead for a more ambitious programme in 1988,' says Crighton.

With sponsorship from Duckhams of oil fame, Trevor Nation and Simon Buckmaster were signed to ride wherever Nortons could get entries. One of the problems in those early racing days was that the powers that be had not yet decided how to calculate the capacity of a rotary engine. Nortons claimed that the twin-rotor unit was 588 cc and eligble for 750 cc events, but the FIM insisted on a 1.7 handicap which turned the 588 into 999.6 cc. This obviously eliminated the Norton from the 750 cc class but meant that it was eligible for 1000 cc and above Open class races and for the 'Battle of the Twins' events which permitted twin-cylinder engines up to 1000 cc.

The 1988 TT was a disappointment. Nation qualified in fine style in sixth place with a lap at 110.9 mph, far and away the fastest ever by a Norton, but retired from the race with bike problems. Buckmaster soldiered on to finish a lowly 33rd. For British racing the ACU allowed the Nortons to race against 750 cc four-strokes and 500 cc two-strokes in a new-look British Formula One Championship, several rounds of which were televised by the BBC. It was in this new series that the Norton threat turned into a winning one.

Andy McGladdery had shown the way when he borrowed a factory Norton and won the 1300 cc Star Championship round at Carnaby on 14 August 1988. Two weeks later Nation won a round of the same championship at Cadwell Park and after that Nortons won three of the four remaining Formula One rounds – Nation finishing first at Mallory Park and Cadwell Park in October and Steve Spray winning on his debut ride at Brands Hatch later the same month. Crighton remembers Spray's ride.

Simon Buckmaster was never able to get the best out of the bike. He was always complaining about something or other

ABOVE **The Norton Commander, launched in 1988, has a twin-rotor with power output of 85 bhp.**

RIGHT **This is the 1991 NRS588 Norton factory racer – lighter and more compact than the RCW588 it replaced though still powered by a water-cooled twin rotor engine.**

and we finally split up. This meant that we had a bike spare for the final round at Brands Hatch and I invited Steve to try it. He'd never ridden the rotary before and it wasn't set up for him but when I asked him after practising if he wanted us to change anything he said everything was fine just fill it up with petrol! He then went out and won the race. A fabulous performance.

This late run of successes literally transformed the British racing scene. Fans at last had something to cheer about and this, coupled with television exposure, led to John Player stepping in with major sponsorship for the 1989 season.

Meanwhile the limited-edition batch of 100 Classic Nortons had been followed by the Commander – a completely different machine with a water-cooled twin-rotor engine, comprehensive fairing and a launch price of £7599 when it was announced in the spring of 1988. One retrograde step was the use of a Yamaha fork in place of the excellent Italian Marzocchi used on the Classic, but after a faulty batch of ignition components had been replaced the Commanders in service have proved fast and reliable.

Frank Westworth, editor of the *Classic Bike Guide*, is an enthusiastic Commander owner and reports a fuel consumption of over 50 mpg 'If you ride it like a BMW', but admits this drops to little over 30 mpg when he uses all the performance of the 85 bhp engine. Demand for the Commander has been steady with production running at around 200 a year.

To boost finances Le Roux organised a share issue and this generated £3.5 million – enough to pay off outstanding debts and to finance the development of an out-and-out sports machine to supplement the fully faired, touring-orientated Commander. While development of this bike, the F1, was going on the new John Player Special team was carrying the Norton banner on the race circuits.

The riders for 1989 were Nation and Spray and both the riders and the bikes were finished in the black, silver and gold colours adopted by John Player during their Formula One car-racing days. Additional staff were signed on and Nick Collis appointed team manager, leaving Crighton free to concentrate on technical matters. The first major change was to abandon the air-cooled RC588 in favour of the water-cooled RCW588. Again the TT results were disappointing. In the Isle of Man, Nation teamed with Ireland's Steve Cull (Spray prefers not to ride in the TT) and both retired from the TT Formula One Race – Nation when he ran

out of petrol and Cull when the gearbox failed. In the final race of the week, the Senior TT, Nation was in fifth place on the fifth lap when the water pump failed, while the chain of Cull's bike broke when he was holding eighth place with just three miles to go. He pushed home to finish 23rd, and got a great ovation from the partisan crowd.

Following the pattern of the preceding year, the Norton team really came to the fore after the TT. Roland Brown puts it well in his review of the British season for *Motocourse*.

> The story of British Racing in 1989 was undoubtedly the return to victory of the Norton. Riding an all-black JPS sponsored rotary that fully lived up to its promise of the season before, Steve Spray roared to win after win to take two major championships amid much patriotic programme waving.

The two championships were the British 750 cc TT Formula One and the MCN/ACU British Championship, and during the season Spray set no less than nine new lap records at British short circuits. On the surface all was well, but behind the scenes the team was split by internal politics and petty squabbles. Unable to keep the peace and to get the team all pulling together, team manager Collis left at the end of 1989 and was replaced by former Honda Britain team chief Barry Symmons.

The F1 sports roadster was launched at the National Exhibition Centre, Birmingham in November 1989 with a price tag of over £12,000! A handsome machine, finished in John Player racing colours, it was powered by an RCW588-type engine which produced 95 bhp at 9500 rpm with a compression ratio of only 9 to 1.

Explained Crighton:

> The 1989 racing engines gave between 145 and 148 bhp at 10,000 and were not critical on fuel. In fact they would run on two-star. We actually used normal pump four-star and did not have to worry about the very high octane special fuels that the rival teams now use.

For the team 1990 began well with Robert Dunlop, signed to team with Nation at the TT, winning the big class at the North West 200 where he went through the radar speed trap at an incredible 189 mph – almost 20 mph faster than the best of the Japanese four-cylinder machines! At the TT Dunlop and Nation finished third and sixth in the opening Formula One race after Dunlop had set the fourth-fastest lap around the island during practice at 119.74 mph and Nation had overcome the handicap of rib injuries sustained at Snetterton just before the TT. Then in the Senior Nation rode a well-judged race in poor conditions to finish second, beaten only by Honda hot-shot Carl Fogarty. Dunlop retired while holding fifth place when a stone jammed the throttle open.

It was at the TT that news came through that the FIM had decided to scrap the handicap imposed on rotary engines and to accept the Norton method of calculating the capacity. This meant that the RCW588 was eligible for the FIM TT Formula One Cup. Dunlop then went to Portugal where he finished second at Vila Real, and back home in Ulster he again took second place in the Irish round at Dundrod to finish third in the overall championship.

On the British circuits things did not go well. The team was still split, with Symmons at loggerheads with Crighton. The performance of the machines suffered and after Spray had made a good start to the new Shell Supercup ACU British Championship series by winning at Snetterton in May, the team did not win another round. The title was won by Terry Rymer (Yamaha) from Brian Morrison (Yamaha) with Nation third and Spray fourth. Nation had the consolation of winning the lesser *MCN* TT Superbike Championship to make it three championship successes out of the four contested in 1989 and 1990.

In December 1990 Nortons launched an extended five model roadster range at the International Motorcycle Show at the NEC, Birmingham – and in addition offered two out-and-out racers for sale plus two versions of the racing engine for sidecar use. Cheapest was the Classic roadster at £7,500 followed by two versions of the Commander – one with permanent integral panniers at £8,400 and the second with detachable German Krauser panniers at £8,250. The F1 sports roadster launched the previous year was retained with the price rising to £13,900 and a new top-of-the-range roadster, the F1, JPS Special, was added at £15,400. This was finished in the black, gold and silver of John Player and looked very like the successful racers.

The genuine racing model, the F1R, cost nearly £10,000 more at £24,881 with normal carburettors or £27,381 with electronic fuel injection – or you could buy the engine/gearbox units alone for £12,500 and £15,000 respectively. But the Show proved a disaster. Rumour has it that only two machines were ordered. Plans to produce the Classic were cancelled; not a single racing model was sold; production of the two Commander models was reduced to a trickle and the work force cut.

It was a time of crisis. The share price, which had risen to a high of over £6 in 1987 plunged to 15p and on 13 January 1991 Le Roux resigned, three days after the Department of Trade and Industry announced that it was to investigate the company and a series of takeover bids involving the Minty furniture group, Pro-Fit (an American piping company) and the German fastener firm FUS.

This investigation is, at the time of publication, still going on and it would be wrong to comment.

Control passed from Le Roux to James Tildesley and in April 1991 he was replaced by David McDonald as Chief Executive. McDonald is determined to keep Norton in motorcycle manufacturing and the first fruits of his thinking were seen in late October at the 1991 NEC International Show – the range had been cut to two models, the Commander and the F1 Sports, and the prices slashed; the Commander from £8,400 to £7,000 and the re-styled F1 (now called the F1 Sports) from £15,400 to £9,000. Throughout this period of change the day-to-day running of the company had been in the hands of Graham Williams who took over as Managing Director early in 1989 when Le Roux, who had previously been both MD and Chairman, split the responsibilities.

The completely separate John Player Special Norton racing team, directed by team manager Barry Symmons and housed in separate accommodation in Lichfield some miles from Norton's Shenstone factory, suffered their ups and downs in 1991. Brian Crighton had left in September 1990 to pursue his own racing plans centred on the Australian-backed Roton machine with Norton type rotary engine, while the John Player team settled down to build a completely new racer for 1991.

Ron Williams designed the new frame and every effort was made both to reduce frontal area and to shed weight. At the same time a revised engine–gearbox unit was schemed out. The basic 588 cc water-cooled twin rotor unit was retained but in order to increase the number of gears from five to six a new gearbox (built by Nortons based on a Kawasaki design) was added. Because this was of the 'cross-over' type with the clutch and primary drive on the right the engine now runs 'backwards'. Interestingly, the primary chain was replaced by a Kevlar toothed belt.

Dubbed the NRS588 (Norton Racing Services) the newcomer weighed around 297 lb (135 kg) compared to the 320 lb (145 kg) of the older model. Power was said to be 'over' 135 bhp at 9,800 rpm with the lowly compression ratio of 9 to 1. This compares to the rival Japanese four-cylinder 750 cc machines which produce similar power but have compression ratios of up to 14 to 1 and rev to 14,000 rpm running on aviation fuel, while the Norton is happy on pump petrol.

After a successful end-of-season ride at Brands Hatch late in 1990 the experienced Ron Haslam joined the squad for 1991. He replaced Steve Spray to team with Nation in the British short circuit events while Nation and Robert Dunlop contested the road races – the NW 200 and the TT. Additionally Haslam, with his wealth of experience (notably as a member of the Elf–Honda, Suzuki and Cagiva grand prix teams), was chief development rider.

Inevitably there were teething problems and it was not until the TT in June that the NRS588 was first raced. There both Nation and Dunlop tried their new bikes in practice but only Dunlop actually raced his – retiring in both races after two laps because his injured shoulder, damaged in a crash at Donington in May, was too weak and painful. Nation reverted to an RCW588 and finished third in the Formula One race, only to be excluded when the tank was measured and found to be .7 litre (just over a pint) over the 24 litre maximum.

Commented Nation: 'It was a flat bottomed tank and under a full load of fuel I think it bulged and increased the capacity slightly – just enough to get me excluded. I finished with ample fuel so there was no question of me running out if the tank had been a little smaller.' In Friday's Senior TT Nation led the race at Ramsey halfway round the first lap but was then slowed by a loose exhaust system. This led to overheating and he eventually retired when the engine seized at the Bungalow on the third lap.

In lesser events the team had been doing well. Haslam had captained the British team to a resounding win in the annual UK versus USA Transatlantic series, winning two of the three races at Brands Hatch, while Nation and Dunlop had dominated the North West 200 in Ulster where Nation won the main event at an average of 120 mph and his Irish team-mate took the Superbike event with Nation second.

After the TT the riders switched to the new machines and when Haslam won on his debut on the NRS588 at Brands Hatch things looked to be going well as far as he was concerned – though Nation was not so happy. 'The bike had been developed by Ron and his likes and dislikes when it comes to setting up a bike are completely opposite to mine. I simply couldn't get on with the new machine and struggled for the rest of the season,' said Nation who left the squad at the end of 1991.

A highlight for British fans was when Haslam took twelfth place in the British Grand Prix at Donington in August 1991 – competing against the full might of the Japanese teams with their vee-four two-strokes. The FIM agreed to allow the 588 cc rotary to compete in the 500 cc class and Haslam rode his normal short circuit machine. Said the team chief Symmons: 'The idea was to show the flag and finish the race so Ron paced himself rather than racing flat out. Later the same day he went out on the same machine and won the MCN/TT Superbike round, lapping faster than he had done in the actual Grand Prix.

At the time Haslam was favourite to take the MCN/TT Championship but then a string of poor starts cost him vital points. In race after race the pack roared away while he struggled in mid-field. It made for incredibly exciting television as he carved his way through the field but cost him vital points as he was unable to score the outright wins needed for championship success. Haslam broke six lap records during these epic rides but could still finish only fourth in the main MCN/TT Superbike series – though he did climax with a flourish when he set a new lap record at 91.99 mph for the Brands Hatch short circuit at the final round of the year in October. In the lesser six-round Superbike Championship Haslam was second.

The year ended with two notable happenings. First David Garside's patient development of the rotary engine was recognised with the award of the MBE and then John Player affirmed their intention to back the Norton racing project again in 1992 with Ron Haslam as number one, with support from Ireland's Robert Dunlop who will also carry the Norton colours in the TT.

Mention of the famous Isle of Man races brings us full circle. For it was Rem Fowler's success in the 1907 TT that first brought the name Norton to the attention of the general public. A string of victories in the twenties and thirties gained world-wide fame for the Birmingham company. There was further success in the forties and fifties – and not just in racing, but also in production. Then came the long decline into near obscurity – a decline shared by so many famous British companies. I cannot help wondering what James Lansdowne Norton would make of it all. . .

Just one year short of the century of the founding of the Norton Manufacturing Company in Birmingham by the 29-year-old James Norton, the successor to that company still exists - the oldest surviving motorcycle marque in the world. But the workforce at the factory in Shenstone has dwindled to five and general manager Bob Haines admits: 'We have been in limbo for three years'.

The cause of this unhappy situation can be traced back to 1993 when David MacDonald, installed as chief executive in 1991 by the Midland Bank in an effort to safeguard an outstanding debt of £7m, sold the company to Wildrose Ventures, a North American company headed by Canadian Nelson Skalbania. Skalbania, an entrepreneur whose financial activities have been varied and interesting on both sides of the Atlantic, re-formed the company as Norton Motors (1993) Ltd with his daughter Rosanda as general manager at Shenstone. But she departed in 1994 when Skalbania was unable to repay money he had borrowed to buy Norton and ownership reverted to the company who had backed him: the Aquilini Investment Group of Vancouver.

Sales manager Bob Haines was left in charge and became general manager. The last batch of ten Commanders was built in August 1993 for export to Portugal and a single machine was assembled from spares in 1994 for a special customer - a courier who covers exceptionally long distances and revels in the complete lack of vibration of the Norton rotary.

Since then Haines and his small team have been 'trying to keep customers on the road.' But the service side was closed at the end of 1996 and transferred to two dealers - Reg Allen Motorcycles in Acton, London and Startrite Motors of Leeds. Now the workers at Shenstone concentrate on machining components for light aircraft engines developed from the Norton rotary.

Luigi Aquilini, boss of the Canadian Investment company who own Norton, has visited the factory once. 'He told me he does want to sell but I'm afraid I don't know what plans he has. We are hanging on and hoping for the best,' said Haines in March 1997.

In contrast the Norton racing effort ended in a blaze of glory. The first really major success for the promising rotary-engined racer came at the 1992 Isle of Man TT when Steve Hislop, having a one-off factory ride on a factory bike with private (not John Player) sponsorship won an epic battle with Carl Fogarty (Yamaha) to take the senior TT at the record avarage speed of 121.28mph - the first TT win for Norton since 1973.

And after John Player pulled out at the end of the 1992 season, during which Robert Dunlop finished second on a Norton in the MCN Supercup series (Ron Haslam's hopes being dashed by a broken leg) Duckhams took over as the major sponsor for 1993 and 1994 with Colin Seeley as team manager and Brian Crighton as the technical brain.

After a 'shakedown' season in 1993 during which Jim Moodie finished second in the British Supercup series the team dominated the 1994 championship which Ian Simpson won with 319 points to Moodie's (now on a Yamaha) 287, Phil Borley on the second Norton only three points behind him.

At the end of 1994 Seeley had to take stock: 'The Norton racing effort was costing £200,000 a year and the team had scored 22 wins, 21 second places and ten thirds. We had some technical help from Nortons but we didn't get a word of thanks or congratulations from the Aquilinis, so when Honda offered us a deal for 1995 we took it.' And that was the end of the Norton racing effort, the 190mph machines wheeled into retirement still the fastest bikes in their class ...

Appendix – Racing successes

Listed here are the racing victories achieved by riders on Norton machines in the major European grands prix and in the Isle of Man TT and Manx Grand Prix races.

1907 Isle of Man TT Rem Fowler (twin cylinder class)

1921 Belgian GP 500 cc Hubert Hassall

1922 Ulster GP 600 cc Hubert Hassall

1923 Belgian GP sidecar George Tucker
Ulster GP 600 cc Joe Craig

1924 Spanish GP 500 cc Achille Varzi
Isle of Man Sidecar TT George Tucker
Isle of Man Senior TT Alec Bennett
French GP 500 cc Alec Bennett
Belgian GP 500 cc Alec Bennett
Ulster GP 500 cc Joe Craig

1925 Belgian GP 500 cc Alec Bennett
Ulster GP 500 cc Joe Craig
Amateur TT 500 cc H.G. Dodds

1926 French GP 500 cc Alec Bennett
Isle of Man Senior TT Stanley Woods

1927 Isle of Man Senior TT Alec Bennett
Dutch TT 500 cc Stanley Woods
Belgian GP 500 cc Stanley Woods
Swiss GP 500 cc Stanley Woods
French GP 500 cc Joe Craig
Ulster GP 500 cc Jimmy Shaw
Amateur TT 500 cc Tim Hunt

1928 Dutch TT 350 cc Stanley Woods
French GP 500 cc Stanley Woods
German GP 350 cc Pietro Ghersi
Amateur TT 500 cc Tim Hunt

1929 Spanish GP 500 cc Tim Hunt
Spanish GP Sidecar Dennis Mansell
Amateur TT 500 cc Norman Lea

1930 Ulster GP 500 cc Stanley Woods
Swedish GP 500 cc Jimmie Simpson
French GP 500 cc Stanley Woods

1931 Isle of Man Junior TT Tim Hunt
Isle of Man Senior TT Tim Hunt
French GP 500 cc Tim Hunt
German GP 500 cc Stanley Woods
Dutch TT 350 cc Stanley Woods
Dutch TT 500 cc Stanley Woods
Belgian GP 350 cc Jimmy Guthrie
Belgian GP 500 cc Stanley Woods
Swiss GP 350 cc Tim Hunt
Swiss GP 500 cc Stanley Woods
Ulster GP 350 cc Leo Davenport
Ulster GP 500 cc Stanley Woods
Senior Manx GP Jock Muir

1932 Italian GP 500 cc Piero Taruffi
Isle of Man Junior TT Stanley Woods
Isle of Man Senior TT Stanley Woods
Dutch TT 350 cc Stanley Woods
Dutch TT 500 cc Tim Hunt
French GP 350 cc Jimmie Simpson
French GP 500 cc Stanley Woods
Belgian GP 350 cc Jimmie Simpson
Belgian GP 500 cc Stanley Woods
Swiss GP 350 cc Stanley Woods
Swiss GP 500 cc Stanley Woods
Ulster GP 500 cc Stanley Woods
Senior Manx GP Norman Gledhill

1933 Isle of Man Junior TT Stanley Woods
Isle of Man Senior TT Stanley Woods
Dutch TT 350 cc Stanley Woods
Dutch TT 500 cc Stanley Woods
Swiss GP 350 cc Tim Hunt
Swiss GP 500 cc Stanley Woods
French GP 350 cc Jimmie Simpson
French GP 500 cc Tim Hunt
Belgian GP 350 cc Jimmy Guthrie
Belgian GP 500 cc Tim Hunt
Ulster GP 500 cc Stanley Woods
Swedish GP 350 cc Jimmie Simpson
Spanish GP 350 cc Jimmy Guthrie
Spanish GP 500 cc Jimmy Guthrie
Senior Manx GP Harold Daniell

1934 Isle of Man Junior TT Jimmy Guthrie
Isle of Man Senior TT Jimmy Guthrie
Dutch TT 350 cc Jimmie Simpson
German GP 350 cc Jimmie Simpson
Swiss GP 350 cc Jimmie Simpson
Swiss GP 500 cc Jimmie Simpson
Belgian GP 350 cc Jimmie Simpson
Belgian GP 500 cc Wal Handley
Ulster GP 350 cc Jimmie Simpson
Spanish GP 350 cc Jimmy Guthrie
Spanish GP 500 cc Jimmy Guthrie
Junior Manx GP Doug Pirie
Senior Manx GP Crasher White

1935 Isle of Man Junior TT Jimmy Guthrie
Swiss GP 350 cc Walter Rusk
Swiss GP 500 cc Jimmy Guthrie
Dutch TT 350 cc Walter Rusk
Dutch TT 500 cc Jimmy Guthrie
German GP 350 cc Walter Rusk
German GP 500 cc Jimmy Guthrie
Belgian GP 350 cc Crasher White
Belgian GP 500 cc Jimmy Guthrie
Ulster GP 500 cc Jimmy Guthrie
Spanish TT 350 cc Jimmy Guthrie
Spanish TT 500 cc Jimmy Guthrie
Junior Manx GP Freddie Frith
Senior Manx GP Doc Swanston

1936 Swiss GP 350 cc Jimmy Guthrie
Swiss GP 500 cc Jimmy Guthrie
Isle of Man Junior TT Freddie Frith
Isle of Man Senior TT Jimmy Guthrie
German GP 350 cc Freddie Frith
German GP 500 cc Jimmy Guthrie
Dutch TT 350 cc Crasher White
Dutch TT 500 cc Jimmy Guthrie
Belgian GP 500 cc Jimmy Guthrie
Ulster GP 500 cc Freddie Frith
Swedish GP 350 cc Freddie Frith
Senior Manx GP Austin Munks

1937 Isle of Man Junior TT Jimmy Guthrie
Isle of Man Senior TT Freddie Frith

Dutch TT 350 cc Crasher White
Swiss GP 350 cc Jimmy Guthrie
Swiss GP 500 cc Jimmy Guthrie
Belgian GP 350 cc Crasher White
Belgian GP 500 cc Jimmy Guthrie
Junior Manx GP Maurice Cann
Senior Manx GP Maurice Cann

1938 Isle of Man Senior TT Harold Daniell
Belgian GP 350 cc Crasher White
Swiss GP 350 cc Harold Daniell
Swiss GP 500 cc Harold Daniell
Swiss GP Sidecar Arthur Horton
German GP 350 cc Crasher White
Junior Manx GP Ken Bills
Senior Manx GP Ken Bills

1939 French GP 500 cc Crasher White

1946 Junior Manx GP Ken Bills

1947 Isle of Man Senior TT Harold Daniell
Dutch TT 500 cc Artie Bell
Belgian GP 350 cc Ken Bills
Belgian GP 500 cc Harold Daniell
Belgian GP Sidecar Frans Vanderschrick
Ulster GP 350 cc Johnny Lockett
Ulster GP 500 cc Artie Bell
Junior Manx GP Eric Briggs
Senior Manx GP Eric Briggs

1948 Swiss GP 350 cc Artie Bell
Swiss GP 500 cc Harold Daniell
Swiss GP Sidecar Hans Haldemann
Isle of Man Senior TT Artie Bell
Dutch TT 500 cc Artie Bell
Belgian GP 500 cc Johnny Lockett
Belgian GP Sidecar Frans Vanderschrick
Junior Manx GP Denis Parkinson

1949 Isle of Man Senior TT Harold Daniell
Swiss GP Sidecar Eric Oliver
Belgian GP Sidecar Eric Oliver
Junior Manx GP Cromie McCandless
Senior Manx GP Geoff Duke

1950 Isle of Man Junior TT Artie Bell
Isle of Man Senior TT Geoff Duke
Belgian GP Sidecar Eric Oliver
Swiss GP Sidecar Eric Oliver
Ulster GP 500 cc Geoff Duke
Italian GP 350 cc Geoff Duke
Italian GP 500 cc Geoff Duke
Italian GP Sidecar Eric Oliver
Senior Manx GP Peter Romaine

1951 Spanish GP Sidecar Eric Oliver
Isle of Man Junior TT Geoff Duke
Isle of Man Senior TT Geoff Duke
Belgian GP 350 cc Geoff Duke
Belgian GP 500 cc Geoff Duke
Dutch TT 500 cc Geoff Duke
French GP 350 cc Geoff Duke
French GP Sidecar Eric Oliver
Ulster GP 350 cc Geoff Duke
Ulster GP 500 cc Geoff Duke
Italian GP 350 cc Geoff Duke
Senior Manx GP Dave Bennett

1952 Swiss GP 350 cc Geoff Duke
Isle of Man Junior TT Geoff Duke
Isle of Man Senior TT Reg Armstrong
Dutch TT 350 cc Geoff Duke
Belgian GP 350 cc Geoff Duke
Belgian GP Sidecar Eric Oliver
German GP 350 cc Reg Armstrong
German GP 500 cc Reg Armstrong
German GP Sidecar Cyril Smith
Ulster GP 350 cc Ken Kavanagh
Italian GP 350 cc Ray Amm
Spanish GP Sidecar Eric Oliver

1953 Isle of Man Junior TT Ray Amm
Isle of Man Senior TT Ray Amm
Belgian GP Sidecar Eric Oliver
French GP Sidecar Eric Oliver
Ulster GP 350 cc Ken Mudford
Ulster GP 500 cc Ken Kavanagh
Ulster GP Sidecar Cyril Smith
Swiss GP Sidecar Eric Oliver
Italian GP Sidecar Eric Oliver
Junior Manx GP Frank Fox
Senior Manx GP Denis Parkinson

1954 Isle of Man Senior TT Ray Amm
Isle of Man Sidecar TT Eric Oliver
Ulster GP 350 cc Ray Amm
Ulster GP 500 cc Ray Amm
Ulster GP Sidecar Eric Oliver
Belgian GP Sidecar Eric Oliver
German GP 350 cc Ray Amm
Senior Manx GP George Costain

1955 Swedish GP 350 cc John Hartle
Junior Manx GP Geoff Tanner
Senior Manx GP Geoff Tanner

1956 Swedish GP 350 cc Keith Campbell
Ulster GP 500 cc John Hartle
Junior Manx GP Jimmy Buchan
Senior Manx GP Jimmy Buchan

1957 Belgian GP 500 cc Jack Brett
Junior Manx GP Alan Holmes
Senior Manx GP Alan Holmes

1958 Swedish GP 350 cc Geoff Duke
Swedish GP 500 cc Geoff Duke
Senior Manx GP Ernie Washer

1959 Dutch TT 350 cc (F1) Bob Brown
Belgian GP 350 cc (F1) Gary Hocking
Swedish GP 500 cc (F1) Bob Brown
Junior Manx GP Eddie Crooks
Senior Manx GP Peter Middleton

1960 Ulster GP 500 cc John Hartle
Junior Manx GP Ellis Boyce
Senior Manx GP Phil Read

1961 Isle of Man Junior TT Phil Read
Isle of Man Senior TT Mike Hailwood
Senior Manx GP Ned Minihan

1962 Senior Manx GP Joe Dunphy

1963 Senior Manx GP Griff Jenkins

1964 Ulster GP 500 cc Phil Read
Finnish GP 500 cc Jack Ahearn

1965 Ulster GP 500 cc Dick Creith
Senior Manx GP Malcolm Uphill

1966 Junior Manx GP Gordon Buchan

1967 Junior Manx GP John Wetherall
Senior Manx GP Jimmy Guthrie (jnr)

1968 Isle of Man TT 750PR Ray Pickrell
Junior Manx GP John Findlay
Senior Manx GP John Findlay

1969 Yugoslav GP 500 cc Godfrey Nash

1973 Isle of Man TT F750 Peter Williams

1992 Isle of Man Senior TT Steve Hislop

Index

Page references in *italic* refer to captions.